The Diplomacy of Silence

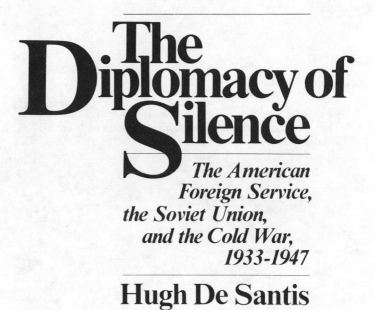

*The American
Foreign Service,
the Soviet Union,
and the Cold War,
1933-1947*

Hugh De Santis

The University of Chicago Press

Chicago and London

HUGH DE SANTIS is the research analyst for the regional political and security affairs of Western Europe at the Department of State.

The University of Chicago Press, Chicago 60637
The University of Chicago Press, Ltd., London
© 1979, 1980 by The University of Chicago
All rights reserved: Published 1980
Printed in the United States of America

87 86 85 84 83 82 81 80   54321

Library of Congress Cataloging in Publication Data

De Santis, Hugh.
   The diplomacy of silence.

   Bibliography: p.
   Includes index.
   1.   United States—Foreign relations—Russia.
2.   Russia—Foreign relations—United States.
3.   United States—Foreign relations—1933–1945.
4.   United States—Foreign relations—1945–1953.
5.   Diplomats—United States. 6.   United States—
Diplomatic and consular service—Russia. 7.   Russia
—Foreign opinion, American. 8.   Public opinion
—United States. I.   Title.
E183.8.R9D46   327.73047   80–16676
ISBN 0–226–14337–6

Contents

Preface

This book was conceived, in its most embryonic form, while I was a student of international relations at the University of Chicago. While I was immersed in the study of systems theory and its application to international politics, it occurred to me at some point that the systems approach, for all its complexity, virtually ignored the most complex variable, namely, the human condition. Later at Chicago, as a doctoral student in history, I came to a similar conclusion about the historiography of the Cold War. Scholars of the so-called orthodox and new left persuasions basically described the developments that led to the breakdown of relations between Washington and Moscow after World War II as inevitable outgrowths of a historically preordained drama. Moreover, they tended to explain these developments monistically: events were culturally, ideologically, or economically determined. For those writers who viewed the Cold War as a tragedy, it was a tragedy of the necessary.

What I have set out to produce in the pages that follow is a humanistic study of international politics that treats the historical drama of American policy toward the USSR as a complex tragedy of the possible. This book is a decidedly heuristic undertaking. It discusses the nature and underlying influences of the perceptions of the Soviet Union formed by American career diplomats. To appreciate how these individuals saw the world in which they lived, I have tried to share in what was existentially real to them. At the same time, to make their views more meaningful to the reader, I have attempted to offer an interpretation of why they perceived reality as they did. In the truly existential sense of the word, this is a study of historical participation-observation.

I am grateful to the University of Chicago for providing the matrix within which my ideas developed and to my professors for advising, assisting, and intellectually nurturing me. My greatest debt is to Akira Iriye, who introduced me to the study of history and who subtly and patiently showed me the way when I was lost. I also owe thanks to William H. McNeill, who taught me European history and who otherwise allowed me to wander in the ecumene of his mind. Barry Karl showed me how to combine history and politics and warmly encouraged the interdisciplinary direction of my work. I am also grateful to Susanne Hoeber

Rudolph for exposing me to the fascinating world of bureaucratic politics and for sensitively considering my interest in psychological analysis when few others would. For helping me to sharpen my understanding of existential psychology, I acknowledge my appreciation to Salvatore Maddi.

Research of this book was a major undertaking. The bibliography acknowledges those individuals and institutions who responded to my queries, welcomed me into their homes, and permitted me the use of research facilities. Beyond this, however, I wish to express my appreciation to those diplomats, or their families, for generously allowing me to see materials that previously had not been made available to the public. They include Mrs. John F. Bruins; Ambassador Elbridge Durbrow; Mrs. Maxwell M. Hamilton; Ambassador Loy Henderson; Mrs. Marjorie Riddle, who permitted me to read the diary of her uncle, Joseph Jacobs; Ambassador H. Freeman Matthews; and the family of H. F. Arthur Schoenfeld. For permission to cite passages from restricted correspondence, I thank Professor George F. Kennan. Special thanks are in order to Ambassador Henderson and Mesdames Bruins and Hamilton for their warmth and trust and for their timely words of encouragement. For making my exile in the catacombs of the National Archives a personally as well as professionally rewarding experience, I extend my gratitude to Salley Marks, Kathie Nicastro, and Ronald Swerczek.

A number of people from various disciplines have read these pages at different stages of completion and have offered useful criticism. I am particularly grateful to Alexander George for his helpful advice. In addition, I would also like to thank Grace De Santis, Waldo Heinrichs, Sheppard Kellam, and David Patterson for taking time from their own work to give me the benefit of their insights.

Finally, I would like to thank Temple University, for providing the facilities that enabled me to complete the book, and Gloria Basmajian, for typing the final manuscript with supreme efficiency and consumate geniality.

The views expressed in this book do not necessarily reflect the policies of the Department of State.

Introduction

It was shortly past one o'clock in the afternoon when President Harry S Truman entered the chamber of the House of Representatives. Senators and congressmen who had jointly assembled there on that warm, sunny March 12, 1947, broke into nervous applause as the president made his way down the aisle to the clerk's desk. Smiling acknowledgment of the legislative reception which greeted him, Truman waited for quiet. Then he began to speak.

"At the present moment in world history nearly every nation must choose between alternative ways of life." One way was that of representative government and individual liberty, the president said; the other, minority rule and political oppression. "I believe," he went on to assert, "that it must be the policy of the United States to support free peoples who are resisting attempted subjugation by armed minorities or by outside pressures." Accordingly, he requested the Congress to approve financial aid to Greece and Turkey in the amount of $400 million and to authorize the despatch of American civilian and military personnel to those countries to assist them in the development of postwar economic and political stability. "Should we fail to aid Greece and Turkey in this fateful hour," he warned, "the effect will be far-reaching to the West as well as to the East." Free nations looked to the United States for support to maintain their independence. "If we falter in our leadership, we may endanger the peace of the world—and we shall surely endanger the welfare of our own nation."[1]

Truman's speech received a thunderous ovation from members of both parties. By now they too had concluded that the world was divided between mutually irreconcilable ideologies. Even so, legislators of both liberal and conservative persuasions, like the larger public and press, recoiled from the idea of political involvement in countries far removed from American shores. But in the end, the fear that Soviet-directed communist subversion in Europe might threaten the security of the United States impelled Congress and the public to support the Greek-Turkish aid bill.

It was precisely this view that administration officials responsible for the conduct of the nation's foreign policy sought to impress on the American people. General George C. Marshall, the new secretary of state, his

1

undersecretary, Dean Acheson, and the service secretaries had concluded during the course of 1946 that the United States and the Soviet Union were locked in an ideological conflict of global proportions. The Greek-Turkish crisis was but a microcosm of that cataclysmic struggle. To deny immediate aid to these countries, they reasoned, was to imperil, in the longer run, American security. In short, as Clark Clifford, the president's special counsel, put it, Truman's address was really "the opening gun in a campaign to bring people to [the] realization that the war isn't over by any means."[2]

Clifford resonated the thinking of American career diplomats. Indeed, no segment of the foreign-policy establishment more enthusiastically supported the president's stand "to stop Soviet efforts to undermine the free nations through subversion," in the words of Charles Bohlen, than the Foreign Service. This is not to say that careerists, any more than the administration, had consistently held to the notion of a perfidious, ideologically expansionist Soviet Union. Impressed by the Russian military effort during World War II, the apparent "democratizing" movement within the USSR signalled by developments such as the dissolution of the Comintern and the success of the Moscow-Teheran conferences of 1943, they had believed their Russian ally would join the United States in constructing a postwar world of peace and harmony. By the winter of 1944–45, however, as Soviet armies planted themselves in Eastern Europe, they began to question anew the Kremlin's motives. Gradually, trust gave way to suspicion and fear, friendship disintegrated into antagonism, and their expectations of postwar cooperation eventually collapsed into the pile of wartime rubble.

Equally alarmed by the unexpected developments in Eastern Europe, President Truman and administration officials increasingly relied on the interpretations of Foreign Service officers to explain Moscow's intentions. To diplomats in the department who helped draft Truman's momentous statement of March 12, and to their colleagues abroad, particularly in Soviet-occupied Eastern Europe, whose reports provided the basis for the decision to aid Greece and Turkey, the Truman Doctrine, as it came to be called, vindicated their estimation of Moscow's postwar objectives.

While Foreign Service officers played a prominent part in the unfolding of American postwar policy toward the Soviet Union, with few exceptions—notably George Kennan and Bohlen—their foreign-policy views have received little scholarly attention. Recent studies of the Cold War, however, have begun to consider the role diplomats played in the shaping of America's Soviet policy. In *The Cold War Begins* (1974), Lynn Etheridge Davis concluded that career diplomats uniformly advocated a policy of cooperation with the Kremlin in support of the Atlantic Charter ideals. Conversely, Daniel Yergin asserted in *Shattered Peace* (1977) that diplomats, especially those who had served in Riga and Moscow in the twenties and thirties, sustained a consistently hostile attitude toward the Soviets and opposed Franklin Roosevelt's policy of postwar cooperation. Independently, both interpretations are overdrawn; but taken together they are instructive. Actually, Foreign Service officers demonstrated considerable vacillation in their assessment of Moscow's postwar objectives. During the early war years, they held competing views of the Soviets, whom they saw, on one hand, as willing adherents to the American postwar order, and on the other, as incorrigible ideologues antagonistic to cooperation with the democratic West. Resolution of this cognitive dilemma did not result in an undifferentiated image of the Soviet Union. Quite the contrary, by the war's end diplomats perceived Moscow's aims in three discrete ways, each of which called forth different foreign-policy paradigms.

This book intends to contribute to a broader understanding of the Cold War in the first place by defining the different images of the Soviet Union formed by American Foreign Service officers. Diplomats who held to the image of *ideological cooperation* assumed that the Russians were willing to subscribe to, if not embrace, the reconstruction of the postwar world based on liberal-democratic values and beliefs derived from universal and absolute principles. They supported a policy of compromise and accommodation. Those who perceived the Soviets in terms of *ideological confrontation* contended that they represented an aggressive, ideologically expansionist threat to liberal-democratic values. They advocated a policy of ideological counteroffensive. To those who adopted the view of *realistic cooperation*, Moscow was indifferent to liberal-democratic values and was disposed to adhere to a world order based solely on national interests derived from the circumstances of relative military and political power. They endorsed the division of the globe into spheres of influence. *Realistic confrontation*, the advancement of Soviet interests by means of militaristic expansion, potentially an alternative view of Soviet objectives, was not seriously considered by professional diplomats. This image would have logically summoned forth a policy of retaliatory confrontation.

These divergent images, which I have presented in the abstract as ideal-types, did not, of course, suddenly spring forth like Minerva during the war years. Nor was a single image continuously paramount in the minds of Foreign Service officers; although at any given time one was predominant, multiple images were frequently held simultaneously. The second and more important purpose of this monograph, then, is to analyze the complex of antecedents which gave rise to these diverse images during the years from 1933 to 1947. As I have defined the term, an image is the subjective reflection of the external world. Stated in the context of phenomenological-existential psychology, on which framework the analysis of foreign-policy perceptions in this study rests, individuals exist at given historical moments in time and space and consciously intend, that is, point toward, material objects which have meaning for them. Another central argument of existential thought is that individuals exist simultaneously in three "worlds": the biological world of nature, which I have extended to encompass commonly held cultural ideas and values; the social-interactional world; and one's own private world. One's predisposition to invest with meaning that which he observes, or one's self-relatedness to the external world in which he participates, derives from one's store of cultural, social, and psychological experiences. Reality, then, is a construct of that which we share with everyone, with some, and with no one. Collectively, these experiences are translated into paradigms of the real world that serve to establish which of the myriad stimuli one encounters are meaningful. However, given different cultural-social-psychological experiences, what is meaningful to one individual may not be meaningful to another. Thus one's intentionality toward the external world, which underlies perception, is irreducible to causal or nomological forms.[3]

By virtue of their rearing and education, diplomats were imbued with American cultural values and beliefs and a liberal-internationalist concept of world affairs which espoused the harmony of interests among nations and emphasized the ideals of free trade, political self-determination, and the inviolability of public opinion. These values and beliefs were further reinforced by the training they received as members of the Foreign Service, which was, in turn, facilitated by the relatively homogeneous class backgrounds they shared and the close personal relations they developed. While they adhered to the same concept of international relations and embraced the same cultural myths, national stereotypes, and recollections of the past, they did not share the same social experiences. The social conditions encountered by careerists in Moscow during the thirties, for example, induced a much harsher image of the Soviet Union than that formed by their colleagues in other parts of the world or in the State Department. Association with the political elites of different countries, ethnocentrism and social-class bias, the existence or absence of creature comforts, and bureaucratic pressures within the State Department all affected the perceptions of Foreign Service officers. Social-situational factors and the psychological effects they produced had a particularly decisive influence on their perceptions of the Soviet Union after 1944. Confronted with the psychologically brutalizing effects of Soviet behavior in Eastern Europe, diplomats in the field increasingly perceived Moscow's postwar aims in terms of ideological confrontation. Removed from these unsettling conditions, diplomats in the department sustained an image of ideological cooperation through 1945.

Personality characteristics further contributed to image-formation. Psychologically predisposed, as a group, toward social conformity, diplomats in the department committed themselves to the American government's policy of postwar cooperation with Moscow along Atlantic Charter lines. Unable to implement this idealistic policy in Soviet-controlled Eastern Europe, their conformist colleagues in the field increasingly despaired of U.S.-Soviet cooperation, which rendered meaningless their professional roles. To redress their anxiety, some of them submitted to the state of affairs in Eastern Europe and lifelessly pursued their diplomatic functions; others retreated, both literally and figuratively, from the Soviet-defined world they inhabited; still others quixotically crusaded for the survival of American ideals in Eastern Europe. Unlike his colleagues, Kennan advocated an alternative policy based on the image of realistic cooperation. His power-political approach to U.S.-Soviet relations derived from his personality make-up and his related worldview, both of which made him atypical of the Foreign Service establishment.

This book also explores relations between the United States and the countries of Eastern Europe, a subject of investigation which American historians have mainly confined to U.S.-Polish relations. Since it was Moscow's behavior in Eastern Europe after 1944 which called into question American expectations of postwar cooperation and which served as the model of anticipated Soviet actions elsewhere, the focus will be on the views of Foreign Service officers assigned to Poland, Hungary, Czechoslovakia, Albania, Yugoslavia, Rumania, and Bulgaria or to the State Department's corresponding geographic divisions of Eastern, Central, and Southern Europe from 1944 to 1946. I have excluded Germany and Austria because the allies shared military and political control there. Furthermore, American jurisdiction in both countries rested in the hands of military authority. I have treated Finland peripherally partly because of her location on the fringe of Eastern Europe and partly because she was neither an ally nor an enemy of the United States during the war.

As to the criteria for sample selection, only those career diplomats of grade 5 or lower in the post-World War II classification system who were stationed in Eastern Europe and Soviet Russia or the appropriate geographic divisions of the State Department between 1944 and 1946 for a period of at least six continuous months were included.[4] Those officers in the entry-level grade 6 (the equivalent of FSO-8 and the "unclassed" grade for the period from 1924 to 1946), whose duties were wholly administrative in nature and whose status was considered probationary; those who spent less than six continuous months in Eastern Europe or the department during the 1944–46 period, whose limited duty might have precluded sufficient time to assess Soviet objectives; and those who served simultaneously as representatives to more than one government, as was the case with a number of careerists in London and Cairo assigned to various governments-in-exile, were excluded. The following brief biographical sketches will serve to introduce the thirty Foreign Service officers who are individually and collectively the subject of this book.

WALWORTH BARBOUR. June 4, 1908. Cambridge, Mass. Attended Phillips Exeter and graduated from Harvard University in 1930. Joined Foreign Service in June 1931. Balkan specialist. Currently lives in Gloucester, Mass.

MAYNARD B. BARNES. June 28, 1892. LeRoy, Minn. Attended Tilford Academy and graduated from Grinnell College in 1919. Entered diplomatic service in August 1919. Geographical focus Near East. Deceased.

BURTON Y. BERRY. August 31, 1901. Fowler, Ind. Attended Fowler High School and received his bachelors (1923) and masters (1925) degrees from Indiana University. Entered service in May 1928. Geographical focus Near East. Currently lives in Rome.

CHARLES E. BOHLEN. August 30, 1904. Clayton, N.Y. Attended St. Paul's School and graduated from Harvard University in 1927. Joined Foreign Service in March 1929. Soviet expert. Deceased.

JOHN H. BRUINS. May 5, 1896. Coopersville, Mich. Graduated from Hamilton College in 1918. Joined diplomatic service August 1923. Geographical focus Central Europe. Deceased.

CAVENDISH W. CANNON. February 1, 1895. Salt Lake City. Attended Salt Lake City High School and graduated from University of Utah in 1916. Studied at University of Paris. Joined service in February 1920. Balkan specialist. Deceased.

JOHN PATON DAVIES, JR. April 6, 1908. Kiating (Lo-shan), China. Attended Shanghai-American School and Yenching University in Peking. Graduated from Columbia University in 1931. Entered Foreign Service in December 1931. Far Eastern expert. Lives in Spain.

JAMES CLEMENT DUNN. December 27, 1890. Newark. Studied law and architecture. Entered diplomatic service in September 1919. Geographical focus Western Europe. Deceased.

ELBRIDGE DURBROW. September 21, 1903. San Francisco. Attended the Shattuck School and graduated from Yale University in 1926. Attended the University of Dijon, l'Académie de Droit de la Haye (Netherlands), and l'École Libre des Sciences Politiques. Joined service in April 1930. Soviet specialist. Lives in Washington, D.C.

WILLIAM N. FRALEIGH. September 21, 1916. Philadelphia. Attended Summit (N.J.) High School and graduated from Haverford College in 1938. Joined Foreign Service in March 1939. Resides in Rome.

W. PERRY GEORGE. November 25, 1895. Gadsden, Ala. Disque High School. Attended Gadsden Training School, the University of Grenoble, and the U.S. Naval Academy. Entered service in September 1916. Deceased.

MAXWELL M. HAMILTON. December 20, 1896. Tahlequah, Okla. Attended Sioux City (Iowa) High School and graduated from Princeton University in 1919. Entered diplomatic service in May 1920. Far Eastern expert. Deceased.

LOY W. HENDERSON. June 28, 1892. Rogers, Ark. Graduated from Northwestern University in 1915. Attended Denver Law School and New York University. Joined service in May 1922. Soviet specialist. Resides in Washington, D.C.

THEODORE J. HOHENTHAL. August 14, 1905. Daggett, Calif. Attended Turlock Union High School and received bachelors (1928) and law (1931) degrees from the University of California at Berkeley. Joined Foreign Service in December 1931. Currently lives in San Francisco.

CLOYCE K. HUSTON. May 12, 1900. Crawfordsville, Iowa. Attended Crawfordsville High School and graduated from the University of Iowa in 1922. Joined Foreign Service in July 1925. Balkan specialist. Resides in Warrenton, Va.

JOSEPH E. JACOBS. October 31, 1893. Johnston, S.C. Attended Johnston High School and graduated from the College of Charleston in 1913. Joined diplomatic service in November 1915. Far Eastern expert. Deceased.

GERALD KEITH. March 13, 1893. New York. Attended Brockton (Mass.) High School and graduated from Amherst College in 1915. Attended University of Grenoble. Entered service February 1927. Deceased.

GEORGE F. KENNAN. February 16, 1904. Milwaukee. Attended St. John's Military Academy and graduated from Princeton University in 1925. Entered Foreign Service in September 1926. Soviet expert. Resides in Princeton, N.J.

ALFRED W. KLIEFORTH. October 10, 1889. Mayville, Wisc. Received bachelors degree from the University of Wisconsin in 1913 and law degree from the University of Manitoba in 1944. Joined service in June 1916. Geographical focus Central Europe. Deceased.

FOY D. KOHLER. February 15, 1908. Oakwood, Ohio. Graduated from Ohio State University in 1931. Joined Foreign Service in December 1931. Near Eastern specialist. Became a Soviet expert after the war. Resides in Jupiter, Fla.

ARTHUR BLISS LANE. June 16, 1894. Brooklyn. Attended the Browning School and École de l'Île de France à Liancourt. Graduated from Yale University in 1916. Entered service in August 1917. Geographical focus Latin America. Deceased.

H. FREEMAN MATTHEWS. May 26, 1899. Baltimore. Attended the Gilman Country Day School and received bachelors (1921) and masters (1922) degrees from Princeton University. Studied at l'École Libre des Sciences Politiques. Geographical focus Western Europe. Resides in Washington, D.C.

ROY M. MELBOURNE. April 11, 1913. Philadelphia. Attended Germantown High School and graduated from University of Pennsylvania in 1935. Masters degree from Fletcher School (1935) and Ph.D. from University of Pennsylvania (1951). Resides in Newberry, S.C.

EDWARD PAGE, JR. July 31, 1905. Ardmore, Pa. Attended Newton Country Day School and graduated from Harvard University in 1928. Attended the Universities of Grenoble and Heidelberg. Soviet expert. Deceased.

SAMUEL REBER. July 15, 1903. East Hampton, N.Y. Attended Groton School and graduated from Harvard University in 1925. Joined Foreign Service in May 1926. Geographical focus Western Europe. Deceased.

MILTON C. REWINKEL. December 7, 1913. Columbus, Neb. Attended Roosevelt (Minneapolis) High School and graduated from the University of Minnesota in 1935. Attended graduate school at Minnesota. Joined Foreign Service in July 1937. Resides in Mexico.

H. F. ARTHUR SCHOENFELD. January 31, 1889. Providence, R.I. Attended the Friends School in Washington, D.C., and received bachelors (1907) and masters (1909) degrees from George Washington University. Attended George Washington Law School and the University of Caracas (Venezuela). Joined service in September 1910. Deceased.

HAROLD SHANTZ. January 10, 1894. Rochester, N.Y. Attended East High School and graduated from the University of Rochester in 1915. Joined service in October 1921. Deceased.

FRANCIS B. STEVENS. April 6, 1905. Norwich, N.Y. Attended Schenectady High School and graduated from Union College in 1926. Studied at the Universities of Berlin, Geneva, and Besancon. Soviet specialist. Joined service in June 1931. Deceased.

LLEWELLYN E. THOMPSON, JR. August 24, 1904. Las Animas, Colo. Graduated from University of Colorado in 1928. Entered Foreign Service in January 1929. Soviet specialist. Deceased.

The narrative proceeds chronologically. The first chapter briefly describes the historical origins of the Foreign Service, analyzes the social backgrounds of career officers, and examines the institutional processes by which the service inculcated in them the culturally-induced concept of American foreign policy, their professional roles, and the organization's behavioral norms. It also considers the factors that contributed to the decline of officer morale during America's isolationist era of the thirties, reinforced social and intellectual conformity, and hence constrained independence of imagination and judgment. Chapters 2–3 discuss the social experiences of diplomats in Russia, Latin America, East Asia, and Europe during the 1930s and stress two main themes: first, that international instability caused diplomats to relate heretofore isolated developments in particular countries to the larger structure of world affairs; second, that their concept of an orderly and harmonious international system, their opposition to foreign political entanglement, their Europo-centric cultural bias, and their state of apathy as a result of the State Department's bureaucratic inertia impelled them to judge sympathetically the rise of authoritarianism, to tolerate the fascist "aberrations" of Italy and Germany and to fear the socially disruptive, anti-modern force of Soviet communism. The next two chapters analyze the fitful transformation of the diplomats' image of the Soviet Union after 1942. Chapters 6–7 contrast the perceptions of ideological cooperation and confrontation respectively held by diplomats in the department and the field in 1945 in the context of the different social-psychological environments in which they functioned. Chapter 8 traces the deterioration of U.S.-Soviet relations after 1946: the reemergence of mutual mistrust and hostility symbolized by Moscow's renewed fear of "capitalist encirclement" and Washington's evolving "containment policy." A summary chapter analyzes the underlying factors that gave rise to the diplomats' images of the Soviet Union. The epilogue takes the story full circle to the Truman Doctrine, where it began.

Throughout the narrative I have attempted to show that the diplomats' perceptions of events in Eastern Europe after 1944 were colored by their ingrained cultural values and beliefs, by historical memories of Bolshevik propaganda as well as Nazi behavior in the region, and by the psychological effects of social-environmental influences. It is my contention that these factors blurred their memory of interwar Eastern Europe and narrowed their vision of Soviet objectives, which, prescinding evidence to the contrary in the still inaccessible Soviet archives, were not globalistic, as American diplomats believed, at least for the immediate postwar period, but rather cautious and limited in both strategy and tactics. Writing about this crucial period in American foreign relations three decades later, and at a time when both powers, armed with weapons of awesome destructiveness, hover on the precipice of renewed Cold War, the historian who perforce lives vicariously the rapidly changing and unsettling developments these diplomats experienced must guard against reading into the past the anxieties of the present. That these Foreign Service officers, honorable and well-intentioned men socially and culturally conditioned to a particular view of the world, misperceived Soviet intentions amid the swirl of events in which they were enmeshed must not be construed as a moral failing on their parts, but rather as a tragic failing which betrays the inescapable frailty of the human condition in which we all share. Finally, then, this book essentially seeks to present a human portrait of American foreign relations.

1. The Social Milieu

During the nineteenth century, when the dominant issues in the United States were domestic rather than foreign, international affairs played an insignificant role in the nation's life. While European statesmen traded other people's real estate with one another to maintain a tottering balance of power, and monarchs helplessly sought to stem the tide of social change, Americans, except for a mid-century attempt at self-mutilation, went about the business of nation building. Imbued with Enlightenment ideas and ideals, geographically insulated from the struggle for mastery of the Old World, they self-consciously based their foreign policy for most of this period on the principles of peaceful commercial expansion and political noninvolvement in the affairs of other states.

Just as the rules of the game were different in Europe than in the United States, the actors who played the game—the diplomats—were also judged differently. Notwithstanding his Machiavellian public image, the diplomat was accepted as a necessary evil by Europeans and accorded considerable social recognition. By contrast, the American diplomat, in the eyes of his countrymen, enjoyed a sinecure at the expense of the national treasury. At best he was a symbolic reminder of the nation's status in the world; at worst an effete "cookie pusher" and "striped pants boy" who had disingenuously fallen prey to the undemocratic ways of the European aristocracy.

Extreme as these unflattering epithets were, they were not without some basis in reality. Although the diplomat did negotiate commercial treaties, report political changes in foreign governments, collect commercial information, and promote trade, his function was primarily representational. Ministers were usually drawn by presidents from the ranks of politicians, wealthy campaign contributors, retired generals, and journalists. Diplomatic secretaries typically entered the service through family connections with newly appointed ministers or through political patronage. For many of these young men, who had still not decided upon careers or who had simply grown weary of the tedium in their lives, a diplomatic fling offered an opportunity for travel, adventure, education, and an entrée into the world of royalty and refinement. There were no formal qualifications; but then, little was expected of them. As late as the 1890s, heads of missions could still be found advertising for polo-playing secretaries. Training in the art of diplomacy, such as it was, emphasized mainly the finer points of diplomatic etiquette and protocol.[1]

During the last two decades of the century, however, a small group of younger officers formed the vanguard of a movement to professionalize the diplomatic service. Their interest in rescuing diplomacy from the rich dilettante or political amateur coincided with the larger reformist aspirations of the "respectable classes" in American society, the old-line elite who detested the spoils system and who wanted to restore the principle of "free trade" in the dispensation of government jobs. These reformers wished to create a body of diplomatic specialists, functionally expert but politically neutral. In their eyes, the ideal diplomat should be someone who possessed the requisite education and breeding; someone, like them, "representative of what is best in American society, of that element in it which gives it its strongest claims to gratitude and respect of the civilized world." This notion of social stewardship found a receptive audience among diplomats like Joseph Grew, Hugh Gibson, Leland Harrison, Jr., and Franklin Mott Gunther, who shared the same background, values and social outlook of the genteel reformers.[2]

Eventually, businessmen, Social Darwinists, and religious groups, all of whom contributed to the growing mood of national expansionism, also joined the movement for a trained, nonpartisan foreign service. But their attention focused primarily on the consular service, which had historically protected the rights of American citizens abroad and promoted trade. Given the nation's preeminent interest in commerce and its ingrained suspicion of traditional diplomacy, diplomats realized that a professionalized service could only be achieved by fusion with the consular service. So they increasingly advertised their potential contribution to the expansion of American trade. Aided by businessmen, chambers of commerce, the National Civil Service Reform League, and others who believed that international commercial intercourse would benefit world peace as well as satisfy American interests, their efforts finally bore fruit in the Rogers Act of 1924, which merged 511 consular and 122 diplomatic officers into the Foreign Service of the United States. While both bodies were to remain functionally distinct, provision was made for the interchangeability of officers in diplomatic and consular assignments to facilitate organizational efficiency and to "dearistocratize," that is, Americanize, the diplomatic branch. To enable individuals of humbler means to enter the service, the measure also provided for higher salaries, travelling and representational allowances, retirement, and disability benefits.[3]

While some scholars, notably Warren Ilchman and Waldo Heinrichs, Jr., have contended that the Rogers Act paved the way for a "democratized" Foreign Service during the 1920s and 1930s, the social backgrounds of the thirty diplomats in this study, which compare favorably with the demographic composition of the service as a whole, suggest that the organization retained its exclusivist character. The composite portrait reveals that they were from native-born, Anglo-Saxon, Protestant, upper-middle-class parents who lived primarily in the northeast. As descendants of early American settlers, some of them traced their forebears to the Revolutionary War period. Although mainly English, a number were of German extraction. Thirteen grew up in New England and the Middle Atlantic states; eight were from the Midwest; four came from the South and Southwest; and four were raised in the Far West. One was reared in China. The sample was evenly divided between urban and rural backgrounds, with the latter predominantly represented by those from the South and the Midwest.

Almost half were the sons of professional men—lawyers, ministers, military officers, and educators. About a third were the sons of businessmen, the majority of whom were banking executives or presidents of companies. One of the thirty came from a farming family; another, the son of a grocery store proprietor, was the product of a white-collar, lower-middle-class occupational background. None came from working-class backgrounds.

Slightly more than half of the group received their secondary education in public schools; somewhat less than half were privately educated. All but two were college graduates; six possessed either masters or law degrees; and eight more received some postgraduate training. In addition, thirteen engaged in study abroad. Three fourths of them attended private universities rather than state schools. Eighteen went to private colleges in the East; nine attended Yale, Harvard, or Princeton. Virtually all were Protestants, half of whom were either Episcopalian or Presbyterian. These faiths, with their emphasis on order, ceremony, and mission, provided symbolic spiritual sustenance for the profession of diplomacy. One was a Catholic and one was Jewish.[4]

To be sure, the demographic characteristics of these diplomats reflect the post–World War I trend toward a broader geographical representation, public versus private secondary education, and the increasing recruitment of candidates from nonelite colleges; but on balance, Foreign Service officers continued to present an Eastern, Anglo-Saxon, Ivy-League appearance. A private income was still an important factor for those who wished to embark on a diplomatic career. Enrollment at expensive Washington "cramming schools," where candidates prepared for the Foreign Service examination, persisted into the 1930s to the disadvantage of applicants from humbler backgrounds. In addition, there are indications that Catholics and Jews, while not denied admission to the service, may have been handicapped in their careers.

During a meeting of the Foreign Service Personnel Board in December

1924, for example, Joseph Grew questioned whether H. F. Arthur Schoenfeld, who gave his religion as Episcopalian, should be considered for a position as chief of mission. Although Grew felt that Schoenfeld was "a very keen and brilliant man," he noted that "he is probably of the Jewish race and that fact might affect his service at certain posts," such as Rome, "where the social and representational aspects of the job were important." On the other hand, Grew had not observed any of the "unfavorable Jewish attributes" in his behavior. In the end, Schoenfeld was unanimously endorsed for a ministerial post. In a letter to Burton Berry in 1937, G. Howland Shaw, then assigned to the division of Foreign Service Personnel, wrote that in his efforts to become division head, he felt personally attacked by Wilbur Carr, one of the founders of the Foreign Service, who reminded him that, among other factors, his Catholic faith would have to be taken into consideration.[5]

At best the Foreign Service of the interwar years was an organization in transition, less aristocratic in appearance than the diplomatic corps of the nineteenth century, but more elite than the institution which evolved after World War II. On the whole, those who were accepted into the service, as opposed to those who sought admission, were still representative of a small and relatively homogeneous segment of American society. "The diplomats of the thirties and forties were cut more or less of the same cloth," said one retired officer. By virtue of their education and background, they were "more of a type." That service, he added, was a better organization than its modern successor, "where you have to have so many blacks, tans or blues." "The old service of the Rogers Act was frankly an elite corps," remarked a colleague. "A superior education, a superior intellectual approach, a superior sense of responsibility and self-reliance, a superior flair for languages, all were important requisites for admission," he recalled nostalgically. "Those who made the grade took immense pride in their abilities and enjoyed a unique sense of camaraderie, akin to that found in the congenial circles of a close-knit professional club."[6]

As a result of the Rogers Act, Foreign Service officers underwent a period of training, acquired a specialized knowledge, displayed an affective neutrality and a lack of self-interest in the conduct of their duties, and based their status on performance rather than ascriptive characteristics. Yet the attempt to professionalize the diplomat was not wholly successful. In the first place, he did not regulate his own behavior. While the new legislation instituted self-control mechanisms such as the Board of Examiners and the Board of Foreign Service Personnel, social control was actually exerted by the hierarchical authority structure of the State Department. Secondly, in contrast to doctors and lawyers, the diplomat did not provide his own discrete body of knowledge.[7] For this he de pended upon the professional expertise of historians, political scientists, geographers, and students of international law.

Foreign Service officers themselves differed over what constituted a professional. To the self-styled generalists within the service, mainly but not all pre–Rogers Act officers, diplomacy was an art; the qualities which distinguished the "professional" diplomat from the amateur were the intangible ones—judgment, imagination, discretion, prudence—qualities that were cultivated and refined through years of experience. A smaller group, mostly younger officers who were trained as Soviet, Near Eastern, or Far Eastern specialists, were more self-conscious of their roles as "experts." Having immersed themselves in the language, history, and civilization of another people, they depended less on intuition and more on objective analysis for their views of international behavior. Although they did not deny the importance of insight or judgment, they conceived their vocation more as a science.

Collectively, the thirty Foreign Service officers assembled in this study represent a cross-section of the diplomatic community by date of entry, geographical experience, and specialization. Thirteen entered prior to the passage of the Rogers Act, when American foreign policy concentrated on the Western Hemisphere and China, and when diplomacy was still the practice of gentlemen; fourteen joined between 1924 and 1932; three entered in the late 1930s—two in 1937 and one in 1939—after the hiatus in new recruitment during the middle years of the decade. Ten received formal training as country or regional experts. Seven of these were Soviet experts; three were Far Eastern experts. Twelve were area specialists with five or more years of experience in the Balkans (three), the Near East (three), Western Europe (three), Central Europe (two), or Latin America (one). Eight possessed no special regional expertise. Half of the sample had served in Eastern Europe prior to 1944; a third had previous experience in the Soviet Union. Twelve had either minimal or no exposure to this part of the world, eight of whom would serve in key positions in the field or the department between 1944 and 1946.

Because of their specialized training, experts were inclined to form cliques, which, as John Paton Davies has noted, were closed even to specialists from other geographical divisions of the department. Foy Kohler, for example, trained first as a Near Eastern expert, recalled the reserved greeting he received from George Kennan when he joined the staff of the Moscow embassy in 1946. Area and country experts, in short, reckoned themselves superior to their nonspecialized colleagues, rather an elite within an elite. As one officer wrote from Riga in 1936, the Russian specialists represented "a somewhat unassimilable element." Their work, which "is not tied up with the daily business of the institution," he stated, "lends itself to the habit of mind of a Ph.D. candidate, whose own little contribution to scholarship is the one thing in which he can perceive any importance." Consequently, "all the members of that group are under the temptation of regarding themselves rather after the manner of prima donnas."[8]

Professionally threatened by the experts, generalists reaffirmed their attachment to a more traditionally defined, hence superior, identity. They contended that excessive specialization limited the Foreign Service officer's usefulness. The diplomat was an actor, not a scholar, one careerist put it, who was broadly schooled in his craft. No degree of scholarly training could substitute for "the assets of perceptiveness, sound judgment, panoramic understanding, and intuition tempered in the fires of practical experience." The backbone of the service, another veteran diplomat explained, was the "general practitioner." Although encouraged to take Arabic language training, Burton Berry preferred instead another field assignment in the Near East. In his opinion, understanding the mentality of a people afforded as much specialization as the "drudgery" of language training.[9]

Regardless of their differences, career officers univocally welcomed their responsibilities as professional diplomats. A triumphant Joseph Grew broadcast from Washington, D.C., on February 24, 1926, that a "new order" had been established in international affairs. Henceforth, the nation's commercial interests abroad would be protected by "a new generation of red-blooded young Americans, straight-thinking, clear-speaking men, whose watchword is 'service' and whose high conceptions of integrity, sincerity and patriotism is steadily raising the standards of effectiveness of the honorable profession they follow." In a speech delivered at Dartmouth several years later, J. Theodore Marriner compared the modern diplomat to a physician, a "healer" who strove to befriend foreign peoples and to cultivate cooperative relations. Foreign Service officers served not just the United States, Secretary of State Charles Evans Hughes pointed out, but the "whole human family."[10]

As these comments indicate, the occupational roles the career diplomat was called upon to play combined traditional values with a new ethos. Clearly, trade promotion and equality of commerical opportunity had directed the course of American foreign policy since the founding of the republic. Adherents to a liberal-capitalist world view, nineteenth-century Americans, like the British, believed that trade relations should be divorced from politics in international as well as domestic affairs. Free enterprise would simultaneously produce individual prosperity and contribute to the general welfare of society; in their view, it was both socially and morally beneficent. The active promotion of harmonious relations among nations, however, espoused most ardently by Woodrow Wilson, was a relatively recent objective. Wilsonian ideology defined the national interest in liberal-internationalist terms. According to Wilsonianism, the United States had a mission to export to other countries the same Lockean blueprint—political democracy, free trade, and the rule of law—from which the American nation was formed. Obversely, the United States sought to transform the European international system, which inhibited political self-determination, fostered national trade rivalries, and resorted to force rather than law to settle international disputes. It was the function of the diplomat, as an expert in statecraft and as an agent in an immutable, rational-historic process in which realpolitik would give way to a world order of peace, prosperity, and harmony, to spread the blessings of free enterprise and constitutionalism, that is, to internationalize the American liberal-democratic national experience.

To learn their roles as professional diplomats and, in so doing, to become familiar with the goals of American foreign policy, new recruits were to receive a year-long course at the Foreign Service School, which was established under the Rogers Act. Coursework in history, international law, and geography was intended to supplement their undergraduate education. As it turned out, however, the importunate need to alleviate manpower shortages in the field reduced the term of study to several weeks or, at most, a few months and shifted the focus of the lectures to administrative and procedural matters—visas, notarials, issuances of bills of health—with which the individual would be immediately confronted upon arrival at his post.

Despite these constraints, senior diplomats and State Department officials presented occasional lectures to impress newcomers with the nature and importance of their duties. Their remarks simultaneously strengthened the group's common social identity, its shared undertaking, and its sense of belongingness. Joseph Grew, Wilbur Carr, and others who led the movement to professionalize the service reminded junior officers of their responsibilities to make the new service work. They encouraged them to develop an esprit de corps, to take pride in their work, and to remain attentive to the sensibilities of Congress and the public. No less stress was placed on career opportunities within the service for ambitious young men, "if they make it pay."[11]

The *American Foreign Service Journal,* which succeeded the *American Consular Bulletin,* reinforced group attachments and shared social values. The publication's stated purpose was "to add to the understanding of the tasks and surroundings of the Foreign Service, to maintain and enlarge the acquaintance with one another of widely scattered colleagues and to preserve and increase the zeal of the officers in the Foreign Service for the protection and promotion of American interests." While its breezy, gossipy format hardly presented the appearance of a professional journal, it served a useful purpose. Commentary on the comings and goings of Foreign Service officers—notices of births, deaths, transfers, and promotions—symbolically lessened the physical distances which separated colleagues, and reinforced organizational cohesion. Pieces on the evolution of American diplomacy and on developments in the diplomatic corps of other countries helped to cement the diplomat's professional identity; and articles of local color, such as coverage of the World Series, strengthened national connections.

Editors and senior officers also used the pages of the journal to stress the importance of the diplomat's role. Modern diplomacy must be wrested from the provincialism of the past, wrote DeWitt Poole, a career officer with considerable experience in Russia. As the globe continued to shrink and as American political and economic contacts grew, he averred, the value of the diplomat-expert would far outweigh that of the highly intelligent generalist. "The time is past," a colleague declared, "when the problem of major diplomatic importance was that of gaining the ear of the king's mistress or in ascertaining to whom he had transferred his affections." Another careerist pointed out that "more and more today the great discoveries are coming from the laboratories of the leading industrial concerns and universities, where many scientists have collaborated on new discoveries and where no one person can lay claim to the whole achievement. So in diplomacy, the laboratory has come to prevail."[12]

But the most important way in which younger members of the service learned their roles was by interacting with experienced diplomats. This took on added significance in the field, where newcomers were daily exposed to the social and intellectual influence of senior officers through a formal hierarchy of work relations. At the head of the organization was the chief of mission; he determined field assignments, established the reporting style, and reviewed the performance of the officers who served under him. Moreover, he and other senior diplomats attached to the mission presented a standard on which younger Foreign Service officers modelled their professional identity.

In spite of this formal organizational structure, there existed at the same time a pattern of informal interaction among diplomats. This was due to the isolated nature of the diplomatic post and its compact size. During the period from 1924 to 1946, the Foreign Service numbered only some 650 to 800 people. Actually, the social character of the field mission was reminiscent of communal relations in traditional, small-town America. Similarities in social backgrounds made diplomats feel comfortable with one another and facilitated the development of intimate personal ties that extended beyond their professional association. They shared similar values, role definitions, and a common social language. "At the average diplomatic Mission or Consulate," observed a British diplomat, "one is on close terms with most, if not all, of the other members of the staff, and there is, especially at small posts, the atmosphere of a large family." Social interaction between "families" was also common, and the more isolated the diplomatic community—physically, socially, or polit- ically—the more likely it was to form close associations with other foreign missions. Diplomats posted in Moscow during the 1930s, for example, developed relationships of "such strong personal sympathy and so much mutual trust that they lasted even beyond the war and its aftermath."[13]

Career officers in the department enjoyed an equally warm and re- warding atmosphere. An air of "old-world courtesy" prevailed that fos- tered personalized relationships. From the coding clerks to high depart- ment officials, all were regarded as "fellow members of the departmental family." The department was akin to one's "home town," to which dip- lomats returning from field assignments were genially welcomed by their Foreign Service colleagues.[14]

Veteran careerists, both in the department and in the field, conveyed to newcomers a sense of pride in the emergence of the United States as an international power. Illustrative of this nationalistic attitude was the speech delivered by John H. Bruins in Singapore on July 4, 1929. Although it was 153 years old today, he exclaimed, "it is only since the Spanish-American War, a mere three decades ago [sic] that our country has taken its present place among the colonial powers of the world." Encouraged by new inventions like electricity, air travel, synthetic goods, and the beauty of modern American architecture, Bruins predicted that the "possibilities of the United States are only beginning to be realized." At the same time, like other Americans of their generation, the pre-Rogers Act diplomats adhered to the goals, if not the means, of Wilsonian inter- nationalism. While they maintained that international bodies and the ef- fect of public opinion held little sway in a world based on competitive national interests, they were hardly apologists for European power poli- tics. Quite the contrary, they subscribed wholeheartedly to the Wilsonian ideals of peace, prosperity, and the rule of law. They lauded their gov- ernment's desire to promote harmonious relations among nations, for which, as Bruins noted, "we may also take pride in our national idealism. Surely the present seems but a turning point into a new and more marvel- lous future." And who, he rejoiced, was in a better position to understand and guide American aspirations than the group of "cosmopolites" living outside the United States. As scions of an old-line, nativist elite, career diplomats felt especially equipped, by virtue of their background and education, to transmit these ideals to a benighted world. Indeed, they perceived themselves as apostles, both as Americans and as elites, of a new day; and they proudly spread the word.[15]

Social attitudes and the prescribed norms of diplomatic behavior exhibited the same mixture of old and new values as the roles into which careerists were socialized. On one hand, the Foreign Service officer was heralded an expert, a professional in foreign affairs. After all, as Secretary of State Hughes had stated, the "days of intrigue to support dynastic ambitions [and] to promote the immediate concerns of ruling houses" were gone. The "new diplomacy" was not based on "the divining of the intent of monarchs [or] the mere discovery and thwarting of intrigues," but on "the understanding of peoples." On the other hand, he was expected, as his untrained predecessor had been, to follow loyally the directives of the State Department. His task was to implement the nation's foreign policy, not to analyze, question, or challenge it. While lower-level officers might disagree with the thinking of senior diplomats or the department, one did not lightly take issue with those of superior rank and status. Indeed, individuals who did not conform to the expectations of the mission chief might not find themselves on the next promotion list. In short, the hierarchical structure of the diplomatic post inhibited intellectual competition among its members. Since opposition to prevailing attitudes entailed the potential loss of a promotion as well as of the emotional support of the community, dissidents were unlikely to receive social approval. Thus the individual's and the group's perceptions of reality tended to coincide.[16]

Senior careerists also taught younger officers correct diplomatic style. To deal effectively with sophisticated diplomats abroad, Grew explained in an address to the Foreign Service class of 1926, one had to present a cultured and courteous appearance, what the French diplomat Jules Cambon called *"une certaine habitude du monde."* A proper command of English was absolutely essential. The varieties of diplomatic etiquette, including cookie-pushing and tea-serving, did no one any harm, according to the *American Foreign Service Journal*. Indeed, diplomatic style was no less important at a formal dinner or cocktail party than at the foreign ministry. Breaches of etiquette could have repercussions damaging to America's international relations, not to mention an individual's chances for promotion. In addition, indiscreet indulgence in wine and women was similarly viewed disapprovingly. Sometimes it provoked a reproach from the chief of mission or other senior officers; occasionally it led to an individual's transfer.[17]

Decorum was especially important in the elegant capitals of Western Europe, which enjoyed the most prominent social standing among American diplomats. Junior officers were advised to emulate the standards of diplomatic style set by European models, especially the British. The presentation of a cultured appearance was less critical in the backward and underdeveloped regions of the world, such as Asia and Latin America. Attitudes toward these climes revealed marked ethnocentric biases. The

February 1925 issue of the *American Foreign Service Journal,* as an example, carried a piece of doggerel extolling a Chinese boy who awakened, dressed, nursed, even suffered the diplomat's abuse, who affection ately snitched food and cigarettes, and who was most missed when the officer was on holiday.

The diplomats' cultural image of Soviet Russia and the Slavic lands of Eastern Europe, notwithstanding the institutional emphasis on understanding peoples, mirrored the ethnocentric and racial prejudices that permeated American society during the early years of the twentieth century, particularly urban, nativist, upper-middle-class American society. Reared in this social milieu, career diplomats carried with them a stereotype of southern and eastern European immigrants as dirty, unruly, inferior, and uncivilized peoples who had vulgarized American social, political, and moral life. The immigration restriction act of 1924, Harold Shantz told the American Women's Club of Toronto early the following year, assured "the continued progressive development of a thoroughly united country and a homogenous American race." Non–Anglo-Saxon types, unfamiliar with the English language and liberal institutions, he pointed out, were simply unassimilable into the fabric of American society.[18]

Considering the fanfare that greeted the new professionalized service, it was hardly remarkable that career diplomats looked forward to certain social and personal rewards. Not only were they repeatedly reminded of the abundant cultural, intellectual, and career opportunities that awaited them, but as Hughes soothingly intoned, they also "had the inspiration and the satisfaction of the assurance that the nature and importance of their service are appreciated at home." But careerists soon discovered that they had a negligible impact on the nation's foreign policy and that the acclaimed importance of their service was neither appreciated by the American public nor its elected officials. The more the chasm between social expectation and reality widened, the more demoralized they became.[19]

Morale within the Foreign Service began to decline in the late 1920s as diplomats came to realize that their function was essentially to observe, report, and, "above all," Bohlen recalled, "don't get involved." Conditions worsened in the thirties. The emergence of political authoritarianism, military expansionism, and world autarchy mocked the Foreign Service officer's ostensible role of apostle of liberal-internationalist principles. Shocked by the destabilizing and destructive tendencies of foreign states, the American government and public attempted to barricade themselves behind the facade of neutrality legislation. As a consequence, the professional diplomat, so-called expert, was reduced to the status of his nineteenth-century predecessor, for the most part a "clerk at the end of a wire." His purpose, as defined by Secretary of State Cordell Hull, was to provide accurate and impartial information, protect the lives and property of Americans in foreign countries, and carry out the department's instructions. "We were merely foreign observers," Elbridge Durbrow remarked. Although Hull did not oppose a "fair interpretation" of what one observed, few diplomats would characterize the field reporting during the interwar years as interpretive.

To make matters worse, a wave of noncareer attachés flooded the ranks of the service in 1939, following the Commerce and Agriculture Departments' disbandment of their foreign installations. Foreign Service officers complained to no avail that the transferees had neither the preparation nor the commitment to a diplomatic career. The establishment of the division of cultural affairs in 1938 and the subsequent wartime transfer of cultural attachés into the service was seen by careerists as a further infringement of their professional status. George Messersmith, assistant secretary of state for administration and former minister to Vienna, contended that cultural attachés merely duplicated tasks already performed by diplomats. As he superciliously reminded the head of the cultural affairs division, the Foreign Service represented "the best there is in our culture and tradition."[20]

The diminution of the diplomat's professional status was further aggravated by the public's untoward view of his social utility. The issue that reignited public resentment of the diplomatic elite was the interchangeability of officers in consular and diplomatic assignments. Based on their interpretation of the Rogers Act, consular officers anticipated the frequent interchange of officers between the two branches; diplomats, however, fearful of losing their organizational distinctiveness, argued that interchangeability was to be exercised judiciously. They maintained separate membership on the Foreign Service Personnel Board and rigidly adhered to different performance-appraisal policies than did the consular service. As a result, diplomatic vacancies tended to be filled by diplomats. Moreover, because there were more vacancies in the diplomatic branch, the number of promotions greatly surpassed those of the consular service. At a meeting of the personnel board in March 1927, then Undersecretary of State Grew asserted that the single list of promotions desired by consular officials would be superfluous since efficiency was the major criterion for advancement. Furthermore, he argued, it would be unfair to diplomatic officers, who were markedly superior to consular people.

Because most consular officers felt that fusion would eventually take place, they initially tolerated the separate but unequal attitude of the diplomatic branch. But by 1926, their patience having grown thin, they began to criticize openly the favoritism demonstrated by diplomatic representatives on the personnel board. Their reaction, along with the outcry across the nation that it set loose, led to a congressional investigation in 1927. While the press and public vigorously backed the inquiry to limit the power of men of wealth and influence, diplomats scornfully referred to it as "the Senatorial inquisition." Perturbed by a Senate proposal to require a definite period of service for all officers in the consular branch, Arthur Bliss Lane sardonically called the measure "a 5-year penal servitude." [21]

Despite the objections of diplomats, Congress passed a bill in 1931 which restricted their influence over promotions and reaffirmed the concept of a combined service. With the issuance of dual commissions from that time forward, the interchangeability of Foreign Service officers became the rule rather than the exception. Still, relations between consular and diplomatic representatives remained "neither close nor cordial." As an illustration, the ceremonial practice of having third secretaries of embassy take precedence over consul generals at international functions persisted into the 1930s as a symbolic reminder of the consular service's second-class status. For some diplomats the levelling effect of interchangeability was a bitter pill to swallow. If the same rewards were to be given to "second-rate men," Burton Berry groaned, the more ambitious and capable officers would be forced to leave the service. Others, however, like Schoenfeld, simply resigned themselves to what appeared to them to be "the vogue." [22]

Resolution of the dispute between the two branches of the Foreign Service only temporarily blunted domestic criticism of the diplomat. A new assault was mounted in the thirties. Caught up in the throes of the depression, the public considered it sheer prodigality to contribute to the economic support of clerks with aristocratic pretensions. Some Americans even suspected the diplomat of harboring totalitarian proclivities. The managing editor of *Nation* excoriated the diplomatic elite within the State Department for their attachment to Victorian diplomacy, their boarding-school, Ivy-League cast and their clerico-fascist sympathies toward Italy and Spain. He saved his most fulsome language for James Clement Dunn, chief of the division of western European affairs. A favorite whipping boy of American liberals for his support of Franco, Dunn was portrayed as one of the most "politically unenlightened and socially reactionary men" in the department. "Rich, snobbish, and flawlessly groomed, cultivated in the social graces and backward in social thought, Dunn is the pattern of the career man who has long dominated the Foreign Service." [23]

Through the pages of the *American Foreign Service Journal* and popular magazines, diplomats defended themselves against their detractors. They emphasized, with some validity, the drudgery of diplomatic life, their overworked conditions, and their economic hardships. Their attempt to disavow the public stereotype of the Foreign Service officer as a member of the Social Register and a model of fashion who knew more about bridge and fine wines than international affairs was less credible. The modern diplomat, they pleaded, was typically middle class, of moderate means, and a Midwesterner with a degree from a Midwestern university. If the Foreign Service appealed mainly to the wealthy, asserted one careerist, it was precisely because American diplomats did not enjoy the same career opportunities and remuneration as their counterparts from even second- and third-rate powers.

Sometimes careerists took the offensive against their critics. They attacked the public's failure to appreciate the complexities of international affairs, criticized its indifference to foreign relations, and scoffed at the popular notion of diplomacy as deceitful, dishonest, and trivial. One diplomat wrote anonymously in *Foreign Affairs* that Americans embraced an unrealistically optimistic view of world affairs. The dignity of the individual, equality of commercial opportunity in foreign markets, and the legal resolution of international grievances, however valid to the United States, he argued, were no longer viable objectives for many governments in the totalitarian world of the 1930s.[24]

While the depression did not force the diplomat into the bread lines as it did many of his countrymen, the federal retrenchment program it prompted clearly impaired his economic security. The combined impact of pay cuts, the dollar devaluation, reduced housing allowances, and the suspension of promotions, post allotments, and representational allowances shrivelled the salaries of Foreign Service officers by as much as 75 percent in some cases. According to one writer, the number of careerists declined from 762 in 1931, when the retrenchment program began, to 688 by the end of 1934. Those who managed to weather the storm did so cheerlessly. Loy Henderson lamented that he was forced to live on an income roughly equal to that which he had earned ten years earlier. W. Perry George complained that the "drastic" and "irrational" economic cutbacks reflected the "deplorable lack of continuity in the government's policy toward the Foreign Service which can only aggravate [and] accentuate the feeling of acute insecurity and further undermine the morale of entire personnel." Berry informed the department that he saw little point in retaining his service affiliation without the expectation of a promotion. Indicative of the diplomat's reaction to the austerity measures, a cartoon in the April 1934 issue of the *American Foreign Service Journal* showed a line of men with placards bearing the acronyms of familiar New Deal programs queued up at the U.S. Treasury. At the end of the line stood a tattered little careerist in a bruised derby with an SOS tag affixed to his sleeve. Although diplomats began to receive some relief in 1935, when salaries were restored and housing allowances raised, their demands for increased representational allowances, home leaves, and an improved promotion system persisted throughout the decade and beyond.[25]

Even more damaging to the diplomat's morale than public condemnation and economic uncertainty was the lack of support, either real or symbolic, from the Roosevelt administration. Vice President Henry Wallace confided to his diary in 1942 that "the State Department is probably the weakest department in our entire government." Although "there have been a great many fine devoted servants in the State Department," he allowed, "the percentage of career diplomats with little to commend them aside from a wealthy background is altogether too high." For his part, Roosevelt displayed an almost contemptuous indifference to the State Department and the Foreign Service. He considered career diplomats "fossilized bureaucrats," frivolous dilettantes, and reactionaries. According to one careerist, Roosevelt believed that the road to minister or ambassador could be travelled by anyone who remained loyal to the service, offended no one, and exercised a reasonable degree of sobriety at public functions.[26]

Of course, Secretary of State Hull was not unsympathetic to the grievances of the service. Unfortunately, he could offer little more than understanding. In the first place, his energies were almost totally invested in programs to promote international trade. In addition, he was by nature a procrastinator and disliked involvement in controversial issues. More importantly, Hull had little influence on Roosevelt. Indeed, he was not shown the crucial Lend-Lease bill, which proposed wartime aid to Great Britain, until four hours prior to its introduction in Congress. Having been bypassed by Roosevelt in favor of Undersecretary Sumner Welles and presidential advisor Harry Hopkins, he seriously considered, on at least one occasion, resigning his office.

Although Roosevelt sustained the trend to appoint chiefs of mission from the ranks of career diplomats, he continued to save the most important European posts—London, Paris, Rome, Berlin—as political plums for worthy campaign contributors and political friends, a practice careerists feared would destroy the service. The professionals he did appoint, moreover, had little role in the conduct of foreign affairs, since he preferred to rely on hand-picked emissaries to deal with important foreign-policy questions. "[Roosevelt] had little or no understanding for a disciplined hierarchical organization," George Kennan explained. "He had a highly personal view of diplomacy, imported from his domestic political triumphs. His approach to foreign policy was basically histrionic, with the American political public as his audience. Foreign Service officers were of little use to him in this respect."[27]

The changing mood of the professional diplomat during the interwar years mirrored the spirit of the entire nation. The optimism and confidence that had animated the Foreign Service of the twenties gave way to disillusionment and dejection in the thirties. Professionally and socially alienated by the public and the government, unable to transfer their skills to other occupations in a depression-plagued economy, career officers retreated into their private institutional world. Collectively an enormous out-group unified against the outside environment, on the eve of World War II they languished in a state of "diplomatic isolation," a reflection of the political and psychological condition of the American people.

As demoralized as they were, the overwhelming majority of diplomats did not leave the service. This was due partly to the strength of their career commitment, but more importantly to the supportive ties of the diplomatic community, which eased their frustrations, anxieties, and disappointments. But the more accustomed the diplomat became to his "life of self-imposed exile," the more he felt estranged from his own country. Still, despite the feelings of cultural disconnectedness, it was comforting for him to know that his colleagues understood and shared his misfortunes. In a way, noted one careerist, Foreign Service officers secretly enjoyed their "martyrdom," and rather derived a "masochistic pleasure" from it.[28]

2. The Soviet Connection

The process of socialization to which Foreign Service officers were con-
tinually exposed imbued them with a shared liberal-internationalist concept of international relations which derived from the American historical
experience by way of seventeenth-century British political dissent, John
Locke, and Utilitarianism. Fundamental to this concept were the ideals of
unrestricted commercial intercourse, noninterference in the political affairs of other countries, and deference to the balancing function of public
opinion. This, of course, was the metaphysical basis of the Wilsonian
world order. In his application of this concept, however, Wilson excluded
Bolshevik Russia, whose concept of the world, derived from the Russian
historical experience by way of Rousseau, Marx, and Lenin, was not only
antithetical to, but also inimical to, his vision. Thus Russia was branded
an international pariah.

Once the scare of global revolutionary disorder subsided, this image of
the new Soviet state that the Foreign Service inculcated into the thinking
of professional diplomats increasingly diminished in intensity. Following
the establishment of diplomatic relations in 1933, diplomats assigned to
the Moscow embassy actually nurtured the idea that the Kremlin had
trimmed sail on a course of international cooperation. However, the purge
trials of the late thirties and the Nazi-Soviet pact soon dispelled their
hopes. By the beginning of the forties, they reverted to the old image of
Soviet Russia as a revolutionary outcast, even more dangerous now as a
result of Stalin's penchant for power politics.

At the beginning of the 1920s, diplomats, like other Americans, viewed
the Soviet Union with mistrust, anxiety, and hostility. Fearful that the
Soviets were bent on destroying the traces of civilization, they considered
the wave of strikes and bombings that afflicted the United States in the
wake of the Bolshevik revolution ominous portents that the cataclysm
prophesied by the Third International was about to take place. Although
the world proletarian revolution did not occur, diplomats remained uneasy about the future. They remembered Trotsky's dire prediction at the
Fifth Congress of Russian Communist Youths in October 1922 that "the
revolution is coming in Europe as well as in America, systematically,
step-by-step, stubbornly and with gnashing of teeth in both camps. It will

be long, protracted, cruel and sanguinary." In the opinion of Alfred Klieforth, who had served with American armed forces in Russia during World War I, "Communism was less dead than ever, unless Germany should develop a stable conservative gov[ernment]."[1]

Alarmed by Moscow's relentless, crusading rhetoric, diplomats opposed recognition of the Soviet Union. Since the Third International and the Soviet government were synonymous, reasoned William R. Castle, Jr., head of the division of European affairs, recognition would simply open American portals, as Europe had unfortunately discovered, to Bolshevik propagandists. As a State Department memo of March 1926 stated, "There has been no change in the essential fact of the existence of organizations in the United States created by and completely subservient to the Bolshevik regime, seeking the overthrow of the existing social and political order of this country."[2]

No one was more intransigently opposed to recognition than Robert E. Kelley, chief of the division of Eastern European affairs. Having studied Russian at Harvard and the Sorbonne, Kelley was a "scholar by instinct and dedication." Under his tutelage, junior officers such as Charles Bohlen, who entered the service with no great interest in or knowledge of Bolshevism, were introduced to the nature and objectives of the Soviet Union. Kelley, Earl Packer, and other senior diplomats lectured on Russian history, politics, geography, and culture. Special emphasis was placed on Soviet ideology and its ultimate goal of world revolution. As a consequence, diplomats in the eastern European division, particularly, developed "a sharply critical view of Soviet activities, policies, and methods, and believed in standing up firmly to the Kremlin on the many issues in dispute."[3]

Meanwhile, by the late 1920s the incubus of communism had gradually faded from the view of most Americans. Businessmen interpreted Lenin's introduction of the New Economic Plan in 1921 and the increasingly nationalistic, production-oriented focus of Stalinist Russia as harbingers of a slowly developing capitalist ethos. Their call for recognition, which grew louder after the onset of the depression, was echoed by liberals and intellectuals, who believed the Soviet experiment in social engineering offered the United States a model for an ethical, progressive, and economically stable society. While Foreign Service officers did not share these sanguine expectations, they moderated their views of Soviet Russia. For one thing, Moscow's baleful rhetoric had considerably subsided. For another, it seemed anomalous for two nations the size of Russia and the United States to remain diplomatically estranged, when all other major powers had already recognized the Soviet state. Thus, with the exception of such unyielding foes of the Soviet Union as Kelley, career diplomats went along with the president's decision to restore relations with Russia.

Actually (not that Roosevelt would have asked), they had no strong opinion one way or the other. In a diary entry of October 24, 1933, Joseph E. Jacobs, who was serving in the department's Far Eastern division, casually noted that "[Foreign Commissar Maxim] Litvinov is coming over to discuss matters with Roosevelt." On November 18, two days after Litvinov and Russia exchanged formal statements of recognition, Grew, then ambassador to Japan, confided to his diary that the Soviet ambassador called for an appointment, "which means we've recognized the Soviet Union; [but] I've heard nothing from the Department." This rather stoical mood of the career service was reflected in the matter-of-fact way news of the momentous decision was carried in the *American Foreign Service Journal,* buried in a column with the heading, "Washington News Items."[4]

It seemed fitting—and historically ironic—that Roosevelt selected William Bullitt as the first American ambassador to the Soviet Union, the same William Bullitt who had so enthusiastically worked for Soviet-Allied rapprochement at the Paris Peace Conference, only to be shunned by President Wilson. No less buoyant than he had been in 1919, Bullitt told the Philadelphia Chamber of Commerce in January 1934 that both the United States and the USSR, despite differences in domestic institutions, were advocates of peace. Russia's economic reconstruction program, her admiration of American technical know-how, and her "pioneer spirit," he observed, symbolized the cultural affinities that united the two nations.[5]

Joining Bullitt in Moscow were George Kennan and Charles Bohlen, the first of a coterie of officers from the "unclassified" rank of the Foreign Service selected on the basis of educational background, personality, career interests, previous experience, and the needs of the department, as trainees in the Russian studies program instituted by Kelley in 1927. Under Kelley's program, these young men received formal training in Russian history and politics at l'École Polytechnique in Paris. The sole exception was Kennan, who studied at the University of Berlin's Seminar für Orientalische Sprachen, the institution created by Bismarck to prepare diplomats for assignment to the Orient. Exposed to his teachers' realpolitik view of international affairs as well as to the intellectual current of Weimar Germany, which pulled against the dominant stream of liberalism in American and British political thinking, Kennan, as we shall see, would interpret Soviet behavior differently than would his fellow careerists. Of the fourteen individuals who were trained as Soviet specialists, only Kennan, Bohlen, and a few others would remain by the 1940s, most of their colleagues having either washed out of the program or quit the service entirely.[6]

Aloof, sensitive, and intensely serious, Kennan had a brilliant intellect and a scholarly devotion to, as well as affection for, Russian history and culture. "I have rarely been so impressed by the ability and character of a man of his age," Bullitt wrote to J. V. A. MacMurray, minister to the Baltic States and Kennan's boss. "His Russian seems to be perfect and he should be, unless I am mistaken, the wheelhorse of the embassy here. That will mean that I shall have to take him away from you. I apologize, but he is to my mind essential." Bohlen, a descendant of the aristocratic Bohlens of Prussia and a cousin of the head of Germany's Krupp arms industry, also possessed "a keen and exceptionally alert mind." Somewhat "brusque in manner and rather self-centered," he shared Kennan's intellectual arrogance, if not his academic style of presentation. Moreover, with a gift for amusing conversation, spontaneous joyousness, and "the capacity to match the Russians drink for drink in the vodka bouts which were an inevitable part of diplomacy in Moscow," the attractive and charming Bohlen, unlike Kennan, enjoyed the popularity of his fellow officers.[7]

Loy Henderson and Harold Shantz completed the nucleus of the mission. Henderson was an intelligent and meticulously conscientious officer, "ever watchful of his country's interests." Although not formally trained as a Soviet expert, he had acquired years of specialized experience in the division of Eastern European affairs. In addition, he had worked in 1919–20 with the Red Cross in the Baltic States, which provided him with a glimpse of the "brutality and torture" in postwar Russia. Because of these early experiences and his compassion for "small peoples" struggling to establish viable democratic states, he was more inclined than either Bohlen or Kennan to view the USSR from the perspective of the Eastern European states. The lively and good-natured Shantz, who remained with the mission for less than two years, was a generalist responsible for the embassy's administrative affairs. Later in the decade, Edward Page, Jr., another Soviet specialist, and Elbridge Durbrow would also join the embassy staff. The charming, handsome, and affable Page was not the intellectual peer of either Kennan or Bohlen. But he had "excellent political sense" and understood well, in Henderson's opinion, the policies and tactics of the Kremlin. Emotionally intense, amusing, and indefatigable, Durbrow, who had served previously in Poland and Rumania, was assigned to Moscow in 1934 as an economics officer.[8]

Kennan, Bohlen, and Henderson had seen service in Riga during the years prior to Soviet recognition, when that tiny Baltic port afforded the United States "a window to the east." In those days, and even after recognition, diplomats assigned to the Riga research post read and analyzed Soviet newspapers, periodicals, and party magazines and reported to the department as best they could on conditions inside Russia. As late as the summer of 1933 the sovietologists in Riga, indirectly exposed to the changing currents inside the USSR, and influenced by the White Russians they met there, had considered the American public's expectations of cooperation with Moscow overly optimistic, if not naive. In Henderson's opinion, the Soviet Union, which continued to seek the overthrow of democratic governments and the establishment of a communist world headquartered in Moscow, hardly represented a democratic experiment. Noting that Moscow's ultimate economic goal—as reflected in the program of forced industrialization and the collectivization of the peasantry—was autarchy, Kennan attributed talk of expanding trade between the two countries to either a "malicious desire to misinform" or ignorance.[9]

Despite their pessimistic utterances, the Soviet specialists did not oppose Washington's normalization of ties with Moscow. In fact, they accepted the agreement with surprising equanimity. By the early weeks of 1934, they actually began to view with guarded optimism the Soviet-American future. The roseate buds they sprouted were due partly to the warm welcome accorded Bullitt when he presented his credentials to the Soviet government, including Stalin's promise to permit construction of a new American embassy. More significant, no doubt, was the overpowering charm and the infectious confidence radiated by Bullitt.

Henderson has called 1934 "a honeymoon period" in U.S.-Soviet relations, and, in many ways, it was. With mobility unrestricted, the Moscow embassy drank up the sights and sounds of Russian life, so unexpectedly accessible to them. On one occasion, Bohlen and Kennan gleefully served as advisors to a Russian stage production of *The Front Page*. Delightfully surprised by the development of "a new cosmopolitan society" of artists, writers, scientists, and industrial managers, Foreign Service officers began to reconsider their old stereotype of Soviet Russia: primitive, xenophobic, culturally barren. It seemed as if the Russians were becoming *embourgeoisés*. Citizens took pride in their personal appearance; the military adopted such conventions as the salute; and the people expressed veneration for Russia's past. Even the government's views toward the West, especially the United States, were in flux, with some leaders openly fostering feelings of genuine cooperation and friendship.

At the policy level, relations between the two countries appeared equally encouraging. Although the thorny questions of imperial Russia's prewar debts to the United States and the confiscation of property owned by American citizens were left unsettled in the Litvinov talks, efforts continued throughout the year to resolve them. The embassy was further heartened in September by Moscow's entrance into the League of Nations, a move which ushered in the "Geneva period" in Soviet foreign policy and contributed to the internationalist-cooperative image of the USSR which American diplomats were gradually forming. Up to this time, Stalin had watched the rise of Nazism with apparent aplomb. The menacing visage of an ambitious Führer and the signing of the German-Polish alliance the previous January, however, had caused him to reassess matters. While embassy officials recognized that Stalin's decision to join the league was motivated by his concern for Russian security, they believed at the same time that it indicated Moscow's support for the West's policy of collective security. More importantly, it gave rise to the hope that the doctrine of two hostile worlds, written into the preamble of the 1923 Soviet constitution, would be replaced by a policy of continued rapprochement with the noncommunist world.[10]

Meanwhile, undetectable to the American embassy, concealed tensions of potential destructiveness were building within the Communist party. Sensitive to the hardships visited on the Russian people by the collectivization program, liberal factions had begun to call for moderation of the regime's domestic policy. Opposition seemed to center on Sergey Mironovich Kirov, secretary of the party's Leningrad Committee and member of the Presidium of the Soviet Central Executive Committee. Obsessed by the threat to his control, Stalin commenced a bloody purge of the opposition on June 30, which culminated in the assassination of Kirov on December 4 and the suppression of the humanizing elements among the "old guard." As the new year dawned, the purge of disloyal and subversive elements within the state picked up steam. The major targets of Stalin's wrath were the remnants of the old Russian nobility, former leading industrialists and estate owners and the party leaders of the "Leningrad Center," notably Lev B. Kamenev and Grigorii E. Zinoviev.

While Stalin reaped his harvest of party heretics, which constituted the threat from within, he became increasingly attracted to the merits of collective security. At the Seventh Congress of the Communist International in July 1935, he abandoned the hostile line of world revolution in favor of a united front of communists, socialists, and left-liberal parties marching together against fascism, the threat from without. During the same year, Moscow consummated alliances with France, following a mutually passionless courtship of two-and-a-half years, and Czechoslovakia.

Stunned by the purge of Kirov and the old Bolsheviks, whom they considered model Soviet leaders, Foreign Service officers feared a repetition of the revolutionary violence of the previous decade. Stalin's determination to liquidate all Trotskyites and Zinovievites, Bohlen informed the department in January 1935, was no more than the internalization of the terroristic techniques applied by the Soviets against their perceived class enemies. The once irrepressibly optimistic Bullitt was now convinced that Kremlin officials were barbarian fanatics bent on imposing communism on the United States and the world, and that the so-called social experiment was really a brutal and inhumane system of pain and suffering. Like the caliphs of Islam, he told the department before leaving Russia in 1936, they committed "heinous crimes with a sense of virtue." While careerists did not advocate Bullitt's proposed Franco-German reconciliation to oppose the "Godless theocracy," they also reevaluated their inchoate internationalist-cooperative image of Soviet foreign policy in the wake of the Kirov episode. Kennan and Bohlen agreed that Moscow would determine its future course independent of its treaty obligations with France, which were based on little more than "cordial distrust and euphemistic self-restraint," and Czechoslovakia. Henderson believed that recent Soviet criticism of fascist elements in the United States and the continued activities of the Communist International suggested that the Kremlin had not abandoned its ideological goal. His view was supported by Shantz and Page, the latter having temporarily joined the mission in 1935, who noted that published letters to Stalin from high-ranking members of the party revealed that the temporarily quiescent proletarian revolution was still the ultimate Soviet aim.[11]

The year 1936 marked a turning point in Soviet foreign policy and a hardening of the American mission's perceptions of Stalin's objectives. As France and Britain watched from a distance, Italy conquered Ethiopia, Germany remilitarized the Rhineland, and the fascist-aided Spanish rebels began to assert their dominance over Republican Spain. Disillusioned and embittered by the timidity of Britain and France, especially in permitting Hitler to seize the Rhineland, Stalin, pausing briefly to render valuable aid to Loyalist forces in Spain, lost confidence in the arid legalism of collective security and in the feckless collaboration of leftist elements in the so-called united front. Realizing that he could not rely on French assistance in the event of a German attack to the east, he set out to build up the Red Army and to strengthen unilaterally the integrity and defense of Soviet territory, a move, undiscovered at this juncture by the American embassy, that would ultimately lead to the Nazi-Soviet pact of 1939. Having decided to abdicate the collective security program and the united front, Stalin next had to deal with the possibility of political repercussions should his new course be challenged domestically. Thus the curtain was rung up for the first of three public purge trials which eliminated all potential opposition and, as we shall see, psychologically alienated the American diplomats who witnessed them.

The August 1936 trial of Zinoviev, Kamenev, and fourteen other key figures of the so-called Leningrad faction was a meticulously produced affair with all the dramatic effects of a Greek tragedy. Four hundred ticket-holders, including embassy and press visitors, filled the theater to watch the "beautifully staged" spectacle. Prosecutor Andrei Vyshinski reminded Henderson alternately of Lionel Barrymore and a "circus director putting a group of well-trained seals through a series of difficult sets." Charged with being Trotskyite enemies of the state and "therefore allies of the Hitler fascists," the accused, to the astonishment of the visitors, admitted their guilt in long and moving perorations to the tearful gallery. To no avail British and French socialist leaders appealed to the Kremlin to commute the death penalty and offer the right of appeal. In response, *Pravda* implacably denounced their intercession, calling them "agents of the Gestapo" equally deserving of liquidation. Twenty-four hours after the trial was concluded, all sixteen convicted "terrorists" were killed.[12]

Members of the American embassy were horrified by the methodical inquisition they had witnessed. While they suspected that the executed leaders had probably contemplated killing Stalin, there was no evidence of an actual plot or of Trotsky's complicity. Furthermore, it seemed incredible that Stalin would attempt to divide the proletarian movement at a time when forces of the right were bent on its destruction. Overcome with disgust, by the end of 1936 diplomats had completely divested themselves of their earlier hopes of Soviet cooperation with the United States and the Western democracies. Summarizing relations between the two countries since 1933, Henderson concluded that the differences between the American and Soviet systems of government were unbridgeable. As a dictatorship, the Soviet Union had more in common with the fascist states than with the United States. But even this was not an apt comparison, in Henderson's view, for Moscow pursued "much more of a progressively aggressive foreign policy than do most powers which are endeavoring by peaceful means to satisfy their international ambitions." Unlike that of other states, he pointed out, Soviet foreign policy was based on "a series of definite objectives," with world revolution and the creation of world socialist republics the main goal and Russia as the foremost world power a subordinate objective. Whereas power operated in the service of ideology to Henderson, just the opposite was the case to Kennan: "It is only the distribution of force which determines the Soviet attitude toward world affairs." In his opinion, the Kremlin was no longer interested in the Third International; this was only a weapon to be used in the larger "battle for power pure and simple." Stalin, like Mussolini, was a dictator for whom "such things as principles, ideals, human lives and even the welfare of entire peoples will be no more than pawns." American pacifists and liberals, he admonished, must not be deluded by Bolshevik propaganda which portrayed Stalin as "a modern Prince of Peace." Soviet goals were no longer defensive; rather, they were becoming increasingly imperialistic.[13]

Career officers became even more estranged from the Kremlin during the final three years of the decade. The hysteria and degradation produced by the purges of January 1937 and March 1938, which resulted in the liquidation of Karl Radek, Nikolai Bulganin, and the remaining influential members of the Bolshevik intelligentsia, strained their credulity. Dismissals, arrests, and executions showered the country. Lesser officials, Stakhanovites, party operatives, artists, writers—no one was immune from the reign of terror. Soviet citizens, urged, as "voluntary workers" for the People's commissariat for internal affairs, to keep their eyes and ears open for potential enemies of the state, viewed one another suspiciously, as the hunt went on for Trotskyites, saboteurs, and antinationalists. The outlying republics of the USSR were charged with conspiratorial connections with foreign agents. A number of officials in Soviet central Asia were arrested or disgraced; others committed suicide. Thousands of ethnic minorities—Poles, Ukrainians, Afghans, Chinese, and Volga Germans—were relocated like cattle in central Asia and Siberia.[14]

To ensure his undisputed domination over Soviet officialdom, Stalin filled the government bureaucracy with nonparty types described by Kennan as youthful "rankers" who had grown up in Stalinist Russia and who carried with them no memories of the czar or Lenin. Stalin won their confidence and, in turn, made them "more useful instrument[s]" in his hands by encouraging them to aspire to positions of authority vacated by purged party members. To control the masses, who at first took "malicious pleasure" in the extermination of bureaucrats and rural party bosses, he constructed xenophobic barriers which effectively ended their contact with the outside world. Citizens who made connections with foreign embassies were arrested, imprisoned, or killed as potential enemies of the state; public officials were humiliated or removed from office. As the public grew increasingly fearful for its own safety, Stalin projected blame for the devastation on lower-level officials and stressed the importance of protecting innocent citizens. Recognizing the widespread acceptance of the liberated 1936 constitution, cunningly contrived to follow the Zinoviev-Kamanev trial, he permitted the electorate to vote for hand-picked candidates by secret ballot in the December 1937 elections to the Supreme Soviet. Equal employment opportunities were stressed, rationing was eliminated, some industrial and agricultural enterprises were decentralized, and patriotism and pride in Russian culture were revived.[15]

Spectators before the convulsive orgy of human sacrifice unleashed by the new round of purges, American diplomats were bewildered and brutalized by Stalin's malevolent disregard for human life and for "the values on which a stable society is based." Seared by their experience, they struggled to understand how one man could be driven to destroy many of the best minds in Russia, to harness the rest in a despotism of conformity, to liquidate thousands of Red Army officers in such an uncertain and threatening international environment. Henderson attributed this apparent madness to Stalin's "semi-oriental nature: vengeful, jealous, suspicious, capricious." Bohlen related it to Stalin's lack of contact with the "human values of Western christian [sic] civilization." Kennan considered it partly due to Stalin's paranoia and partly to the Russian character, conditioned by centuries of backwardness, inferiority, and xenophobia.[16]

Relations between the embassy and the Kremlin were now almost nonexistent. Diplomats denounced the "democratic" elections to the Supreme Soviet as a farce, "a gigantic dumb-show," with the Supreme Soviet nothing but a "mechanical and pompous tool of the ruling Stalin clique." Gazing at the sea of faces in the Supreme Soviet, Henderson and Bohlen found it difficult to suppress their ethnocentrism. "Judging from appearances," the intelligence level of the House of Soviets was "considerably lower" than in the West; that of the House of Nationalities seemed even lower. Even more disturbing, Page pointed out, it was a "sad omen" that the reign of terror continued after the elections. Embittered by the hideous blood bath they had witnessed, they discharged their hostility on the newly appointed ambassador, Joseph E. Davies, whose predisposition to see the bright side of the "Soviet experiment," in spite of the purge trials, produced a near mutiny.[17]

Isolated from the people as well as from Soviet officials, careerists likened themselves "to the passengers from a ship which had been wrecked on a desert island surrounded by a shark-infested sea." The culture, the topography, the people themselves—almost everything outside their own island community—seemed, as before 1934, forbiddingly primitive and depressing. To purchase currency, import food, to enter and leave the country, to meet with American citizens, they were no less dependent on the whim of the regime than the Russian people. Their personal effects were searched, their goings and comings closely watched; and they were frequently portrayed to the public as foreign spies. In the summer of 1938, Kennan wrote that conditions were unlikely to revert "to their former state of comparative liberality" for some time. And they did not.[18]

The purges and the attendant internal reorganizations of the party and the army had a pronounced effect on the embassy's perceptions of Soviet foreign policy. The embryonic internationalist-cooperative image formed by the Soviet specialists during the Geneva period was replaced by the old image of Bolshevik Russia: revolutionary, isolationist, and dangerously manipulative. Such symbols of cooperation with the West as the united front, Henderson stated, were merely maneuvers to conceal the regime's world revolutionary objectives. At variance with foreign diplomats like the French ambassador, Robert Coulondre, who presciently argued that the Soviets might forego their isolationist-revolutionary posture for an agreement with Nazi Germany, Henderson wrote to a colleague in Riga: "If Hitler thinks the Soviet will drop their revolutionary aims, he will be disappointed." The recurrent theme of "capitalist encirclement," Bohlen observed, suggested Moscow's return to the revolutionary program of the pre–united front period. Noting the Kremlin's increased antifascist rhetoric, which gradually included fascist sympathizers and bourgeois tolerators in the United States as well, he pointed out that the regime's preoccupation with internal affairs and its indifference to the more formal aspects of international affairs had led to the decline of its relations with every European and Near Eastern power. Kennan reported to department officials that Moscow's hostility toward the capitalist world, as evidenced by the Communist International's manifesto commemorating the twentieth anniversary of the October revolution, remained unaltered and that the Comintern, in repudiation of the Litvinov pledge of 1933, continued to seek "the overthrow of the political and social order of the United States."[19]

This isolationist-revolutionary image of the Soviet Union embraced by American diplomats was conjoined with a realpolitik view—cynical, deceitful, amoral—which gained increasing strength as the world edged closer to the brink of war. Despite Russia's alliances with France and Czechoslovakia and her earlier support for collective security, Kremlin officials, in their judgment, now appeared perfectly content to watch Europe and Asia go up in flames. Moreover, Moscow would surreptitiously attempt to fan those fires of friction. Antifascist propaganda would keep Europe divided and hasten war in the west; encouragement to the Chinese to resist Japan, as evidenced by the Sino-Soviet nonaggression treaty of August 1937, would keep the Japanese bogged down in China, thereby diverting their attention from Soviet territory, and possibly embroil the United States in the Far Eastern conflict. Once she succeeded in manipulating a world conflagration, Russia would cynically bide her time until the combatants weakened themselves, at which point, Kennan observed, she would intervene, "if only in the capacity of a vulture." The Soviet Union stood poised for the revolutionary kill. "Moscow has tasted the wine of proletarian imperialism after [World War I]," he noted, "and though the cup was promptly snatched from her lips, the flavor has not been forgotten." As the hour of war in Europe began to knell, and it became more apparent that Stalin would side with the forces of destruction, the suspicions of Soviet perfidy harbored by American diplomats became reality.[20]

While the Japanese and Chinese obligingly played their parts in the Soviet scenario, European states took steps to avoid a conflict. Thanks to the appeasement policy of Britain and France, Germany had managed to expand her sphere of influence in central Europe without firing a shot. Having recently signed an anti-Comintern pact with Japan, Hitler now cast covetous glances eastward. Understandably apprehensive, the Kremlin turned a conciliatory cheek toward the Third Reich. Rumors of a thaw in Russo-German relations started to infiltrate the American embassy as early as the spring of 1937. By early 1938 Stalin began intimating to Hitler that Russia might be receptive to friendly ties provided the security of Soviet territory were guaranteed. At this stage, considering the ideological onslaught they had just witnessed, American diplomats attached no importance to these innuendoes. Neither did the British and French, who vainly tried to pacify Hitler later in the year. However, with Germany's seizure of Prague in March 1939, it became clear to Western governments and American diplomats that the policy of appeasement had failed.[21]

Thus it was that Britain and France initiated talks with Russia in April to reconstruct the anti-German alliance of World War I. Mindful of the West's recent efforts to propitiate Berlin, Stalin was wisely cautious. Meanwhile, having begun relatively minor economic discussions with Germany, Soviet representatives in Berlin tentatively approached the Wilhelmstrasse on broader political issues. In May the German ambassador, Count Friedrich Werner von Schulenberg, was summoned from Moscow by Hitler, who, intent on avoiding a two-front war, had decided to pursue earnestly the Soviet probings. Recognizing the reciprocal hatred which existed between Russia and Germany, but justifiably suspecting, at the same time, that the British and French ultimately desired to see the two come to blows, Stalin continued to chart a delicate course between Scylla and Charybdis. In Henderson's view, he presented to both sides "the attitude of a woman being wooed by suitor[s] to whom she was in no hurry to give an answer." But this was no dalliance on Stalin's part; he was completely serious about selecting a partner. He simply wanted to be sure that he chose the one who offered the least precarious peace.

Throughout these tension-filled months, the American embassy, in addition to staying abreast of Soviet talks with Britain and France, kept informed of the Russo-German negotiations through a contact in the German embassy. In July, while Britain and France temporized, pourparlers between Moscow and Berlin began to show promise. By mid-August Bohlen reported to a skeptical State Department that details had been worked out for a German-Soviet agreement. On August 23 Joachim von Ribbentrop, Hitler's obsequious and bumptious minister of foreign affairs, met with Molotov in Moscow, where they affixed their signatures to a nonaggression pact. More importantly, the embassy later learned that in the secret protocol to the agreement, Germany had consented to precisely what Britain and France refused to concede: a territorial division of Eastern Europe that included within the Soviet sphere the Baltic states (save, for the time being, Lithuania), the eastern half of Poland, and Bessarabia.[22]

Henderson, who had returned to the department as assistant chief of the European division a year earlier, was nonplussed by this volte-face in Russian foreign policy. Here was the Soviet Union and her avowed ideological enemy throwing themselves together in an unfathomably absurd demonstration of friendship. Noting the sudden absence of revolutionary references in Soviet speeches, he pondered the possibility that Moscow had abandoned its struggle to impose communism on the world. Still, he wrote University of Chicago professor Samuel Harper, the inflammatory rhetoric of the Comintern had not abated. To him, then, the pact only indicated a change of Soviet tactics; the revolutionary goal remained the same. Bohlen and Page, the latter having joined Henderson in Washington, emphasized more the amoral realpolitik element in Stalin's thinking. Bohlen asserted that the Kremlin's decision, above all else, was motivated by its desire to preserve the Soviet system. Had Britain and France been willing to match Germany's concessions, and had they been able to provide the assurances of military support in case Russia were attacked, the Kremlin might very likely have chosen to cast its lot with the democratic states. "It would in fact now appear that many of the Soviet Union's much heralded theories of collective security and corrective action against fascist states," Page had stated at the outset of the talks with Germany, "were advanced with the idea in view that the resistance to the fascist powers should be borne mainly by countries other than the Soviet Union. This has become more and more clear in the light of recent events."[23]

Once the initial shock of the German-Russian bombshell had passed, careerists began to assess the implications of the agreement. Henderson and Kennan believed the compact was, at best, a *mariage de convenance*. Referring to the economic agreement between the two states by which Germany would obtain badly needed agricultural products in exchange for manufactured articles, Henderson acknowledged that the Reich's willingness to sell national defense goods might indicate "that it has no intentions to attack the Soviet Union." But it would be a mistake to view the agreement as a political alliance of an aggressive nature, for both sides continued to mistrust each other. Although the setting and characters had changed, mused Kennan, who had followed the events of the past two years from central Europe, both powers would continue to act out the imperialistic confrontation of 1295 when the Knights of the German Order and the horsemen of Alexander Nevsky battled on the frozen surface of Lake Peipus.[24]

After Germany's invasion of Poland on September 1, Bohlen, who remained in Moscow, came round to the view that the Nazi-Soviet accord was a much more serious affair than he had at first thought. When the Red Army entered the country on the 17th, he reported to Washington that "this morning's invasion of Poland by Russian troops convinces me that the recent [understanding] between Russia and Germany has reached the stage of active cooperation between the two countries." Since the Soviet press praised the liberation of White Russians and Ukrainians and condemned the "reactionary" policies of France and Britain, he concluded, "I see no prospect of an hostile attitude on the part of the Soviet government towards Germany in the immediate future. All evidence appears to foreshadow an extended period of Soviet-German cooperation." A second economic agreement between the two countries in February 1940, which involved a massive exchange of Russian raw materials, particularly grains and petroleum, for German manufactured goods, confirmed his expectations. This "far-reaching step," he wrote, created a condition of mutual self-interest that would make Soviet political collaboration with Germany a practical necessity. Bohlen's assessment was quite on the mark. By virtue of this agreement, Russia became Germany's chief raw materials supplier; in turn, Germany became the primary source for Russia's importation of arms and machine tools.[25]

With the destruction of Poland, the secret protocol of the Nazi-Soviet agreement was brought into grim focus. This was cordially modified in the aftermath of the fighting: Germany received a larger chunk of Poland; and Russia, as a *quid pro quo,* incorporated Lithuania into her sphere. On the surface the victors appeared quite satisfied with the results. However, clearly frightened by the swiftness and strength of the German war machine, Stalin decided to secure control of his sphere while Germany was still savoring the fruits of victory. Between the end of September and the middle of October, representatives of the Baltic states trekked to Moscow at Stalin's command to sign nonaggression pacts with the Soviet Union and to provide naval bases and military fortifications for Soviet forces.

The refusal of Finland to agree to similar demands met with a Soviet invasion in November. Coincident with this action, Soviet troops began to occupy the military installations relinquished by the Baltic governments. By the summer of 1940, three more states had been erased from the map of Europe.

Foreign Service officers and other officials in the State Department were aghast at the barbarous manner in which the totalitarian powers set out to transform the face of Europe. To Henderson, who had married a Latvian, the demise of the Baltic states was particularly tragic. He remembered their efforts to build viable societies following World War I. Now, he thought, would come the inevitable process of sovietization: the midnight searches, the executions, and the long, silent train rides into the white Siberian wasteland. In a memorandum of June 30 drafted to prepare Hull for a meeting with Soviet Ambassador Constantine Oumansky, he denounced the Kremlin's decision to abandon the principles of peace "for which it led us to believe it stood" and its collaboration "by deed and word with the advocates of the rule of armed force." At the same time, he recognized that Roosevelt, Hopkins, Hull, and Secretary of War Henry Stimson, given the unpredictable state of world affairs, sought to avoid any precipitous behavior which might alienate Moscow, a consideration which grew in importance as the possibility loomed that the United States might be drawn into war, probably against Japan. Thus he advised Hull to tell Oumansky that, "in spite of the disillusionment which we have suffered," it was still "not too late to save civilization from the calamity that is threatening us," provided Moscow and Washington would work "for those principles in which my Government believes and which it is still difficult for us to believe that you have irrevocably abandoned."[26]

In the months ahead, Henderson, Page, and their colleagues in the department, befitting their training, dutifully implemented the administration's policy of restraint and caution, which included supplying Moscow with machine tools, limited quantities of gasoline, and other commodities and permitting Soviet engineers to visit factories in the United States to learn American production techniques. They loyally defended these measures against the criticism of congressional leaders such as Senator Arthur Vandenberg and officials from other government agencies, who feared that the sudden infiltration of Soviet agents in the United States would be detrimental to national security, "since it was the desire of this Government to maintain as cordial relations as possible with the USSR." But their animus against Russia had not waned. At the end of August, Henderson unsuccessfully recommended that the department publicly impugn the validity of Soviet gains in the Baltic region, as it had condemned German and Japanese aggression. Of course, Page stated in October, the Kremlin insisted that it stood for peace, but its violent actions in Poland and the Baltic area were "ethically indistinguishable from the aggressive acts committed by Germany, Italy and Japan." Combining images of power and ideology, he added that "the principles of revolution and class warfare" continued to direct the Soviet leaders, who "have never departed from the ultimate aim to enlarge their domain and to include under the Soviet system additional people and territories." In view of this, "it becomes apparent that no action or policy should be based upon the word of the Kremlin, however solemnly pledged."[27]

This was precisely the message Bohlen was trying to get across to Sir Stafford Cripps, British ambassador to Moscow, early in November concerning the impending talks in Berlin between Molotov and Ribbentrop. Bohlen had suspected during the summer that relations between Russia and Germany were cooling, an obvious departure from the views he had held earlier in the year. The cession of Bessarabia and northern Bukovina to Russia and the subsequent decision by Germany and her Italian ally to modify the Hungarian-Rumanian border were unmistakeable signs of tension to him. The anti-Comintern pact between Germany, Italy, and Japan (which was actually directed against Britain) provided him with a more emphatic signal. Listening to Cripps anguish about how the talks might strengthen Nazi-Soviet collaboration, Bohlen concluded that the British had learned nothing from their experience of 1939. Concessions, he stated, whether from Germany or the Western democracies, meant little to the Soviets. If anything, they diminished one's status and prestige in Moscow's eyes. Lest Washington might suffer a similar misperception, he advised against making any concession until the embassy learned the results of the conference.[28]

While they were not visible to foreign observers, fissures in the Nazi-Soviet alliance actually began to appear after the Russo-Finnish War. Stalin's demands of territory and bases from Helsinki were clearly intended to provide a strategic buffer against Germany. The speed and power of the Nazi sweep through western Europe in the spring and early summer magnified in Stalin's mind the possibility of a German attack in the east. Thus the Soviet leader began to establish contacts with Yugoslavia, which had abstained from entering into relations with Moscow, stepped up his claims in Rumania and Bulgaria, and occupied the Baltic states. Disturbed by Soviet actions, Hitler tightened his grip on the Balkan areas under his control. In the meantime, diplomatic communications between Berlin and Moscow, undertaken to define more precisely their respective spheres of influence, proved unsuccessful. Finally, in mid-October, Ambassador Schulenberg handed Stalin a letter from Ribbentrop suggesting that Molotov visit Berlin.

The Nazi-Soviet discussions stalemated. Molotov's demands for Russian control of the Black Sea, the Straits, and the Baltic region were completely unacceptable to the Germans. Of far greater significance, the persistent conflict of interests between the two countries confirmed Hitler's long-held belief that, sooner or later, he had to crush Russia. Now that she represented Germany's only remaining military threat on the continent, that time had arrived.

Although Bohlen, who had been transferred to Tokyo at the end of November, surmised that the talks had broken down, he had no inkling of Hitler's decision. Neither did the Moscow embassy. Similarly, despite rumors of a German military offensive, Kennan and others in the Berlin embassy found it difficult to believe that Hitler, having failed to defeat Britain, would suddenly attack eastward. Henderson, Page, and their colleagues in Washington remained equally skeptical. Indeed, Henderson felt that Moscow's policy of playing off Germany and the United States seemed to be working effectively. "If the aftereffects of the Molotov visit do not throw the Soviet Union further into the German sphere," he wrote to Laurence Steinhardt, the new ambassador to the USSR, Washington might offer "more sweeping concessions" as a reward to Moscow. "One has to admire the success of the Soviet policy. By remaining noncommittal and whispering here and there and by back door methods, it is able to gain concession after concession from all quarters without sacrificing anything. I must tell you frankly," he closed, "that I personally have some grave doubts that our policy of so-called appeasement will get us any place. However, as long as that is our policy I am endeavoring loyally to cooperate in carrying it out and I sincerely hope that my misgivings are without basis."[29]

By the spring of 1941, however, sources in Berlin had disclosed German plans to the American embassy. These were conveyed to officials in the State Department, who vainly attempted to warn Stalin. On June 22, 1941, the months of waiting ended. In the early hours of the morning, Wehrmacht tanks stole across the Soviet border and set the Russian sky ablaze with the fire from their guns. Awakened by the news, Kennan excitedly stared at a map in the embassy and reflected that the Germans had attacked at the Neman River on almost the same day as had Napoleon nearly 130 years earlier. "Can the Red Army survive?" Henderson wondered. American military officials gave them until August 1, he wrote to Steinhardt, but added the observation that Hitler might have made a fatal mistake.[30]

The implications of the German invasion were far-reaching to the American government. It was simply unthinkable that Hitler could be permitted to control all of eastern Europe. Once Russia were defeated, Germany would be able to concentrate her full attention on Britain. The defeat of Britain, in turn, would place the United States between the pincers of Germany in the Atlantic and Japan in the Pacific. In March Congress had approved Lend-Lease aid to Britain to safeguard American security; President Roosevelt now ordered similar aid to Russia, whose survival was also deemed crucial to the defense of the nation.

It was clear as well to Kennan and the other Soviet specialists that Washington had to prevent a German victory in the east. Their approval of Roosevelt's decision did not imply a change of heart toward the Soviets. It would have been better, in Henderson's opinion, had Germany not attacked. Not only did this create the possibility of Russian control of central and eastern Europe, but "it meant the Soviets would be our allies." Kennan feared that Washington might extend moral support to Russia, whose attack on her neighbors, in his view, scarcely hearkened to democratic ideals. As he had earlier observed, Russian foreign policy, unlike that of the United States, was dominated by the next war. Impervious to the idea of friendly relations, the Kremlin would continue to treat other countries as "little more than pawns in the constant juggling for position which goes on in preparation for renewed military hostilities." Having attempted to purchase security by her agreement with Germany, Russia deserved little sympathy from the West for playing "a lone hand in a dangerous game." For that, he coldly stated, she "must now alone take the moral consequences."[31]

But the United States did eventually offer moral support to Soviet Russia; and, as time would reveal, the two powers were to become less the "fellow travellers" Kennan had hoped, and more the allies he and the other Soviet specialists had feared.

3. Particularism, Globalism, and the Politics of War

Throughout most of the 1930s Foreign Service officers assigned to other diplomatic posts were little concerned with the Soviet Union. Like the Russian specialists, the social-psychological worlds they inhabited were particularistic ones, formed in part by the different social, cultural, and political conditions they encountered. Just as they imposed on their environments a set of culturally defined values and beliefs they held in common with their colleagues in Russia, so too were they informed by their diverse social experiences. Until 1937 the desultory state of international relations served to reinforce their particularistic experiences. Secure in the belief that the American fortress was invulnerable to attack, diplomats in Latin America, Asia, and Europe generally sustained the government's and the public's preference for avoiding foreign political entanglements. Thereafter, however, as the countries in which they resisted began to choose sides with either the forces of change or the forces of order, they were impelled to connect their once circumscribed experiences to the larger structure of world affairs. The cataclysms of the late thirties shrank a once horizonless globe and shattered the myth of American impregnability. With the nation's entry into World War II, time and space had reached a point of convergence. To view a single event was to view the entire world at the same time. Everything touched on everything else. Europe was Asia. Asia was Europe.

Latin America

The undulating political crises in Latin America were commonplace occurrences to career diplomats. Since the end of the nineteenth century, the United States had attempted to create conditions for political stability in the region, both to obviate the intervention of foreign powers and to safeguard the lives, property, and investments of American citizens. In the years following the Roosevelt Corollary of 1905, which sanctioned Yankee intervention in the area, American marines were frequent but uninvited guests of these Hispanic states. By the end of the 1920s troops still remained in Haiti and Nicaragua; and as late as 1937 American warships drifted watchfully in Cuban waters. Meanwhile, Latin American resentment toward the imperialistic behavior of the "colossus of the north" intensified. Faced with unrest south of the border, mounting opposition within the United States, and the realization that military intervention contradicted its policy renouncing force in the settlement of international disputes, the administration of Herbert Hoover took the first steps to realign Washington's relations with its southern neighbors in conformity with the liberal-internationalist ideals enunciated by Woodrow Wilson. These efforts, continued and extended by Roosevelt and Hull, culminated in the repudiation of military intervention and political interference in the region. This was the policy of the Good Neighbor.[1]

During the summer of 1933, while the State Department was completing plans to announce formally its new Latin American policy, Arthur Bliss Lane received word that he had been designated minister to Nicaragua. At thirty-nine, the youngest officer to have served as chief of mission, Lane was nonetheless displeased with his assignment, begging Undersecretary of State William Phillips to transfer him "to a better post, presumably in Europe, before too long." A combative, opinionated person, he was also a Wilsonian idealist who staunchly supported the Good Neighbor policy. At the same time, he embraced the department's paternalistic view of the Latin American peoples, whom he considered "volatile, immature and insufficiently versed in the art of self-government."[2]

Lane arrived in Nicaragua following the evacuation of United States marines, who had been sent to restore peace between the government of Juan Sacasa and the opposing rebel faction, led by General Augusto Sandino, and who had trained a new constabulary force, La Guardia Nacional, to maintain domestic order. Upon learning early in 1934 that Sandino's forces had not relinquished all their arms and that the chief of the Guardia, Anastasio Somoza, had presidential ambitions of his own—and the military force to realize them—Lane began to worry that the delicate political balance was on the verge of collapsing. Shortly thereafter, local rumors started to circulate that Lane had conspired with Somoza in the February 21 murder of Sandino. Since the United States had established the Guardia, Nicaraguans reasoned that it could not operate without the consent of the American minister.[3]

Although Hull, at Lane's request, publicly condemned the unjustified allegations of American complicity in the assassination, he refused to become entangled in the Nicaraguan imbroglio. As political tensions in Managua rose, Lane grew increasingly concerned about the possible decline of American trade and prestige in the area were the United States to be made the scapegoat for the breakdown of civil order. Irritated by the State Department's inaction, Lane wrote privately to Undersecretary Sumner Welles in May that "the 'good neighbor' and 'hands-off' policies could be reconciled if the state department were ready to use our good offices or extend calming advice should it appear to us that a crisis, imperiling the peace of the country, is impending." Sensing the imminence of a government takeover by Somoza, Lane urged the department in September 1935 to reaffirm the policy denying recognition to governments which assumed power by force. "Everyone is looking to the United States," he told Edwin C. Wilson, chief of the Latin American division. "I do not mean to interfere with their politics. It is a question of law and order. You have to assume the responsibility of American interests and the protection of them. I shall do what you want, but I absolutely assume no responsibility for what may happen."[4]

Managua's fears of communist subversion made Nicaraguan instability appear even more threatening to Lane after 1936. On February 11 a chauffeur's strike in the capital ignited widespread rioting. Interpreting this as the beginning of revolution, Lane attributed the upheaval to the influence of the Mexican chargé, Dr. Reyes Spíndola, whose inflammatory speeches and articles "expounding Socialistic theories" had incited Nicaraguan workers. In a letter to Welles, Lane accused the Mexican of having "alienated the confidence of the Government and of General Somoza, both of whom, I feel, are sincerely opposed to communistic and subversive movements." While Spíndola had not attacked the United States, Lane noted, "we will be more seriously affected than any other country in case the working classes get out of hand."[5]

Discouraged by Washington's unwillingness to proffer a little "friendly advice" to the unruly Nicaraguans, and disgusted by the corruption and weakness of Sacasa, who criticized the "premature" withdrawal of the marines as a major factor in the current unrest, Lane accepted with alacrity his transfer to the Baltic States.[6]

The mercurial world of Central American politics provoked an equally emphatic, though less vehement, reaction from Lane's pre–Rogers Act colleagues in the area. H. F. Arthur Schoenfeld, named minister to the Dominican Republic in 1931, was a tactful, amiable, and exceptionally hardworking officer who demonstrated little of Lane's infatuation with the Good Neighbor policy. His objective in the Dominican Republic, as it had been in Mexico, where he had previously served, was to direct that state's policies along the road of political and economic freedom. "Each case of dealing with a Latin American country in our immediate sphere of interest should stand on its own bottom," he had asserted in unqualifiedly nationalistic terms, "being considered in the light of our interests, then in the light of our considered view of that country's interest and only lastly from the standpoint of any alleged solidarity among Latin American countries." H. Freeman "Doc" Matthews, formerly assistant chief of Latin American affairs, became minister-counselor at Havana late in

1933. His stated mission was to bring "peace, prosperity and stable government" to a country historically afflicted by internal disorder and unscrupulous leadership. Cautious and reserved, "dry-mannered and prosaic" to some, Matthews evinced no especial enthusiasm for the policies of nonintervention and noninterference.[7]

Schoenfeld and Matthews were no more pleased than Lane with their posts. Reflecting the ethnocentrism of the Foreign Service, Schoenfeld considered Santo Domingo a most "primitive" capital. Like their colleagues in other "backward" areas outside of Western Europe, however, careerists in Latin America found shelter from their primitive surroundings in the company of the social elite, including, of course, by virtue of their positions, prominent government officials, whose class backgrounds were much like their own. Social life in this part of the world, Matthews noted in his memoirs, centered around the Anglo-American club; friends numbered among the local elite and American corporation executives. The agreeable social life of the Dominican Republic, Mrs. Arthur Schoenfeld explained, psychologically removed the diplomatic community from the unpleasantness of civil unrest. One evening, while dancing with President Rafael Leonidas Trujillo, or "el jefecito," as only she was permitted to call him, she found herself bumping against a hard object. The source of the difficulty, she recalled with amusement, was a concealed revolver which the president good-naturedly displayed.[8]

Actually, in the early years of their Caribbean confinement, Matthews and Schoenfeld discharged goodly optimism about local developments. This they generously attributed to the guiding light of two rising stars in the galaxy of Central American dictators. Fulgencio Batista, who had led the army mutiny against the government in late 1933, was "the saviour of Cuba," in Matthews's judgment, "the one man able and willing to maintain a semblance of order." Amidst ceaseless plotting, street fighting, and intermittent bombings, he had built rural schools, put down labor strikes, protected foreign and native-owned sugar plantations from sabotage, and pledged his support for democratic elections. For his part, Schoenfeld was delightfully surprised to find things "under the strong hand of President Trujillo [so] remarkably quiet politically." Despite criticism from the press and the business community against the government's severe social and economic measures and exploitation of the courts, Schoenfeld maintained hope that the "relatively serene and consistent course" adhered to by Trujillo would be sustained.[9]

By the middle of the decade, domestic conditions in both countries had deteriorated. The announcement of new conscription and antisedition laws in the fall of 1933, aimed at combating mounting antigovernment sentiment, sent Trujillo's enemies scurrying to neighboring countries. The increasing fear of internal conspiracy and foreign invasion, nothing more than the "angry impotence" of an impulsive leader, in Schoenfeld's altered view, heralded the beginning of the government's disintegration. Fearing that Trujillo might sever relations with the United States financial advisor, and thus postpone debt payments to American creditors, Schoenfeld advised the government, in a "friendly spirit," of its obligations and special relations with Washington, for which he suffered, like Lane in Nicaragua, its reproof. Notwithstanding the policy of the Good Neighbor, he confidentially wrote Welles, "unofficial influence" would be "a desirable means" to bring about free elections in the Dominican Republic in 1934. "Perhaps its technical violation of sovereignty would be more than counteracted by material benefits." The results of the election did not change the political complexion of the country. Once again, Schoenfeld informed the department, Dominican affairs teetered on the brink of disorder: arrests, expulsions, confiscations of property, and anti-Trujillo cabals combined to reinforce the image of instability.[10]

The political climate had also dramatically changed in Cuba. The elections of January 1936 caused dissension among the various political factions, including the victorious coalition ticket of center-right parties. At first Matthews clung to the "moderate optimism" that the new president, Miguel Mariano Gómez, and Batista could restore domestic tranquility. But when Gómez was impeached later in the year, Matthews became disillusioned, calling the decision a "mere pretext for his elimination." By the spring of 1937, he reported to the department that the continuing presidential crisis, scandal, patronage, and the generally ineffectual government had produced a "wholesome disgust" among the Cuban people.[11]

As did Lane, Schoenfeld and Matthews found especially alarming the appearance of leftist movements, which were seen less as an indigenous outgrowth and more as an ideological import from neighboring states, Europe, and Russia. Influenced by local officials, conservative social elements, and the press, Schoenfeld reported as early as the fall of 1933 that revolutionary activities in the Dominican Republic were inspired by Cuban communists and apparently financed by the Soviet Union via Mexico. The subsequent deportation of several Poles suspected of communist agitation, the rise of terrorist bombings, and the formation of a secret organization in the Dominican Republic were perceived as portents of a communist-instigated plot to topple the Trujillo government. Distressed by the recent wave of strikes in Havana, Matthews despatched word early in 1934 that Cuban unions had fallen prey to a left-wing workers' confederation that operated "solely for the purpose of creating, through paralysis of industry, a situation of chaos in which its radical program of government may flourish." The bloody clash between demonstrators and the military on May Day convinced him that radical students and communists were "only too ready to take advantage of every opportunity to create trouble and weaken the [Carlos] Mendieta Government." While the stabilizing influence of Colonel Batista and other rightist forces had temporarily saved the country from a communist takeover, the government was unmistakeably "fighting for its life." After the outbreak of the Spanish Civil War in the summer of 1936, American diplomats began to define unrest in the Caribbean in global terms. While Schoenfeld hoped "that ultimate calamity in human stupidity" might be avoided, he feared that a revolutionary upheaval "may even be possible in our country."[12]

East Asia

However ominous the political convulsions in the Caribbean, the uncontested dominance exerted by the United States in the Western Hemisphere comfortably reduced the likelihood that they would seriously threaten American security. This was not the case in East Asia, where the source of instability—the powerful and expansionist Japanese army—loomed as a menace not only to regional peace and to American financial interests in the area, but to the security of the United States as well. Contrary to the interventionist tactics employed in the Caribbean, the United States had, with few exceptions, historically foresworn political and military involvement in Asia. This traditional policy was reaffirmed in the Washington Conference treaties of 1921 and 1922, which stipulated that international disagreements in the region were henceforth to be resolved through peaceful, multinational cooperation. The main signatories to the treaties—the United States, Japan, China, and Great Britain—further agreed to adhere to the principles of equal economic opportunity in China and to safeguard that country's territorial integrity. The new order of trade, stability, and peace in East Asia prevailed until September 1931, when Japanese army extremists invaded Manchuria. Their decision, which reflected their repudiation of Tokyo's cautious foreign policy in the depression era, marked the abandonment of multilateral cooperation and adherence to treaty obligations in favor of an independent policy of militarism and pan-Asian expansionism. The era of the Washington Conference system was over.[13]

Senior Foreign Service officers like Maxwell Hamilton, assistant chief of the division of Far Eastern affairs, considered Japan's emerging militaristic posture potentially disruptive of the tenuous stability in East Asia and a threat to American cultural ideals and commercial interests in the region. At this point, Hamilton did not perceive Japan to be a danger to American security. If an Asian war were to break out, he argued, it would more likely involve Japan and Russia. However, during a visit to the Far East in the winter of 1933–34, which included talks with Chinese and other foreign officials who believed in the inevitability of war between Japan and the United States, his attitude began to change. While retaining the view that the Manchurian crisis had not abrogated the Washington Conference system, which, he asserted, rested on inviolable legal-moral principles rather than on the balancing of national interests, he now anxiously envisioned Japanese encroachment on the Philippines. Following Tokyo's publication in April 1934 of the Amau Doctrine, which emphasized Japan's special position in China and proclaimed her mission to maintain peace and order in Asia, he accordingly recommended as a precautionary measure that the United States shore up her Pacific naval defenses. At the same time, Hamilton steadfastly opposed any political involvement in the Asian crisis, either independently or in combination with other states. In a departmental memorandum the previous year, he had pointed out that America's consent to "sit with" the advisory committee established by the League of Nations to assess the Far Eastern situation should not convey the misleading impression that the United States was a member of the committee in any way bound by its decisions.[14]

Hamilton urged the department to mollify Tokyo for a variety of reasons, not the least of which was the paucity of American commercial interests in China. In his view, it seemed prudent to acquiesce in Japan's desire for a larger share of the China market, to impress upon Tokyo the pacific nature of American foreign policy. The absence of any genuine wellspring of cultural sympathy for China was another reason to steer clear of Sino-Japanese affairs. Foreign Service officers saw China as backward, inefficient, and uncultured. Most of her leaders, in Hamilton's opinion, lacked "any dominating and purposeful ideology" or "force of character." By contrast, modernized Japan was identified with the civilized world of Western Europe. Rickshaws had been replaced by Chevrolet and Ford taxis, old shops supplanted by the gleaming iron and steel faces of new department stores. "Is this really Japan?" Hamilton puzzled. Tokyo's wide avenues, broad steps, and extensive use of granite gave the city a new appearance of "massiveness, strength and size." American diplomats further believed that the chaotic and undisciplined state of Chinese society posed as much, possibly more, of a threat to the international stability of Asia as did Japanese imperialism, especially when one considered that "communism might yet succeed." Thus Hamilton and his fellow officers were willing to tolerate Japan's "orderly" presence in Manchuria.[15]

But even if diplomats in the Far Eastern department had been sym-pathetically inclined toward China, they were bureaucratically encum-bered by Washington's policy of political nonentanglement. Additionally, they had to contend with the rising isolationist sentiment among the American people, which they shared in less extreme form. Alluding to the League of Nation's reluctance to endorse Secretary of State Stimson's proclamation forswearing the fruits of Japanese oppression in Manchuria, and the American government's subsequent hesitancy to coordinate its policy with the league, Hamilton confided to Hull in March 1934 that "experience has show the difficulty of getting other countries to act when the United States has thought desirable and of getting the United States to act when other countries have wished to take action." The department's reluctance to "stick its neck out" took on added significance after 1935, as parallels were drawn between Japan's aggression in China and the Italian invasion of Ethiopia.[16]

Hamilton's thinking was further influenced by his personality. He was a "selfless" but "dutiful" bureaucrat. "Prim, meticulous, and most re-spectful toward higher authority," he was more disposed, as were his service colleagues, to support an existing policy rather than to suggest an alternative approach. Withal, he was a peaceful man. And while others in the department—notably Stanley K. Hornbeck, advisor to the secretary of state on Far Eastern political relations—came to advocate a harsher line toward the Japanese, Hamilton persisted to the end to seek some rapprochement.[17]

Following a clash between Japanese and Chinese troops in July 1937, the once localized conflict over Manchuria escalated into full-scale hos-tilities. Disturbed by the combative statements of Henry E. Yarnell, commander-in-chief of America's Asiatic fleet, Hamilton reminded the latter's superior that the most practicable way for the United States to undermine the military's hold on the Japanese government would be to assure Japan's economic security in the area, in part by giving her a greater share of the China market. Eventually, he continued in good Wilsonian fashion, Tokyo would discover that the absorption of China was an unprofitable venture. After 1938, however, as the Japanese army began a southerly advance toward French Indochina, Hamilton's and the department's fears intensified. What made this move so alarming was its coincidence with the decision of France and Great Britain to propitiate an acquisitive German Reich at the Munich Conference. In view of the fact that Tokyo had already joined forces with Hitler in the anti-Comintern pact of November 1936, the Japanese thrust, the department concluded, was not an isolated phenomenon, but now constituted a full-fledged secu-rity risk. "Today in many parts of the world various foreign governments are embarked on courses of action definitely prejudicial to American rights and interests," Hamilton argued. "These courses of action have force as their mainspring; they are the negation of the procedure of orderly process."[18]

But apart from this globalistic rhetoric and the suggestion that Washington adopt retaliatory restrictive-trade measures against foreign aggressors, there was no significant modification in American policy. Even though the Asian war was now connected with unrest elsewhere in the world, Hamilton stolidly opposed Nanking's requests for aid in 1938, which ultimately produced a modest loan of $25 million from Washington. In his judgment, this would contravene the spirit of the neutrality legislation, conflict with America's treaty obligations to respect the Open Door and the independence of China, and possibly push the United States and Japan to the precipice of armed conflict. Disagreeing with the power-political view of Eugene H. Dooman, American chargé in Japan, who recommended in June 1939 that the United States either acquiesce in the course of events in China or inform Tokyo that further infringement of American rights and interests would be met with force, Hamilton argued instead that Washington should continue to impress on Tokyo the American government's commitment to the fundamental principles of international relations. "We believe in those principles, we can't ignore their disregard in one half of the world, and we consider that they should be regarded as applicable to all parts of the world." Fearful of inciting an indecisive Japan into unintended hostilities, Hamilton advised the Japanese embassy to enter into a new most-favored-nation trade agreement with China, which "would contribute substantially to general prosperity and healthy relationships among nations." And when Admiral William D. Leahy proposed that the United States establish a naval base on the Tuamoto Archipelago in the South Pacific, Hamilton rejoined that such a move, considering the American presence in Hawaii, would be seen by Tokyo as an attempt at encirclement, and that the Japanese might then feel compelled to join Italy and Germany in warfare against Britain and France. This, in turn, would jeopardize American security in the Atlantic and the Pacific.[19]

The more American diplomats linked Japan with Germany and Italy, the more they mentally transformed China into an associate of democratic Europe. To be sure, this was a decidedly gradual transition, since careerists could not easily divest themselves of their ingrained image of a hopelessly undisciplined Chinese people. Rising Chinese nationalism and the raging civil war between the communists and Chiang Kai-shek were frequently reported by diplomats in the field as little more than petty jealousies between rival warlords. John Paton Davies, for example, a keenly intelligent and, as time would show, independent-minded observer of Chinese affairs, filled his despatches as late as 1938–39 with routine information on social and economic conditions. If their reports lacked analysis and interpretation, it was because they served little purpose for department officials; career diplomats, particularly in an era of isolationism, were not asked to formulate a foreign-policy strategy, but to dissociate the United States from the impending world conflict.[20]

With the outbreak of the European war, however, and Tokyo's adherence to the Axis pact a year later, American diplomats conceived China's struggle against Japan as a struggle against world aggression. No longer a feckless, incorrigibly divided nation, China was now a democratic island in a totalitarian sea. The feelings of profound sympathy and admiration for the Chinese people expressed by Davies and other diplomats in the field echoed the sentiments of careerists in Washington. Hamilton lauded the Chinese government's ingenuity in meeting economic contingencies with sparse materials and the people's spirit of social cooperation. Now a strong proponent of American assistance, he told an audience at the Army War College on January 9, 1940, that Nanking could not continue to resist for long, much less stage a counteroffensive, without the implements of war. The following year the United States government embarked on a massive program of financial, material, and technical aid to China. Unintentionally, Washington had become directly involved in China's internal affairs.[21]

The Japanese threat to American security also affected Congress' decision to grant independence in 1946 to the Philippine Islands, that tarnished trophy of the Spanish-American war. The political and administrative transition in the colony's status was entrusted to the office of Philippine affairs. In 1936 Joseph Jacobs, a "shy and retiring" veteran careerist and Far Eastern expert who had spent fifteen years in China, was named to head the office. Unlike Hamilton, who disliked service in the field—and who was disliked for that—Jacobs abhorred the political headaches and bureaucratic confinement of the department. "However, I have to be a good soldier and go on with it," he remarked about his new duties, "hoping some day that I shall have work more to my liking."[22]

At first Jacobs was primarily concerned that the liquidation of America's commitments would neither jeopardize the status of the country's trade and investments in the islands nor necessitate a costly intervention in Philippine affairs to ensure the safety of American interests. Mirroring the paternalism of his colleagues in Latin America, Jacobs believed that the United States should continue to provide her adolescent child with benign parental supervision, including a demand of assurances from President Manuel Quezon that monies surrendered by Washington in the form of relinquished tax revenues would be used for "constructive purposes," especially the retirement of Filipino indebtedness to the American government and its citizens. By 1938, however, Philippine independence, like China aid, became increasingly tied up with considerations of national security. Jacobs now feared that precipitous disengagement would upset the balance of power in the Far East by facilitating Japan's demand for trade, if not territorial, concessions from France, Britain, and the Netherlands, which countries needed to ensure the security of their strategic raw materials in southeast Asia in the event of a European war. Moreover, social and economic disturbances in the Pacific chain following independence might provoke American intervention and trigger war with Japan. "The most profitable, the most honorable and, in the long run, the safest course" for Washington to pursue, Jacobs concluded in January 1939, was independence in 1946.[23]

During the suspense-filled winter of 1940–41, department and administration officials anxiously watched Japan's unremitting southern advance. Having identified American security with the survival of the British Empire, the Roosevelt administration considered it imperative to prevent Japanese incursions into British possessions in southeast Asia. For a brief moment in 1941, following Germany's attack on Russia, the State Department entertained the possibility that Japan might turn her attention northward and join the Nazi offensive. By this time, however, Tokyo's course was set. So, as it turned out, was Washington's.

Tension between the two nations climaxed in July 1941 when, in response to Japan's deployment of troops in southern Indochina, the American government froze Japanese assets and declared a total embargo on fuel oil. Foreign Service officers voiced no disapproval. The reactions of Davies and Hamilton to Japan's thrust were indicative of the ebbing hopes of diplomats and high government officials alike. "The foregoing situation," they gravely stated, "would seem to be an additional reason for the taking of strong action in the event of the Japanese occupation of the French colony."[24] In the remaining months of 1941, representatives of both governments engaged in a denouement of fruitless discussion. On November 26 all talking ceased. Now everyone simply waited.

Europe

European developments during the 1930s followed the same fateful course toward war as events in China and the Pacific. Before 1939, however, Foreign Service officers believed that the civilized, economically developed states of Europe, their penchant for power-political solutions aside, would reconcile their differences. "As for totalitarianism," Schoenfeld declaimed in 1936, "though it is in a militant stage at present, does it not seem natural that it will wane when the political and economic consolidation it is designed to bring about is further advanced and that its more abhorrent phase will then disappear?"[25] In addition, given the Roosevelt administration's preoccupation with domestic affairs, diplomats tended to drift with occurrences abroad, treating them as isolated squalls that would eventually blow over without affecting conditions on remote American shores. Furthermore, they supported Washington's traditional practice of noninvolvement in European politics, which was resumed following World War I. Of course, the American government had cooperated with various League of Nations committees, sent representatives to the World Court, and in the twenties helped to stabilize the parlous European economic situation. But its contribution was indisputably more that of an interested and self-consciously humane bystander than of an active participant in European politics.

For most Americans in the twenties and thirties, including career diplomats, Europe meant the modernized, industrialized western extremity of the Eurasian land mass, the cradle of the civilized world. East of the Elbe was another Europe, one which scarcely existed in the minds of Americans. Stretching from the Baltic Sea southward to the Black Sea, and westward across the Carpathian Mountains and the great Danubian plain to the northeastern corner of the Alps, Eastern Europe was an almost completely foreign world of ethnically diverse peoples, each with their own language, history, and culture: mainly Slavs, but including as well Letts and Lithuanians, Mongol Magyars, Bulgars and the related Finns and Estonians, Romanized Dacians in Rumania, Ghegs and Tosks in Albania, as well as Jews, Turks, Ukrainians, Greeks, and still others.

Having imbibed the heady wine of nineteenth-century romantic nationalism, the peoples of Eastern Europe buoyantly established themselves as sovereign entities following the military and political collapse of the area's ruling Ottoman, Hapsburg, and Romanov empires. But self-government was a burdensome undertaking for these new states. With the exception of Czechoslovakia, the region's political life was, at best, semifeudal. Socially and economically these were still largely peasant societies with low yields of agricultural productivity, considerable underemployment, high rates of illiteracy, and little urbanization. Moreover, linguistic and ethnic differences did not neatly conform to political boundaries, a condition that revived the old nationality conflicts of the multinational empires and inflamed the irredentist passions of "host" governments to unite with their ethnic kin in neighboring countries. Since the new states were easy prey for the exploitative practices of German and, in smaller measure, Italian autarchy, and so for the insemination of Fascist ideas, the region's experiment in democratic government slowly disintegrated during the depression years into demagogic chauvinism, dictatorship, and bogus corporativism. Political and economic disunity further militated against the establishment of defensive alliances. To be sure, the Little Entente of Czechoslovakia, Yugoslavia, and Rumania and the Balkan Entente of Greece, Turkey, Rumania, and Yugoslavia gave some indication that Eastern European countries were willing to collaborate in defense of their homelands. However, these *combinazioni* were created to inhibit intraregional revisionism rather than to deter the possible expansionist designs of the European powers. Following the Polish-German and Soviet-Czech agreements of the thirties, centrifugal tendencies within the area intensified. Caught between the vise of German and Russian power, the policy of *sauve qui peut* ultimately embraced by the Eastern European governments only aggravated the "balkanization" of the area, which was again destined to be a battle ground for rival imperialisms.

Since the United States had never established any significant interests in Eastern Europe, American diplomats remained aloof from its politics during the interwar period. Still, considering their idealistic concept of an orderly and harmonious international system and the disparaging image of Eastern European immigrants in the United States during the early twentieth century, they found the region's social chaos and instability disconcerting. Thus they were inclined to tolerate the emergence of authoritarian governments and the political influence of Germany and Italy as safeguards against further disorder and even as harbingers of democratic conditions. After 1939, however, when Germany began to assert her predatory dominance over Eastern Europe, the isolated rumblings Foreign Service officers once heard in these countries became increasingly louder reverberations of an impending world disorder.[26]

The Baltic Region

Life in Riga presented a welcome change from the turbulent conditions Lane had experienced in Nicaragua. If his work was not especially interesting, neither was it dangerous. Alluding to the authoritarian right-wing governments established in Latvia, Lithuania, and Estonia between 1926 and 1934, he remarked to a friend that there was no chance of any personal political involvement. "Here politics has been abolished, at least theoretically." In fact, Lane's only source of annoyance was the presence of Russian experts Page and William Gwynn on the legation staff, whom he found insufferably arrogant, undisciplined, contentious, and incapable of treating the Soviet Union objectively. Lane found their "Ph.D. complex" all the more nettlesome because Eastern Europe was "perhaps the least important of all the areas in the world with which the United States has to deal," and because he felt he knew better than the inexperienced sovietologists, "even if I do not [have their specialized training]," what type of information to send the department.[27]

However limited the scope of the mission's activities, Lane's assignment afforded him an opportunity to become acquainted with the "colossus of the east" and the "colossus of the west." Politically, he saw little difference between Germany and the Soviet Union: both were dictatorships bent on expanding their spheres of power without recourse to war. Possible Nazi-Soviet rapprochement seemed logical enough, since Russia desired to increase her influence from the Baltic region to Czechoslovakia and Germany sought to isolate France militarily and politically. At the same time, Lane considered it "superficial and possibly inaccurate" to base one's estimate of European affairs on the polarities of power versus ideals or dictatorship versus democracy. The main problem, he wrote Dunn, was one of "capitalism versus communism." Though he spurned German totalitarianism, Lane contended that Hitler's apprehension of "the Soviets [sic] disruptive designs was sincere." Referring to a recent editorial in the conservative Le Temps, which elaborated on the idea of a central European block to stem the tide of Soviet communism, he observed that this may be "the dawning realization in France of this new orientation."[28]

But Lane was not prepared to throw down the ideological gauntlet to Moscow. At this stage he still held out hope that Stalin would "[lead] the way in Russia back toward if not to a capitalistic regime and that the differences will soon merge with each system compromising with the other." In his opinion, the transition in Soviet society since 1917 compared favorably with the gradual melioration of U.S.-Mexican relations between 1925 and 1933. Even though the "[Soviet] system of government is abhorrent to the American concept of liberty," he noted, Washington should attempt to "sell" itself to Moscow, much as a businessman did to a prospective client, without, however, "losing our dignity," in an effort to cultivate the same friendly relations it maintained with Britain.[29]

Alas, the wave of Soviet purges in 1937 quickly extinguished Lane's hopeful rhetoric. He and Page were chilled by the terrifying events they followed in the Soviet press. With the corresponding arrests and trials of Moscow-trained Communists in Riga, Lane began to worry about the spread of communism to the Baltic States. The image of revolutionary disorder he carried with him from Nicaragua seemed ready to explode into reality in this scenic Baltic port. Taking advantage of growing anti-Semitism and popular dissatisfaction with President Kārlis Ulmanis's economic restrictions, the Communists were "making considerable leeway." The tendency of Ulmanis and other Baltic leaders to "lean toward" the USSR gave him further cause for concern. Despite fears of Communist revolution in Lithuania, he wrote President Roosevelt, Moscow enjoyed a not inconsiderable influence "over the rather weak petticoat government" of President Antanas Smetona. But since the shock waves of Baltic disorder were far less likely to reach the United States than similar upheavals in Latin America, Lane continued to urge a policy of noninvolvement to avoid the misinterpretation that the American government was taking a political role in the region.[30]

When Lane arrived in Riga in 1936, his former neighbor in the Caribbean, Arthur Schoenfeld, was just getting settled in his new position of minister to Finland. Rid of the political chaos and sweltering heat of Santo Domingo, Schoenfeld was delighted to be in this Nordic clime among such a "sturdy, upstanding race" as the Finns. Under the coalition government of Social Democrats, Agrarians, and National Progressives, the country's political life, plagued during the twenties by frequent clashes between Communists and a homegrown Fascist organization, was now a model of peace and order. Schoenfeld also judged approvingly the "democratic spirit" of Finland's foreign policy, which "[found] expression in sympathetic cooperation with [her] Scandinavian neighbors and with the Western Democracies."[31]

By the end of 1938, however, signs of internal unrest reappeared. Neofascist groups, impressed with Hitler's exploits in Austria and the Sudetenland, demanded the government's disengagement from traditional attachments to the Scandinavian countries in favor of closer relations with Germany. Influenced by the accentuated ideological rhetoric of Soviet Russia, leftist elements reemerged with their own panaceas for Finnish society. Clashes between rightist and leftist students and sporadic bombings forced an apprehensive Schoenfeld to conclude that perhaps not all Finns were committed to a democratic system. But the major threat to this fledgling democracy, Schoenfeld discovered, was not internal. As a consequence of the Ribbentrop-Molotov pact, the Soviet Union had become, so it seemed, undisputed master of the Baltic area. The Soviet demand of nonaggression treaties with Latvia, Lithuania, and Estonia, Schoenfeld notified Washington, was fraught with more significance than any action undertaken by Moscow since the Bolshevik Revolution. Although the Communist International had failed to spread the revolution, Russia was now getting maximum gain out of minimum effort. While the westward thrust of Soviet policy might ultimately be directed against Germany, at whose expense, he wondered, would the next move be?[32]

It did not take long to find out. On November 30, having refused to comply in full with the Kremlin's exaction of a nonaggression treaty and certain territorial concessions, the Helsinki government found itself in a state of war with the Soviet Union. Appalled by Stalin's action, Schoenfeld conveyed unfeigned admiration for the Finnish defense. Encouraged by the British minister, Thomas Maitland Snow, who observed that a rupture of relations between Washington and Moscow would have a good effect in Germany, where the "sense of outrage" was pronounced, and on Finnish Prime Minister Risto Ryti, Schoenfeld unsuccessfully appealed to Hull that "it may well be that diplomatic action under the leadership of the United States might affect Soviet morale and the political situation in Germany thereby facilitating early help for the Finns from various quarters." In December he requested the department at least to issue a statement explaining Washington's reluctance to offer Finland economic aid while it continued to export gasoline to Russia.[33]

With Finland's cession of the Karelian Isthmus and the establishment of a Soviet naval base on the Hangö peninsula, peace between the two countries was restored in March 1940. From Schoenfeld's perspective it was a tenuous peace, for the unsettled social conditions in Finland that were the residue of war bade fair to trigger Communist agitation far more serious than he had witnessed in the Dominican Republic. "So long as the Soviet Government choses [sic] not to interfere with internal affairs in this country," he pointed out, "the situation is not likely to become dangerous"; but "the picture would obviously change if outside pressure were brought to bear on the Finnish Government to tolerate Communist activity." As 1941 wore on, it became clear to Schoenfeld that Finland would cast her lot with Germany in the event Hitler decided to attack the Soviet Union, since "the cardinal element of Finnish policy is security against the Russians." Even so, "there is no reason to doubt the basic sympathy of the Finnish people with the cause which Britain and ourselves are now defending."[34]

When the Nazi-Soviet war finally broke out, the Finns, as expected, quickly joined the fray, jesuitically explaining to Schoenfeld in the process that they were fighting against bolshevism, not with nazism. While Schoenfeld's sympathy for the Finns had not waned, he was nonetheless annoyed by Helsinki's obdurate refusal to see the connection between its actions and the Anglo-Russian war against Germany. Vainly he tried to impress on Finnish leaders the danger of their "passive policy," reminding the foreign minister early in 1942 that they had "surrendered all pretension of exercising their own free will." Following the closing of American consular offices in July, Schoenfeld poignantly wrote that Finland had behaved like the "captain of a ship intent on following a set course no matter what winds might blow or what shoals might be ahead. If in following this fixed course they ran aground on a reef, despite American warning, it was the fault of the reef and not of the ship." Finding life "daily more drab and dreary," Schoenfeld left Helsinki at the end of the year pessimistic about the effects of wartime social dislocations on this "granitic people."[35]

The Balkans

Of all the states in interwar Eastern Europe, Bulgaria was the most open, progressive, and socially cohesive. The method of land distribution was remarkably egalitarian, social mobility was high, and education free and accessible to all classes. Yet the nation's political life, excepting the short-lived radical agrarianism of Aleksandŭr Stamboliiski in the early twenties, revolved around individual personalities rather than ideology, and was just as chaotic as that of its neighbors. Having observed the turbulent state of affairs in Sofia since 1930, Maynard Barnes, an outspoken and intense veteran diplomat, informed the department in March 1933 that the country had become dangerously fragmented. Both the Liberals and the Agrarians, constituting the two major parties, were embroiled in internecine feuds; and there were indications that a protofascist party, led by professor and ex-premier Aleksandŭr Tsankov, had formed to combat the left-wing Agrarians and the Communists. Although the National Bloc government had taken measures to deal with the Communists "in a firm manner," including arrests, the denial of civil rights, even the expulsion from parliament of those freely elected, their revolutionary ideology had spread throughout the country ever since the onset of the depression and the general elections of June 1931, Barnes explained, affecting not only the desperate masses, but the army and other segments of society as well.[36]

As the months passed, conditions within Bulgaria approached the precipice of insurrection. The nation was overwhelmed by labor unrest, a violently irredentist Macedonian population, police brutality, political corruption, and a stagnant economy. In November Barnes wrote that the "sands of power are fast running out for the National Bloc." "The feeling is therefore growing that the parties are worn out and that a new basis for government must be found." Faced with the imminent threat of a Tsankov-led fascist takeover, a group of army officers and technocrats, the latter members of the nationalist and authoritarian Zveno (Link) organization, staged a coup d'état on May 19, 1934. As it turned out, they were better conspirators than politicians, and in the following January, King Boris overthrew the military-technocratic alliance and established a royal dictatorship. Having returned to Washington as assistant chief of the division of Near Eastern affairs, Barnes expressed veiled support for the authoritarian order imposed by the king. He felt certain that the regime would seek harmony with the "Bulgarian national tradition" and "the strongly entrenched democratic sentiment of the Bulgarian people."[37]

His views were shared by Cavendish Cannon, an imperturbable "Austro-Hungarian royalist" who had studied music in Paris and Vienna before joining the diplomatic service in 1920. Remaining in Sofia after Barnes's departure, he supported the king's institution of a "neutral" government removed from party affiliation. Not only did this represent a more orderly alternative to the fractionalized and directionless party politics of the precoup period, but it also demonstrated that "the new Government is definitely committed" to a representative democracy rather than rule by executive fiat. While Cannon remained uneasy about political conditions in Bulgaria as 1937 dawned, pointing out that the regime's continued suppression of the press and party system, delay of the promised general elections, and the growing strength of the Communists did not augur well for democratic government, he remained remarkably confident that popular enthusiasm for King Boris, who was now an absolute ruler, would sustain order and stability and facilitate the reinstitution of representative government.[38]

The same scenario was acted out in neighboring Greece. Unable to cure the ills of the depression-wracked economy, the Liberal government of Eleutherios Venizelos, which had stabilized the country from 1928 to 1932, eventually lost public support. The ensuing conflict between Royalists and Venizelists further divided national sympathies and set the stage for the August 1936 coup d'état, led by General Joannes Metaxas. Like Barnes and Cannon, Harold Shantz, who arrived in Athens from his Moscow post at the end of 1935, viewed the Metaxas dictatorship as a potentially healthy corrective to the political instability of the preceding years. Echoing the Metaxas line, he explained to Washington that the dissolution of parliament, the imposition of martial law and press censorship, and the suspension of constitutional rights were intended to counteract the proposed general strike by communist elements. To be sure, he was not pleased with the appearance of these totalitarian practices, exclaiming at one point, "Shades of Soviet Russia!" But the regime did promise to suppress the "communist menace," as it had been stifled elsewhere. Moreover, the dictatorship seemed to be "benevolent and paternalistic and to have the sincere support of the King [George II]," who was restored to the throne at the end of 1935. "The Metaxas Government," Shantz said, "has a great opportunity to effect much needed reforms; and if it uses its power wisely it may perhaps engender considerable popular support."[39]

Weeks after the coup, Shantz continued to wax optimistic about the regime. "Greece has been as quiet as a lamb," he informed the department. Although conceding that small merchants and other sectors of Greek society had cause to grumble over higher taxes, exchange control, travel restrictions, and censorship, he noted that the regime had reduced the farmers' debts, put more people to work, instituted minimum wage contracts, and improved social welfare services. "Even if fascist methods of converting opponents have been used," he said, "the regime seems strikingly mild by comparison with older fascist governments," adding that no political opponents had been killed. Thus, while most Greeks privately expressed great dissatisfaction, he perceived their state of mind as really a "contented discontent."[40]

Foy D. Kohler, Jr., an ambitious and highly intelligent Near Eastern expert, concurred with Shantz's observations. Mindful of the many constraints on popular government under the authoritarian Metaxas regime, he nonetheless found a hopeful sign in its educational reforms. Unlike the old system, he stated, which favored the well-to-do and ignored the country's high rate of illiteracy, the new program expanded educational opportunities for the masses and created badly needed technical schools. "It is true that the present regime has taken such fascist measures in education as the censoring of the classics and the revision and issuance of textbooks by a government monopoly"; but "the present reorganization of the schools does not in itself constitute a vital part of the dictatorial program or any threat to democratic ideals."[41]

A year after his arrival in Tirana late in 1932, Cloyce Huston, a pleasant and dependable officer, concluded that Albania appeared ready to explode in another round of violent disorder. In this tiny and predominantly Moslem state, long a backwater of the Ottoman empire, tribal vendettas and regional insurrections had rained with annual, if not seasonal, regularity until 1924, when the warrior-chieftain Ahmed Zogu returned from exile in Yugoslavia. Under Zogu, later self-styled King Zog I, Albanians seemed to have rid themselves of these chronic episodes of violence. A closer look, however, revealed that the peasantry, despite the government's efforts to modernize the clan-structured society, still lived in abject social and economic conditions. Heavy taxation, embezzlement by government officials, and Greek minority agitation combined to arouse the public's ire; and the regime's secularistic educational policy antagonized Catholics in the north. Far more serious in Huston's opinion were the growing alienation of the military, whose salaries the government failed to pay, and Zog's inability to rule the state effectively. Though an able and clever man, Zog was basically a Turk with old ideas, the young diplomat observed, a peasant who felt uncomfortable with Albanian leaders of "a more occidental turn of mind." In 1935 sporadic rebellions broke out in various parts of the country. By employing the familiar techniques of mass arrests, executions, and the institution of martial law, the government temporarily restored peace.[42]

In view of the maelstrom of Albanian internal affairs, Huston thought that a new alliance with Italy might solve the country's social and economic woes and help to maintain order. Recognizing that the state's interwar economic development, such as it was, was heavily subsidized by Italian capital, he noted that Zog and his followers "have not yet forgotten the sweet clink-clink of Italian gold." But the king, having already refused to renew the 1926 pact with Italy guaranteeing Albania's territorial and political independence, demurred. Meanwhile, internal conditions worsened. Amidst more arrests, tortures, and executions, the cabinet resigned in October. Huston now believed that a full-fledged revolutionary organization existed in the country. Although some Albanian officials contended that the movement was financed by Italy, Huston informed the department that there was little proof of this allegation; the recent outbreaks were fomented internally, he noted, by years of poverty and government neglect.[43]

During the spring of 1936, Zog finally succeeded in suppressing the insurrections. Subsequently, he liberalized his regime somewhat, allowing more freedom to the press and accessibility to political life. Furthermore, in March an agreement was reached with Italy by which Albania relinquished certain administrative and economic prerogatives in exchange for a badly needed loan. By this time Huston had left behind him the turmoil of Albania for the equally chaotic environment of Rumania.

However tenuous the political equilibrium in the area, there were as yet no indications that the great powers or the Balkan states themselves, notwithstanding their irredentist ambitions, intended to alter the regional status quo. Although Bulgaria, as an example, cast covetous glances at the Dobrudja and Greek territory along the Aegean, she was obliged "to follow a neutral and colorless foreign policy," Barnes explained, "hoping that time and a sense of justice on the part of the Great Powers," especially the Soviet Union, "will ultimately rectify the wrong that Bulgaria itself has not the power to right." But with the formation of the Rome-Berlin Axis in October 1936, which signalled the decline of French influence in Eastern Europe and the emergence of a new combination to defend civilized Europe against barbaric communism, the Balkan governments became restive. Sensitive to the changing balance of power, Yugoslavia, still allied with France, signed a pact of friendship the following January with Bulgaria, whose revisionist ambitions had received Mussolini's endorsement. Foreign Service officers now also began to give pause to their earlier hopes for "a new order of things" in the region. Lane, who arrived in Yugoslavia later in 1937, suspected that Germany aimed to push southeastward. Cannon speculated that Macedonian Bulgarians, regardless of the rapprochement between Sofia and Belgrade, would intensify their efforts to unite with their conationals in Yugoslavia and thereby provoke discord between the two states. And Shantz noted that the Greek press, in marked contrast to its earlier fulsome praise of Italy and Germany, had initiated a campaign critical of the Axis powers.[44]

Despite these signs of unrest, American diplomats saw no cause for alarm as long as order was maintained. Shantz and Kohler responded favorably to the annual conference of the Balkan Entente in December 1938, even though Italy and Germany had imbedded their talons—first economically, but gradually politically as well—deeply into the innards of southeastern Europe. Rumors that Yugoslavia and Rumania had agreed to make irredentist concessions to Bulgaria at Greece's territorial expense elicited no cries of dismay from the American embassy. Shantz pointed out that this Balkan brand of "appeasement" was understandably intended to forestall German-supported Bulgarian demands. Withal, they remained sympathetic to the Greek dictatorship's efforts to establish domestic stability. While Metaxas had failed to arouse popular enthusiasm or intrinsically alter Greek institutions, Kohler wrote in the summer of 1939, he was appreciated by some "for a sincere and reasonably successful attempt to bring the country through a difficult period, both internally and externally, when the endless and excessive political strife of republican Greece might have proved disastrous."[45]

Huston conveyed similar sentiments from Rumania, where the failure of Liberal and National-Peasant governments led to the establishment of a royal dictatorship in 1938. Since King Carol took control of the state, the diplomat noted, he had established internal order, which the fascist Iron Guard, rumored to be receiving aid from Germany and Russia, had disrupted, ended political strife, and fostered the development of a national spirit. "Few careful observers are wont to criticize King Carol for the road he has followed in the circumstances; rather he has undoubtedly gained new admiration and respect." Political leaders who attempted to obstruct the formation of Carol's monoparty, the Front of National Renaissance, notably Iuliu Maniu, the passionately romantic head of the Peasant party, and Liberal leader Gheorghe Brătianu were dismissed as unimpressive, "die-hard oppositionists" who refused to recognize the dissolution of Rumanian party politics. The NRF, although undeniably totalitarian, "has none of the passion or fanaticism or frenzy of such total ideologies as Fascism, Nazism or Communism," wrote Huston in December 1939. Despite the iniquities, the peasants seemed pleased with the absence of party squabbles and with the general increase in national prosperity.[46]

But Carol's gossamer order could not withstand the strains of Nazi-Soviet competition for supremacy in the Balkans. Barraged by criticism from Maniu, cabinet dissension, and continued subversion by the Iron Guard, and disgraced by the loss of Bessarabia and northern Bukovina to Russia in June and the subsequent Axis-contrived cession of northern Transylvania to Hungary and southern Dobrudja to Bulgaria, Carol abdicated nominally in September in favor of his small son, who thence came under the control of General Ion Antonescu. Distressed by the arrests and outright seizures of property that followed, a subdued Huston wrote in November that the situation was deplorable, the more so for fear of bolshevism, particularly among the white-collar class and the "thinking people," who imagined "wholesale deportations into 'darkest' Russia." Although he derived some comfort from the Balkan Entente's reaffirmation of solidarity, it was unlikely that these states, which had displayed little reciprocal trust in the best of times, would remain united now that their very survival was at stake.[47]

Unlike his Balkan-based colleagues, Lane exhibited no sympathy for the Yugoslav government that succeeded the royal dictatorship of assassinated King Alexander in 1934. There is "virtually a Fascist state here at the present time," the Skupština (Yugoslav National Assembly) and Senate being virtually inarticulate, he wrote in January 1938. The people, however, "are not in favor of dictatorships and primarily not in favor of the present Prime Minister," Milan Stojadinović, a man of "primitive mentality," in Lane's opinion, an "entirely ruthless, clever and unscrupulous politician desiring only to increase his power." Actually, Lane held Yugoslavian leaders as a whole in low esteem, with the exception of Anglophile Prinçe Paul, head of the government's three-man regency, "a very charming person, very fond of the arts and a delightful conversationalist."[48]

Treated indifferently, so he thought, by Belgrade officials, who truckled to the Italian and German missions, the sensitive Lane became palpably irritated. As the Axis powers, each trying to outdo the other, paraded their art exhibits, theater, opera, and other forms of cultural propaganda before local audiences, he expressed unconcealed annoyance with the State Department, which had paid little heed to Yugoslav developments, for not presenting the democratic alternative of American culture. "One is impressed by the ignorance regarding American cultural achievements and by the general mistaken belief," he protested, "that citizens of the United States are money makers, radio crooners, or jazz artists." But Lane's displeasure was really symptomatic of a deeper concern, namely, Belgrade's growing attachment to the Rome-Berlin Axis. Disputing official statements to the contrary, he anticipated that Yugoslavia would inevitably loosen her ties with Czechoslovakia and Rumania, as she had with France, thereby rendering the Little Entente "absurdly impotent" and further destabilizing the area. Yet, as desperate as the Balkan situation appeared, he was inclined to believe that Germany would satisfy her objectives peacefully. As he told Dr. Ivo Andrić, assistant minister of foreign affairs, "I too have been optimistic for the last two years, for the simple reason that in my opinion no nation except perhaps one really wished war." That nation, he and the Yugoslav agreed, was the Soviet Union, waiting hungrily to feed on the carcass of Western Europe. The

Munich agreement in the fall of 1938 reified Lane's hopes. "There is no doubt in my mind regarding the propriety of the course which was taken in reaching a settlement," he wrote his uncle. "I do not feel that any man can face the responsibility of throwing the whole world into war merely because he thinks that the other man is bluffing."[49]

As was the case elsewhere in the region, things went from bad to worse for Yugoslavia after 1939. The twin bogies of Axis expansionism and communist subversion loomed ever larger in Lane's mind. Fearful of an attack by Italy and Germany, Belgrade voiced no disapproval when Mussolini occupied Albania in the spring of 1939. In addition, the extreme right-wing Croatian Ustaša (Insurgent) movement continued to act as an Axis-abetted destructive force within the state. Scornful of the Yugoslav government, which was "almost cringing with respect to Germany," Lane simultaneously worried that the traditional sympathy of the Serbs for mother Russia "will provide a fertile field for the dissemination of communist propaganda." Radical students and younger professors at Belgrade University were being joined by "an amorphous, somewhat inarticulate but nevertheless real pan-Slav sentiment," expressed by "the man in the street in Belgrade." While the populace mistrusted the communist ideology, Lane pointed out, if given the choice, they would prefer to be dominated by Russia rather than Germany.[50]

By the spring of 1941, it had become more likely that Yugoslavia would join the Axis pact. Persistently, Lane encouraged Prince Paul and government officials to remain neutral in the European war. At the same time, he recalcitrantly opposed their repeated representations for American military aid, a reflection of Lane's anger over Belgrade's indifference toward the embassy and its decision in 1939 to award Germany an oil concession sought by Standard Oil of New Jersey. Now vitally concerned with the state of international affairs, the department accepted the ambassador's recommendation to refuse Yugoslavia credits. "Deeply gratified," Lane felt Washington's "strong stand" had vindicated United States prestige and ensured "the protection of American interests here." However, his judgment, which revealed his easily wounded amour-propre, was questionable, considering that he believed "the [military] danger for the United States was fast approaching." Indeed, he presently informed Roosevelt: "We must, repeat must, wake up to the necessity that we must be willing to give every thing we have to save the situation. This is for the sake of religion, democracy, and civilization."[51]

In the meantime, Lane continued to exhort Belgrade to resist the Axis, but Yugoslavs resented his moralistic meddling in their affairs. On the evening of March 20, 1941, Lane dined with Prince Paul and made, as it turned out, his final appeal to keep Yugoslavia from signing the Tripartite pact. "You big nations are hard," Paul said with exasperation. "You talk

of our honor, but you are far away." On the 23d Lane reported to Undersecretary Welles that Paul had "capitulated." The Yugoslav military tried
to undo the decision three days later by ousting Paul. Unimpressed, Germany invaded the country on April 6.[52]

In due course, the United States and Yugoslavia were allied in common
cause. Just as diplomats responsible for U.S.-Asian affairs had reformed
the image of China once it became clear that America was destined to
travel the same road to war, Lane now perceived the country he had
chastised for her chaotic and antidemocratic ways as a model of national
unity and a citadel of democracy. "Yugoslavs—Serbs, Croatians, and
Slovenes—wherever you may be, let me express to you the admiration of
the United States who fully realize what your attitude means to this
country and to the world," he proclaimed on February 27, 1942, before a
gathering at the Freedom House in New York. "As one who had the
privilege of being in Belgrade during those tragic and momentous days
following March 27, 1941, I wish to say that as long as I live the word
Yugoslav will always connote to me self-sacrifice, courage and the love,
even to the point of death, of democratic freedom."[53]

The Danubian Region

Endowed with rich farmlands and a thriving industry in the historic territories of Moravia and Bohemia, with an educated population and a
well-trained bureaucracy, Czechoslovakia easily enjoyed the highest
standard of living of any state in Eastern Europe. At the same time, as
evidenced by her disgruntled Polish, Magyar, and especially Sudeten
German minorities, she was ethnically the least homogeneous. Prague's
relations with its overwhelmingly peasant Ruthenian and Slovakian
provinces, which experienced disproportionately few of the benefits of
modernity enjoyed by the western part of the country, were also
troublesome. Resentful of Czech paternalism and unable to compete economically with Bohemia and Moravia-Silesia, the Slovaks yearned for
political autonomy. More disturbing still were the fissiparous tendencies
of the Sudeten Germans, who had suffered most from the precipitous
economic decline of the thirties and who were increasingly attracted to
the polestar of Nazi Germany. Open sedition of the Sudeten Germans, led
by Konrad Heinlein, and misguided Czech reliance on her undependable
French ally culminated in Germany's annexation of the Sudeten territory
in September 1938.

John H. Bruins had watched these events unfold since the end of 1934.
Reserved and paternal in bearing, this veteran careerist, like his colleagues, sympathized with British and French efforts at Munich to mollify
Hitler and to assure, despite the "shameful sacrifice" of Czech land,
"peace in our time." Admitting that Germany dominated the Eastern

European region politically and economically, he foresaw no adverse impact on American interests in Czechoslovakia. Since the United States had higher import duties on German goods, he stated, Sudeten products would now be costlier, hence noncompetitive, in American markets. The loss of territory might even provide an opportunity for the United States to finance a Czech reorganization.

After Reichswehr forces marched into Prague, Bruins began to reconsider German objectives. "Up to this time," he noted, "Hitler's announced policy was to obtain justice for 'Germans'. He said he wanted no Czechs." This was in keeping with the policy supporting boundary rectifications along ethnic lines enunciated by Woodrow Wilson after World War I. However, the events of March 15 portended "the first direct evidence of predatory, expansionist action against a non-German people." Still, cognizant of Europe's traditional realpolitik approach to international affairs and America's insubstantial interests in the area, he remained unruffled by the demise of Czechoslovakia. When the puppet Slovakian state was established under Nazi aegis, he impassively informed Washington that German control would be as extensive as that "normally exercised by a great power over a protectorate."[54]

George Kennan, who had arrived in Prague just before the Munich fiasco, remained equally detached from the tragic turn of events in Czechoslovakia. In the first place, he was affected, as were his fellow officers, by the bureaucratic inertia of the department. Second, the "state of Europe was so rotten" during the interwar years, and the "artificial" states created out of the Hapsburg Empire "so little deserving of preservation," that it was difficult to feel outraged when Hitler set his course of expansionism in 1936. Moreover, he found German occupation behavior in Czechoslovakia "surprisingly mild and conciliatory" in comparison to what he had experienced in Russia. Though conceding that this moderate policy could take a brutal turn, he was "encouraged to hope that [Germany's] attitude toward the mass of the Czechs may turn out to be a more reasonable one than many had anticipated." As for the Nazi protectorate in Slovakia, the Germans simply had taken advantage of Prague's failure to acculturate the pedantic Slovak leaders, who had worked with Berlin and Warsaw for years to topple the government of Tomas Masaryk and Edvard Beneš. He averred in realpolitik terms that Slovakian autonomy would be "only an incidental and temporary outcropping of the slow shift of power in the Central European area from Vienna and Budapest northwards to Berlin." The Reich's absorption of the territory "will have to be regarded as an inevitable reversion to the natural state of affairs."[55]

Only after it became clear to Kennan and his colleagues that German policy threatened to disrupt "the natural state of affairs" did they begin to grow uneasy. "We didn't begin to realize until 1938 what we were up against with the Nazis," he explained.[56] Even then they regarded European unrest as a localized phenomenon from which the United States should stay removed.

Western Europe

Although the Axis powers gave every indication that their acquisitive appetites would not be sated by the territorial crumbs European statesmen permitted them, even helped them, to ingest, Foreign Service officers persisted in the notion that these bastions of Western civilization might still prove reasonably disposed to spare the world another tragic war. It was not that Alfred Klieforth, who spent the first part of the thirties in Vienna, condoned the Nazis; rather, it was his hope that a saner leader than Hitler, or the German people themselves, might rise up and moderate Berlin's domestic and foreign policies. Concerned that a breakdown of social order in Austria might trigger German intervention, he defended Chancellor Englebert Dollfuss's suppression of the Socialists with such vigor that diplomats in the department questioned the objectivity of his despatches.

Packed off in the summer of 1935 to a consular post in Cologne, Klieforth sought to improve German-American relations. He joined various cultural institutions, sent his children to German schools, mingled with the social elite, including Herr Krupp von Bohlen, from whom he received a "standing invitation" to skeet shoot at the Krupp estate, and occasionally attended Nazi round-table discussions. The more familiar he became with domestic political conditions and the temper of the German people, who were increasingly dismayed by higher living costs, shortages of consumer goods, and the talk of war, the more he believed Hitler's days were numbered. He informed Washington in the summer of 1938 that leading business, church, and military figures all agreed that the regime was fated to collapse, and that even workers and shopkeepers had lost their enthusiasm for Nazism.[57]

Meanwhile, the German war machine quietly and confidently geared up for its showdown with the Western democracies. Ironically, when its hateful fury was finally unleashed, Klieforth, who had gone out of his way, by his reckoning, to reconcile Germany and America, was called to account by the Wilhelmstrasse on charges of espionage. Embittered by this unconscionable display of Nazi "ruthlessness and cruelty," he vowed never again to accept another German post. Shortly after Germany declared war on the United States, Klieforth unburdened his resentment in the pages of the *Saturday Evening Post*. "Hitler has you card-indexed," he warned agitatedly, "and he will not omit the Western Hemisphere from his blueprint for world domination."[58]

The Foreign Service's reaction to Fascist Italy during the thirties was even more conciliatory. Some diplomats like W. Perry George, an old-line careerist with an impulsive turn of mind, actually defended Rome's military plans prior to its attack on Ethiopia. If guerilla activities continued to threaten Italian possessions, he told the department, Italy would be "reduced, in my opinion, to the inescapable necessity of applying force." Furthermore, given the "backward nature of Ethiopia's population," George believed that Italy's occupation would benefit the country economically and socially, secure the frontiers of nearby Italian and British possessions, and improve Rome's trade balance.[59]

No less sympathetic to the civilizing force of Italian expansionism, James Clement Dunn, among others in the department's European division, raised no objections to Italy's action. Charming, glib, "a total aristocrat in every sense of the word," Dunn admired the European nobility. His attitude was also influenced, however, by the foreign-policy views of Cordell Hull, with whom he enjoyed an especially close relationship, their different social backgrounds notwithstanding, which extended to Dunn's regular attendance at the secretary's frequent croquet parties. Like his mentor, Dunn wished to avoid political entanglements abroad. Despite persistent efforts of the League of Nations to gain Washington's support for a partial economic boycott of Italy, he opposed the idea of "directing our policy so that it may relate constructively to what the League is doing." If it appeared that the continued supply of United States goods was prolonging the war, he stated, revulsion among the American public would produce "a strong independent action by this Government" to rectify such a condition. Annoyed by a British press account in November 1935 reporting Washington's support of an oil embargo, he advised the American ambassador in London to remind the Foreign Service that "what the other nations do with regard to the sanctions program does not concern us all." Dunn was no more in favor of taking collective measures to protest Italy's unconcealed assistance to the rebel side during the Spanish Civil War, preferring to believe that Mussolini would eventually see the error of his ways. Following Rome's agreement in January 1937 to remove its forces from Spain, he felt certain that Mussolini now was "sincerely on the side of peace."[60]

So did the American embassy in Rome, including Samuel Reber, an articulate and conscientious young diplomat who, given his Foreign Service training, "ably followed policy." No proof existed to substantiate the rumors of Italy's continued military involvement in Spain, he reported in the summer of 1937. Il Duce himself assured the embassy that only nonmilitary supplies had been provided. Echoing Klieforth's views, he thought it unlikely that the Italian people, distressed by rising unemployment, a growing trade imbalance, and the lack of conspicuous success in

Spain, would tolerate further acts of aggression. Rather than sing paeans to the Fascist cause, he wrote Dunn in 1938, the poorest classes of Naples chanted, "Non vogliamo Tunisia, vogliamo panettone." Well into 1939 Reber remained sanguine that Rome would continue its peaceful ways. The recent soccer match between Britain and Italy, he noted in May, had been played in an encouragingly friendly atmosphere. The British team had even given the fascist salute when the Italian national anthem had been played. Embassy informants said it had met with great enthusiasm.[61]

Matthews and Barnes, assigned to the Paris embassy in 1937, embraced the same hopes for peace. Caught up in the social whirl of that elegant French city, enjoying weekend rambles in the countryside, they found it difficult to conceive that the gay and civilized world they inhabited would crumble into the abyss of war. Two years later, with the German invasion of Prague, the Italian occupation of Albania, and particularly the Nazi-Soviet pact, it was hard to think otherwise. Worse yet, influenced by the inflexible views of Ambassador William Bullitt, who had not forgotten his experiences in Moscow, they believed the Molotov-Ribbentrop agreement portended the expansion of communist ideology. Soviet complicity in the dismemberment of Poland magnified the embassy's fears. Reflecting the attitude of the Russian specialists, Barnes stated that "Stalin portrayed himself in all his true colors by [his] aggressive actions against Poland, France's ally." It was, therefore, perfectly understandable to him, given the Kremlin's hypocrisy and deviousness, that the government of Edouard Daladier had proscribed the French Communist party, which "placed ideological considerations above national interests at a moment when the very existence of the state was in the balance." As for Matthews, who, like Dunn, had supported the recognition of Franco to terminate the communist-inspired disorders in Spain, Soviet military action signalled the "probable eventual 'Bolshevization' of Germany, and maybe more of Europe, too."[62]

During the spring and summer of 1940, however, it was Germany that captured the embassy's attention. Careerists were stunned by the Wehrmacht's unimpeded march through Scandinavia and the Low Countries and its humiliatingly easy conquest of France. Unable to dissuade President Paul Reynaud from surrendering to German occupation, embassy officials wired the department that France had meekly accepted the status of a second-rate power. Installation of the timorous and obsequious French government at Vichy, headed nominally by General Henri Philippe Pétain, but actually led, at German bidding, by Pierre Laval and Admiral François Darlan, confirmed their opinion. What made the attitude of the new government so upsetting to American diplomats was not its desire to rejuvenate the ancien régime. Quite the contrary, Matthews, who evacuated the Paris embassy with most of the staff for Bordeaux, believed Pétain to be a man of integrity and courage who sought a "new, conservative, orderly France." And Barnes, who remained with Bullitt in Paris, where his "social life was at its acme," actually sympathized with some of Laval's ideas. Rather, it was Vichy's unwillingness to assist the British, "who are fighting our battle," in Matthews's words, and who were now forced to fend off the Nazis singlehandedly. Recognizing Britain's desperate predicament and the implications for American security if she fell, it now seemed likely to Matthews and Barnes that the United States would be drawn into the struggle.[63]

As this reality became clearer to them—and to their Foreign Service colleagues—they altered their interwar image of Germany. Once a model of order and stability, she was now a destructive force bent on the disruption of the established order and the impoverishment of liberal-democratic values. While the United States remained neutral, Barnes told an audience in Paris on Washington's birthday, President Roosevelt recognized that Americans were not neutral in thought. If Washington were still alive, he would unquestionably have underscored the president's stated aversion to the loss of liberty, property, and personal rights. Possibly, he added, Washington would have said something even stronger. By the end of the year, no one doubted that Roosevelt also had something stronger in mind. Commenting on the president's speech of December 29, in which he proclaimed America the "arsenal of democracy," Matthews cabled the department that it was received "with particular delight as a complete vindication of what we have been endeavoring to impress upon our Foreign Office and other French friends is the real policy of our Government and the real pulse of our nation."[64]

At this stage, Dunn, Henderson, Ray Atherton, and others in the division of European affairs also sensed that it was only a matter of time before the flames of war would spread to the United States. The conclusion of the Tripartite pact left no doubt as to the global objectives of Germany, Italy, and Japan. Even if the United States escaped actual involvement in hostilities, it was apparent that American security would henceforth be jeopardized. It thus became increasingly clear that Britain's cause was America's.

As word of Germany's impending attack on Russia reached the department, it also began to dawn on Foreign Service officers that the Soviet Union and the Anglo-Saxon powers might, by this unfortunate quirk of fate, be thrown together in a common struggle. To fight once again on the side of Britain, should it come to that, was one thing. Americans and Britons shared similar traditions, ideals, and values. But to form a partnership with the Soviets, whose beliefs were repugnant to all that was historically sacred, and whose unpardonable treachery in the waning hours of Europe's peace displayed their contempt for order and stability, to say nothing of democracy, was—almost, but not quite—a fate worse than death. The enduring enmity of Dunn and his colleagues toward Moscow was vividly demonstrated in the policy statement prepared by the European division on June 21, 1941, one day before the German invasion. "We should steadfastly adhere to the line that the fact that the Soviet Union is fighting Germany," the statement read, "does not mean that it is defending, struggling for, or adhering to, the principles in international affairs for which we are fighting." Provided Soviet leaders approached the American government, it continued, Washington should relax restrictions on exports and even offer military aid, if it was badly needed, without any commitment regarding future American policy. Special precaution should be taken to avoid the impression that the United States was acting in bad faith if, following the defeat of Russia, "we should refuse to recognize a refugee Soviet Government or cease to recognize the Soviet Ambassador in Washington as the diplomatic representative of Russia."[65]

Clearly, American diplomats were hedging their bets. Since Germany was the primary disturber of the peace and the all-but-declared enemy, they were willing to offer the Soviets a modicum of assistance, short of abandoning American neutrality. However, they did not expect Russia to withstand the encounter, a likelihood that they faced, notwithstanding their awareness of America's ebbing neutrality, with near equanimity. Even as the German army devastated the unprepared Russians with its lightning offensive, careerists continued to view the Kremlin with mistrust and resentment. In July Dunn and Henderson advised Welles to carefully monitor Soviet commercial transactions in the Western Hemisphere, which might be used to finance subversive activities. Disturbed by the department's lack of faith "in the staying power" of the Soviets, John Hazard, principle liaison officer in the Soviet supply section, noted regretfully that a number of officials were simply unprepared to cooperate with the Bolsheviks. As it turned out, the decision was made for them by Japan, Germany, and Italy, whose declaration of war against the United States propelled the country into alliance with Britain and Russia.[66]

Exposed to diverse and sometimes idiosyncratic social experiences during the interwar years, American diplomats tended to filter their experiences through a mutually shared conceptual framework of international affairs. Collectively, they adhered to the principles of free trade and the rule of law and disavowed political interference in the affairs of other states. Withal, they unwaveringly embraced the image of America as "a glorious example of Christian virtue and leadership" and as a beacon of democratic values in a benighted world. Although attentive to the disquieting currents in the sea of world politics, they plied a traditional course in American foreign policy, culturally defined by the nation's his-

torical experience and reinforced by the continuous socializing process of
the Foreign Service. Confident that the American island was safely removed from attack by another power, they, in fact if not in rhetoric,
sustained the isolationist attitude of the American public during the thirties. Bohlen, like others, considered "unfortunate" Secretary of the Interior Harold Ickes's purported remarks favoring a legal ban on the expor-
tation of petroleum to belligerents during the Italo-Ethiopian war. Even
after the German invasion of Prague in 1939, Dunn firmly opposed termination of American neutrality laws, which some, notably Bullitt, advised.

Such parochialism was encouraged by the diplomats' expectations that
the European states would take measures to maintain international stability, if only to avoid another wrenching upheaval such as that of 1914–18.
"To be sure, there are alarming indications that German imperialism may
require to be checked again by the western powers," Schoenfeld wrote in
the spring of 1936, "but that this will necessarily involve war still seems
somewhat doubtful to me." Should war break out, however, he hoped
Americans could be dissuaded from the belief "that it is our duty to save
the world from something or other." Lane judged league sanctions against
Italy "incredibly stupid," for they converted a small colonial war into an
international incident. Henderson admitted to Samuel Harper in mid-
1937, "regarding our friend [columnist Edgar Ansel] Mowrer," who had
predicted war by that time, that "if I see him I may be tempted to say 'I
told you so.' Of course, it is quite possible that if he keeps on prophesying
imminent war and I keep on saying that Europe will be able to dodge it, he
will be able sometime to turn the tables on me."[67]

After 1938 diplomats began to question whether war would be averted
after all. Distressed by the escalation of fighting in China, civil war in
Spain, and German pressure on Czechoslovakia, Schoenfeld feared the
spreading contagion of a world conflict. Preoccupied until this time with
the collection of Near Eastern objets d'art, Burton Berry wrote from
Athens in September 1938 that many Greeks believed the decision for war
was fast approaching. For the time being, their forebodings were allayed
by the Munich agreement. But as the world spun dizzily out of control in
the coming months, Foreign Service officers were jarred by the anxiety
that it would consume itself in a frenzy of disorder and destruction. It was
"an unhappy time," George Kennan recalled, "full of darkening clouds,
vague fears and disturbing premonitions." Recalling the pain and suffering in the aftermath of World War I, a gloomy Henderson predicted that
"if a war does take place the world will be a rather bleak place in which to
live, at least during the remainder of our lifetimes." By this time, though,
he and his colleagues felt certain of its arrival. "Eventually there will be a
fight," Berry soberly concluded in the wake of the Nazi-Soviet accord,
"and when it starts it promises to be a whooper [sic]."[68]

When it came, careerists still entertained the belief that the United States would be spared this calamity, that is, until the German blitzkrieg in Western Europe, the Japanese advance toward French Indochina, and the Tripartite pact made it clear to them that British resistance, hence American security, was imperilled. Outraged by the prevailing spirit of cynicism and opportunism, Henderson replied with the same moral fervor which had preceded past American involvement in wars. "After all the noble utterances that our Government had been making since the days of Woodrow Wilson in support of accepted principles of international intercourse," it was simply inconceivable that the United States could react dispassionately to Soviet and German acquisitiveness. Inspired by President Roosevelt's condemnation of the world conflict, Lane noted that it would "[bolster] the confidence of the civilized world that we too are fighting for freedom of thought, religion and expression." Schoenfeld rejoiced over passage of the Lend-Lease Act, which officially recognized American material assistance to Britain and unofficially drew the two closer together in common cause, lauding the idealistic spirit of unity in the country and the tenacity with which both the United States and Britain defended the principles of democracy in a lawless world.[69]

Apart from traditional foreign-policy attitudes, institutional inertia also influenced diplomats' perceptions. In outlook and style, Dean Acheson disclosed in his memoirs, the State Department of the 1930s operated no differently from its nineteenth-century precursor. Infested with suspicion and jealousy, the system was fractionalized among competing feudal barons. Drifting with the tide rather than steering its own course, department officials evolved policies from specific events rather than the other way around. Since Roosevelt was preoccupied with domestic problems during most of the decade, the department tended to ignore Germany, Italy, and Japan, or at best to avoid them. One diplomat in Germany was astonished at the department's reaction to his reports that Hitler was bent on war. "Oh well, he doesn't mean it," Washington would say; or, "Make this concession and everything will be all right." When the State Department suddenly found itself in a war for which it was unprepared, it was divested of its functional role by the president, who then parcelled this out to various other departments and agencies.[70]

The combined impact of the culture of American foreign policy, bureaucratic barriers, an isolationist public and Congress, an unsupportive president, and the depressing effects of economic cutbacks served to inhibit alternative ways of seeing the world. This was, in turn, reinforced by the informal culture of the Foreign Service, by the desire for favorable performance ratings and group support. Distressed by the lack of intellectual independence, one officer contributed an article to the *Foreign*

Service Journal beckoning the dissenting individualist to show himself from behind the bureaucratic thicket of the service. The appeal went unheeded. "Well, you know, the Foreign Service is a very disciplined outfit," one careerist explained; "And we were compelled to go along a lot." Until 1942, Durbrow pointed out, "we were all slow, pedestrian foreign correspondents, and that's all we were. And the secretary of state couldn't do a goddamn thing about it!" The lack of financial and psychological support and the absence of stimulating work thoroughly demoralized Maynard Barnes. "What can I do with him?" wrote his wife in 1937. "He isn't fulfilling himself." Bored by his wartime experience in Cologne, Klieforth felt "like the man who was ordered to guard the family orchard while the rest of the outfit went out to fight the forest fire, or sidetracked on a dead freight line." Kennan was embittered by Washington's dilatory manner in removing interned diplomats from Germany. Henderson was so depressed that he discouraged his nephew from joining the service.[71]

The Soviet specialists were an especially discontented lot. The alienation and professional indignity they suffered in Moscow heightened their feelings of status deprivation. They fought a constant rearguard action to divest government and military officials, businessmen, liberal journalists, and Jews of what they considered their naive impressions of Russia. Alas, mindful of the need to stay on speaking terms with Russia, the administration silenced the Soviet critics in June 1937 by abolishing the Eastern European division. Organizationally integrated into the Western-oriented division of European affairs, the sovietologists had thereafter considerably less access to the secretary of state.[72]

Foreign Service attitudes were also affected by ethnocentric, professional, and class biases. Acculturated in an industrialized, modernized society, they tended to identify positively with the socially advanced states of Western Europe. As a self-perceived professional elite, they readily formed associations with other professionals: foreign diplomats, political leaders, journalists, writers, and intellectuals. Representative as well of an upper-middle-class or upper-class society, they were attracted to the well-to-do and the socially prominent in other countries. Since most career officers either derived from or at least were inculcated into Anglo-Saxon ideals and traditions, they felt special bonds of affinity with the English-speaking world. "I'm of English origin," Durbrow remarked, "so naturally I was sympathetic to the British." Schoenfeld gushed with pride that "many of the deepest and doubtless the noblest currents in American life have their diverse or most obvious inspiration in the experience of the Anglo-Saxon people." Even though Britain occupied the seat of honor in the American cultural pantheon, France, Italy, Germany, and the rest of

Western Europe also enjoyed prominent places. Diplomats defined this part of the world as elegant, prosperous, civilized, industrious, and tasteful. Though expressed with greater reserve, cultural images of modernized Japan were also favorable.[73]

By contrast China, Latin America, the Near East, and Eastern Europe were regarded as backward, inefficient, and disorderly. Appalled by the amoral conduct of her people, Durbrow considered Rumania a profession, not a country. Burton Berry found "disgusting" the impassably muddy streets of Teheran; dilapidated countryside hotels featured "chickens strolling through the corridors" and toilets which "were really the last word in simplicity." Witness to an innocuous crowd display in Addis Ababa, George termed their behavior "savage," the appearance of barefoot Ethiopian troops simply "pitiful." Unavoidably distracted by the prevalence of nude bathing in Riga, Klieforth opined: "It must have been the Lettish women who made [God] decide to clothe women in garments and jewels!" A colleague described Lithuania as a "God-forsaken country," her people "a bunch of aborigines with an incomprehensible tongue, no manners and no morals." Despite the abundance of ballet, opera, and theater, Moscow was a "dreary" city to Bohlen. Rarely did Henderson see "an attractive or sensitive face." The people's clothes, filled with lice and bed bugs, reeked of a foul ordor. Public buildings were "shabby and depressing"; shops and department stores carried few consumption goods, often displaying merchandise not yet for sale. Some stores specialized in foodstuffs: cuts of meat "beautifully made of rubber"; bread of inferior quality; no fruits or vegetables in the winter months. Travel conditions were something "the traveller would not expect to encounter in a civilized country." Even the horses they rode, recalled Durbrow, were "sorry looking underfed animals."[74]

Some diplomats, of course, "spoiled children" to Hull and others in the department, emitted such shrill cries of anguish that they were reassigned. Most, however, managed to survive the conditions of their existence by isolating themselves from the disorder and primitiveness of foreign peoples and limiting their circle of acquaintances to the aristocracy and to those of their professional and class standing. In spite of Hungary's semifeudal conditions, there was a plentiful aristocracy in Budapest with whom Matthews regularly consorted. Although Lane considered Poland "decidedly primitive" in contrast to France and Italy, he too mingled with the beau monde, dining on one occasion with Princess Radziwill, who recounted wistfully the good old days in czarist Russia. Commenting on the anxiety exhibited by a Yugoslav doctor and his wife—"both highly civilized and cultivated"—following the 1939 invasion of Prague, Lane observed that the physician's attitude was nonetheless "characterized by natural dignity and reserve." In the Soviet Union, however, where the purges had removed or bludgeoned into a politically and socially insensate state the intelligentia and professional class, the diplomatic community supplied its own diversions at a rented dacha outside Moscow. Their impression of those public officials who survived the purges was a stereotypically unflattering one. Bohlen described the delegates to the Soviet congresses, many of whom comprised "the primitive races" (Georgians, Kazaks, Volgans), as "frightened," "bewildered," "phlegmatic." They possessed singularly "non-intellectual faces," impassively listened to the Soviet speakers, and cheered wildly each time Stalin's name was mentioned.[75]

The ethnocentrism of Foreign Service officers had two major effects on their attitudes during the thirties. Because they embraced a favorable cultural and social image of Western Europe, they tended to tolerate the fascist governments of Italy and Germany. Both countries had contributed materially and intellectually to the world's cultural heritage; both were modern, "civilized" countries which, they believed, would gradually abandon their repressive systems of government. Diplomats were especially taken by Mussolini, whom some officers called "courtesy itself." Unlike Hitler, who was at best "a mere house painter" and at worst "insane," Il Duce was "one of those rare people who makes you speak better than you know how to speak, who forces you to use your own mind to its maximum, and whose intensity of intellectual interchange exercises a genuine charm on his listeners." Hardly dismayed by Mussolini's Ethiopian adventure, one careerist noted that "from a technical point of view the Italian effort was magnificent, the road construction was superlative, the health of the Army something that had never been seen when Westerners were fighting in tropic conditions."[76]

By the same token, Foreign Service officers found little with which to identify culturally and socially in less developed countries. As long as order was maintained, they simply ignored the conditions with which other peoples had to contend. They considered the establishment of authoritarian governments a vital antidote to the contagion of social and political disorder. Although they fundamentally disapproved of dictatorship and political repression, they accepted, if not welcomed, these regimes as stabilizing, modernizing, democratizing, even Americanizing forces. Most disturbing to the diplomats' sociocultural sensibilities was the Soviet Union. The revolutionary Soviet ideology was the very antithesis of everything they believed. By severing itself from its traditions, Moscow, despite the rhetoric of historical dialectics, was an insidiously antihistorical monster to them. Unlike the authoritarian—even fascist—governments in other countries, which Foreign Service officers believed arose in part to defend against the communist menace, and which, for all their excesses, seemed committed to order and progress,

Soviet totalitarianism was a destabilizing, antimodern phenomenon, which, if permitted to spread, would heinously destroy centuries of human and material progress.[77]

Such were the images—beliefs, myths, prejudices, irrationalities—of American diplomats amidst the kaleidoscopic and disorienting world of the 1930s, images born of a complex of historical, cultural, institutional, social, and personal experiences. Now they would be tested against the reality of war.

4. Diplomatic Euphoria

Unlike Congress and the American public, which erected barriers to escape the baleful effects of international politics, and the diplomatic community, which clung to the hope that Germany, Italy, and Japan would avert their descent toward war, Franklin Roosevelt recognized at the end of 1937 that the Western Hemisphere would be an endangered island were Hitler and his allies to conquer Europe and Asia. Though acutely sensitive to the mounting isolationist sentiment within the United States, Roosevelt skillfully persuaded Congress to alter American neutrality legislation and to extend material assistance to Britain, Russia, and China by giving public assurances that such measures would keep the nation out of war. These steps, endorsed by Foreign Service officers after 1939, were realistic responses on his part to the geopolitical threat posed by the Axis powers.

By the summer of 1941 Roosevelt had unmistakably identified American security with the survival of Britain and Russia. Mainly to galvanize public support for the war, but also because he possessed an idealistic streak, Roosevelt, with encouragement from Secretary of State Hull, decided that the three nations should anoint their association with a declaration of principle to guide their common cause during and after the war. So in August the president arranged a secret rendezvous with Prime Minister Winston Churchill off the coast of Newfoundland, where together they conceived the Atlantic Charter, which affirmed, among other things, their renunciation of territorial aggrandizement, respect for the political self-determination of all nations, and opposition to territorial changes that did not accord with the popular will. In the wake of Pearl Harbor, the American government extended the principles of the Atlantic Charter to a larger body of states—including the Soviet Union—all of which signed the Declaration of the United Nations on January 1, 1942.

Whereas Hull and official Washington viewed the Atlantic Charter in neo-Wilsonian terms as a *sanctus corpus juris* that trumpeted the dawn of a new world order, it was clear from the outset that its commandments would meet resistance from America's allies. Churchill served notice that he considered the compact little more than a fallible expression of righteous purpose by exempting the British Empire from the unconditional applications of the principles of self-determination and equal opportunity of trade. Quite impervious to idealistic pronouncements, Stalin limited his acceptance of the charter to its "practical application" to the reality of the specific needs and historical conditions of its signatories. Like Hull, Roosevelt was keenly aware of these differences, but he realized that Britain no longer possessed the might to obstruct American postwar plans. The Soviet Union, however, both militarily and ideologically, did. Roosevelt had not forgotten the Kremlin's repudiation of the Litvinov pledges, its disregard of human freedoms, or its cynical agreement with Germany in 1939. Even as Washington prepared to authorize Soviet aid following the German invasion, the president made it plain that "the principles and doctrines of communist dictatorship are as intolerable and alien to American beliefs as are the principles and doctrines of Nazi dictatorship."[1]

Now, in the spring of 1942, here was Foreign Minister Molotov indifferently mocking the lofty principles of the Atlantic Charter by audaciously dictating allied compliance with Stalin's demand to retain the Baltic, Finnish, Rumanian, and Polish territories acquired after 1939. Clearly, approval of Soviet claims would violate the principle of self-determination; a negative reply might induce Stalin to seek peace with Germany. Determined to sustain the military alliance, but loath to abandon the universalistic approach to peace spelled out in the Atlantic Charter, around which the American people had rallied their support, Roosevelt sought some middle ground. He proposed the postponement of territorial questions in exchange for Anglo-American assurances to expedite the shipment of war materials to the USSR and to open a second front in Europe later in the year. Molotov's concurrence delighted the president, for it gave reassurance that the Russians were committed to the overriding allied objective of defeating the Axis powers. As for the acceptance of American principles, Roosevelt felt confident that he could resolve conflicts among allied leaders, when the time arrived, through the sheer force of his personality.[2]

During 1943 Roosevelt grew increasingly sanguine about the prospects of U.S.-Soviet, hence allied, cooperation. Despite Stalin's oft-stated resentment of the temporary suspension of war-material deliveries and the delayed opening of the second front, the Russian army, which had courageously borne the brunt of the fighting up to this point, won the president's respect and admiration. Moreover, the favorable coverage of the allied war effort in the Soviet press, the revival of Russian nationalism, Moscow's sanction of religious worship, and the dissolution of the Comintern in May nourished the image—both in the minds of administration officials and the American public—that the Soviets had decided to abandon their revolutionary goal for peaceful cooperation with the United

States and the democratic West. Illustrative of this ebullient mood, *Life* devoted a special issue to the USSR in March, which portrayed the Russians as "one hell of a people," eulogized Kremlin leaders, and minimized the illiberal aspects of the Soviet system. Amidst the din of jubilation that swept the country, critical voices like Bullitt's, who considered it "wishful thinking" to suppose that Stalin had been converted, like Saul on the way to Damascus, to Atlantic Charter ideals, were drowned out.[3]

Roosevelt shared neither Bullitt's passionate antagonism toward the Russians nor the American public's illusion that Kremlin leaders would repudiate their totalitarian system of government. Yet he could not dispute the reality that the Soviet Union was proving a worthy ally. Moreover, assuming that the United States satisfied legitimate Russian security needs, the Kremlin might well relinquish its historic mission to communize the world in favor of postwar peaceful coexistence. Thus it was that Roosevelt, encouraged by Moscow's willingness to coopeate with America and Britain, and grandiosely confident of his own abilities to reconcile political differences among the alliance partners, fashioned his "grand design" for a new world order after the termination of hostilities.

At one level Roosevelt's envisioned new order was influenced by the liberal-internationalist ideology of Wilsonianism. Like Wilson, he believed that universal adherence to self-determination and multilateral trade would eliminate the political and economic tensions that had led to two world wars. At other levels, however, Roosevelt's plan diverged from the Wilsonian model. In contrast to the negotiated peace of World War I, the doctrine of unconditional surrender announced by Roosevelt in January 1943 was intended to nullify the war-making potential of the Axis aggressors. But it was in Roosevelt's conception of a postwar security system that the "grand design" fundamentally departed from the Wilsonian order. Recognizing that the collective security system of the League of Nations had failed to prevent aggression, Roosevelt advocated a kind of international trusteeship in which the United States, Britain, Russia, and eventually China, by virtue of the preponderance of military force they would possess after the war, would ensure the peace that had eluded the architects of the Versailles settlement. These "Four Policemen" would eventually assume leadership roles in a new collective security organization that would serve as a forum to resolve international disputes. For the foreseeable future, however, each of the four would be responsible for maintaining order in their respective spheres of influence.

Mindful of the American public's repugnance to realpolitik, Roosevelt was careful not to publicize even this limited or "benign" balance-of-power policy. Nor did he make his intentions apparent to officials in the State Department, who, as will become clear, perceived the postwar international order in neo-Wilsonian rather than power-political terms. Thus Foreign Service officers considered the consummation of the Atlantic Charter principles, which were enunciated by Roosevelt at least in part to conceal his realpolitik objectives from domestic scrutiny, to be the ultimate goal of American postwar policy. In the end, these principles would circumscribe the president's strategic flexibility with the Soviets and, in so doing, destroy his "grand design."[4]

At this stage, of course, Roosevelt's "grand design" was quite literally that, a blueprint for the postwar world. Before it could be approved by the allies and put into effect, it had to be developed and refined. To conduct this task, Roosevelt turned to the State Department, not because he recognized that such an activity logically fell within its purview or because he suddenly felt confident in its ability to manage such an important undertaking; rather it was because other government agencies were preoccupied with more critical military matters. Actually, the secretary of state was usually the last to know of policy and strategy decisions made in connection with the military effort. In fact, during the early war years, the president preferred to transmit highly classified communications to Churchill through Navy Department codes. And even now that the State Department had overall responsibility for postwar planning, its prerogatives were encroached upon by the Board of Economic Warfare and most cabinet officials. Nevertheless, the department did have a role in foreign-policy planning. Happily for them, so did Foreign Service officers assigned to Washington.[5]

Department planning had actually begun secretly in September 1939, when Leo Pasvolsky, special assistant to Cordell Hull, was asked by the secretary to initiate ideas for the postwar world order. Shortly after the European war started, an ad hoc committee was established, which gave way in 1941 to the Advisory Committee on Postwar Foreign Policy. This committee, which functioned through the summer of 1943, transformed postwar planning from the stage of discussion to the stage of formulation. To ensure secrecy, its work was divided among six subcommittees, the three most important of which concentrated on political, territorial, and security problems.

Professional diplomats participated in the deliberations of these working groups as well as sundry intradepartmental and interdepartmental committees spawned by the hydra-headed postwar planning organization to breathe life into the Rooseveltian blueprint. Career diplomats affirmed the administration's position that international adherence to the precepts of political self-determination, territorial changes in accord with national desires, and equality of trade offered the best chance to ensure postwar peace. Their commitment to the realization of these ideals was influenced partly by the spirit of optimism infused into the department bureaucracy by the president, Hull, and others (notably Harry Hopkins, Roosevelt's special advisor and secretary of state in all but name), and partly by Roosevelt's reluctance to reveal completely his "grand design." In addition to these factors, which were not inconsiderable, diplomats were psychologically inclined, as individuals, and institutionally conditioned, as a group, to embrace the American government's declaration of principle.

Foreign Service officers also recognized that their envisioned postwar world would not materialize without continued U.S.-Soviet cooperation in conformity with the Atlantic Charter. While they too welcomed the Russian military performance and the apparent moderating trend within the Soviet Union, jaded by the memory of Soviet rhetoric and behavior during the interwar years, they responded cautiously to the Soviet-American rapprochement. This evoked no surprise from administration proponents of U.S.-Soviet amity like Sumner Welles, who quipped to Vice President Wallace one day at lunch that three fourths of the Foreign Service, with Dunn among its leaders, preferred to arm the Poles as a safeguard against Soviet expansionism.

Those who had served in the Soviet Union were still more skeptical of Moscow's motives. According to Wallace, the "Riga group" of Bohlen, Kennan, and Henderson "felt that Russia was the real enemy in 1942." Upset by Litvinov's success in winning Welles's confidence, Henderson had admonished the undersecretary in the spring of 1942 not to base America's Soviet policy on the struggle against a common enemy. "We have no information which would cause us to believe that [the Comintern] is not continuing quietly to function with headquarters in the Soviet Union," he noted. Concerned about the diplomat's presence in Washington, Litvinov told Admiral William H. Standley, then ambassador at Moscow, and Eleanor Roosevelt that improved relations between the two nations would be impaired if Henderson were to assume charge of Eastern European affairs as the department had planned. Sent briefly to Moscow at the end of 1942, where, as we shall see, his views underwent a significant change, Henderson departed for Iraq the following summer.[6]

Despite the persistence of the past, career officers had to contend with the equally powerful reality of the present. Pulled one way by the memory of a deceitful Soviet state devoted to inevitable and unconditional ideological warfare, still another by the Kremlin's ostensibly war-chastened attitude and by the Edenic future world of peace, prosperity, and collective security that intruded ever more powerfully on their minds, they struggled to reconcile their conflicting images. Though his mistrust of the Soviets was still pronounced, Cannon had declared to the Rumanian chargé in Washington late in 1941 that Hitlerism was now the public enemy. By 1942 Bohlen found it difficult to ignore the indications of "a less suspicious and more friendly attitude towards the United States and Great Britain on the part of the Soviet Government." He pointed out that Stalin's November 6 speech commemorating the twenty-fifth anniversary of the Bolshevik revolution "stressed the growing collaboration between the 'Anglo-Soviet-American coalition' not only for the prosecution of the war but by implication for the post war period." A week later he wrote Professor Samuel Harper: "I look forward with confidence to the steady growth of fruitful cooperation between the United States and the Soviet Union." Even Elbridge Durbrow, no more favorably disposed toward the Soviets than Henderson, moderated his views. Although the economic systems of the United States and Russia were not complementary, he allowed that a new trade agreement "might be advisable from the point of view of expressing our good will and determination to foster Soviet-American trade by all means possible."[7]

Whereas diplomats in the department actively participated in postwar reconstruction planning, diplomats in the field performed essentially the same role they had during the interwar period: to observe and report. And since Washington preferred to defer discussion of political issues until victory was assured, the information they supplied dealt mainly with war-related issues such as the availability of food supplies in occupied countries, the morale of the people, political conditions, and the like. Because of their military-support function, they focussed only indirectly on the postwar world and on allied political relations. Even so, like officers in the department, they enthusiastically supported the war-of-principle America was fighting; and they too had to reconcile similar conflicting images of the Soviet Union. While their colleagues in Washington constructed their wartime perceptions of the USSR against the backdrop of global policy formulation and high-level cabinet diplomacy, however, diplomats in the field were influenced by the narrower reality of their specific geographical location and by the observations of foreign nationals and local officials they encountered there.

From their vantage point in Colombia, Lane, who was made ambassador in 1941, and his chargé Gerald Keith, a post–Rogers Act diplomat who had won Lane's confidence and affection, fixed their attention through 1943 on strengthening inter-American solidarity in the postwar period. While they expressed concern about the continued appearance of radical leftist organizations and their state-directed social reforms, they did not link these movements with the Soviet Union as they had in the thirties. At this juncture, the presence of "leftish" groups was perceived as an impediment to Latin American collaboration with the United States and her allies against Germany.[8]

Closer to allied policy-making circles, Matthews, in his telegrams from London, revealed greater preoccupation with the postwar world and with potential obstructions to the fulfillment of the Atlantic Charter. The British, not unexpectedly, presented adamantine opposition to lower trade barriers; liberals even envisioned a planned social-welfare state, not at all what their cousins across the Atlantic had in mind. A more formidable obstacle, in Matthews's opinion, was Charles de Gaulle, hero of the French resistance and symbolic leader of the nation. While de Gaulle enjoyed Churchill's confidence and support, partly because he had stood by England when Vichy France caved in to German pressure, and partly because he represented a counterforce to American political influence in Europe after the war, he was quite clearly *l'enfant gâté* to Washington. Not only had his criticism of American policy in North Africa caused friction between London and Washington, "with all that it means for the future of the war and the peace," but he had deceitfully masqueraded before all the liberals of the world as "the 20th century Joan of Arc," a feat, Matthews declared, even Hitler had failed to accomplish. Matthews contended that the British had closed their eyes to de Gaulle's "boring from within tactics" and to the inevitable *révolution sanglante* he would foment. Faced in the end with "an Adolph of their own in Paris," the French people would blame the United States "for saddling them (through our support) with a Fascist de Gaulle regime."[9]

At other times, curiously enough, Matthews was "inclined to attribute much importance to communist influence" in de Gaulle's appeal for sabotage and open resistance against the Vichy French, a concern that was aggravated by the accounts of American and Free French military officers, who pointed out that Moscow considered the general a "fellow traveller." Enduring suspicions of Soviet ideological aims also prompted the diplomat to view uneasily the growing popularity of the Communist party in England, which stood to gain politically from its responsible contribution to the war effort. But in light of the Red Army's impressive contribution to the allied cause, Matthews, who admitted that his "own knowledge of Russian mental processes in general and those of Stalin in particular is nil," tended to compartmentalize past Soviet actions and intentions. When the British contended that Soviet territorial demands in Eastern Europe were intended to sow the seeds of allied friction, since Stalin knew full well that " 'the British would never go to war to take that region away from them,' " Matthews stated reassuringly that "[Soviet] demands would have been far more extensive than they are" if Moscow was really spoiling for a fight. Desiring to avoid at all costs their "haggling tactics" of 1939, Foreign Office representatives finally conceded the point. Even after the Russian victory at Stalingrad, the skittery Foreign Office continued to voice unofficial misgivings about

Soviet intentions, particularly in Yugoslavia. So long as Russian sensibilities and interests were not ignored, an unruffled Matthews observed from the State Department the following summer, there was no reason to believe that Stalin would not carry over to the postwar world the same cooperative spirit he had displayed on the battlefield.[10]

American diplomats in neutral Turkey conformed to the general view of the allied effort as a common struggle against a common villain. Having served in Greece during the occupation of 1941, Burton Berry, consul general at the listening post in Istanbul, could not forget the horror he had witnessed: the rapes, the expropriation of property, the twisted and contorted corpses piled perfunctorily into cavernous grave sites by Nazi executioners, and the childlike helplessness on the faces of the friends and relatives who were invited to watch the festival of death. The invasion of Greece had also introduced William Fraleigh, Berry's young colleague in Athens, to the destructive regularity of war. Assigned to Istanbul in the summer of 1941, he was joined a year later by Roy Melbourne, another novice diplomat. Serious and scholarly, Melbourne had passed the previous two years as a consular office in Japan, where he caught the Nipponese overture to war.

Contemptuous though they were of the Axis aggressors, Berry, Fraleigh, and Melbourne were noticeably less restrained in their reactions to the prospect of postwar U.S.-Soviet cooperation than their counterparts in the State Department and London. Doubtless this had much to do with the nature of their mission. Because of their geographical proximity to the primary theater of operations in Europe, they were primarily concerned with gleaning information which might contribute to the war effort. But it was also due to the frequently conflicting views about Soviet Russia and communism in the Eastern European press and in the accounts proffered them by refugees.

Recognizing after Stalingrad that Germany's defeat was only a matter of time, and increasingly more anxious about a Soviet-dominated peace settlement, Hungarians and Rumanians began to characterize their complicity in the war exclusively as a struggle against the "anti-European power of Bolshevism" and the "Asiatic hordes" of Russia. While not unmindful of the opportunist nature of Magyar and Rumanian politics, motivated as always by "the cold realism of power politics," Berry and Melbourne found it difficult just the same to disregard the recurrent pleas for Anglo-American protection against the Soviet army. Yugoslav expatriates stated that the partisan forces of (Josip Broz) Tito, who were engaged in an internecine conflict with the exiled government-backed charges of General Draža Mihailović, intended to liquidate Serbian business, professional, and political leaders and to impose communism on the country. While Fraleigh condemned partisan actions as severely damaging to the integrity of the nation, he noted at the same time that Tito appeared to enjoy the support of Serbian refugees in Egypt, who, along with other Yugoslavs, were willingly transferring their allegiance to the communist camp. Upper-class Bulgarians in Istanbul also gloomily awaited the imposition of communist rule in their country. There were indications, however, that the peasantry harbored different feelings. According to a Jewish merchant from Varna, 90 percent of the Bulgarian people supported communism. By virtue of geography, traditional Bulgarian affinities for Russia, and the impressive performance of the Red Army, it was inconceivable to Berry that Russia would not seek to exert her influence in the country. Still, as a former member of the Bulgarian Assembly (and a man "well disposed to American ideas and institutions") cheerily asserted, Russia's association with the bourgeois West nullified the possibility of world revolution.[11]

Because of the confused state of affairs in Eastern Europe and the biases of informants, Foreign Service officers in Istanbul tended to withhold judgment about Soviet objectives. Indeed, they were inclined to question the authenticity of many of the reports they received. In Berry's opinion, the events of November 1917 appeared to have cut too deeply into the Russian weltanschauung to expect any real change of attitude on the part of the Soviets. Nevertheless, neither he nor his colleagues dissented from the growing image of ideological cooperation characteristic of the diplomatic establishment during this early phase of U.S.-Soviet wartime relations. In May 1943 he wrote Cannon that he had not yet consolidated his view of Soviet intentions. "Communism is something about which I have been trying to learn as much as possible and talk as little as possible." While communist elements were in a position to increase their influence in the Balkans, Moscow had thus far given no indications of expansionist aims. Moreover, in his opinion, much of the internal unrest in the region was a product of historical Balkan divisiveness.[12]

Meanwhile, in Moscow, a skeptical Henderson warily assessed Soviet intentions. Occasional expressions of friendliness notwithstanding, he wired in the fall of 1942, Kremlin authorities "are not yet prepared to permit the Soviet people to have feelings of confidence in, or wholehearted friendliness for, any of the so-called capitalistic nations." Despite his unequivocal surface utterances, however, Henderson harbored a hope, albeit barely alive, that the Kremlin might yet seek some ideological rapprochement with the West and with the principles of the United Nations Declaration. Gradually, the hope survived and matured. Of the fifty-two slogans in the Soviet press honoring the twenty-fifth anniversary of the revolution, he informed the department on October 31, most were intended to arouse patriotism and to augment the war effort. More significantly, "There is nothing of an international revolutionary content in any of them." Like Bohlen, Henderson was further encouraged by Stalin's anniversary speech, which "represents another step forward in the direction of closer cooperation between the Soviet Union and its allies. I believe and already have received indications Soviet officials are interpreting the speech as a directive for the display of greater friendliness toward the United States and Great Britain." A month later he reported: "The tone of the Soviet press and radio during the last month make it appear that the Soviet Government has decided to present war developments in such a light as to influence the Soviet population to have a more friendly feeling towards the United States and Great Britain, in particular toward the United States."[13]

Henderson's nascent image of ideological cooperation, reminiscent of his attitude in 1934, was clearly evident in his observations of Soviet society. The citizenry was better fed and clothed than they had been before the war and there was a greater abundance of fuel oil to heat buildings. Once idle factories now energetically stamped out the implements of war. Even the gray Moscow sky seemed less somber. While the city was still drab compared to Western capitals, "the atmosphere seems to have become slightly more western than it was five years ago," he remarked. "At times cheerfulness almost reaching the point of gaiety has been noted." As for the people themselves, free to worship again at Russian churches, they "are beginning to hope, as they did in 1936 when the new constitution was first announced, that they may live to enjoy personal freedoms under a more benign regime."[14]

Some months later, after Henderson had returned to Washington, the department received a wire from Ambassador Standley urging Secretary Hull to correct the impression given by the Kremlin that Russia was singlehandedly fighting the Germans. Henderson opposed the recommendation partly to avoid a breakdown in the alliance, but also because he had modified his perceptions of the Soviets. Ironically, Soviet officials were unaware of his softened image; by this time, they had succeeded in having him transferred from Washington.[15]

Having never before served in the USSR, Maxwell Hamilton was less encumbered by memories of the interwar years than Henderson. When he arrived in Moscow as counseller of embassy in June 1943, allied relations were fast approaching the high point of wartime collaboration; and the many Soviet expressions of friendship formed a kind of palimpsest on the revolutionary invective of the past. Somehow, he revealed to his wife, with the reinstitution of "first-class" ballet, opera, and theater, and the elegant Russian dinner parties, the Soviet Union seemed to be transforming right before his eyes into a new society, or rather the old society of czarist Russia. Graded coeducational schools, the establishment of an officer classification system in the armed forces, respect for parental authority, and an emphasis on moral virtues all bore striking similarities to cultural forms in the United States. Stalingrad became "Russia's Valley Forge." As for Stalin, he was precisely what Hamilton expected him to be: strong, powerfully featured, and "direct in manner and speech." His new book on the Russian war effort, Hamilton wired the department in September, conveyed a sense of "liberating mission," support for the Atlantic Charter, and a commitment to cooperate with the West, as already evidenced by the dissolution of the Comintern.[16]

Hamilton's cheerful outlook for continued Big Three cooperation was matched in kind, if not degree, by others in the embassy. Notwithstanding his "taciturn, grim" demeanor, sovietologist Francis Stevens, whose studies had been abruptly terminated by the department in the thirties because he had "committed the reprehensible act of contracting marriage with a nice Polish lady" and daughter of czarist officials, was heartened by a recent Soviet publication that sympathetically reviewed United States foreign policy during the interwar years and praised America's fighting spirit and productive capacity. Llewellyn Thompson, a patient, soft-spoken, and highly regarded diplomat who had gone to Moscow late in 1940, stated in a review of Soviet foreign relations during 1943 that Russia, both militarily and politically, had embarked on a course of "international collaboration." Although Stalin remained suspicious about the absence of a second front, declined to exchange military and technical information, and refused American aircraft permission to operate on Soviet soil, there was a growing appreciation in the Soviet press for the Anglo-American war effort. The dissolution of the Comintern and the Kremlin's expressed intention to participate in the forthcoming United Nations Relief and Rehabilitation Association were further reassuring indications of Moscow's growing identification with the democratic powers. Like Hamilton, Thompson was especially encouraged by Stalin's willingness to confer with Churchill and Roosevelt at the end of the year, which signalled, in his view, a diminution of mistrust and a personal commitment to the policy of collaboration.[17]

George Kennan, appointed counsellor of legation in Lisbon in mid-1942, also subscribed to the democratic ideals of the Atlantic Charter and supported the administration's policy of U.S.-Soviet cooperation in the postwar world. He was even more skeptical than Roosevelt, however, that the tenets of the Atlantic Charter would form the basis of U.S.-Soviet cooperation. Given America's congenital weakness for subjectivity and parochialism in foreign affairs, he asserted, both Washington and the public had become carried away by Soviet wartime collaboration, just as they had caricatured the Russians after World War I as the embodiment of all evil. Unlike the American government, which perceived its relationship to the world as "we *and* they," the Kremlin saw it, beginning at its own doorsteps, as "we *or* they." Since Russia was not fighting America's war, Kennan pointed out, Washington should base its participation in the joint undertaking purely on self-interest. But even as he perceived the Soviets in terms of realistic cooperation, Kennan could not easily abandon his own idealistic predilections. Assuming Berlin and Moscow were to establish humane regimes, he stated, "I could see no objection to dividing all of eastern Europe (except Finland) up between them;" if only one humane regime survived, it should enjoy a dominant position. However, if dictatorship prevailed in both countries, power should then be returned to the "small peoples," provided they adhered to a more effective security system than in 1919.[18]

During the course of 1943, Kennan consolidated his views of realistic cooperation and, in the process, gravitated farther away from an idealistic perspective on foreign policy. His overriding preoccupation with security and international stability inclined him to tolerate the Portuguese dictatorship of Prime Minister Antonio Salazar. In Kennan's judgment, the likelihood of a democratic form of government, however preferable, was an unrealistic expectation, since Portugal's problems were not "susceptible to solution by any of the clichés for social progress that find currency in greater and more advanced countries." With an eye for maintaining political equilibrium in the postwar world, he thus found it advisable to support Salazar and to refrain from "messianic remedies for social progress foreign to his own world of thought." He deemed it equally important to impress upon Washington Portugal's strategic significance. In a long disquisition to the department, in which he traced the history and significance of the ancient Anglo-Portuguese alliance, Kennan pointed out that a war-weakened England could no longer fulfill her relationship with Portugal any more than she could combat the Axis without American technological and economic assistance. The United States, therefore, in the interests of Anglo-Saxon security, must accept her share of the responsibility for the continued defense of Portugal. "For over a hundred years, American diplomatists have resided as passive and frequently bored observers in this remote capital of a languishing but long-lived empire," waiting for some event which would seize American interests. "This day, I believe, has at long last arrived; and we should be lacking in perspicacity if we failed to perceive it." Alluding to the latest invocation of the Anglo-Portuguese alliance, Kennan expressed his "personal hope that I may consider myself—among the long succession of predecessors and successors—if not the first of the participants, then at least the last of the observers."[19]

It was at the end of his intellectual evolution that Kennan learned of Roosevelt's desire to obtain certain facilities for the U.S. army and navy—including a naval base—in the Portuguese Azores. Horrified at the effect this might have on Portuguese neutrality, Kennan refused to enter into such negotiations without an order from the president, explaining to Welles and Matthews on October 20 that a demand of this magnitude, which surpassed what the British had requested of Lisbon, would confirm Salazar's suspicion that the United States had designs on the entire archipelago. Three days later, after the department had rejected his recommended quid pro quo to respect Portuguese sovereignty and to return all facilities after the war, Kennan himself, in direct violation of his orders, provided these assurances to the Portuguese government.

Insubordination was obviously a risky business in a career service that stressed the norms of discipline and discretion. But, fundamentally a scholar who "spent most of his time in the world of ideas," Kennan did not "fit comfortably in an organization that is weighed down by inertia and in which the ambitious foreign service officer is inclined to play safe." It was not that Kennan was unambitious. Quite the contrary, his inability as a child to gain recognition from his father and a sense of worthiness produced in him a burning desire to succeed, to affirm his own existence, or as he put it, to "acquit" himself. It was not surprising, then, that Kennan chafed at his assignment as administrative officer in Berlin at the end of the 1930s and his later transfer to Lisbon. As he had explained to G. Howland Shaw in August 1942, he had "no right to waste" the years of his "maximum strength as an individual plugging away at administrative jobs," when his knowledge of German and Russian affairs were as broad as "many men who have achieved public prominence in them." Nor was it surprising, in view of his consuming need to establish his professional competence, hence his personal identity, that he contradicted the department's instructions concerning the Azores.[20]

Puzzled and irritated by the young man's impertinence, military and civilian officials in Washington called him home. "By this time," Matthews recalled, "George's nerves—never very strong—had reached the borderline of hysteria." Tired and jittery, Kennan was driven to the Pentagon, where he was interrogated by the secretary of war and military officials. "Frightened and confused as he was, George did not make his explanation of Salazar's attitude convincing to that high-powered jury," Matthews related, "and Stimson's suggestion that a career ambassador be sent promptly was accepted." Devastated by the experience, but resolved to make himself heard, Kennan managed, after a series of intermediate conversations, to gain access to the president. In the end he had his way. Roosevelt agreed to give him a letter for Salazar guaranteeing Portuguese sovereignty over the Azores. Before the negotiations could be completed, however, Kennan was notified of his assignment to the newly created European Advisory Commission in London.[21]

Committed to the ideals of the Atlantic Charter and the United Nations Declaration, heartened by the Kremlin's manifestations of cordiality and the apparent "democratizing" trend within the USSR, Foreign Service officers, including Kennan for a time, as we shall see, became increasingly sanguine about the vision of U.S.-Soviet ideological cooperation after the war. Most diplomats defined that cooperation on the basis of self-conceived international principles rather than on the mutual reconciliation of national interests. From their perspective, these were not mutually exclusive phenomena, since it was in the interests of all states, including Soviet Russia, to support the principles of peace, security, and prosperity. Seemingly antipodal concepts such as "realism" and "international morality" were confusing to the likes of Henderson, who, at times, believed that "the most realistic policy is that of the highest international morality and adherence to established principles." That the Soviets would actually adhere to American postwar objectives was still questionable. Through the summer of 1943, as the telegrams from diplomats in the field suggest, vestigial memories of Soviet behavior during the interwar years, obscured but never wholly dissipated by the glow of allied unity, weighed against the developing image of U.S.-Soviet cooperation.[22]

This slow and desultory process of image transformation was particularly evident in the conflicting attitudes of careerists in the department who participated in shaping United States postwar policy. The residue of mistrust was plainly obvious in their deliberations to reconcile Moscow's interwar behavior with the cardinal tenets of the Atlantic Charter. Would the Soviets uphold the territorial integrity of other countries? Would they accede to the principles of self-determination and noninterference in the internal political and economic affairs of other states?

From the outset American diplomats voiced misgivings about Soviet willingness to respect the territorial integrity of other nations. They regarded Moscow's insistence on the restoration of its prewar borders less as the prophylactic measure it was presented to be and more for what it might portend: a sinister design to weaken the integrity of the Atlantic Charter. On December 29, 1941, Llewellyn Thompson reported to the department from London that the Soviets had unequivocally stated their demands, for which they were prepared to concede, as a quid pro quo, the establishment of British bases in Holland or on the Atlantic Coast. Dunn and European division chief Ray Atherton flatly asserted in a memorandum prepared for Hull that the Soviet government intended to become the dominant force in Eastern Europe, and that it further had "tremendous ambitions with regard to all of Europe." Acquiescence to this objective, they feared, would weaken the principles of the Atlantic Charter and alarm the small states of Europe, especially those to whom communism was most repugnant. Durbrow felt just as strongly, especially after learning that the secret clauses to the proposed Czech-Soviet mutual assistance pact called for a common frontier between the two countries. In his view, this would establish Prague as "spokesman for the Soviet system in Europe in both economic and political fields." As far as Cannon was concerned, "Russia would not dissociate itself from the affairs of Central and Eastern Europe." Neither would she forego the opportunity to assert her influence in the Straits region of the eastern Mediterranean, where she had long desired a *point d'appui*.[23]

Apprehension about Russia's territorial ambitions intensified in 1943. Soviet exactions on eastern Poland, which had sparked a series of verbal clashes between Moscow and the Polish government in London throughout the previous year, continued unabated. His suspicions obligingly fed by the Polish embassy in Washington, Durbrow noted in January that the Kremlin's refusal to grant Poles of White Russian, Ukrainian, and Jewish descent exit from the USSR demonstrated its desire to lay ethnic claim to eastern Poland. Tensions increased in April, following Moscow's break in relations with the London Poles, a decision ignited by the latter's request for an investigation into the deaths of thousands of Polish officers near Katyn forest. Thenceforth, Poland would become the crucible of the United States-Soviet future: "Would that future be the enlightened and Christian American formula of the Atlantic Charter," queried Henderson, "or the imperialist one of the Congress of Vienna?" If Russia were to succeed in her territorial objectives, he admonished, the world would be visited with "a revival of tsarist imperialism and super-nationalism." Moreover, it would bankrupt the United Nations and, in a war-chastened reversal of his former position, tragically "mark the return of appeasement." For the "Four Freedoms" to survive the "Freedom to Grab," it was imperative to assert "a truly virile policy of blunt warning."[24]

Apart from their anxious rhetoric, however, professional diplomats offered no concrete plan to meet the anticipated Soviet advance. Had they done so, they might well have incited the very grubby game of territorial shuffling they sought to avoid. Moreover, they would have precluded the possibility that the Soviets would not further extend their territory. When the Polish National Council sought American support for its proposal to occupy militarily eastern Poland, Durbrow, Bohlen, and Cannon turned deaf ears for fear that the atavistic principle, "'possession is nine-tenths of the law,'" would later render meaningless the resolution of frontier problems on the basis of "logical and practical economic, ethnic and political considerations." They recommended instead that the Poles and Russians iron out their territorial differences between themselves.[25]

Given the Kremlin's world-revolutionary program of the interwar years, career diplomats also understandably questioned whether Moscow would permit other countries to determine their own political fates. Considering their repudiation of the Litvinov pledges of 1933, there was no reason to assume that the Soviets would honor their decision to abolish the Communist International, Durbrow told Joseph Davies in February. Bohlen and Henderson surely saw nothing routine in Moscow's appointment of Constantine Oumansky as minister to Mexico in May 1943. Since Mexico had been the center of Comintern activities in the Western Hemisphere, they suspected that his appointment betokened an expansion of Soviet publicity and propaganda institutions in the region. Lest the American government become too enraptured by its Soviet ally, Bohlen admonished it to recall the concept of the "two hostile worlds" expounded in the first Soviet constitution of 1923. Ever since that time, Soviet leaders "have taken the attitude that fundamentally the Soviet system of government must be in a permanent state of discord with the systems prevailing in all other countries." Moscow had never considered the Soviet Union part of the family of nations, "but rather as a beleagured socialist fortress surrounded by a hostile capitalist encirclement." The decision to dissolve the Comintern, he pointed out, was undertaken primarily to eliminate an unnecessary bureaucracy, since foreign communists now received guidance directly from Stalin.[26]

While the principles of self-determination and noninterference, long hallmarks of American foreign policy, were intended to encourage other peoples to emulate the American national experience of selecting governments of their own choosing, they were also meant to remove the United States from foreign entanglements. At a security-and-technical-subcommittee meeting in April 1943, Cannon affirmed that Washington was obliged, from the standpoint of international morality, to recognize the legitimacy of all duly authorized governments, including those in exile, pending determination of their future by the popular will. At the same time, apprehensive about the internationalization of the United States, specifically that Washington might fall prey to the self-aggrandizing territorial and personal ambitions of "low grade" exiled leaders like the Yugoslavs, he proposed that "a definite 'United Nations' character" be given to liberation operations, and that a military administration be established afterwards to avoid unnecessary political complications should new leaders assert themselves in opposition to the provisional governments.[27]

Nowhere was the division between the principle of noninterference and the diplomats' lingering suspicions of Moscow's intentions more clearly illustrated than in the Polish-Soviet dispute. Despite Stalin's ultimatum that the London Poles excise the "fascist" elements from their government as a prerequisite to the resumption of diplomatic relations, Bohlen, Henderson, and Durbrow bridled at the thought of bringing pressure on Prime Minister Wladyslaw Sikorski, who had cooperated on behalf of the common cause. Apart from efforts to help resolve certain irritating problems such as the citizenship of Poles in Russia, they advised against participation in discussions on the composition of the Polish government to avert breaching the principle of noninterference.

As a result of their commitment to principle, American diplomats—unwittingly perhaps—were indirectly gainsaying Moscow's demand for a reconstituted Polish government. Considering their persisting suspicions of Soviet objectives, however, they may have unconsciously intended this outcome. Henderson and Durbrow speculated that Soviet interference in Polish affairs symbolized Stalin's desire to warn his neighbors that "their continued existence depended on a willingness to accede to Soviet demands." Their mistrust was aggravated when, two days after Moscow's break with the London Poles, the Union of Polish Patriots, supposedly composed of Polish prisoners of war and refugees, was formed in the Soviet Union. This development, along with the activity of communist partisans in Poland, noted Durbrow, "indicate[s] that the Soviet Government is at least keeping the way open to establishing a Communist Poland if it should prove advantageous."[28]

Bohlen, Dunn, and Cannon were similarly troubled by the thought that Russia would attempt to assert political dominance in the Balkans after the war. "Whenever Soviet troops enter a country," Bohlen exclaimed in a long exegesis on the Soviet government, "the lights go out and certain processes begin to take place which result in the substitution for the ideals which we consider to be those of a civilized world the materialistic ideology of the Moscow regime." Not only would European liberalism be extinguished, but there would arise in its place "a dark continent inherently hostile to western civilization." Already there were indications, he noted, that some groups in England advocated an arrangement "whereby the Soviet Union may have a free hand in Eastern Europe while the British are to dominate Western Europe." But the disproportionate strength the Russians would wield, he hastened to add, would render England powerless to protect her sphere "without resort to another war into which we would almost inevitably be drawn."[29]

To counteract the emergence of power blocs, and particularly Soviet domination of Europe, Kohler and Bohlen considered the adoption of Churchill's plan for an Anglo-American invasion of the Balkans (until the war department rejected the idea as strategically impracticable). Provided the United States sought "to live up to the spirit of the Atlantic Charter" and did not "intend that Europe will be divided into spheres of influence," Bohlen argued, the Balkan states would "accept us with open arms as saviours from both Germany and the Soviet Union." In particular cases such as Albania, where the fight for liberation from the Axis yoke was compounded by intense civil war between the nationalist forces of King Zog (Balli Kombetar) and the communist-influenced liberation movement of Enver Hoxha, diplomats advocated some form of international mandate over which, Cloyce Huston felt, the United States could exert a prominent or leading influence.[30]

The situation in Yugoslavia, equally complicated by civil conflict, was still more distressing. To gird themselves for war against the partisans, the Četniks of Mihailović were receiving supplies and equipment from the Italians, and if they were not fighting with the Axis, they were certainly not fighting against them. British assistance to Mihailović provoked Soviet charges of internal interference and complicity with the pro-Axis proclivities of the Četniks. For their part, the Soviets continued surreptitiously to support the partisans and to inflame anti-Mihailović sentiment. Since the partisan movement, Cannon argued, was incontrovertibly infiltrated by communist elements (Matthews estimated the figure at 70 percent), "Isn't it all to the good that [the Četniks] are collaborating with an enemy that is the lesser evil against an enemy that is the far greater evil?" Sensing the Russian desire to strengthen communist influence in Serbia, which Durbrow attributed to Pan-Slavism, the ideological aphrodisiac of nineteenth-century Russia revived after the German invasion of 1941, some careerists at first contemplated Washington's dispersal of military aid to Mihailović. "Then there would be point in saying with emphasis to the USSR," Cannon had stated in August 1942, "that we want one war, not two, in Serbia, and Mihailović is its leader."[30] A year later Durbrow still suspected that the Kremlin planned to use the nationalistic Pan-Slav movement—simply a refinement of the "popular front" policy of the thirties, in his opinion—as a wedge "to gain substantial, if not complete, control over [the Balkan] countries."[31]

All this rhetoric of mistrust and resentment aside, at the level of behavior diplomats were not inclined to advocate measures which would have simultaneously weakened allied military collaboration and abrogated the principles on which the postwar world order they helped fashion was predicated. As the rift between London and Moscow widened, and as the Tito-Mihailović/Serb-Croatian conflict threatened to impede the war effort and, by polarizing Serbian and Croatian hyphenates in the United States, to disrupt American national unity, an overworked, tired-eyed Cannon strongly recommended a cautious course, "if we expect to exert an American influence" in the Balkans. That course, Cannon, Dunn, Kohler, and their colleagues agreed—the formation of an Eastern European federation—would entail United States participation in the postwar reconstruction of the region, without any direct involvement in its turbulent internal affairs.[32]

Cannon hoped that the little states of the region, notwithstanding nationalistic barriers, might gradually develop common economic interests, coordinate transportation systems, and integrate their military establishments as part of the inevitable development of a postwar organization. Members of the postwar advisory committee on political problems contended that this would not only alleviate Soviet concerns about a revival of German expansionism, but redound socially and economically to Russia's benefit. Since the Soviet Union would no longer be justified in demanding additional territory, rasped Durbrow, "it might be persuaded to drop its claims to these areas of eastern Europe." As an added inducement to Moscow, Cannon and Bohlen were prepared to recognize Russian occupation of Bessarabia, to which the Rumanians were gradually becoming reconciled anyway, and on which the United States had never taken an official position. Matthews suggested concessions as well in Finland and Poland. By granting legitimate Russian claims, Bohlen pointed out, the United States would be in a position to resist later excessive demands. Advocating power-political means to achieve idealistic ends, he maintained that Moscow employed both a "limited" and "unlimited" policy. Just as Soviet leaders in 1940 had accepted limited gains in Finland to avoid a clash with Britain and France, they might eventually compromise all territorial demands with the exception of the Baltic states so as not to alienate their Western allies. Even in the case of the Baltics, Matthews held out hope that the Soviets, considering their "sincere efforts for peace in the League of Nations," would be willing to trade off the independence of these states for assurances that they would be completely disarmed. But what if Russia refused? Should the United States go to war or excommunicate her from future international accords? "These questions, to my mind, answer themselves," he declared. "We must work with Russia through thick and thin."[33]

Almost as soon as the idea of a regional grouping germinated, policy planners in Washington received information from the Russian embassy of Moscow's unalterable opposition to it. The Kremlin confirmed this judgment later in the year by its proposed treaty of alliance with Czechoslovakia. Certainly Cannon had no objection to Czechoslovakia's desire to reach some "understanding" with Russia after hostilities terminated, but an alliance "would be a step backward in our efforts toward international understanding." The British alternative—a tripartite Russo-Polish-Czech pact, "while certainly less objectionable than a tight alliance," was no more palatable. Despite Moscow's unequivocal repudiation of a regional structure, American diplomats persisted in the hope that Washington might yet convince Soviet leaders by affirming its intention to include them in all decisions affecting Eastern Europe. As for the Czech-Soviet treaty, Matthews reassured the British embassy on August 24 that the United States government had not modified its opposition to bilateral agreements. Two days later Bohlen informed Dunn of an article in the Soviet periodical *War and the Working Classes* which "assails any 'schemes' for federation in Eastern Europe as the work of anti-democratic and semi-Fascist elements whose real aim is hostile to the Soviet Government." Regardless of American aims, Bohlen could hardly mistake the inference "that the Soviet Union will insist on dealing bilaterally with the various countries in that area thus assuring predominant Soviet influence over such countries as are to be 'independent' in that area."[34]

Further adding to the diplomats' apprehensions of Soviet intentions was the formation on Russian soil of "the 'Free Germany Committee'" in July. Bohlen interpreted Freies Deutschland's manifesto urging the German people to cast off their Hitlerite chains for a democratic government as a euphemism for a Moscow-controlled dictatorship. Durbrow thought this avatar from the Soviet revolutionary past "another indication of the new tactics of the Soviet Government since the 'dissolution' of the Comintern; in other words, appealing to nationalist groups to have them adopt a friendly attitude towards the Soviet Union against the Western powers." Moreover, the manifesto's appeal, which conflicted with the unconditional surrender principle enunciated by Roosevelt at Casablanca in 1942, portended a possible Russian compromise peace with Germany. Certainly Henderson found it curious that the American communist press employed rhetoric similar to that of the manifesto in its report of an alleged clandestine Soviet-Nazi meeting in the Rhineland. However, the sovietologists also considered that Moscow's ultimate objective may have been either to prod the Anglo-American allies to embark on the long-awaited second front or to intimate Soviet policy vis-à-vis Germany. In any event, along with Dunn and other careerists in the department, Bohlen advised against taking any position on the German committee until Soviet intentions crystallized. Meanwhile, Henderson wired the embassy in Moscow to be attentive to the formation of other national groups in the USSR. This may not be merely a gambit in psychological warfare, he pointed out, but part of "a concerted plan" tied to the Polish Patriots, the dissolution of the Comintern, "and other moves made or contemplated with regard to various European countries."[35]

The effect of these unsettling developments on Foreign Service thinking gave momentum to the prewar rumblings of uncertainty and apprehension. Nevertheless, diplomats were loath to dismiss the likelihood that

Moscow's military collaboration with the allied powers, its toleration of certain "democratizing" features within the USSR, and its ostensible abandonment of revolutionary objectives adumbrated the emergence of a more benign regime seemingly inclined toward harmonious relations with the Western world. Withal, having participated in the State Department's postwar planning sessions during the previous two years, they became increasingly wedded to the universalist ideal of a peaceful international order based on common acceptance of the principles of free trade, self-determination, and the rule of law. Faced with the alternatives of adjusting their developing image of ideological cooperation in conformity with the reality of Soviet intentions and behavior or transforming Kremlin leaders into proponents of the Atlantic Charter principles, Foreign Service officers—admittedly more reservedly than the administration, the State Department, and the American public—chose the latter, compartmentalizing as they did so the more intractable and divisive characteristics of Soviet foreign policy.

"Maybe I couldn't see the woods for the trees," Durbrow would recall, "but I was influenced by the Atlantic Charter—and the Boss [Roosevelt] was for it. So I figured give them another chance." Charles W. Yost, another careerist assigned to the department, said that diplomats were "neither less hopeful nor more determined to make [U.S.-Soviet postwar cooperation] work than Roosevelt." Robert H. McBride described the attitude of professional diplomats as "neither hopeless nor antagonistic." Basically, "they were for the United Nations approach." Henderson, Kennan, Matthews, Dunn—they were all willing to give the Soviets the benefit of the doubt. Following the Moscow conference of foreign ministers in October, Foreign Service officers began to conclude that their hopes had not been in vain. Delighted that the Soviets had announced their commitment to the idea of a postwar international organization, Bohlen remarked to Hull that the talks had engendered a "mood of trust." By the end of 1943, the skepticism and anxiety that remained were all but washed away by the flow of good feelings produced by the Big Three parleys at Teheran.[36]

No sooner had the American delegation arrived in Moscow for the conference of foreign ministers than they were welcomed with a reassuring note from Assistant Commissar of Foreign Affairs Andrei Vishinsky. During intermission of a ballet on the evening of October 18, Vishinsky informed Bohlen and General John R. Deane that Moscow had no territorial interests beyond Soviet frontiers, and that it believed the future of the world rested on continued Big Three collaboration. He further intimated that the Soviet Union would join the Pacific war after the defeat of Germany. This agreeable attitude carried over to the formal talks begun the next day. When they ended on the 30th, each party could take satisfaction in the results. The Soviets had received Anglo-American assurances of a cross-channel attack on France the following spring and Washington's agreement to initiate discussions relating to postwar credits; the British had obtained approval to establish a European Advisory Commission to formulate surrender terms and occupation machinery and to consider political issues in the liberated countries; the United States had succeeded in securing Stalin's promise to join the struggle against Japan and, as enunciated in the Four Nation Declaration signed by the Big Three and China, Soviet consent to enter a postwar international security organization.[37]

The conference broke up in a froth of brotherhood and good cheer. Even Molotov, "old stone-ass" himself, could not hold back the words of warmth, which danced from his lips with an unexpected ease and grace that belied their infrequency of utterance. Harriman called the conference an "historic" affair. The idea of mutual understanding had been implanted, he told Hamilton; now it had to be capitalized. General John Deane was impressed by "the kindly expression" on Stalin's "deeply wrinkled, sallow face." No less captivated by the Soviet chief, Hull remarked "that any American having Stalin's personality and approach might well reach high public office in my own country." Hamilton felt that the "praise and exultation" was "warranted." Although "much hard and tireless effort, patience, and wisdom" lay ahead, he scribbled to his wife, "there has been established a solid framework for collaboration." He was especially gratified by the Four Nation Declaration, "the first document I have yet seen which I believe will really command the support of the American people, not just spasmodically but as a continuing policy."[38]

What made the achievements of the Moscow Conference so significant was Stalin's personal imprimatur, which he applied verbally following the conference and symbolically at a banquet he hosted on the evening of the 31st. Like everything else Russian, this was done on a grand scale and with the spirit of incontinent good cheer the Soviets had shown on past celebratory occasions. After consuming an endless variety of hors d'oeuvres, Stalin and his guests gorged themselves alternately on morsels of caviar, fish of assorted kinds and preparations, and cold suckling pig, washing them down one by one or as part of a gustatorial medley with liberal quantities of vodka. This Russian antipasto was followed by the main course of soup, chicken, and a game bird served with red and white wine. Mountains of ice cream, succulent cakes, and fruit also joined the parade of comestibles which disappeared in unhurried course from the gold and silver plates. Periodically through the feast, glasses of wine, brandy, champagne, pepper vodka—whatever struck one's fancy—were hoisted in respectful and fraternal salute to the scores of toasts which were proposed. No one enjoyed the evening more than Stalin, who, grinning his black, irregular teeth, joked, charmed, and intermittently needled the humorless Molotov, much to the amusement of his guests. At one point, obviously elated by Deane's toast to the future meeting of allied forces in the streets of Berlin, Stalin "walked clear around the table to the other side where General Deane's seat was to chink glasses with him."[39]

An even more lavish diplomatic reception was thrown on the evening of November 7 at the Spiridonovka Palace by the dour and heavily posteriored Molotov to commemorate the anniversary of the revolution and to send Marshall Stalin off for Teheran in proper style. Having brought no formal attire to wartime Moscow, the American contingent dressed in dark suits. This became less and less noticeable as the "exceedingly drunken affair"—the last Molotov was to give—wore on. The presence of bejewelled Soviet ladies, Russian celebrities from the world of art, literature, theater, and music—including the composer Dmitri Shostakovich—and the diplomatic corps in this palatial setting seemed strangely reminiscent of "that wild and irresponsible extravagance of pre-revolutionary Moscow."

Yet, in spite of the social and political transformation of Russian life, some things had not changed. This was evidenced as the evening proceeded by the popularity of the recumbent position—usually prostrate rather than supine—and by the periodic removal of the guests by Russian factotums, barely able to suppress their malicious glee. Ever the gracious host, Molotov circulated about the throng, toasting his guests along the way, under the motive power of two strong-armed aides pressed into temporary service as bookends. As it turned out, however, no one outdid British Ambassador Sir Archibald Clark-Kerr for histrionic effect. Draped in medals, a great red and blue sash and a stiff shirt borrowed from the neutral and obliging Swedes, he proceeded to fall in the middle of a toast—not gracelessly, all things considered—on a table littered with bottles and glasses, incurring only minor abrasions and, given the horizontal attitudes of many of his crapulous colleagues, no great loss of dignity.[40]

While Moscow diplomats recovered from their celebratory spree, preparations went ahead for the Teheran Conference, which began on November 28. For the most part, a genial and cooperative mood prevailed between the heads of state, continuing the tone set a month earlier at the Moscow meeting. This is not to say that there were no sharp exchanges. Indeed, on more than one occasion, Churchill and Stalin tangled verbally. However, military considerations, a sense of statesmanship, and the mediatory presence of FDR, even if he did bend over backwards—frequently at Churchill's expense—to try to win over Stalin, kept the ocasional provocative sallies from discharging into heated disputes. What was incapable of resolution was simply held in abeyance until such time as they might meet again.

As was the case at Moscow (and as it would be at Yalta), each came away from the talks pleased with the outcome. In the military area, strategic plans were laid for the cross-channel attack on northern France and for the tandem landing in the southern part of the country, and Stalin reaffirmed his promise to enter the Pacific war. (During separate talks at Cairo, which Stalin refused to attend, Roosevelt, Churchill, and Chiang Kai-shek agreed to strip Japan of all territories but her four small main islands.) As to political questions, the Big Three agreed to form a permanent international organization, to preserve the independence of Austria and Finland, and to remove military forces from Iran after the war. Although no decision was reached, they also leaned toward dismemberment of Germany. Progress was made as well on the Polish question. While the thought of possibly jeopardizing the votes of six to seven million Polish-Americans in the forthcoming elections caused Roosevelt to abstain from active participation in the discussions, Churchill and Stalin proceeded to define the Curzon Line in the east and the Oder River in the west as the new boundaries of the Polish state, an arrangement to which Roosevelt by no means disagreed and indirectly probably agreed.

Indicative of the spirit that had obtained throughout the conference, at its conclusion the leaders praised one another for their courage, dedication, and commitment to the common cause. Although different customs and philosophies set apart the three nations, Roosevelt intoned, "We have proved here at Teheran that the varying ideals of our nations can come together in a harmonious whole." Churchill was also "well content" with the results, even though his proposed military strike in the Balkans had failed of allied support.[41]

The rainbow of cooperation painted by the allied leaders was also visible, albeit in more muted hues, to Foreign Service officers. It was reasonably clear, Bohlen wrote on December 15, that Moscow would steadfastly oppose any federation scheme in Eastern Europe, demand the dismemberment of Germany, and insist that France be stripped of her colonies and strategic bases beyond her borders. Assuming this pattern were to take shape, "the Soviet Union would be the only important military and political force on the continent of Europe." Despite these disquieting premonitions, Bohlen, who had ably interpreted for the president at Teheran, was optimistic about the future. "A realist on Soviet policy always has his doubts," he said in his memoirs, "but there are times when he is hopeful." Similarly affected by the friendly atmosphere of Moscow and Teheran, Durbrow felt the timing propitious to negotiate a licensing agreement with the Soviets in anticipation of postwar trade. Hamilton

observed that the Soviets were entering into agreement for the first time
"as friends on a basis of individual and mutual self-interest. That is the
revolutionary thing that has occurred." Problems would doubtless remain,
particularly with respect to questions of individual rights and the future of
the small states of Europe, he allowed, but this was natural for such "a
politically young people" as the Russians.[42]

Meanwhile, as American diplomats contemplated the political future of
U.S.-Soviet relations with mounting optimism, the Red Army was relentlessly advancing westward along a front stretching from the Baltic Sea
to the Balkans. The paths of political ideals and military realities were
about to converge.

5. Distress Signals in Eastern Europe

The feelings of warmth and intimacy that animated the Moscow and Teheran Conferences had little diminished as the new year rolled around. Secretary of State Hull believed that U.S.-Soviet relations were better at the beginning of 1944 than at any time before. In his annual message to Congress on January 11, President Roosevelt reiterated to the nation his faith that the allied powers would unite in a "just and durable" system of peace, prosperity, and security after the war. Their sentiments, in turn, were symbolically reciprocated by the Soviets. The Anglo-American decision to embark on the long-awaited European offensive the following spring touched off a cavalcade of praise in *Pravda, Izvestia, War and the Working Class,* and other more or less official organs of the state. Equally, if not more, propitious was the growing coverage devoted to American culture and politics, even if Roosevelt's adversaries were stereotyped as reactionaries.

Lurking below Moscow's sea of cordiality, however, was a current of lingering suspicion. This suddenly emerged on January 17, when *Pravda* carried a Cairo report from TASS, the Soviet news agency, that British and German officials had met surreptitiously in the Pyrenees to discuss a separate peace. Two days later *Pravda* printed a denial by the British Foreign Office and, for all intents and purposes, retracted the charge. Although the "Cairo rumor" had no effect on U.S.-Soviet relations, it suggested to Bohlen, Kohler, and other diplomats that Stalin was reluctant to let the post-Teheran euphoria mesmerize the Russian public. Clearly, Foreign Service officers had not ceased to harbor similar undercurrents of mistrust toward the Soviets, which had surfaced earlier in the month after the first phalanx of Red Army divisions lumbered across the Russian frontier into Poland. On January 18 the Kremlin issued a statement unilaterally declaring the Curzon Line the eastern boundary of Poland. Averell Harriman, recently named ambassador to Moscow, conveyed the embassy's concern in a cable to Churchill. "The Russian bear is demanding much and yet biting the hands that are feeding him," he remarked. "I agree with your comment," answered the Prime Minister, "but he is biting others at the same time."[1]

Partly because the Red Army was biting the Nazis so fiercely, partly because of the Teheran afterglow, and partly because of the perceived "democratizing" trend within Russia, American diplomats, even as they suspected Moscow of sinister motives, remained hopeful of continued U.S.-Soviet cooperation. By the close of the year, they were predisposed to view Soviet behavior in the liberated countries of Eastern Europe as confirmatory evidence of the Kremlin's adherence to the envisioned liberal-democratic postwar order.

Throughout the spring and early summer of 1944, reports from the Moscow embassy reinforced the image of ideological cooperation. Because so many changes in Russian life had taken place, Hamilton had become convinced that there was a sound basis for postwar amity. "Then the Moscow and Teheran Conferences established that basis." Owing to the favorable treatment accorded the United States and Britain in the Soviet press, the continued emphasis on the Russian national past, the toleration of religious worship, and the "glorious" performance of the Red Army, Thompson and Stevens shared his optimism. It was significant "for the trend of Soviet thinking," Stevens stated on January 24, that socialist themes were subordinated to the need for industrial and agricultural development and the establishment of amicable relations with the various peoples of the USSR. In May Stevens wrote that Stalin's willingness to allow the Russian church to strengthen its organization, and his meeting with Fr. Stanislaus Orlemanski, an obscure Catholic priest from Massachusetts, indicated his "desire to remove an obstacle to closer cooperation with other countries, including the United States." Withal, Stalin had expressed interest in a strong and independent Poland; even Soviet criticism of the London Poles remained "unusually moderate," in the embassy's view, further indication of the "mature restraint Moscow had demonstrated in its foreign relations."[2]

Of course, the byzantine ways of Soviet officialdom had not relieved the customary headaches that went with diplomatic life in Moscow. It took several weeks and considerable persuasion on Harriman's part to get Stalin to approve American shuttle-bombing flights over Germany from Russian bases in the Ukraine. Furthermore, the Soviet leader still refused to establish air bases in the Maritime Provinces in preparation for the final assault on Japan and failed to justify requests for additional Lend-Lease aid in accordance with Washington's instructions. Irritating as these pinpricks were, they did not dispel the auspicious impression of continued allied collaboration. The Kremlin's announcement of the first shuttle-bombing raids on June 1 were eagerly welcomed by the embassy as "most helpful and constructive in laying solid bases of cooperation." "There will be difficulties, of course," Hamilton allowed to his wife, "but there is a solid core on which real friendship can build steadily."[3]

In the meantime, on the military front, the advancing Russian forces pushed farther into eastern Europe. Through February and March the relentless Soviet offensive buckled enemy defenses all along the Baltic and Ukrainian perimeters. On April 2 the Red Army crossed the Prut River, which Molotov immediately declared the new Soviet-Rumanian frontier. This meant that the Soviet Union had reannexed Bessarabia and acquired as well the former Austro-Hungarian province of Bukovina. At the same time, Molotov's press release stated that the Kremlin sought neither additional Rumanian territory nor alteration of the prevailing social system in the country. Both Washington and London publicly acknowledged the declaration and accepted Moscow's proposed armistice terms.

News of the Russian victories sent a chill of fright through the Balkan nationals with whom Berry and his staff in Istanbul came into contact. Upper-class Bulgarians and Rumanians voiced fears of pro-Soviet uprisings, radical changes in the social system, and the emergence of a "Soviet orbit." Editorials in the Rumanian paper *Curentul* exhorted Britain to defend against the slavification of the continent and "to stave off the Asiatic avalanche." Exiled Yugoslavs and Greeks—military personnel, businessmen, professionals, and other "progressive-minded" observers—repeated the same refrain: indigenous communist groups planned to take advantage of the Russian military push to seize control of their countries as soon as the Germans were defeated.[4]

Berry and Fraleigh did not dispute the view that local communists sought to increase their influence in southeastern Europe. They further recognized that Russia might well annex Bulgaria—especially if Britain and the United States attempted to gain favor in that area—and establish the Balkan hegemony she historically desired. For the time being, however, they were preoccupied with the spectacular Soviet military successes on the eastern front. Moreover, they perceived no deviation on Moscow's part from the political objectives enunciated in the United Nations Declaration. Notwithstanding the appeals of Rumanians to save them from communism, American diplomats had not detected a single instance of misbehavior in those parts of Rumania the Soviets occupied. "Of course the end of the war in Europe does not mean the end of difficulties, even in Europe," Berry explained to his mother in July. "In all the occupied countries the restoration of the freedom of speech and press will bring some violent conflicts of points of view and in many of these countries there may be many and bitter internal struggles. But these will work themselves out and none of them are [*sic*] likely to endanger peace in the larger sense."[5]

Curiously, career officers in the western European theater of military operations expressed more concern about Soviet intentions. Startled by Moscow's undisclosed recognition of the Badoglio government in March, Reber and others attached to allied military headquarters in Algiers were certain that the Soviets, uninvolved in the formulation of Italian armistice terms, sought to exploit the growing leftward trend in Italy. It was not that Reber suddenly despaired of U.S.-Soviet cooperation; yet the impropriety of Moscow's demarche, which gave rise to doubts as to whether Italians would be free to choose their own broadly based representative government, did merit the State Department's close attention. On March 31 Reber explained to Dunn that American "directives and aspirations must be clear so that we do not by accident rather than by design embark on a course" inconsistent with the Atlantic Charter. Washington's refusal to grant cobelligerency to Italy had permitted Russia to enter Italian affairs, which "cannot fail to diminish Anglo-American influence in the ultimate political solution. We were handed the ball nearly two months ago and through our apparent failure to adopt a constructive policy have let it drop. The Russians have now picked it up and are running down the field with it."[6]

Further monitory observations were made by Kennan, who was serving as political advisor to Ambassador John G. Winant, the American delegate to the European Advisory Commission. On February 7, as the Red Army neared the Bessarabian frontier, he suggested to Winant that the EAC invite the Russians to discuss surrender terms in Rumania. It would "constitute an important breakdown of tripartite collaboration in the termination of hostilities," he stated, "if they were to determine unilaterally peace terms." But Winant ignored his protestations. So early in March, disregarding his earlier instructions from Dunn to offer the department counsel only if it were requested, Kennan took his case to Hull. "I feel I should tell you that I have noted with considerable uneasiness" the inclination of "our authorities" to equate the surrender of Rumania, Hungary, and Bulgaria with that of Germany. Unlike Germany, he wrote, there were strong democratic opposition movements in these countries that could succeed to power, and considerable popular sentiment favoring the allies. Yet, no provision existed to relieve allied and Soviet high commands of posthostilities responsibilities. Since the policy of unconditional surrender would have lasting political effects, "any lack of flexibility and realism in our approach may later become a serious cause of criticism of our handling of these questions." Moreover, Kennan disputed the practicability of unconditional surrender for Germany. This, he told Winant, would create a thirst for revenge among the German people, entail indefinite American military obligations, impede the reconstruction of a united, prosperous Western Europe crucial to the survival of the Anglo-Saxon world, and disproportionately benefit Russia, whose only interest in Western Europe was to keep it weak.[7]

As Kennan eventually learned, however, the American delegation had neither the latitude nor the guidance from Washington to consider the kinds of measures he proposed. To make matters worse, Winant, a rather disorderly man anyway, was incapable of giving full attention to his new duties, inasmuch as he was serving simultaneously as ambassador to Great Britain. Several weeks passed without a response from the department to a British proposal on occupation zones in Germany. Given his need to be heard and recognized, Kennan agonized over the delay. To accept passively the vagaries of wartime bureaucratic government was to deny his own existence. But he realized at the same time that to exceed the accepted norms of organizational behavior might result in further alienation and possibly exclusion from the Foreign Service group from which he derived his social identity. Angered by Washington's cavalier attitude toward his and the commission's efforts, he considered resigning from the service. On March 8 the department finally responded with a one-sentence directive, which, had it been implemented, would have considerably reduced the Russian zone to which the British had already assented. Once again Kennan balked at the order; once again he nervously journeyed across the Atlantic to see the president. Kennan's anxiety was understandable, for the president, the ultimate symbol of authority, was in a position to dispense or to deny the approbation Kennan desired. But upon hearing the nature of the confusion, Roosevelt merely broke into laughter. "Why, that's just something I once drew on the back of an envelope," he roared. And with that this seeming *peu de chose* was quickly rectified. By now the pertinacious Kennan had worn thin the patience of department officials. Sensing his physical and emotional exhaustion, they were only too happy to recommend that he take a vacation, which he did.[8]

Diplomats in the State Department embraced both the optimism and intermittent suspicion of their colleagues in the field. Flush with the success of Teheran, they too operated on the overriding assumption that U.S.-Soviet military collaboration would spill over into the political sphere as the European war entered its final stages. At the same time, old doubts, fears, and obsessions remained tucked away in the recesses of their minds. That they were closer to the surface than the diplomats may have realized was made perfectly clear once the Red Army invaded Poland and Stalin decided to take political advantage of the changing military realities.

Bohlen and Durbrow averred that Moscow's unilateral determination of the Soviet-Polish frontier contradicted America's policy of deferring territorial settlements until the end of hostilities and "[imperilled] the newly formed association" between the allied powers. "Long-standing differences in points of view and particularly in methods," noted Durbrow, presented obvious difficulties for the Soviet Union "to guide its policy into new channels which will bring it into harmony with the democracies." Realizing "the brilliant action of the Red Army, which has rightly increased Soviet prestige abroad," Moscow was in "a most favorable position to seize the popular imagination" in the Balkans, Scandinavia, France, and Italy as well. Lest the United States forget, he admonished, "a basic revolution has been and is still going on in Europe." While the commitments undertaken at Moscow and Teheran "have undoubtedly tended to modify [the] concept of irreconcilability between the two worlds," added Bohlen, now chief of the Eastern Europe division, it still existed to a large degree in the Kremlin's thinking on international affairs. If the "two worlds doctrine" were to survive, as Reber's reports from Algiers suggested, Soviet relations with the Western world would "continue to be based exclusively on the self-interest of the Soviet state untrammeled by any basic feeling of community with or obligations towards the powers with which it is temporarily associated." Thus, along with Durbrow, he urged the department to stress its interest in social and economic progress and to assist the liberal and left-democratic governments in Europe as a counterweight to communism.[9]

Diplomats in the department expressed further concern that Soviet behavior in Poland would suggest to an American public only recently freed from the shackles of isolationism that the proposed postwar security organization was a facade for power politics rather than a forum for the peaceful settlement of international disputes based on the principles of the Atlantic Charter. On February 9 Bohlen stated in a secret cable for transmission to Harriman that the combination of the Kremlin's Curzon Line dictum, the Cairo dispatch, and signs of renewed truculence in the Soviet press had "mystified and alarmed the American public" as to "the real motives" of the Soviet government. If Moscow continued "to deal unilaterally" with Eastern Europe, the American public might conclude "that despite Teheran and Moscow the Soviet Government is not disposed to play a constructive part as a full and equal member of the family of nations in the movement of international cooperation," and that the world organization was simply a cover for force majeure. "We share your view that it is of the utmost importance that the principle of consultation and cooperation with the Soviet Union be kept alive at all costs," but Moscow would have to demonstrate some regard for world opinion.[10]

Judging from public opinion surveys taken at the time, however, the diplomats' worries appear to have been exaggerated. Prescinding the views of former isolationist senators and Polish-Americans, whose fears for the fate of Poland intensified after 1944, there was as yet no hue and cry from the American public concerning Russia's behavior in Eastern Europe or the future of the postwar international organization. At best there were indications of a possible change of public attitude on both counts; but the evidence was hardly conclusive. Yet, for several reasons, diplomats in the department chose to ignore the vague and even contradictory soundings of popular opinion. In part, they resonated in a generalized way at lower levels of the department bureaucracy the president's personal uneasiness about Polish-American attitudes. Furthermore, mindful of public sentiment during the interwar years, they were obsessed with the possibility of a neoisolationist impulse. But, even more importantly, they tended to concentrate on those public views which reflected their own anxieties. As Matthews and Barbour were later to state, public opinion did not have a major influence on Foreign Service thinking at this time. The real influence came from within the government, from the State Department, and more precisely, from the personal and bureaucratic relationships formed with respected colleagues. Committed to the policy of postwar cooperation, diplomats tended to overreact to external developments as indications of potential obstacles to the achievement of the government's objectives. Consequently, they selected out of the amorphous public reaction to U.S.-Soviet relations those attitudes which accorded with—indeed reinforced—their own anxieties about Soviet intentions and the implications that lay therein for postwar collaboration, screening out in the process those views which deviated from their own.[11]

Throughout the spring of 1944, Foreign Service officers remained acutely sensitive to Soviet war aims. It was clear that Stalin, motivated by security considerations, wanted to retain the Baltic States as constituent republics of the USSR, render Germany powerless, if not politically dismembered, and establish Russia's predominant interest in the "middle zone" from Poland to Albania. As the easternmost parts of Poland fell to the invading Soviet armies, Stalin pressed his territorial and political demands on the exiled London government with greater obduracy. Much to the dismay of the London Poles, Dunn, Durbrow, and Bohlen continued to spew a steady stream of official solicitude for an "equitable and just solution" of Russo-Polish differences. The personal forebodings of the three diplomats, however, continued unabated.[12]

The Russian military advance toward the Bessarabian frontier produced similar anxieties about Soviet objectives in Rumania. "While we recognize the Soviet Union's preeminent military and political interest in Rumania, both as regards the immediate military phase and long-range political aspect," stated a memorandum from the division of Southern European affairs, "we think that both the United States and Great Britain should maintain their interest in that country and should apply to Rumania the general principles underlying our conduct of the war." Huston and division chief Cannon argued that the United States should maintain Rumania's independence and territorial rights by proposing plebiscites in Bessarabia and northern Bukovina. Although the department, they pointed out, had assumed that surrender terms were to be determined jointly in the EAC, the Soviet armistice, accepted by Churchill and Roosevelt, left "the matter of the Rumanian surrender exclusively in Russian hands." They also maintained that the Kremlin's proposal to have the Rumanian army change fronts and join forces with the Russians against Germany, which Marshal Antonescu rejected, departed from the unconditional surrender principle. Similarly troubled, Matthews, deputy director of the newly formed office of European affairs, suspected that the Kremlin's plan to obtain Rumania's surrender through King Carol masked Stalin's real aim to create a new Rumanian regime. After all, Carol was no "friend of Democracy," and he did not appear to have popular support.[13]

Bohlen thought it significant that the incorporation of Bessarabia and Bukovina gave Russia a common frontier with Czechoslovakia. While Stalin made plain from the war's inception his intention to regain Polish territory once part of the Romanov empire, no similar historical claims could be made of Czechoslovakia. In Bohlen's judgment the future of Czechoslovakia symbolized "the acid test" of Moscow's willingness to coexist with the non-Soviet world. Weeks before the Russian sweep into the Balkans, he had articulated his views on this subject in meetings of the special subcommittee on problems of European organization. If the Kremlin proved incapable of amicable relations with Czechoslovakia, he pointed out, "it would be reasonable to conclude that the [Soviet and non-Soviet] systems were incompatible in the long run." Subcommittee members Leo Pasvolsky and University of Chicago economist Jacob Viner pressed for a more precise estimate of how much "control" Russia would likely exercise in Eastern Europe.

"Inasmuch as Czechoslovakia was a small country," Viner stated, "the test you propose might not indicate much as to the compatibility or incompatibility of the two systems but merely that large and powerful countries tended to dominate their smaller and weaker neighbors."

"The central point," Bohlen responded, "was really whether or not the Soviet Union intended permanently to abandon its missionary attitude so far as its relations with neighboring countries were concerned."

"My reading of history has not convinced me that harmony was any more likely to prevail between similar social systems," Viner shot back, "than between dissimilar systems."

"The Russian attitude was that the small border states must never be allowed to become bases for aggression by a great power hostile to Russia," Pasvolsky joined in.

"The question was whether other states were to share the fate of the Baltic States," Bohlen asserted. Assuming a maximum Soviet program, he explained, Europe would be dominated by a one-power aggregation after the war. But since this would antagonize the world and possibly lead to international complications, he believed that Stalin was more likely to pursue a minimum program, at least for the immediate postwar period, and permit foreign governments to operate freely provided they posed no threat to Russian security.[14]

Yet, even as Foreign Service officers contemplated the politically insalubrious influence of Russia in Eastern Europe, they did not begin to disparage U.S.-Soviet cooperation. Reinforced by Russian military accomplishments and the Kremlin's cordial reaction to American postwar plans at the Moscow and Teheran discussions, the image of ideological cooperation they had gradually formed over the past two years had superseded in importance the image of confrontation built up during the interwar years. As this newer image gained strength, it tended to resist the dissonant impressions produced by Soviet behavior during the first part of 1944. This was precisely the opposite of the diplomats' reaction to the Soviet Union before 1943, when the combination of Moscow's prewar ideological rhetoric, the purge trials, and the Ribbentrop-Molotov pact obstructed the formation of a more positive mental picture.

Thus it was that Durbrow could express hope that the common interests and aspirations of the United States and her allies would lead to the postwar world of peace, freedom, and international cooperation. Or that Bohlen could portray the United States, Britain, and the USSR "as one" in their "fidelity to the principle of international cooperation." Or that Matthews could dismiss rumors that the Soviets, in spite of their agreement with the Italian government, appeared ready to dissociate themselves from the common cause of the United Nations. Or that Dunn, tactical considerations aside, could caution against giving Russia the impression that Washington opposed severe surrender terms for Germany, lest postwar cooperation might be impaired. As Bohlen put it, the United States should "endeavor to bring the Soviet Government to the realization in its own interests and for the peace and stability of the world of the advantages of cooperative rather than unilateral action." To avoid giving Moscow the impression that "we wish to have their armies encounter maximum resistance from the satellite countries," he recommended modification of the unconditional surrender principle, which Roosevelt subsequently agreed to alter in specific cases. As did Kennan, Bohlen also advised against unconditional surrender. The reason in Bohlen's case, however, was to avoid friction that would impair postwar ideological cooperation; in Kennan's it was to restrict Soviet prerogatives to set peace terms in Eastern Europe, hence to minimize Russian postwar political control of that region.[15]

The image of U.S.-Soviet cooperation was further bolstered by the optimism that permeated the Washington bureaucracy. At a time when

Roosevelt, Hull, and other high officials in the government were preaching the gospel of the Atlantic Charter and successfully proselytizing the American public to the postwar millennium of peace and good will that awaited them, diplomats in the department could not avoid being affected by the administration's hopes for the future. More significantly, they were actively helping to plan that future world, a far cry from their interwar years of passive observation. Acolytes at the altar of the administration's *novus ordo saecolorum*, they were personally and bureaucratically committed to continued U.S.-Soviet collaboration.[16]

As Russian troops relentlessly marched westward and D-Day approached for the Anglo-American invasion of Normandy, career diplomats worked closely with other State Department officials in the interdivisional and interdepartmental country and area committees to formulate United States policy vis-à-vis the occupied and axis satellite states of Eastern Europe. Cannon, Huston, and Theodore Hohenthal, a post–Rogers Act officer with previous service in Yugoslavia, joined Bohlen, Durbrow, James Riddleberger from the division of Central European affairs, Near Eastern division chief Kohler, and others to study, draft, and review the policy statements. Each of the position papers—starting with Rumania on April 15 and ending with Poland on June 20—contained the precepts of self-determination, deferral of territorial changes until peacetime, and support for some form of regional grouping. Additionally, to accelerate economic progress and minimize political conflicts in Europe, the statements stressed the importance of multilateral trade and equality of commercial opportunity.

Professional diplomats believed that the American government, without interfering in the domestic affairs of the Eastern European states, should encourage political and economic decentralization, the creation of representative national assemblies, and the development of non-discriminatory trade within the region and with Western Europe. Of course, they had no illusions that their policy preferences would be readily realized. In some cases, they were willing to tolerate the continued existence of authoritarian systems until such time as democratic forms of government could be developed. Cannon, Huston, Hohenthal, and Bohlen acknowledged that postwar governments in Bulgaria, Hungary, or Albania "will be primarily authoritarian in character." "The United States should have no fundamental objection to the existence of an authoritarian regime" in Albania, Cannon and Kohler noted, "provided it had the assent of the Albanian people and was not imposed from the outside, and provided it respected international obligations and did not menace the security of other states." Furthermore, while diplomats continued to endorse some form of regional structure to remove political instability, reduce trade barriers, and obviate "special alliances," as Bohlen and Durbrow pointed out, they were cognizant of Soviet opposition to a large confederation and of the long-standing boundary disputes in the region. Nevertheless, despite Moscow's desire for "friendly governments" on its western borders, Cannon, Huston, Bohlen, and Durbrow remained optimistic that Rumania, Poland, and their neighbors would establish postwar governments favorably disposed toward the Soviets and, "in harmony with the spirit of the Moscow Agreements" of 1943, simultaneously representative of the popular will.[17]

Meanwhile, on the other side of the Atlantic, the British found it difficult to conceive how the rule of allied consent could be effectively applied in the rapidly changing European military situation. On account of their historical rivalry with Russia, they had tended all along to be more circumspect than the Americans in their approach to Moscow. Now, his mind burdened with the thought of a communized Europe on one hand and Roosevelt's categorical refusal "to police France and possibly Italy and the Balkans as well" on the other, Churchill decided to take to heart the president's affectionate reproach "to bring up and discipline your own children." Early in May he disclosed to Foreign Minister Anthony Eden what he had in mind: concede to the Soviets primary military and, implicitly, political responsibility in Rumania in exchange for British control in Greece.[18]

Several days later, Churchill gingerly requested Roosevelt's approval of overtures to Russia. He assured the president that his proposal applied only to wartime responsibilities in the Balkans, and that it was not intended to carve the region into spheres of influence. Roosevelt asked the State Department to prepare a reply. Opinion was divided. Matthews considered the British proposal "the equivalent of telling the Russians that they may have Rumania as their sphere of influence if they will give Greece to the British," an arrangement which would "[depart] from the principle adopted by the three Governments at Moscow, in definite rejection of the spheres of influence idea," and "prejudice the efforts toward directing the policies of the Allied Governments along lines of collaboration rather than independent action." Still, recognizing the greater military contribution of Anglo-Soviet forces in the Balkans, he advised against an adverse reply. Kohler and Cannon, conversely, fearing that the political division of Europe would abort American plans for a broad general security system "in which all countries big and small will have their part," vigorously urged a negative response.[19]

In the meantime, Churchill cabled the president again on June 8. While this transmission repeated his earlier repudiation of postwar spheres of influence, it added Bulgaria to the Russian military zone and Yugoslavia to the British. Now more adamantly opposed to the British proposal, Cannon argued that allied interference in the Tito-Mihailović dispute threatened to disrupt the war effort and implicate the American government in Yugoslav problems. Were it not for his concern about giving the enemy the impression of allied disunity, Dunn would have preferred despatching a strongly worded message to the Yugoslav government-in-exile dissociating the United States from British involvement in Yugoslavia. In any event, on June 12, while Hull was away from Washington, Roosevelt secretly agreed to Churchill's request for a three-month trial period, carefully adding, to avoid alienating the American public and the State Department, that this did not imply United States support for postwar spheres of influence. The president never notified Hull, who, given the abysmal communications channels between Roosevelt and the State Department, learned of the decision from Lincoln MacVeagh, the American ambassador in Greece, who was, in turn, informed by his British counterpart in Athens. World finally filtered down to Cannon by the end of June, and on July 15 the State Department repeated Roosevelt's "official" injunction against postwar spheres to the Soviet government. For the time being, however, preoccupied with the fast-changing military developments on the continent, Churchill and Stalin deferred action on the proposal.[20]

Coincident with the department's advanced preparation for the postwar world, allied military successes during the early weeks of the summer signalled the final stages of hostilities in Europe. On June 4, after months of bloody combat, Rome fell. Two days later, Canadian, British, and American forces stormed the beaches at Normandy. Finally the second front was underway. Stalin bubbled with childlike excitement. Considering "its vast scale, its vast conception, and its masterly execution," the annals of warfare knew no undertaking like it, he rejoiced to Churchill.[21]

At the other end of the continent, the prodigious Russian summer offensive hammered at the Germans from Finland to the Balkans. By the end of June all the railways from Leningrad to Murmansk had been recovered. Like a raging sea, Russian armies farther south swept the enemy's flank, engulfing German placements from Vilna to the Pripet Marshes. On July 7 General Dwight D. Eisenhower repaid Stalin's compliment of the previous month. "I have been tracing Red Army progress on my map," he noted to Harriman. "Naturally I got a tremendous thrill out of the rate at which they are demolishing the enemy's fighting power. I wish I knew how to express properly to Marshal Stalin and his Commanders my deep admiration and respect."[22]

As the summer wore on, the Russian war machine won new plaudits every day. Notwithstanding Moscow's repeated refrain of "friendly governments" along its western flank, Foreign Service officers anticipated no major problems in allied political relations. As Harold Shantz observed from Cairo, where the exiled governments of Yugoslavia and Greece prepared to return to their homelands, "it should be within the realm of possibility to have Balkan governments friendly to all powers." Thus far, he saw no faults in the "solid framework" of cooperation forged by the allies; those fissures that might later appear, he felt confident, would be compromised in the international security organization. At the same time, welcome changes were taking place within the Soviet Union. Moscow's recognition of the family as the foundation of Soviet society, a move intended to encourage wartime national unity and the replenishment of the male population, signified to Stevens "another step in the long chain of developments indicating the increasing conservatism of the present regime and its tendency to restore many of the traditional pre-revolutionary aspects of Russian life." Even Kennan, struck by this apparent social transformation in the Soviet Union, began to reassess his pessimistic views of Moscow's intentions.[23]

Kennan's return to Moscow on July 1 was occasioned by a number of factors. In the first place, Harriman wanted a Soviet-language expert, which Hamilton was not, to administer the embassy during the final stages of the war. There were also bureaucratic considerations. Bohlen, Harriman's first choice, was badly needed in Washington to complete work on postwar planning. More importantly, whereas Dunn "absolutely refused" to part with Bohlen, he was just as insistent on transferring the recalcitrant and outspoken Kennan from Washington, especially now that the administration sought to win Moscow's consent to the new United Nations Organization. From Dunn's perspective, the decision was a judicious one; for no sooner had Kennan left than he resumed his criticism of the government's postwar policies.[24] News of his assignment as chief administrative officer did not sit well with Kennan. He understood, of course, that the Roosevelt administration preferred to consult with the military establishment in wartime on policy matters, and that General Deane was serving Harriman in this capacity in Moscow. Even so, Kennan was annoyed by the department's decision, and he departed for his professional—and personal—"exile" in a rebellious mood. In June, during a stopover in Lisbon en route to Moscow, he told the legation officer staff that American postwar planning, as evidenced by his experiences with the EAC, was "shallow and often unrealistic." Rather than "impose" an unnatural order on Europe based on the United Nations, he hoped that the United States would opt instead for some kind of European federation that would more accurately reflect the continent as it was rather than as the United States wished it to be.[25]

These views hardly diminished Kennan's attachment to the same idealistic spirit of harmony and brotherhood embraced by other Americans. Influenced by the tenor of feeling within the Foreign Service, he could not help but admire, if only from a distance, the castles of hope built by his associates from the rubble of a common war effort. Perhaps he had misunderstood Soviet intentions? After all, he had not been in Russia since 1937, and colleagues who had—Bohlen, Thompson, Henderson, Stevens—had reconsidered their earlier impressions. Unlike them, however, Kennan anticipated little change in Soviet internal affairs; and, as his ruminations at the time suggest, he never really wavered in defining U.S.-Soviet relations in the realpolitik terms of peaceful coexistence. "Perhaps the great traumatic experiences of Russia in the war—the intimacy between people and regime and the association with foreign allies in a common military undertaking—had brought to the Soviet leaders what no other experience had succeeded in bringing to them," he thought, an awareness of the unrealistic antagonism perpetrated by Marxism, a new-found sense of collaboration with noncommunist states, "a readiness to believe that differences in social systems might not, after all, be the final determinants of relations between sovereign states, that other more hopeful factors might also be involved."[26]

The suddenness of Soviet actions in Poland demonstrated all too plainly to Kennan the form that peaceful coexistence would take. By the latter part of July, the Russian army had crossed the Curzon Line into ethnic Poland and captured the city of Lublin. On the twenty-seventh the Polish Committee of National Liberation, formed behind Russian lines, declared Lublin the capital and signed an agreement with the Kremlin to undertake civil administration of the country. Two days later Prime Minister Mikolajczyk and his entourage reluctantly arrived in Moscow at the urgence of Churchill and Roosevelt to confer with Stalin. The Polish leader's discontented frame of mind was understandable. During his talks in June with Roosevelt, who was preoccupied at the time with the upcoming November elections, and who was hardly about to reveal to an anguished Mikolajczyk his receptivity to a Soviet sphere, he had received little more than unctuous assurances about America's unflagging interest in an independent Poland. Uncomfortably, Kennan went through the motions of offering official encouragement to Mikolajczyk, although he felt it would have been more dignified "to bow our heads in silence before the tragedy of a people who have been our allies, whom we have helped to save from our enemies, and whom we cannot save from our friends."[27]

It was clear as well to diplomats in the department that no hope remained for the London Poles. However, the diplomats were afraid they would bankrupt American ideals if they severed ties with them. As a prerequisite to recognition of the rival Lublin government, Dunn stated to Hull, the United States required "substantial proof," either by reports of observers or a general election, "that the new organization commands the support of the majority of the Polish people." In the meantime, he suggested that Washington watch events in Poland closely and "avoid any positive statement which would bind us irrevocably to the permanent support of the Polish Government-in-exile per se."[28]

The forebodings of American diplomats in Washington and Moscow intensified in the weeks ahead. On July 21 the Polish underground had seized upon the Russian advance across the Vistula River to rise against German forces in Warsaw. Despite repeated appeals by Britain and the United States for Soviet assistance to the Warsaw insurgents, Stalin refused to help, probably at first because Russian forces had overrun their supplies, but in the end to break the resistance of Polish forces loyal to the London government. Finally, on September 13 Soviet planes dropped some supplies to the insurgents. But it was much too little too late to do any good.

Incensed by Moscow's malevolent passivity, and so all the more impatient with Washington's insistence on keeping military and political issues separate, Kennan fumed to Harriman and General Deane that the administration should terminate further Lend-Lease aid to Moscow. As he had thought all along, the Kremlin would not be deterred from its goal of carving a sphere of influence in Eastern Europe. Consequently, postwar cooperation between the allies would only be possible if the United States and Britain established their own sphere from which the Russians would be excluded. No less appalled, Harriman fretfully complained to Hopkins that the Soviet Union would become a "world bully" unless Washington clarified to Moscow "the price of our goodwill." Yet, even though it seemed clear that the Soviets desired a "positive sphere of influence" in Eastern Europe, he paradoxically clung to the belief that Stalin and the principal Soviet leaders remained faithful to the spirit of cooperation established at Moscow and Teheran. Believing that British and American representations had ultimately forced the Kremlin to assist the beleaguered Poles, he recommended similar forceful measures in the future whenever Soviet behavior offended American standards.[29]

Harriman's ambivalence mirrored the attitude of diplomats in the department. As the Warsaw slaughter neared its tragic end, Bohlen stormed that the Kremlin had misinterpreted American friendliness for weakness. The time had come, he asserted, when the United States had to impress upon the Soviets, even at this risk of their displeasure, the importance of observing "the accepted principles of international conduct." Equally outraged, Dunn now envisaged the possibility of "a Russian-dominated Europe, [which] would threaten western civilization." Lane, in Washington at the time awaiting reassignment to the Polish government in London, urged Roosevelt to intercede militarily until the president suggested that this might lead to war with Russia. At the same time, diplomats in the department considered Kennan's proposal to terminate aid unrealistic. It would not alter the Kremlin's position, Bohlen reasoned; and it could adversely affect future Soviet-Polish negotiations and possibly entangle the United States in the dispute. Like Harriman, they too were reluctant to conclude that Moscow had retreated from its commitment at Teheran to help construct a new postwar order. Even as the Warsaw massacre was taking place, they took solace from the perceived success, however finely drawn in reality, of the Dumbarton Oaks Conference, which met from August 21 to September 28 to discuss plans for the United Nations Organization.[30]

State Department officials, from Hull on down to the cadre of professional diplomats who worked on provisional proposals for the international organization, eagerly awaited the discussions with the British and the Russians. Diplomats in the field, heartened by Teheran and the apparent moderating trend within the USSR, were also optimistic about the outcome of the talks. Of course, there were exceptions.

As far as Kennan was concerned, the concept of a rule of law which underlay the new international organization, as it had the Holy Alliance and the League of Nations, was incongruous with the realities of power that had historically defined the actions of nation-states and the organic and constantly changing nature of international relations. In his judgment, it was fanciful to think that Stalin would not lay claim to Eastern Europe as his sphere of influence—just as he would acknowledge Anglo-American hegemony in the western sectors—or that he would be restrained by the United Nations should he later decide to expand Soviet influence elsewhere. The fundamental objective of the Kremlin was no different from that of Czarist Russia: the establishment of a protective glacis against the West by a program of political and military expansion, including domination of Slavic Europe, Finland, and the Baltic States and control of the Dardanelles. Although Soviet leaders preferred to realize their goal by collaborating with the West, the course of military operations in Eastern Europe made it likely that they would achieve "most of these objectives whether the Western powers liked it or not." As to the communization of the region, this, Kennan noted, was only of secondary importance to the Russians.[31]

Kennan's skeptical views of the United Nations were shared by John Paton Davies, who had been influenced by Kennan during a visit to Moscow in the late thirties as to the role of power and ideology in the Soviet weltanschauung. Having served in China for the past decade, and since 1943 as political advisor to General Joseph H. Stilwell in the China-Burma-India theater, Davies had watched the ebb and flow of political and military conflict between rival warlords, between communists and Kuomintang, between China and Japan. Affected by the unremitting conflict in China, and convinced that Britain and Russia sought political control in their military spheres of influence, he reckoned that America's idealistic postwar goals were incompatible with the realities of war. "We are not heading for a brave new world. For the conduct of the war is shaping the conditions of the peace. Nowhere does Clausewitz's dictum that war is only the continuation of politics by other methods apply with more force than in the Asiatic theatre." However, less comfortable than Kennan with the values that underlay European power politics, he found it distressing that British and Soviet imperialism had attenuated the noble conceptions of the Atlantic Charter. Accepting that reality, nonetheless, he concluded that the "opportunity for a moderate, humane, and equitable transition to a better world has passed. The lines of future conflict are being formed by the course of the present one. We can now be assured of further war and revolution in our time. Like it or not, we are up to our necks in power politics." [32]

This image of realistic cooperation met with disfavor among careerists in the department, including Soviet experts such as Bohlen, who scorned cynical power politics. "Our overall objectives in our relations with the Soviet Union had undergone no change," Bohlen stated in September; they were still postulated "on the closest, most cooperative relations" based on "the mutual acceptance and observance of the essential principles of good international conduct." To be sure, he was not insensible to realpolitik; but having thrived personally and professionally in the Washington bureaucracy, owing largely to the patronage of Harriman and, particularly, Harry Hopkins, who had been impressed with him ever since the Teheran Conference, Bohlen, though still suspected of anti-Sovietism by Vice President Wallace and the liberal left within the bureaucracy, became a staunch advocate of the United Nations and the "grand design," as he understood it, for postwar peace and security. Through that "accident of my fate," he later wrote of his Teheran experience, "my career had been fundamentally altered." Thereafter "I had more or less what you might call an 'in' at the White House. No longer was I just a junior Foreign Service officer who happened to be able to speak Russian; [far more importantly,] I was asked for advice on Soviet affairs." While Bohlen shared Kennan's misgivings about Soviet intentions in Eastern Europe, he did not think Kennan "would be so pessimistic if he had a wider perspective on the whole war." [33]

As it turned out, the Dumbarton Oaks Conference did not establish the great power consensus Bohlen and the department had hoped for. While a number of lesser questions, such as the composition of the security council, were settled, the Russian delegation's request that all sixteen Soviet republics receive separate membership and its insistence on retaining veto power even in disputes in which the USSR was directly involved were left unresolved. For the first time since the Moscow Conference, Hull began to wonder whether Stalin had departed from the policy of cooperation. Yet it was difficult to conceive that Russia, having fought so gallantly on behalf of the common cause, would subvert the postwar peace and plunge the world anew into a struggle for power or ideological supremacy.

To avoid an unfortunate reaction from the American people and other nations, Dunn recommended that the three powers publicly announce only those issues on which they agreed. "We must not allow any disagreements to creep into our relations," or the world community would cease to believe in the future cooperation of the Big Three. While the Russians scoffed at the American delegation's concern with world opinion, they went along with the public statement, more perhaps because they appreciated the import of Dunn's exhortation "that we not consider that we have failed." Privately, however, Dunn was unhappy about the deadlock over the veto question. This would "vitiate the very spirit which we are all trying to set up in an International Organization." In the event the Russians remained intransigent to a compromise proposal, he proposed limiting the organization's aegis to social and economic cooperation or, deviating from his neo-Wilsonian worldview, entering "into some arrangement with the principal nations of the world to maintain peace and security." Although it was left unstated, the ultimate form the postwar organization would take appeared to rest with the Russians.[34]

Notwithstanding this impasse, Foreign Service officers tended to perceive Dumbarton Oaks as one more step toward their ultimate goal of postwar peace, security, and cooperation. The effect of this was to treat in vacuo the obvious incongruity of Soviet behavior in Poland with American principles. To challenge Stalin's position there or to accede to his demands for a revision of the Polish frontier and a reorganization of the London government, both of which offered realistic policy alternatives, and both of which were considered, would have attenuated U.S.-Soviet cooperation and the larger principles which had guided Washington's conduct of the war. So diplomats sustained the posture of recognizing the Mikolajczyk government while simultaneously extending good offices to help resolve the Polish-Soviet dispute.

While Washington policymakers struggled to reconcile allied interests and ideals, Soviet armies methodically hammered out a sphere of interest in Europe. Rumania surrendered in August. The following month Finland

signed an armistice agreement with Russia. Bulgaria, formally not at war
with the Soviet Union, attempted to negotiate a surrender with Britain
and the United States, but the Russians preempted this by declaring war
on September 5, which immediately produced a cease fire. Although half
the country was still occupied by Germany, Hungary, after a desperate
appeal to the Anglo-Americans for moderate terms, gave up the battle to
the Russians in October.

Churchill was deeply troubled by these events. As the Red Army prepared to invade Yugoslavia and, as far as he knew, Greece as well, he
anxiously visualized the possibility of postwar communist governments in
both countries. Talks with Roosevelt in Quebec proved of little avail;
Washington, motivated purely by military considerations, would not oppose the advance of Russian armies into central Europe and the Balkans.
Thus Churchill notified the president on September 29 of his intention to
confer with Stalin in Moscow, commenting vaguely on the nature of the
proposed meeting and suggesting that Harriman, Stettinius, or General
George Marshall, U.S. army chief of staff, attend on Roosevelt's behalf. The president wired a tepid reply, stating that he would direct
Harriman to provide assistance.[35]

Diplomats in the department were uneasy. Throughout the summer,
Kohler, Cannon, and others responsible for American policy in the Balkans had voiced disapproval of Britain's efforts "to back its favorite
horses" in Albania, Yugoslavia, and Greece in contradiction of the principle of self-determination. To avert the impression that Washington was
"tagging along in willing acquiescence," they recommended a more
forceful exposition of American views. Fearing the forthcoming talks
would result in a "first class British-Soviet row over European problems
or the division of Europe into spheres of influence on a power politic
basis," on October 3 Bohlen persuaded Hopkins to have an American
representative attend "to insure that this government is not, even by
inference, committed to policies or decisions not of its own making" and
to impress upon Stalin that the United States would not be bound by any
decisions without the president's approval. The next day Roosevelt
cabled Stalin to that effect.[36]

In Moscow, convinced that an immediate arrangement had to be
reached with Russia to deter future political unheaval in the Balkans and
possible allied conflict, Churchill seized upon Harriman's absence from
the first meeting with Stalin on the evening of October 9. On a half sheet of
paper, he scribbled a proposal which gave Russia predominance in Rumania and Bulgaria and Britain the same advantage in Greece. Political
influence was to be shared in Hungary and Yugoslavia. Stalin paused,
then took his blue pencil and ticked his concurrence. This minor Euro-

pean surgery, as Churchill stated, "was all settled in no more time than it takes to set down."[37]

Bothered by feelings of guilt, Churchill leaked the decision piecemeal to Harriman. Although no one in the State Department knew at this juncture precisely what had transpired, Matthews informed Hull that the talks appeared "to forecast a spheres-of-influence arrangement." In due course Roosevelt learned the full significance of the conference. Relieved that Churchill had not implicated him in any political discussions, particularly in regard to Poland, and pleased to hear that Stalin had promised to join the fight against Japan within three months after Germany's defeat, he reacted impassively to the spheres agreement. Not surprisingly, he did not communicate the Anglo-Soviet division of Europe to Hull. Even though career diplomats surmised what had occurred, they received no official confirmation of the "cynical and unrealistic" division of Europe, as Bohlen later termed it, until early 1945. Consequently, they continued to operate on the assumption that the Atlantic Charter remained inviolate. Nevertheless, the Churchill-Stalin meetings magnified in their minds the potential for Anglo-Soviet collusion in Europe and the subversion of American postwar objectives.[38]

While the Soviet Union, both ideologically and militarily, represented the greater potential obstacle to the achievement of the State Department's aims in Europe, Foreign Service officers, particularly those in the Southern European division, were more concerned with British behavior during the waning months of 1944. They contended that Britain's schemes to revive her sagging empire bade fair to incite old Anglo-Soviet feuds in the Balkans, particularly in Yugoslavia, where both Stalin and Churchill appeared to be courting the partisans. Worse yet, they might convey the erroneous impression to Moscow that Washington was using Britain as a cat's paw to establish an American zone of influence in the region. Partly to stifle possible Soviet suspicions, partly to avoid "risking an impairment of our national prestige," Cannon and Hohenthal urged a scaling down of Lend-Lease and relief aid to Yugoslavia. Likewise, Kohler recommended that the United States steer clear of the political shoals of Greek internal affairs.[39]

Significantly, despite Soviet arbitrariness in Poland, the impasse at Dumbarton Oaks, and intermittent vituperations in the Soviet press, careerists, notwithstanding periodic skepticism, remained hopeful that Stalin would ultimately endorse Washington's liberal-internationalist blueprint for postwar peace. Indeed, Matthews commented how Stalin "had gone out of his way to be friendly and conciliatory" toward the allies during his meeting with Churchill, how he had toasted America's vital role in the war. It was as though the British, experienced in world affairs and culturally sophisticated, should have known better, while the Soviets, xenophobic and culturally retarded, were delinquent and potentially destructive children who needed to be educated. The essential problem with the Russians, Harriman contended, was that they were backward, insecure, and ignorant of the Western world. One had to remember, Cordell Hull stated, that Soviet Russia had been isolated from the world for a quarter of a century. Even so, he felt sure that the two nations would eventually combine their efforts on behalf of the international organization.[40]

After October, however, as Russian armies began to implant themselves in Eastern Europe, Soviet educability seemed increasingly more dubious to diplomats in the field. It was clear to Kennan that Moscow intended to make Rumania "pay through the nose." Red Army expropriations of petroleum refinery equipment, some of which was American-owned, and the inability of allied representatives on the Soviet-dictated control commission to do much about it, hardly presaged the spirit of allied collaboration Washington anticipated. Since Stalin was likely to take similar advantages by right of conquest in Bulgaria and Hungary, Kennan advised the department to remove its representatives from the armistice commissions in Eastern Europe, which they were embarrassingly powerless to influence, and to direct future communications regarding civil and military affairs to Moscow. Not only would this conform to the reality of allied relations in those countries, he reckoned, but it would dissociate the United States from moral responsibility for Soviet actions. Cooperation with the Russians was still viable, in his judgment, provided the United States recognized the inevitable military, hence political, division of Europe into Anglo-American and Soviet spheres.[41]

Although the department planned to question Soviet leaders concerning difficulties on the control commissions, Thompson, Matthews, and Dunn were prepared neither to withdraw American participation if they received unsatisfactory answers nor to acquiesce in a political division of Europe. The department's attitude was supported by reports from the recently formed American diplomatic missions in Bulgaria and Rumania. To be sure, Burton Berry, head of the mission in Bucharest, was as provoked as Kennan by the arbitrary removal of American property and by the highhanded Soviet behavior on the allied control commission. However, he and Roy Melbourne were not persuaded that Moscow wished to sacrifice Anglo-American cooperation in the long run for short-term political spoils of war. Thus far, there were still "frequent good personal contacts between Soviet, British, and American officials based on respect for our common effort," Melbourne noted. And though Maynard Barnes found conditions in Bulgaria, where the communist-led

Fatherland Front had overthrown the regency installed by the short-lived Muraviev government, "in a hell of a state," a "natural doubt" existed in his mind as to Moscow's ultimate aims.[42]

Influenced by local pressures with which the Moscow embassy did not have to contend, Berry, Melbourne, and Barnes also differed with Kennan over America's role in the Rumanian armistice. Almost from the start the American mission in Bucharest received indications from "trustworthy sources"—John H. Lerougetel and Donald F. Stevenson (respective heads of the British political and military missions), King Carol, and Iuliu Maniu (leader of the National Peasant party)—that the Soviets intended "to bring about a dissolution of the Rumanian state." This view was most forcefully presented by Maniu, who explained that he would not have advised Carol to sign the armistice if he had known that Russia "was deliberately planning to communize Rumania while the democratic powers silently watched." While it appeared to Berry that "the three principal Allies [still] expected Rumania to be an independent and sovereign state," Maniu's emotional intimations of abandonment gave all the more reason not to quit the country, as this would have "cast doubt upon our sincerity" in signing the armistice, nullified Roosevelt's expressed objective of fostering the American way of life, and forsaken Maniu, that "champion of pre-Allied action and sentiment" during the Antonescu dictatorship (which, of course, Maniu was, but only after Germany's demise became certain). "Because of what he has been and what he is," Berry said of the Peasant party leader, "it seems important that he be preserved from slipping into sharing the general conviction that the dissolution of the Rumanian state is now in progress." Thus, for Berry and Melbourne, American ideals—symbolized by the Atlantic Charter and personified by Iuliu Maniu—were American interests.[43]

Conversations with the minister for foreign affairs and "with numerous prominent Bulgarians" similarly affected Barnes, who notified Washington that the Communists "are on the make and have every intention of gaining full control of the country." Both the Agrarian party and the bourgeoisie bitterly censured not only the Communists, but the government as well, which, Barnes noted, had cravenly compromised the country's interests. Influenced by the noncommunist political elite, who detected covert Soviet support behind the purge of the Bulgarian army and the designation of "people's courts" to try fascist sympathizers, and unable to enlist the sympathies of General Sergey Semenovich Biryusov, Russian representative on the control commission, in the plight of the Bulgarian people, he and General John A. Crane, head of the American military mission, grew increasingly restive. "It is 'shameful' for the Anglo-Saxon powers to have signed an armistice and exercise no power in the execution of that armistice," he stated, especially since Bulgarians recognized that "America and Britain represent one set of political, economic and social ideas and Soviet Russia another set." By the turn of the year, he began to view Bulgaria as the touchstone of U.S.-Soviet postwar relations. While the Russians continued to "play their cards close to the chest," it was anyone's guess what the future would bring. "As matters go here," however, he wired the department, "certainly will they go in Yugoslavia and probably also in Hungary."[44]

The threat of Soviet political expansionism to which Barnes alluded emerged more prominently in the reports from Moscow and other diplomatic posts during the winter of 1944–45. As the Red Army thundered victoriously westward, Kennan and Stevens were at once impressed and disconcerted by Soviet military strength and by the proportionate increase in the Kremlin's sense of its own political prestige and influence in the world. Despite Moscow's unmistakeable interest in allied cooperation, they suspected that Soviet control in Bulgaria, Rumania, and Hungary would surely be followed by demands to revise the Straits regime, possibly interference in Greece, and conceivably influence-peddling in the Middle East. As a result of wartime arrangements between London and Moscow, the Red Army had already established control in northern Iran, and Loy Henderson reported signs from Iraq that Moscow aimed to exploit the highly charged question of a postwar Jewish home in Palestine to increase its influence in the Arab world. Davies's reports from China, where political power had shifted to the Communists, also conveyed a preoccupation with Soviet expansion. If the United States continued to underwrite the bankrupt regime of Chiang Kai-shek, he warned, the Communists would eventually turn to the Russians for assistance. Thus "the Soviet Union may stand to gain a satellite North China. The Kremlin is not likely to be unaware of what is at stake in this situation—the future balance of power in Asia and the Western Pacific."[45]

These distress signals caused the ripples of doubt produced by the Warsaw uprising and Dumbarton Oaks to heave with perceptibly greater force against the breakwater of optimism in the department. Matthews reacted impatiently to the Kremlin's decision to negotiate the Bulgarian armistice "in the interests of," rather than "on behalf of," the United Nations. American acquiescence in the matter, he pointed out, would amount to an admission that "we are unwilling to object to anything the Soviets may propose." Durbrow, Cannon, and Bohlen shared his irritation over Soviet reparations claims against the former German satellite states. Moscow's intransigence on the subject reified in Durbrow's mind its equally implacable attitude over the settlement of Lend-Lease accounts several weeks earlier at the Bretton Woods talks to reinstitute postwar international economic stability. But by now the months of assiduous preparation for the postwar peace had created a reservoir of hope to contain these undulations of apprehension. To protect the integrity of their expectations, and to preserve their influence within the department, which was directly tied to their support of the administration's policy of postwar collaboration, they abstracted their perceptions of Russia's intentions from the reality of her behavior. Despite Russia's unwavering commitment to reabsorb eastern Poland and the Baltic States, despite her apparently unilateral control of Bulgaria, Rumania, and Hungary, despite her indifference to the envisioned liberal world economy, diplomats in the department persisted in their expectations of postwar harmony between the two nations, ostensibly to demonstrate to a skeptical American public and world opinion—but really to assure themselves—that the principles enunciated in the Atlantic Charter and reaffirmed at Moscow and Teheran remained undiluted and viable.[46]

In a December 11 memorandum summarizing U.S.-Soviet relations since 1933, Bohlen pointed out that the difficulties of the past had resulted less from specific political or economic issues than from the ideological differences between a democracy and a dictatorship that pursued a dual program of national and revolutionary expansionism. After 1941, however, relations between the two powers had entered a new phase of military collaboration that had carried over to the political sphere, Bohlen went on, as attested by the Moscow and Teheran conferences and the meeting at Dumbarton Oaks. Real advances had been made to integrate the USSR into the family of nations; accordingly, American policy "remains unchanged in its objective of working out the fullest cooperation with the Soviet Union," both politically and militarily, "without making any concessions which would compromise our basic principles." The following January a top-secret memorandum approved by Matthews noted that Moscow's suspicions of the West and its preeminent quest for security suggested that it would seek to establish friendly governments on Russia's borders and to support communist parties and front organizations in other countries, especially in Eastern Europe, the Straits region, northern Iran, Mongolia, and Manchuria. However, if convinced that no threat to its security existed, the memorandum stated, "there is no reason to anticipate that the Soviet Government would be disposed to destroy this peace and stability by embarking on a calculated program of territorial expansion."[47]

As 1944 slowly expired, the tranquil world of peace and harmony in which Washington-based diplomats reposed their hopes for the future contrasted sharply with the emerging politics of war in Europe. In Bulgaria, Rumania, and Hungary the Russians took charge of the armistice controls with a triumphant arrogance that befitted the primordial struggle they had suffered and survived. Success was savored with equal relish in

Albania by the communist-led National Liberation Movement of Enver Hoxha, which seized the reins of government on November 28, and in Yugoslavia, where the British-instigated agreement between Tito and Ivan Šubašić, the new prime minister of the exiled government, masked the preponderant influence of the partisans. On December 3 a new round of fighting broke out in Greece between Communists and nationalists, dissolving the gossamer truce arranged by the British in May.

Diplomats in the department ascribed these repercussions less to the nascent political metamorphosis of the Balkan-Danubian region than to the confused and unstable conditions of war. With the fighting in Europe in its final stages, they believed that these aberrations of war would gradually be reconciled with the larger issues for which the common struggle had been waged. During the early days of 1945, plans were already underway in the department for the forthcoming Big Three meetings at Yalta in preparation for the postwar peace conference. Foreign Service officers were cautiously optimistic. As Dunn had told newsmen on Christmas day, "The Atlantic Charter is still there."[48]

6. Shaping the Postwar World:
From Yalta to Potsdam

The American contingent departed for the Crimea on January 31, stopping
first at Malta, where military discussions were already underway between
the combined chiefs of staff, before finally setting down at an airfield
eighty miles from Yalta on the evening of February 3. After an official
welcome by Molotov and a refreshing repast of vodka and caviar, the
delegation was escorted to the Livadiya Palace, former residence of Czar
Nicholas II, where the Russians had taken great pains to arrange comfortable quarters for President Roosevelt.

Bohlen, who attended the summit meeting as interpreter and advisor,
was gratified by these manifestations of friendship. Like other career
diplomats in Washington who had participated in the preparation of the
conference briefing papers, he had a personal stake in the success of the
talks. It was not surprising, then, that he reacted with disquietude to the
Cassandra-like missive from Kennan that greeted his arrival at Livadiya.
While the United States pursued a quixotic quest for a new League of
Nations, Kennan pointed out, "wandering about with our heads in the
clouds of Wilsonian idealism and universalistic conceptions of world collaboration," Moscow had politically and economically penetrated Eastern and Central Europe, without so much as a murmur from Washington
and, owing to the futile presence of American missions there, partly in its
name. "We must get it out of our heads that we are going to have anything
to do with the immediate future of eastern and southeastern Europe," he
asserted, "unless we are willing to go the whole hog and oppose with all
the physical and diplomatic resources at our disposal the domination of
this area by any other single power. Lacking the will to do this, we should
write these territories off." Despite this bleak prognosis, Kennan believed
that cooperation with Russia was not impossible, provided the American
government "bury Dumbarton Oaks" and "divide Europe frankly into
spheres of influence."[1]

Annoyed by Kennan's renunciation of the United Nations and his
thinly veiled mockery of American postwar objectives, Bohlen dismissed
his gloomy colleague's prescriptions as "frankly naive": fine in the
abstract, but practically "utterly impossible." The United States was a
democracy, not a totalitarian society, he rejoined, in which foreign affairs
leaders had to create "a climate of public opinion" to support policy and

in which power had to "justify itself within the framework of the general good." In short, "the *Soyuz* [Soviet Union] is here to stay as one of the major factors in the world. Quarrelling with them would be so easy—but we can always come to that."[2]

Roosevelt felt the same way about the Russians, and even more so about Stalin, whose efforts to moderate Russian social conditions suggested to the president a sympathetic quality in his nature. When the two leaders met privately on February 4, Roosevelt greeted the Soviet premier as a friend, warmly shaking his hand. Stalin reciprocated the gesture, a thin smile breaking across the craggy topography of his ruddy, peasant face. For his part, he too hoped to strengthen relations with the allies.

So reminiscent of Teheran, this genial mood, into which Churchill also was drawn, persisted throughout the eight-day conference, despite periodic wrangling and even occasional bitterness between the prime minister and Stalin. Substantive discussions were characterized by a spirit of compromise on all sides. Stalin approved the discussion of international disputes in the United Nations Security Council with majority approval and acceded to Churchill's insistence on an occupation zone for France in Germany. Churchill assented to Stalin's territorial claims in eastern Poland and to the possible dismemberment of Germany, and Roosevelt conceded to Stalin the retrocession of the Kurile and southern Sakhalin Islands, the lease of Port Arthur as a naval base, recognition of Soviet preeminent interests in Dairen, joint Sino-Russian control of the Manchurian railways, and the establishment of an autonomous Outer Mongolia. Finally, all agreed to the creation of a special commission to study the question of German reparations.

These agreements were reached because they were not incompatible with political and military realities. Considerations of principle, however, proved another matter. Here, the American goal of free elections and political self-determination conflicted with Stalin's insistence on "friendly governments" in Eastern Europe. As it had in the past, debate centered on Poland. Although privately amenable to a Soviet sphere of influence in Eastern Europe, Roosevelt, pressed by Mikolajczyk and sensitive to Polish-American opinion, advocated the formation of a new and broadly representative Polish government. Concerned about Soviet military expansion in the Balkans, Churchill supported this proposal. Stalin was willing to expand the provisional government so long as the Soviet-backed Lublin Poles maintained primacy of control. After days of haggling, the allied leaders finally subscribed to a vaguely worded placebo accommodating both positions and agreed to create a tripartite commission to assist in the reorganization of the postwar Polish government. At one level, the ambiguity of the statement obviously signified the impasse reached by the heads of state; at another, it conveyed their reluctance to impair the agreements already concluded in the interests of preserving postwar cooperation on a realpolitik basis. The pious-sounding "declaration on liberated Europe" presented by Roosevelt and signed by Churchill and an amused Stalin was really a diluted version of the Provisional Security Council for Europe proposed by Hickerson, Matthews, Bohlen, Durbrow, and others, which purported *actively* to participate in the formation of popular governments.[3]

Even though divisions still existed between them, the three heads of state left the Crimea in high spirits. The conference strengthened their personal attachments and enhanced the prospects of postwar allied harmony. With the possibility of peace for years to come so near at hand, Chruchill stated, it would be tragic to let it slip away.

Yalta also kindled the hopes of Foreign Service officers. Matthews, Kohler, Riddleberger, and their colleagues were all heartened by the results. As Durbrow put it, "The Yalta accord was a damn good document." It was clear to Bohlen that Stalin "genuinely wished" to compromise allied differences. "In short," he said, "there was hope, as we left Yalta, of genuine cooperation with the Soviet Union on political questions after the war. Kennan's gloomy assessment had not yet proved correct."[4] Never fully comprehending Roosevelt's "grand design," however, career diplomats perceived the Yalta agreement to be something different from the power-political accommodation the president intended. Encouraged by the Kremlin's ostensible abandonment of its revolutionary objectives and by the apparent democratizing course it had set upon during the war, they now awaited Soviet actions in Eastern Europe as further evidence of Moscow's adherence to the liberal-democratic postwar order.

While the department savored the success of Yalta, diplomats in Soviet-occupied Eastern Europe grew increasingly disturbed by Moscow's behavior. In contrast to their colleagues in Washington, who had helped formulate America's neo-Wilsonian postwar policy, they were called upon to implement it. That proved far more problematic; for rhetorical courtesies to the Atlantic Charter and the "declaration on liberated Europe" aside, the Soviets had not altered their objective of establishing a security zone in postwar Europe and imposing political dominance in those areas they militarily controlled. As Stalin had explained before Yalta to Milovan Djilas, Tito's then trusted lieutenant, this war was different from past conflicts. "Everyone imposes his own system as far as his army can reach. It cannot be otherwise."[5] Nevertheless, Stalin did not self-consciously set out to impose a policy of *Gleichschaltung* on Eastern Europe. On the contrary, his approach was cautious and irresolute. To guard against another military invasion, those countries along the immediate perimeter of Russia, with the exception of Finland, were either annexed or rendered politically inert. However, those states in the Danubian region or on the eastern Adriatic, which geographically presented less of a threat to Soviet security, were allowed to retain control of their domestic institutions so long as they remained politically docile. Sandwiched between American expectations and Soviet aims were the peasant peoples of Eastern Europe, who desired primarily to return to their farms, fill their stomachs, and even as they hoped for more humane social conditions, to restore their lives as best they could.

Diplomats in Rumania helplessly watched the Russian army impose censorship on the press, denounce the indigenous political parties, foment rioting, and continue its pell-mell expropriation of petroleum equipment. More ominous was the February 26 visit of Vishinsky, who demanded the dismissal of the government of General Nicolae Radescu in favor of one headed by Petru Groza, a Transylvanian businessman, political opportunist, and leader of the peasant party known as the Ploughman's Front. In light of Rumania's antibolshevist-philofascist history, the intensity with which her armies had fought on the Russian front, and the Russophobic attitudes of the Peasant and Liberal parties, none of this was really surprising. But these considerations were little reflected in the mission's cables, which focused apprehensively on Moscow's evident intention to install a "puppet government," unless the United States were able to "translate its principles into action."[6]

Cannon, Huston, Thompson, Matthews, and Dunn all reacted cautiously to these "disquieting factors." Molotov had given his assurance in April, observed Cannon, that the Soviets did not intend to change the internal structure of Rumania, and there was no reason to expect a departure from that position. But since it appeared that local Soviet officials had "afforded encouragement to disruptive actions," Huston requested Harriman to inform Moscow of Washington's interest in a coalition government in Rumania, the preservation of order, and full consultation on the armistice commission. Diplomats in the department simultaneously directed Berry to notify Vishinsky that the United States backed no political elements in the country and desired only the formation of a broadly representative government in accordance with the "declaration on liberated Europe."[7]

The Soviet response was unequivocal: Vishinsky presented King Michael with an ultimatum to recognize Groza. Lacking any real support from the United States, on March 6 Michael reluctantly yielded to the silent coup d'état. Disheartened by this turn of events and affected by Maniu's plaintive admission that Rumania was now virtually "lost to the Russians," Berry upbraided the department for not encouraging Rumanian leaders to resist the communization movement and for helping to power a Soviet-sponsored government. But careerists in the department responded to the Rumanian coup by calling for more consultation with Moscow. Despite another unencouraging reply from Molotov, who likened the Soviet armistice role in Rumania to that of the Anglo-Americans in Italy, they persisted in their search for some "common ground on which we could build a structure suitable to all." So on the twenty-sixth, following Huston's suggestion, Cannon drafted a cable for Harriman to ascertain from Kremlin officials what motivated their suppression of the "historic" (translated "noncommunist") National Peasant and Liberal parties and to stress the principle of tripartite responsibility in Rumania under the now irrelevant "declaration on liberated Europe."[8]

The diplomacy of principle was not faring any better in Bulgaria. Without so much as a murmur from the Russian representative on the armistice commission, communist elements within the Fatherland Front steadily gained control of the country. Like some medieval inquisitors, public prosecutors combed the countryside in search of fascist heretics. Hundreds were incarcerated; hundreds more condemned to die. Appalled by the "macabre tableau" presented by these so-called "people's courts," Barnes and his British counterpart, William E. Houstoun Boswall, sadly concluded that the severity of sentences meted out was intended to liquidate all democratic opposition. As the weeks passed, Barnes, like Berry, grew increasingly more sympathetic to the doleful cries of the Bulgarian people, or, at least, some of the people. Nearly every day since publication of the Yalta accords, he telegrammed Washington on February 27, "some prominent Bulgarian, frequently a member of the Government or a leading military figure," had asked whether "the United States really [intended] to make its influence felt in this part of the world" or whether Washington's refusal to discuss Bulgarian cobelligerency at Yalta demonstrated its willingness to surrender "to Russia 'the key to the Balkans.'"[9]

Finding it difficult to conceal his frustrations, he wrote in March that "being an ally at close quarters with the Russians might be likened to something in the nature of matrimony with a good provider but whose personal habits and disregard for the sensibilities of the other member of the union grate constantly on one's nerves. The inability to modify the partner's character and manners," he went on, "can in time lead only to a suppressed sense of frustration and impotence, or separation." Because the United States had thus far done nothing to modify Russia's character or manners, Bulgaria now viewed the world "largely through a Russian window, just as formerly," he well-remembered, "the government here saw the world picture through German tinted glass." Nevertheless, the combative Barnes was prepared neither to abandon the Bulgarian people, 60 percent of whom, he reckoned, supported the peasant-based Agrarian party, nor abdicate his responsibility to the liberal-democratic ideals of the Atlantic Charter.[10]

On principle, diplomats in the department were not opposed to Barnes's recommendations for Bulgarian cobelligerency status; in practice, however, they refused to take the initiative without Anglo-Soviet concurrence. Neither were they inclined to acknowledge a Soviet sphere of influence in the region. Still, heedful of Barnes's predicament and the possibility that the Agrarian party would be denied the right to present a separate slate of candidates in the forthcoming elections, on March 19 Cannon suggested that a number of them—Dunn, Bohlen, Thompson, Matthews—meet to discuss American policy in southeastern Europe. Ten days later Cannon, Huston, and Theodore Hohenthal drafted a message to the Moscow embassy directing Harriman to remind the Kremlin of its obligations to ensure free elections in Bulgaria and to express the American government's readiness to participate in their supervision. As a kind of diplomatic fillip, they further instructed Harriman to explain to the Soviets the American public's "intense interest" in the matter.[11]

Careerists in Washington struck an equally circumspect posture in the case of Yugoslavia, where Tito, fresh from his triumph over the Četniks, and Ivan Šubašić had agreed the previous December to form a provisional government. Despite British efforts to gain United States recognition of this union, Cannon, Hohenthal, Dunn, and Matthews, in support of the new secretary of state, Edward R. Stettinius, opposed an "activist policy" that might interfere with the Yugoslavs' right to work out independently their own form of government. It was still unclear to Cannon that Tito enjoyed greater support than Mihailović. Furthermore, he perceptively noted, it was illusory to believe that the British or the Russians cared a wit about the Yugoslav people. "One cannot but feel that their anxiety to have us go along is in large part a design to prepare a facade of "'Allied' action" to conceal their political maneuvering. So on January 27 Dunn, now assistant secretary of state, and Grew told London that Washington wished to withhold full recognition of the Tito-Šubašić government until it had determined whether the new coalition would work.[12]

No sooner was the Tito-Šubašić agreement consummated than disagreement ensued between the partners as to which members of the former exiled government would be included in the Anti-Fascist Council of National Liberation (AVNOJ), the legislative body set up by the partisans in 1942. By the end of February Tito and Šubašić resolved their difficulties and took their places in the communist interim government as premier and foreign minister, respectively. Diplomats in the department looked forward to elections in accordance with the popular will. The British, *per contra*, held out little hope for the evolution of Anglo-American political ideals in Yugoslavia. As Brigadier Fitzroy Maclean, head of the British military mission in Yugoslavia, told William Fraleigh in March, the coalition government would inevitably come under Moscow's domination. Even so, he believed that Tito's self-confidence and the support he enjoyed throughout the country promised a stable regime.[13]

At this juncture, however, diplomats in Washington set aside Balkan problems and turned their attention toward the disconcerting reappearance of the Polish albatross. Unlike Rumania and Bulgaria, both former Nazi satellites, Poland was an ally; and unlike Yugoslavia, seemingly on the way to political self-determination, she was saddled with a Soviet-imposed government. Moreover, as the first European country to be attacked and despoiled under the Nazi-Soviet pact, Poland was a highly charged symbol of freedom to the American government and public. Poland, as Stettinius and Dunn put it, "was the big apple in the barrel." The issue that triggered the department's concern was the failure of the Moscow Commission—composed of Harriman, Molotov, and British Ambassador Clark-Kerr—to agree on which Poles should be invited from London and Warsaw to form an interim government. Fearing a complete breakdown of the talks, Thompson urged flexibility on all sides. "We do not agree that you should assume Molotov is the advocate for the Lublin [now in Warsaw and hereafter so cited] Poles and that you and Clark-Kerr represent other Poles," he wrote to Harriman. "Whatever Molotov's position may be in fact, we believe it important that the Commission should endeavor to operate as a unit." This "was the intent of the Crimea decisions and that [sic] it is only in this way that success can be achieved." Bohlen underscored these views, noting that agreement on Poland "will be watched by the entire world as an indication of the reality of the unity [Yalta] so successfully established between the three principal Allies."[14]

Again American optimism proved unsettling to the British. Churchill bitterly complained to Roosevelt that the Moscow Commission represented a mere facade to give the communist regime in Warsaw an aura of respectability. He and the Foreign Office proposed that Anglo-American representatives on the Commission demand Societ acceptance of all Poles nominated unless unanimously rejected, the formation of a presidential council of Polish leaders, freedom of movement for Mikolajczyk and his associates in Moscow, and the cessation of Communist-inspired terrorism in Poland. Alarmed by Churchill's pugnacity, Bohlen told the president that he could not agree that "we are confronted with a breakdown of the Yalta agreement until we have made the effort to overcome the obstacles incurred in the negotiations at Moscow." In the end, Roosevelt acceded only to the first of Churchill's points. Compromises were reached on the others, which effectively softened the thrust of British demands. However, adhering to the view that the legal Polish government resided in London, Thompson urged Harriman to oppose the Soviet position that consultations with the Warsaw government should precede those with other Poles. Having done so, he and Matthews felt hopeful that a unanimous decision would now be reached. Alas, these proposals were rejected by Molotov at the end of March. Discussions in the Moscow Commission had deadlocked.[15]

A series of nearly concurrent developments—the Kremlin's refusal to permit Americans to inspect prisoner-of-war camps in Poland and the appearance of an article in *Cahiers du Communisme* by Jacques Duclos attacking the nonrevolutionary attitude of American communists—induced career diplomats to assign a still direr connotation to the breakdown of the Polish negotiations. But the most distressing incident took place on the military front. Having received word that Anglo-American forces in Italy were about to entertain overtures for a German surrender in Berne, Stalin suspected that his partners might conspire with Germany to permit continued fighting in the east for a surrender in the west. He therefore requested Soviet participation in the talks. After airing the matter with Admiral Leahy, head of the Joint Chiefs of Staff, and other military officials on March 13, Bohlen, Dunn, and Matthews agreed that the Soviets should be invited to join subsequent discussions only if preliminary talks in Berne proved eventful. His suspicions ever more inflamed upon hearing this news, Stalin protested violently and insultingly to Roosevelt, implying that he and Churchill were guilty of deceit. Diplomats in the department joined Churchill in condemnation of Stalin's scurrilous outburst. Equally infuriated by the Russian's personal attack, but intent on sustaining the accommodation reached with Stalin in the Crimea, Roosevelt chose to dismiss it as a "minor misunderstanding." Indeed, just before departing for his Hot Springs, Georgia, retreat, he confided to Churchill his continued commitment to the cause of postwar cooperation. As fate had it, this was the President's last official statement. On April 12, 1945, while the world grieved Roosevelt's death, the legacy of the Atlantic Charter, Yalta, and the United Nations passed unnoticed to Vice President Harry Truman.[16]

It was symbolic of his inconspicuous presence in official circles that the "little man from Missouri" was all but ignored by mourners who gathered at the White House for Roosevelt's funeral service. Having had little, if any, prior contact with Truman, whom Roosevelt had kept amazingly in the dark on foreign policy, career diplomats and other State Department officials wondered whether he was capable of leading the nation at this critical moment in its history.

During the next two weeks, however, several factors combined to allay their worries. For one thing, Truman heeded the views of his foreign-policy advisors—notably Grew, Leahy, Stimson, Bohlen, and Dunn, all of whom had become more disturbed by Soviet behavior in Eastern Europe, now likened by Harriman to a "barbarian invasion." Moreover, the president's humble admission that "he was not up on all the details of foreign affairs," and that he would have to "rely on the secretary of state and his Ambassadors to help in this matter," gratified career diplomats. For the first time since Secretary of State Hughes sang encomiums to the new "peace diplomats" two decades earlier, an exalted government official had expressed confidence in the Foreign Service. It was not merely that Truman, unlike the enigmatic Roosevelt, "was playing the game according to the rules," as Henderson put it; more importantly, observed Charles Yost, the Missourian was "dependent" on the department and the Foreign Service for policy guidance.[17]

A further encouraging sign was Truman's assertiveness with the Russians. Shaken by Roosevelt's death, "more disturbed than I had ever seen him," Harriman recalled, Stalin had accepted the ambassador's suggestion to send Molotov to the United Nations Conference in San Francisco, scheduled to begin on April 25. On his way, the Soviet foreign minister stopped in Washington to meet with Truman. Preliminary pleasantries had barely been exchanged when Molotov peremptorily challenged the president's willingness to honor the Far Eastern territorial commitments agreed to at Yalta by Roosevelt. Probably insecure in his first meeting with the Russians, hence all the more ruffled by Molotov's bullying tactics, Truman argumentatively returned the favor by inquiring when the Russians planned to honor their Yalta obligations in Eastern Europe. The question was not an invitation for further discussion. Curtly, Truman dismissed the startled Molotov, acridly requesting the foreign minister to relay his comments to Stalin. Surprised to hear how the inexperienced Truman stood up to the obdurate Russian, Henderson rejoiced that "departmental morale began to soar."[18]

Understandably, Truman's verbal barrage suggested to Molotov and Stalin that the United States had abandoned Roosevelt's policy of cooperation. Resolved to gain the Warsaw government's admission to the new United Nations Organization at the San Francisco Conference, Molotov quickly took the fray to the American delegation. Irritated by Molotov's demanding manner, Stettinius, an amiable organization man with only rudimentary knowledge of diplomacy, marshalled the necessary support to oppose Poland's inclusion in the postwar organization. Unfortunately, his endorsement of Argentina, which remained loyal to the Axis until the final weeks of the war, further aroused Moscow's suspicions of American intentions. By the same token, reports that sixteen Poles invited to Moscow for talks on the postwar government had been arrested similarly aggravated the American government's growing mistrust of the Soviets.[19]

As the haggling at San Francisco continued, military plans went forward for the final assault on Germany. Churchill's recommendation that Anglo-American forces push as far east as possible was rejected by Marshall and Eisenhower, who were determined to adhere to the established military spheres in Europe. On May 8–9 the long-awaited Nazi collapse finally arrived. While allied soldiers jubilantly received news of V-E Day, American officials, mindful of Soviet actions in Rumania and Poland, voiced concern about Stalin's political objectives in Europe. Grew, for one, found Soviet tactics "strikingly reminiscent" of those employed by the Japanese and the Germans in the thirties. Nevertheless, they continued to regard the Soviets as their ally. As Stimson had pointed out to Marshall a month earlier, "we simply cannot allow a rift to come between the two nations without endangering the entire peace of the world." Sensitive to British and Chinese efforts "to play off" the United States and the USSR against each other, Bohlen felt that Washington had to dispel the Kremlin's suspicions that it might face another Munich or that the United Nations, in the manner of the League of Nations, might serve as a forum to isolate Russia from the West. Thus it was that Truman, ignorant of Roosevelt's "grand design" but wishing nonetheless to preserve U.S.-Soviet postwar harmony, accepted, through Harriman, Bohlen's suggestion to send Hopkins, now gravely ill, to confer with Stalin in Moscow.[20]

The Hopkins-Stalin meetings produced mixed results. Appeals to release the jailed Polish leaders evoked little more than polite indifference from the Soviet leader. Moreover, in spite of his respect and probably even affection for Hopkins, Stalin assailed the admission of Argentina to the United Nations and Truman's abrupt curtailment of Lend-Lease aid—a product of bureaucratic bungling—following Germany's surrender. On the other hand, consistent with his Yalta statement, Stalin waived Soviet veto power in the discussion of issues before the Security Council, thereby reversing the position Molotov had taken at San Francisco. Furthermore, he announced the addition of four non-Lublin Poles, including Mikolajczyk, to the Warsaw government.

Hopkins was generally encouraged, as were Harriman and Bohlen, who also attended the talks. Stopping off in Berlin on the way home, Hopkins informed American military personnel there that Churchill's fears of Soviet intentions were exaggerated. For their part, officials in the State Department were pleased by Stalin's stand on the veto question, which helped pave the way to a successful conclusion of the San Francisco Conference. Formulation of the UN Charter even dashed the morose presentiments of Grew, who told Dunn that he was justified, in view of the hard-won victory at San Francisco, to return to Washington "on the crest of the wave."[21]

As for Poland, a coalition government formed on June 28 brought to a close the London-Lublin period of that country's history. Nonetheless, the London Poles refused to accept their fate. In Washington, Ambassador Jan Ciechanowski—stubbornly, courageously, quixotically—tried to get department officials to prevent the formation of the new government. Bohlen, Dunn, Grew, and Matthews all were suddenly "too busy" to see him; and Henderson was now head of the Near Eastern division. So he presented his case to Durbrow, the new chief of the Eastern European division. But Durbrow, who believed that "a definite step forward has been taken in complete conformity with our interpretations of the Yalta agreement," refused to entertain proposals antagonistic to American postwar plans. A "negative attitude in this matter," he explained, "would get us nowhere, would give the Lublin Government time to consolidate its position." For the same reason, Ciechanowski's unveiled proposal that the United States employ military force was also rebuffed. Moreover, Durbrow doubted the American capacity "to impose her will on Soviet Russia." The best course, in his view, was for the State Department to work through its ambassador to assist the Poles in forming a government of their own choice.[22]

Assured by Warsaw that the Yalta agreement would be implemented, Washington recognized the Provisional Government of National Unity on July 5, despite Ciechanowski's accusation that the United States had "[sold] Poland down the river." While administration officials and diplomats in the department held out hope for free elections and a more democratic government in Warsaw, in effect if not intent, they had cut themselves loose from the Polish albatross.

The chord of guarded optimism that sounded in the department during the late spring and early summer of 1945 harmonized with the views of Maxwell Hamilton, who had assumed charge of the American political mission in Helsinki at the end of 1944. Although Finland had to don the same sackcloth of war worn by other defeated states, including the cession to Russia of military bases and a strip of northern territory, she was not militarily occupied by the Red Army. Moreover, even though it controlled the armistice commission, Moscow stayed punctiliously aloof from Finnish national elections in March, which produced a noncommunist socialist government. Encouraged by Soviet behavior, which seemed to mirror the American government's and public's enduring spirit of cooperation, Hamilton told Soviet theoretician Andrei A. Zhdanov that both "the United States and Soviet Union," in spite of different socioeconomic systems, "had the same ideals of democracy and freedom for people." The discovery of arms caches the following summer, presumably hoarded by rightest elements, did result in two peremptory notes of protest from Moscow and the subsequent resignations of a number of Finnish political and military figures. Still, in contrast to what happened in Rumania, the Soviet response was mild. This was partly because the Finns, as the Russians remembered all too well, were a fiercely independent people not easily subdued. More importantly, Stalin recalled how the American public (and the British) had admired the Finns for their stand against the Russians during the winter war of 1939–40. Furthermore, Roosevelt had indicated his support for an independent Finland at Teheran. In Hamilton's opinion, swift action on Helsinki's part to suppress local anti-Russian and fascist elements and the conclusion of a Finnish peace treaty would further reduce tensions between the two countries and promote friendlier relations.[23]

In Soviet-controlled Eastern Europe, however, incipient perceptions of ideological confrontation scrambled the rhythm of cooperation. The resulting discordance was least pronounced among Foreign Service officers in Albania, Czechoslovakia, and Hungary, countries in which indigenous elements, notwithstanding the presence or the shadow of the Red Army, still held political control. In Rumania, Bulgaria, and Yugoslavia, where political life was dominated by the Soviet Union or Soviet-influenced forces, the tone of their despatches was more strident and tendentious. American diplomats posted in these states waged a lonely, anxious struggle to reconcile democratic principles, writ large in the Atlantic Charter and miniaturized in the declaration on liberated Europe, with the reality of the conditions they experienced. To preserve the integrity of American aims in the postwar world, career officers exhorted the department to adopt new means to achieve them, namely, the vigorous assertion of America's rights and responsibilities in Eastern Europe.

Assigned to Tirana in April to assess local conditions, Joseph Jacobs considered impoverished, backward Albania a most unseemly place to satisfy his long-standing desire for his own post. But he decided that it could not be worse than the eight years of frustration he had endured in the department. As it turned out, the political situation was not unpromising. Indisputably, the regime of Enver Hoxha, which enjoyed the patronage of Tito, was a one-party dictatorship. On the other hand, Hoxha was calling his own political tune; and however jarring to American ears, it met no opposition from either the landed gentry or the masses. While leaders of the National Liberation Front were "ignorant of the science of government [and knew] little of international relations," Jacobs found them "a sincere, patriotic group of individuals." Actually, the only potential source of unrest was the presence of the British military mission, which was conspiring with anti-Hoxha forces. Distressed by Brigadier Dana Hodgson's recommendation late in May for an Anglo-American military landing to spur opposition efforts, Jacobs concluded that the British were not committed to determining whether the National Liberation Front merited recognition, "but rather to talking about how the peasant regime may be overthrown." This "would belie everything we were trying to do to solve the world's problems by peaceful means."[24]

On July 1, after making several trips in the country, Jacobs wired his preliminary recommendations to the department. Although half the cabinet was comprised of Communists, he wrote, they had not gone so far as Russia or Yugoslavia "in the regimentation of human activity." As evidenced by the equitable distribution of Lend-Lease aid, they appeared "more considerate of the well being of the Albanian people than any other regime Albania has ever had." Furthermore, there was no indication that the present leadership was unfriendly toward the United States or Britain. He therefore recommended American recognition, pending free elections and the accordance of diplomatic rights and immunities to American representatives.[25]

Newly appointed Ambassador Laurence A. Steinhardt, "a vain and highly egocentric" New York lawyer and former ambassador to Moscow from 1939 to 1942, and Klieforth and Bruins found a more fertile field for the growth of American liberal-internationalist objectives in Czechoslovakia, where the seeds of democratic government had already been planted during the interwar years. Furthermore, the wartime diplomacy of Beneš bade fair to produce amicable postwar relations with all three allied powers. If Czechoslovakia represented the test of allied cooperation, as Bohlen had indicated to Steinhardt prior to his departure, the signs augured well for the future.[26]

Of course, Foreign Service officers like Klieforth, who had served in Russia and Riga during and immediately after World War I, remained wary of Moscow's intentions, particularly since the Red Army still exercised considerable influence in the country. At the same time, he vividly remembered the spectacle of Nazi expansionism in the thirties; and in his view, a resurgent Germany posed far more of a threat to Czechoslovakian independence than Russia. "I cannot agree with those who believe there are millions of decent Germans," he had written to Leo Pasvolsky in 1943. "I have seen the Russian Reds, the Finnish Whites and other elementary mob forces in action, but in none have I seen as little of the milk of human kindness as in the Prussian military caste." Bruins, on the other hand, though having served in Prague during the thirties, felt more of an animus against the Soviets. As yet, however, neither the Soviets nor the Czech Communists had given cause for alarm. To be sure, the Red Army engaged in the same rapacious acts in the eastern sections of Czechoslovakia under its control as it had elsewhere in Eastern Europe. But, in Bruins's judgment, Russian occupation behavior was not "intentionally malicious but merely primitive." And although Communists dominated the Czech national committees, he and Klieforth contemptuously attributed this to the "weakness" and the "natural timidity" of the Czech people, who allowed themselves "to be pushed around." Moreover, local Communist leaders such as Klement Gottwald and sympathizers like Zdenek Fierlinger, head of the Social Democratic party, had demonstrated their desire to cooperate with the other National Bloc parties.[27]

Conditions in the country remained tranquil through the spring and early summer. Then, at the end of June, Communist party members of the provisional government, presumably at Moscow's insistence, pressured Beneš to request the withdrawal of American troops. Privately, the Czech president informed the British ambassador that he desired the simultaneous departure of Soviet and American forces. Klieforth emphatically supported this position, both to preserve Washington's postwar objectives of international peace and harmony and to avoid "a serious and almost irreparable loss to America's reputation and 'western prestige,' not only in Zecho but throughout eastern Europe." The State Department readily concurred. As the Potsdam briefing papers on Czechoslovakia stated, simultaneous withdrawal was necessary to ensure that country's postwar independence. It remained to be seen whether Moscow would comply.[28]

Like his fellow diplomats in Prague, Arthur Schoenfeld arrived in Budapest just as the European war came to an end. He found the city's once beautiful Gothic-Romanesque buildings, tree-lined avenues, and wide squares battered into a grotesque collage by the ravages of war; its people homeless, ill-fed, and disconsolate. Adding to the grim spectacle was the presence of the victorious Red Army, looting, raping, and seemingly indiscriminately destroying the artifacts of civilization that momentarily survived. Although the Hungarians had formed a provisional national council, real political authority, as in Bulgaria and Rumania, was exercised by the Soviet-dominated armistice commission, whose control of newsprint and travel permits constrained the activities of the noncommunist parties. Overtures by Schoenfeld and Alvary Douglas Frederick Gascoigne, his British counterpart, to exert some enlightened influence on the commission were stoically dismissed by the Russian representative, Marshal Kliment Efremovich Voroshilov.[29]

Partly because of his disrespect for the Magyar people, who, unlike the sturdy Finns, displayed "timid fear" and "rabbit-like squeaks of pain and terror" with each sudden movement of the Russian interlopers, Schoenfeld avoided involvement in the nation's political affairs. At the same time, he could not ignore the repeated entreaties of Hungarian leaders for the formation of a democratic government in accord with the Yalta compact. To abandon this duty, he reasoned, was to compromise American ideals and interests. So, in contrast to Gascoigne, who had by mid-June forsaken hope of equal Anglo-American participation on the allied control commission, Schoenfeld vigorously contested Voroshilov's formulation of an electoral decree which sanctioned leftist-influenced local councils to identify alleged Fascists. Since he believed this would bias national elections in favor of the "radical parties," and since Hungary "was not yet mentally, morally, economically or politically prepared to participate in European reconstruction, he considered it vital to American interests— assuming, he told the department, "that real stabilization of Hungary is an American interest in this part of Europe"—to join in the drafting of Hungarian electoral laws. Schoenfeld became even more adamant after learning from Reber that the British Foreign Office, having resigned itself to Soviet control of the armistice commissions in the former enemy countries, recommended the establishment of peace treaties with Hungary, Bulgaria, and Rumania. To accept the British view, Schoenfeld wrote Grew on June 25, was to risk "forfeiting such respect on [the] part of [the] USSR as we painfully gained during [the] European hostilities" and to eschew the "fundamental principles previously agreed on at Yalta and in [the] Hungarian armistice negotiations at Moscow." Free elections, he argued, would only be guaranteed if the allied powers jointly supervised them.[30]

Meanwhile, anxious not to antagonize Stalin just before the summit conference in Berlin, Harriman advised the department that a contretemps at this time might lead Moscow to the erroneous conclusion that Britain and the United States had formed an anti-Soviet bloc, an impression Roosevelt had carefully tried to avoid. Unhappy with the department's acceptance of Harriman's view, Schoenfeld wired back that the Hungarians had grown increasingly more doubtful that the United States would implement the Yalta agreement. Although Gascoigne believed the agreement "out of date," he went on to say, "we presume this is not our Government's view." On July 13 Grew, Reber, and Dunn sent a flaccid message to Budapest confirming the department's faith in Yalta, but firmly opposing the supervision of elections unless the Hungarians clearly intended to conduct them unfairly. Frustrated by this response, Schoenfeld looked forward to the Big Three talks at Berlin to ameliorate conditions in Hungary. On July 26 he informed Árpád Szakasits, leader of the Social Democrats, that he anticipated the unimpeded development of American political and economic objectives in Hungary. "My replies were guided by the confidence," he informed Washington, "that cooperation among the principal Allies in the European war was desired equally by all for the postwar era and [it] would find expression in harmonious policies."[31]

Actually, conditions in both Hungary and Czechoslovakia were quiescent in comparison to what was taking place in the Balkans. Still licking the wounds of humiliation inflicted by his submission to the Groza government, King Michael vainly tried in April to assert his authority by refusing to sign various Communist-sponsored decrees, including the execution of persons affiliated with "pro-Fascist" organizations. Although Berry offered the beleaguered King words of comfort, "we must admit to ourselves," he moaned to the department, "that the encouragement that comes from words expressed in Bucharest at a time when action is desired in Moscow forms but a fragile bulwark for resisting the pressure of powerful groups." But Berry proposed no counteraction. In fact, like his colleagues in Washington, he opposed the developing Rumanian resistance movement, partly because it stood little chance of success against the Soviets, partly because of its extralegal character.[32]

For a brief time following the end of the European war, Berry's and Melbourne's hopes for a democratic Rumania brightened. Titel Petrescu, leader of the Socialist party, had expressed his intent to dissociate himself from the National Democratic Front; the Rumanian peasantry had become progressively more aroused by the presence of the Red Army; and glaring divisions suddenly appeared within the Communist party between the "comintern" faction of Anna Pauker and Vasili Luca and the "nationalist" faction of Gheorghe Gheorghiu-Dej. Furthermore, recently concluded free elections in Finland gave added reason to believe that a modus vivendi with the Russians in Rumania was also possible, Berry stated, provided Washington shifted "from a passive to an active role on the ACC." But diplomats in the department, "more interested in getting Soviet agreement to apply in the future the principles of the Yalta declaration," as Bohlen put it, "than in insisting on a review of the Soviet action of last February or on a drastic reorganization of the Rumanian Government," wished to avoid verbal jousting with the Russians.[33]

Given Moscow's unalterable aim to control Rumania, it made little difference whether the Americans engaged in the rhetoric of protest or conciliation. In any event, by early summer, faced with continuing press censorship and denial of political assembly, war criminals trials, army purges, and undiminished commercial exploitation, the Bucharest mission ruefully concluded that Rumania, once part of the German political and economic sphere, was gradually being absorbed into the Soviet orbit. According to Melbourne, conditions were not likely to change. While some Rumanians hoped for an Anglo-American–Soviet conflict to rid themselves of their Russian masters, and others pessimistically awaited their incorporation into the USSR, most realistically accepted their historical lot "in what they consider to be a power politics trading game." Of course, there still was a chance that the Russians would relax internal conditions; but it would be done probably less in the interests of worldwide cooperation, as Melbourne and Berry had hoped, and more, as was the case with Nazi Germany, to "keep the country to the Soviet heel."[34]

The outlook for U.S.-Soviet cooperation appeared even bleaker in Sofia. Psychologically bludgeoned by the sanguinary activities of the Bulgarian "people's courts," which he equated with the Bolshevik Revolution, Barnes wrote in April, "We should not delude ourselves into believing that three-cornered collaboration here is going to pay dividends, that is, dividends as we understand the term." As Soviet efforts to eliminate the leaders of the Agrarian and Social Democratic parties from the Fatherland Front intensified, politically conscious Bulgarians questioned whether Bulgaria would "go the Russian way under communist domination" or continue as an independent state. To retain "a shred of respect" in the country, Barnes, like Schoenfeld, advised the department to insist on tripartite supervision of the forthcoming elections. This at least would force the Russians to set aside their "brickbats, brass knuckles and all [the] other paraphernalia of the gas house gang." Even though they had already received Moscow's refusal to permit the supervision of elections, diplomats in the department nonetheless remained hopeful that the Soviets would eventually implement the Atlantic Charter principles and the Yalta accords on Eastern Europe. While conceding that "Soviet interests in Rumania and Bulgaria are more direct than ours," Cannon, Matthews, and Reber reaffirmed, in a memo to Truman, Washington's commitment to "joint Allied action in the political sphere and non-exclusion in the economic sphere."[35]

In the meantime, things went from bad to worse in Bulgaria. Late in May Georgi Dimitrov, secretary general of the Agrarian party, escaped from house arrest and received asylum in Barnes's home. Outraged by the "police state" tactics employed against Dimitrov and the apparent murder of his private secretary, Barnes exhorted the department "to save the life of this popular leader and convince the Bulgarian populace that we really mean what we have declared publicly so many times since Yalta." However, Cannon, Matthews, and Reber, fearing that Washington's involvement would compromise its avowed principle of political non-interference, advised against any action beyond the request for assurances that the Bulgarian leader would be permitted safe exit from the country. Miffed by the State Department's caution, humiliated by the presence of the milita from "a defeated nation" surrounding his house, Barnes persisted in his efforts to enlist Washington's support, hinting cryptically at one point that the time might have arrived for "a radical solution" of the Bulgarian problem. Although Barnes had actually dissuaded Agrarian leaders from fomenting an internal irruption, alarmed department officials repeated their earlier admonition to abstain from extreme measures. Now incensed by Washington's seeming indifference to his cables, Barnes sharply retorted that it was imperative, with the general election scheduled for August 23, to impress upon the Bulgarian people through the Voice of America that the democratic powers would not recognize any minority government that received its authority by means of rigged elections.[36]

Receiving no reply from the department, Barnes attempted to infuse a combative spirit in local democratic elements. But the Bulgarian minister of foreign affairs reminded him (as Yugoslav leaders in the 1930s had reminded Lane) that "when the big horses in the barnyard begin to kick and cavort it is only the poor little fleas [sic] who is injured." Barnes disapprovingly observed that the same argument was used when Germany dominated the country. The allusion to Germany was no rhetorical flourish. By the end of June, owing to the Russian troop build-up in the country, rumors bruited about that Moscow further intended to use Bulgaria as a stepping stone to seize the Dardanelles and to establish predominance in Turkey and the eastern Mediterranean. Barnes proposed that the United States act immediately to stem the growing belief in Bulgaria of Russia's overwhelming power. "If we are in the poker game of world affairs, and I assume we are," he wired on June 23, "then we should play the game to the best of our ability. I believe that we have more chips than any one at the table." Reflecting on his earlier service in France, he reminded the department that it was precisely this view of German invincibility that led Pierre Laval to cast his lot with Hitler. Confessing that some might regard his attitude as "unpardonable" on the eve of the Berlin Conference, Barnes nonetheless hoped that the department "can assure those of us who represent the United States here and elsewhere under similar conditions imposed by Russia that a strenuous effort will be made at that meeting to correct the situation responsible for the misconception of those in this part of the world who today see Russia sitting in the seat of world dictatorship." To persist in the "diplomacy of silence," he noted, was to demonstrate American "impotence" to the Bulgarian populace "as compared to the virility of Soviet Russia." In his view, "the war in Europe had not ceased but has developed into a new phase" in which "the old line up of Britain, the United States and Russia together against Germany has become Russia against Britain and the United States." This time, however, he hastened to add, the instruments of war were "ideas rather than men and arms."[37]

Barnes's protestations, along with those of Schoenfeld and Berry, served to reinforce Truman's and the department's opposition to the recognition of Hungary, Bulgaria, and Rumania. Considering Soviet domination of the Groza government, the Dimitrov case, and Communist control of key positions in Hungary, Durbrow argued in late spring, American recognition would be tantamount to "telling the world that they were really democratic governments." It would further imply "that the Soviet Union can run things to suit itself in all areas east of the Stettin-Trieste line." Along with Cannon and Thompson, he pointed out that the United States had "made too much of a fuss about a Democratic Government in Poland to through [sic] it all down the drain by this move." Just the same, as talks in Berlin were about to begin, Walworth Barbour, the portly Near Eastern and Balkan specialist assigned to the department after Yalta, considered it advisable, though himself outspoken, to keep Barnes on a short leash. Accordingly, Barnes was directed on July 17 not to communicate the American government's position on recognition to Bulgarian political leaders.[38]

American diplomats in Yugoslavia—Shantz, Fraleigh, and Ambassador Richard C. Patterson, the former NBC and RKO executive and a diplomatic tyro—reported similar distress signals in the spring and early summer of 1945. In contrast to the situation in Bulgaria and Rumania, however, the source of their consternation was not a Soviet-designated camarilla of Stalinites, but Tito, or *Stari,* "the old man," as he was known to his followers, a Communist with intensely nationalistic sentiments and objectives, who, as time would show, presented a formidable obstacle to the Soviet Union's policy of informal empire in Eastern Europe. But at this stage, insensible to the early ripplings of dissension within the Communist camp, diplomats viewed Tito as little more than a handmaiden of Soviet ideological expansionism. Consequently, they recommended increased American medical assistance to the Yugoslav people and a stepped-up cultural information program to counteract partisan propaganda.[39]

Preoccupied with the Polish question, the San Francisco Conference, and plans for the Berlin meeting, diplomats in the department devoted little attention to internal Yugoslav affairs. When former ambassador Constantin Fotić wrote to Stettinius on April 20 requesting the exclusion of Yugoslavia from the San Francisco gathering until Tito implemented the Yalta declaration, Cannon simply advised Matthews and Dunn to ignore the letter. Belgrade's territorial aims, however, prompted a different reaction. As early as January, Huston and Hohenthal had expressed opposition to a possible Yugoslav-Bulgarian Union for fear that it would likely invite Soviet influence and, a fortiori, domination of the other Balkan countries. Yugoslav ambitions in the northeastern Italian province of Venezia-Giulia proved still more disconcerting. To careerists in Washington, Tito's intractable refusal to place partisan forces in Trieste and Pola under allied command impugned the principle of postwar territorial settlements by peaceful and orderly means and threatened to provoke an outburst from Italo-Americans; more significantly, since, in Matthews's opinion, Tito's action was doubtless "based on Russian guidance," it established a potentially dangerous Soviet presence in the area. For Yugoslavia to serve as a pawn of Moscow's strategy in southeastern Europe was bad enough, but to establish a foothold for Soviet ideological expansionism in Italy, which fell militarily in the Anglo-American sphere, was worse yet.

While officials in the War Department, who were less than impressed with Italy's military performance, were reluctant to make a *cause célèbre* of the situation in Venezia-Giulia, Foreign Service officers considered it crucial for the postwar political order they envisioned to protect Italy's territorial integrity. "It is not a question of taking sides in a dispute between Italy and Yugoslavia, or of becoming involved in internal Balkan politics," explained Cannon. "The problem is essentially one of deciding whether we are going to permit the Soviet Government to operate through its satellite Yugoslavia in the Mediterranean theatre, to set up whatever states and boundaries look best for the future of the USSR." If Tito and, by incrimination, the Soviet Union were to succeed in Italy, he went on, the United States would be faced with similar claims, with equally sinister implications, in the Carinthian and Styrian sections of Austria, the Banat region in Hungary and Greek Macedonia, including Salonika. The fact that each of these areas had been contested by Yugoslavia since World War I, long before Tito, the Soviet Union, and communism gave them contemporary importance, was overlooked. In any event, intent on upholding the principle of peaceful territorial settlements, and thereby preventing the "land grabbing" tactics reminiscent of Hitler and Japan, on May 10 Reber successfully recommended the issuance of instructions to allied headquarters in Venezia-Giulia "to establish effective control even if it becomes necessary to use the overwhelming force of Allied military strength." Several days later, at the urgence of Dunn and Thompson, Stettinius conveyed his government's profound distress over the matter to Šubašić. The combined effect of these representations, similar statements from the British Foreign Office, and the forceful allied posture in Venezia-Giulia finally led Tito at the end of the month to withdraw his forces from the disputed zone.[40]

Although Tito's recalcitrance left a residue of bad feelings in the State Department, once the tense situation had ended, career diplomats resumed their sanguine outlook for the postwar world. Thus even as Cannon told Truman that the Yugoslav regime appeared "thoroughly totalitarian," he remained hopeful that it would take steps to align itself "with the principles for which the United Nations have solemnly adopted for their guidance in the war and in the establishment of the peace." These steps, the improvement of political conditions in Yugoslavia, Dunn and Thompson reminded Šubašić, would have to precede Belgrade's requests for American economic assistance.[41]

For Americans assigned to the Belgrade embassy, however, the seeds of ill will already planted sprouted more bitter fruit of suspicion and resentment. Having received word early in June of Belgrade's intention to pack AVNOJ with Communist members, Shantz observed that the "obvious object of the Communist Party, which behind the screen of the National Liberation Front, is in control of the Government, is to enact laws which will enable it to consolidate its control and at the same time make it appear to the western world that it had done this through 'free elections.'" Later in the month, still smarting from Yugoslav Vice Premier Edvard Kardelj's remark that his country sought "the political backing of Russia" and "the economic backing of the United States," he informed a Soviet diplomat in Belgrade that Yugoslavia "was heading straight towards Soviet Russia and a totalitarian economy." Patterson's and Fraleigh's hopes for postwar cooperation with Tito and his Soviet mullah in the spirit of the Atlantic Charter and Yalta were also fast vanishing. While Belgrade officials, they wrote Washington, unctuously promised democracy and free enterprise, they were simultaneously attacking private business and encouraging the secret police [OZNA] to terrorize "the prosperous classes." Further persuaded by the prewar Yugoslav elite—such as Šubašić, Milan Grol, and former minister of justice Lazar Marković—of Soviet-Yugoslav intentions to communize the country, Shantz cabled on July 14, "I am convinced there is no hope of free democracy here and that new [AVNOJ] laws will be window dressing for [a] totalitarian communist regime." In his view, the Berlin Conference represented "perhaps a last opportunity for the great powers, especially ourselves and the British, to manifest our support for the principles for which Grol and a few others in government are still fighting" and to arrest the oppressive conditions "in which we would seem to have a responsibility to the people."[42]

Disturbed by the growing entrenchment of Russian power in the Balkans, career officers in Moscow likewise concluded that the diplomacy of silence would not conduce to the realization of American postwar objectives. But they also believed that the rhetoric of confrontation was an ineffective tactic to employ with the Kremlin. Whereas Barnes, Berry, and Shantz, influenced by the particularistic effect of Soviet actions and the cries of local "democratic leaders," considered the Russians an ideological threat to American values and ideals, they perceived them from their global vantage point in Moscow as a geopolitical rival in the traditional game of power politics. Instead of advocating a more forceful defense of the Atlantic Charter–Yalta principles, the Moscow embassy counselled the secretary of state to adopt a posture coeval with the military realities of Europe.

Deeper into the stygian mood that had fallen upon him after Yalta,

Kennan vainly attempted to impress upon the department that the Roosevelt administration and the public had allowed themselves to be seduced by the chimera of Soviet postwar collaboration, "which has no substance except in our wishful thinking," when it was clear that the Kremlin would undertake no commitments without some political quid pro quo. Nonplussed by Berry's and Barnes's rage over Soviet control of the armistice commissions, particularly since the United States and Britain had assumed similar authority in Italy, he pointed out that American diplomats would continue "to be given the run around," while the Soviets proceeded to assert their control in Eastern Europe. When Matthews and Grew conveyed in April their dismay that Moscow had unilaterally established a provisional government in Soviet-occupied Austria, Kennan reacted with undisguised incredulity. "I assume that this communication is being made for the record," he stated, for it was "scarcely conceivable" that American protestations "would alone suffice to induce the Russians to withdraw support of this provisional regime, as long as they continue to find it to their liking." Russia's assurances of political non-interference that attended the mutual assistance pacts with the Baltic States in 1939 and the more recent manifesto of the Polish Committee of National Liberation, the Czech-Soviet pact, the Rumanian armistice, and the endorsement of the Georgiev government in Bulgaria amply demonstrated "the wisdom of judging pledges of democracy and independence in contemporary eastern and central Europe rather by their long-term interpretation and application than at their initial face value in the English translation."[43]

While allied soldiers bathed themselves in the friendship of a common victory, Kennan brooded to an unreceptive State Department that the Russians intended to strip eastern Germany of her assets just as they had raped the Balkan states. "In the end," he allowed, scoffing at Washington's proposed reparations commission, "it will come down to a simple horse trade. How much are we going to make available to the Russians from our zone, and what price are we going to demand for it?" He therefore advised Washington and London to express publicly that "we now consider ourselves free to dispose of German territory in the west to our Western Allies on similar conditions, without reference to the views of the Soviet Government." Rather than continue to assume indirect responsibility for policies inimical to American interests and ideals, Kennan advocated "the preservation of a realistic balance of strength" between the United States and Soviet Russia "and a realistic understanding of the mutual zones of vital interest." A division of Europe into spheres of influence, he noted, would far more "assure stability among the great powers" in the future than fantasies of intimate collaboration, which he judged at once unnecessary, impossible, and, given Moscow's atavistic urge to expand territorially, injudicious. Secondarily, mindful of the strength of Communist parties in Western Europe, he urged a stance of moral firmness to deny Moscow an ideological foothold beyond its sphere of interest.[44]

Kennan's colleagues in Moscow—Stevens, Page, and sinologist Davies—did not go so far as to propose a division of Europe. At this level of realpolitik, Kennan stood alone. Nevertheless, they supported the idea that geopolitical considerations made official policy, based as it was on the continued perception of ideological cooperation, impossible of attainment. It was clear to Stevens that the Soviets sought to consolidate politically their military position in Eastern Europe. He contended that efforts to negotiate with them for a new Polish government would only produce a facade for their dictatorial actions. Unlike Kennan, however, he had not disavowed the American government's universalistic postwar objectives in Eastern Europe. What he mainly foreswore was his government's flaccid bargaining attitude.[45]

Like the sovietologists in the embassy, and particularly Kennan, with whom he "had a feeling of kinship," Davies too viewed dimly the State Department's vision of U.S.-Soviet cooperation. He was especially unnerved when Major General Patrick J. Hurley, his former boss and bête noire at Chungking, visited Moscow in mid-April, waxing enthusiastic about Stalin's agreement to conclude a pact of friendship and alliance with the Chinese nationalists. Along with Kennan, Davies promptly conveyed to Harriman that Hurley's optimism was naive in light of Moscow's unquestionable desire to regain the former czarist possessions on the Asian mainland, control North China, and dominate the Chinese provinces along Russia's central Asian border. "It would be tragic if our natural anxiety for Russian support [in the Pacific war]," they said, "coupled with Stalin's cautious affability and his use of words, which mean all things to all people, were to lead us into an undue reliance on Russian aid or even Russian acquiescence in the achievement of our long-term objectives in China." Intent on disabusing the department of its roseate expectations, Davis told Bohlen that the Kremlin, regardless of its promises to Chiang, would continue to pursue a unilateral, revisionist policy in East Asia. In the first place, this policy militated against the possible emergence of a Chinese threat to its security. Second, it satisfied the need for bases (notably Dairen and Port Arthur) to accommodate an expanded Soviet navy and merchant marine. Finally, it permitted Moscow to take political advantage of the struggle in China, the likely postwar chaos in Japan, and the power vacuum in Korea. Given the dual nature of the Soviet system, he observed to Harriman, Moscow's political conciliation in Chungking would be parallelled by ideological infiltration in Yenan. But even if the Kremlin remained ideologically aloof, the Chinese communists would surely outlast Chiang, as they resisted him from 1927 to 1937 without foreign support "save huzzas and poor coaching from the comintern bleachers."[46]

While Davies's admonitions probably heightened Harriman's (and Bohlen's) anxieties about Soviet intentions in East Asia, they little altered his overall thinking on American policy toward Russia. Singlemindedly committed to his own lights, and with no great confidence in the Foreign Service anyway, Harriman, for all his apprehensions to the contrary, remained a "stern supporter" of the American government's liberal-internationalist blueprint for postwar cooperation. It was his view rather than that of the experts on his staff which resounded most audibly in the department as officials there prepared for the final wartime summit conference in Berlin.[47]

7. Between Cooperation and Confrontation

Although the breakdown of the Yalta agreements on Eastern Europe had pricked the bubble of optimism in the State Department, career diplomats expectantly awaited the impending talks in Berlin. For the past several weeks, they had served as an informal foreign-affairs advisory board to their neophyte president, cramming him full of information on U.S.-Soviet relations and introducing him to the arcane art of diplomacy. And many of them—Bohlen, Dunn, Matthews, Cannon, Thompson, Riddle-berger—joined Truman, Admiral Leahy, and James F. Byrnes, the former Supreme Court judge and South Carolina senator appointed secretary of state on July 3, at Potsdam, the Berlin suburb where the heads of state met from July 17 to August 2.

The atmosphere at Potsdam was at once relaxed and tense. Now that the European conflict was over, and the end of the Japanese war clearly in sight, the air of compulsion that overlaid the earlier allied conferences was lifted. By the same token, the absence of a common foe glaringly exposed the elemental differences in the foreign policies of the allied powers. For Churchill, who was the prime mover behind the parleys, which he likened to the Munich Conference of 1938, the Potsdam convocation represented the last chance to limit the advance of Soviet power and arrest "the descent of an iron curtain between us and everything to the eastward." Recognizing that Great Britain lacked the power and the United States the public will to contest militarily Soviet control of Eastern Europe, Stalin was primarily interested in German reparations, which would substantially defray the cost of postwar Soviet reconstruction and prevent the revitalization of a powerful German state. Prepared neither to pressure Moscow into moderating its tactics in Eastern Europe nor willing, as Roosevelt had been, to recognize a Soviet sphere of influence, Truman went to Berlin to reaffirm Washington's universalistic policy of postwar cooperation, which he was in no position to alter anyway, and to ensure Russian participation in the Pacific war.

The discussions that ensued proved frustrating and inconclusive. Recriminations between Stalin and Churchill over Poland, Greece, and Yugoslavia flowed freely. Truman, too, anxious to prove to Stalin, now adorned with the bombastic title of Generalissimo, that he was his own man, joined in the verbal jousting. Perturbed by Soviet violations of the

Yalta agreement on Eastern Europe, he opposed recognition of Bulgaria, Rumania, and Hungary and blocked Stalin's demand for a fixed sum of German reparations. Psychologically, notification on July 17 of the successful atomic bomb test at Alamagordo, New Mexico, stiffened Truman's resistance to Russian demands, although the president and his advisors fully realized that its use against Japan would not prevent Russian entry into the war.[1]

In the end, Potsdam did little to resolve allied differences. It was finally agreed that each power should satisfy its reparations claims against Germany from its respective zone of occupation; in addition, industrial equipment from the Anglo-American zones was to be exchanged for food and coal supplies from the Russian zone. To obtain this concession, Truman and newly elected British prime minister Clement Attlee, who replaced Churchill midway through the conference, acknowledged the boundary of western Poland—at German territorial expense—at the confluence of the Oder and Western Neisse Rivers. A Council of Foreign Ministers was established to draft peace treaties with Italy, Bulgaria, Rumania, Hungary, and Finland. However, it was left for each government to determine the conditions for recognition, a solution to which Churchill vainly objected as antithetical to the notion of joint allied responsibility. Moreover, references to the declaration on liberated Europe, which diplomats in the field had exhorted Washington to press upon the Soviets, were not included in the final communiqué. In practice, then, though not in principle, Truman was forced to accept the existence of a divided Europe. Withal, a proclamation of surrender drafted by the United States and Britain was issued to Japan. And, finally, Stalin renewed his promise to join the war in Asia.

As was the case at Teheran and Yalta, a host of lesser questions were simply deferred for resolution at later summit discussions. Now, however, as mutual trust was increasingly giving way to suspicion, time was fast running out for the alliance partners. No longer at the British mast, Churchill grumbled privately over the revised Polish border, just as he had gloated over news of the bomb. Stalin interpreted Anglo-American opposition to his reparations claims as callous insensitivity to the devastation wreaked on Russia by the Nazis. Harry Truman joylessly sailed back to the United States, dismayed by Soviet aggressiveness but still unwilling to abandon the goal of postwar cooperation.[2]

Foreign Service officers reacted ambivalently. On the one hand, they applauded Truman's decisiveness, his pertinacity, his unflagging defense of American principles. On the other hand, in marked contrast to Yalta, they were plagued by nagging doubts that the United States had conceded too much to the wily Stalin. Bohlen considered it a mistake for Truman, now armed with the atomic bomb, to have asked the Soviets to join in the war against Japan. Durbrow felt that the president had erred in accepting the Oder-Neisse boundary for western Poland. Dunn, on the other hand, took umbrage at Durbrow's remark, which he construed as an attempt to sabotage U.S.-Soviet cooperation. His rejoinder was instructive. Having participated in planning the postwar world, having nurtured the image of an ideologically reformed Soviet Union for the past two years, diplomats in the department expected some recompense, some payoff for their personal and professional investment in the future world of peace, prosperity, and harmony. In the twilight of Potsdam, however, their hopes for an amicable Soviet-American future—assailed by the odious police-state conditions in Eastern Europe and the increasingly vivid memory of a ruthless, ideologically predatory Russia—frayed to the breaking point.[3]

While Truman's gritty resolve to stand his ground with Stalin may have offered some solace for the frustrations and tattered hopes of diplomats assigned to Eastern Europe, it did nothing to change the conditions of their existence. Besieged by the undiminished shadow of the Soviet presence, oppressed by appeals for deliverance from the noncommunist political elites in the region who had not resigned themselves to their fate, and helpless to respond meaningfully to either problem, they could not escape the anxiety that their anticipated postwar world had crumbled.

In those countries where the Russians had not significantly exerted their presence, there still existed a shred of hope for the survival of the Atlantic Charter principles. Public repudiation of extremist elements by Social Democratic party chief Fierlinger and the optimistic statements of Beneš and other Prague officials kindled Klieforth's and Bruins's expectations of a democratic Czechoslovakia. Even more encouraging was the departure of all Soviet occupation forces on December 1. Similarly, in Albania Jacobs reported that Hoxha was enjoying widespread popular support and sincerely sought to inaugurate a new system of government dedicated "to the welfare of the common man." On August 15 Jacobs recommended recognition of the Tirana government under his previously stated conditions that it hold free elections and adhere to all diplomatic rights and privileges accorded under international law. Failure to recognize Hoxha, he warned department officials, would likely drive him into "a Soviet-Yugoslav combination."[4]

Offsetting these encouraging signs, however, were a number of disquieting developments. Klieforth observed that leftist elements in Czechoslovakia, their rhetoric of restraint notwithstanding, were intensifying their program of economic nationalization and intermittently intimidating and terrorizing the Czech people just as the Nazis had done in the late thirties. Moreover, Russia's absorption of Ruthenia in July suggested to embassy officials that the Soviets wished to establish a beachhead to undermine the political and economic reconstruction of Hungary. Meanwhile, Jacobs was dismayed by the Southern European division's position obligating Tirana to honor its prewar treaty obligations as a precondition to recognition, especially since Britain and Russia had already extended unconditional recognition. Given the overwhelming endorsement of Hoxha in the December 1 national election, which was conducted in "an orderly manner without evidence of intimidation," and the Albanian leader's refusal to discuss the treaty question prior to the establishment of diplomatic relations, Jacobs urged the department to issue a new note which "more reassuringly" stated its views. Likewise, Bruins admonished Washington to provide Czech moderates with some indication "that the western powers will not abandon them to the extremists or Soviet influence."[5]

Elsewhere in east Central Europe and the Balkans the post-Potsdam mood was more somber. As the combination of inequitable land reform, nationalization of industry, Russian expropriations of property, reparations payments, and the cost of supporting Red Army troops brought the Hungarian economy to its knees, Schoenfeld set adrift his hopes for U.S.-Soviet cooperation. At the same time, he grew more scornful of Budapest's passivity, which he likened to its behavior with the Nazis. Following the government's trade agreement with the USSR in August, he requested permission to air his disapproval in the control commission. Although diplomats in the department reacted with inquietude to the Soviet-Hungarian agreement, as they had to the Soviet-Rumanian pact, both of which ensured virtual economic domination by Moscow and threatened to vitiate the postwar program of unrestricted world trade, they felt it more appropriate to reserve comment for government-level discussions among the tripartite powers. They maintained this posture even after Moscow refused talks, notifying Schoenfeld secretly that private measures to assist Hungary were under consideration. Meanwhile, the Russians ignored Hungarian appeals to moderate their policies because, in Schoenfeld's disconsolate view, "those policies are deliberate."[6]

Just as depressed by the state of Hungarian political affairs, Schoenfeld told the department that the threat of Red Army intervention and the pusillanimous conduct of Hungarian politicians made free elections a virtual impossibility. But Dunn, Reber, Thompson, and Matthews replied that the department was prepared to consult with Britain and Russia in accordance with the Crimea agreement only if Hungary requested assistance or if it seemed clear that free elections would not occur. Wishing to remain removed from internal Magyar politics, they further directed Schoenfeld to refrain from divulging these views to Hungarian leaders. Chagrined by the department's response, Schoenfeld urged the Hungarians to assert their rights in the spirit of the Magna Carta and the Yalta agreement, while he simultaneously exhorted Washington to participate "in the political stabilization of Hungary along democratic lines," or face further Communist intrusion in Magyar society. "I presume the Department does not agree with Gascoigne who goes so far as to state that the Yalta declaration is out of date."[7]

To be sure, Byrnes and the team of Foreign Service officers who left for London in early September to attend the first foreign ministers conference had not abandoned the Yalta declaration. Moreover, now that the United States was in a position to flex atomic muscles, the secretary of state decided to contest more forcefully Russia's imposition of unrepresentative regimes in Eastern Europe. Although Byrnes at no time confronted Molotov with the threat of atomic reprisal, he believed that the very possession of the bomb, which symbolized the preeminent power of the United States, would induce the Russian to be more receptive to American demands in the liberated states of Eastern Europe. But Molotov's Moloch-like demeanor and his refusal to be intimidated by the bomb unnerved Byrnes. The Soviet foreign minister realized all too well that the United States would not provoke an atomic showdown over Eastern Europe. Days of bitter accusations followed. Fearful that his aggressive rhetoric had alienated the Russians, the unpredictable Byrnes, who shared Roosevelt's improvisional style of diplomacy, determined to break the impasse by establishing some accommodation with the Soviets. Largely due to pressure from Dunn, who had been assigned, much to the displeasure of liberals within and without the department, as the permanent American representative on the Council of Foreign Ministers, he decided to moderate his tactics and recognize the provisional government of Hungary pending free elections.[8]

Schoenfeld reacted pessimistically when he received Cannon's announcement of the decision. "I cannot see that we lost anything by recognizing [the] present Provisional Government in Hungary," he wired back, "but I remain skeptical of [the] value of any pledge to be given by [the] Provisional Government as to point (c) of [the] Crimea declaration [stipulating free elections]." Much to his surprise, however, municipal elections in Budapest, held early in October, were freely conducted. More importantly, the Smallholders, the major Hungarian peasant party, won a majority vote. En route to Moscow from the London conference, Harriman stopped off in Budapest and found Schoenfeld and General Key "much bucked up." Indeed, Schoenfeld now looked forward to "free and unfettered" national elections, especially after Baron Zoltán Tildy, leader of the Smallholders, refused to run a common slate with the Social Democrats and the Communists. The results of the national election of November 4 returned an even larger Smallholder majority. Tildy was elected president of the new coalition government, which included Ferenc Nagy of the Smallholders as premier and Matthias Rákosi, general secretary of the Communist party, as vice premier.[9]

Despite this unexpectedly favorable outcome, Schoenfeld once again lapsed into gloom. The growing Communist strength in labor circles, Communist control of the ministry of interior, and Voroshilov's aversion to reducing the size of occupation forces made it difficult to exult over the democratic victory. Affected as well by the recent memory of Nazi depradations, the recollection of Russian behavior during the interwar years, and the indelible imprint of American values and beliefs on his thinking, by now he had completely altered his perceptions of the Soviet Union. On November 23 he wrote that there "appears to be conclusive evidence that notwithstanding all endeavors during the last six months, there has never been [the] slightest possibility that [the] three Allies could participate here on [an] equal basis in any matters the Soviets believe important." In the end, he feared, world opinion would likely place partial blame on the United States for "a lack of aggressive foreign policy." Yet, save for repeated urging of expanded American economic aid, he recommended neither a realistic accommodation to Soviet influence in Eastern Europe nor military confrontation; by his reckoning, both alternatives would be antithetical to American liberal-internationalist objectives.[10]

Across the Carpathians in Poland, the same dreary montage of wartime devastation and human suffering unfolded before Lane. Partly because of his argumentative personality, and partly because the prospects for democracy in Poland were almost hopeless, Lane, reproducing his stormy response to foreign developments in the thirties, reacted far more intensely than Schoenfeld to Soviet actions. Distressed by the breakdown of talks on the Moscow Commission, the arrest of the sixteen Polish leaders, and the State Department's unwillingness to demand Moscow's compliance with its agreement on Poland, he had admonished Stettinius and Grew in the spring to defend American principles in Eastern Europe. "Appeasement or apparent appeasement can be as dangerous to United States interests in 1945 as it actually was in 1940 and 1941." When he arrived in Warsaw on July 31, the recollections of an intoxicatingly gay city which cascaded on his mind failed to obscure the chilling sight of ragged, sickly people huddled together outside his hotel and little children orphaned by war whose amputated limbs made them smaller still. Moved by this doleful scene, Lane determined to protest vigorously further violations of American rights, regardless of Warsaw's feelings or Washington's instructions. Characterized by *Life* shortly before his departure as an undistinguished diplomat "who has kept himself out of trouble," he was really St. George about to meet the dragon of Soviet communism.[11]

During the weeks that followed, Lane tirelessly enunciated the American doxology of free elections and free markets to Polish officials. But the Warsaw government was indifferent to his protestations. So, it seemed, was the State Department. "Britain has greatly lost prestige here as [a] result of Munich and [the] failure to live up to [her] pledge to Poland in 1939," he wired on August 18. "It would be tragic for the United States to be put in such a position in a country where our prestige has always been of the highest." Intent on gaining Washington's ear, Lane flew to London in September, where he elaborated on the situation to Byrnes and Dunn. While receiving little encouragement, he was nonetheless relieved to have escaped "the mental strain of continued surveillance and the never-ending fear lest some of our political friends be imprisoned because they had the temerity to speak to us." Upon his return to Warsaw, Lane and Gerald Keith, who loyally served as counsellor of embassy in Warsaw as he had in Bogotà, continued to reproach Polish officials. Lane caustically reminded President Boleslaw Bierut that neither he nor the American people could entertain Warsaw's request for long-term credits of $500 million in light of the repressive political conditions in the country. Recent speeches of Vice President Wladislaw Gomulka, he wrote on October 27, made it transparently clear that the Soviets intended to submit a single list of candidates to the electorate, eliminate Mikolajczyk, and increase their political control in flagrant abuse of the Yalta agreement. Moreover, since Warsaw's restrictive commercial agreement with the Soviet Union con-travened America's policy of multilateral trade, he called for a credit ban and a freeze on all current transactions with Poland, just as the United States had done in the Baltic States and Yugoslavia in 1941–41. "I realize that our policy in Poland must be in harmony with that carried out by us in other areas in which the Soviet Government is likewise exerting its in-fluence," he cabled Washington, but further delay would only make it more difficult "to insist on our point of view."[12]

Although distressed by the "economic blackout" in Poland, and by Moscow's apparent intention to control economically all of Europe east of the Stettin-Trieste line, Bohlen, Matthews, and Durbrow refused to tie political strings to American financial aid. Influenced by the visit of Mikolajczyk, who argued that Washington's assistance would help to ensure Polish independence, they proposed a modest reconstruction credit of $25 million for the purchase of war surplus materials. "I agree fully with the Department that, in general, economic rather than political considerations should control the granting of Export-Import credits to foreign governments," Lane replied on November 13. But "if we relax in our resistance, and certainly the extension of a credit would be inter-preted as such, against the despotic rule which is now being perpetrated here we shall not succeed in fulfilling our publicly expressed policy: the maintenance of a strong, free and independent Poland."[13]

While the department deliberated, conditions inside Poland worsened. Political arrests and indiscriminate raping and looting by Soviet troops intensified. Angered by British Ambassador Victor Cavendish-Bentinck's "acquiescence" to the planned exclusion of National Democratic and Social Democratic candidates from the elections, Lane challenged Washington to rise up in protest or "be faced with the same charge which is now being made against the Polish government of not permitting democratic parties to participate in the elections." Durbrow thought this course of action ill-advised, as he did Lane's desire to present his views in Washington the following spring. However, he did inform the embattled ambassador that the department had decided against any long-term financial arrangements beyond the $25 million reconstruction loan. In the meantime, Lane persevered in his personal war with Polish officials, who accused him, as had Nicaraguan leaders in the thirties, of interfering in their internal affairs. Durbrow offered encouragement, noting that "we shall keep up the good fight from our end." But Lane no longer embraced any illusions as to the ultimate fate of Poland.[14]

Lane's hardening image of U.S.-Soviet confrontation mirrored the perceptions of his fellow diplomats in the Balkans as 1945 drew to an end. King Michael's thrice-spurned requests for Groza's resignation convinced Melbourne in the weeks following Potsdam that the Communist regime "will continue by default and expressed American political desires for Rumania will be buried beneath [the] Soviet initiative." In an effort to stave off collapse of the monarchy, he proposed the establishment of a technician government, which would include nominal representation of the four main political parties under a program prescribed by the armistice powers, and Washington's issuance of a public statement reiterating its aims in Rumania. Desiring to avoid actions in the wake of Potsdam that might further erode allied relations, the department instructed Melbourne temporarily to refrain from further contact with Rumanian political leaders. "The principle of [the] United States Government," Dunn and Matthews agreed, was "to keep the road open to a solution of [the] Rumanian political crisis which will be acceptable to all three Allied Governments. We hope no action will be taken which might seem to give ground for Soviet suspicion that [the] crisis was brought about by 'Anglo-American intervention.'"[15]

Melbourne and Berry responded impatiently to Washington's directive. With the press, radio, police, courts, and army controlled by the Communists, King Michael and the democratic parties were fighting for their political lives, Melbourne argued. To prevent further erosion of the King's position, rigged elections, Communist dictatorship, and future conflict in the Balkans, he implored the department to consult immediately with Britain and Russia or suffer "the disastrous undermining of our moral position in this country." Berry urged the department to lift its ban on his mission's activities and publicly repudiate the "colossal distortions" of the facts by Soviet officials. "I fear the continuation of our present tactics will assist in bringing about the defeat of the policies to which the American Government has publicly adhered."[16]

Struggling to reconcile the reality of his existence with American ideals, Berry made a final, futile appeal to Washington, in anticipation of the Moscow conference of foreign ministers, to bring "direct pressure" on the Soviet government, while simultaneously "preserving its attitude of absolute inflexibility" in Rumania. "A backdown from the principles which were enumerated at Yalta and upon which we have stood since, such as is suggested by British under [sic] Secretary Sargent," he wired on December 11, "would net us little in Rumania except the contempt of a vast majority of the Rumanian people." Although the British had wearied of Maniu's "negative maneuvering," he was still "the unquestioned symbol of Rumanian democracy," Berry pointed out. But the best that could be obtained at Moscow was an agreement to add two representatives from the Liberal and Peasant parties to the Rumanian government. Though this somewhat eased the psychological strain of Foreign Service officers in Bucharest, it did not alleviate their disconsolation that the Communists would continue to control the country.[17]

Distressed by the State Department's reluctance to censure more forthrightly Soviet excesses in Bulgaria, as well as by its failure to keep him informed, Barnes too plunged deeper into despair after Potsdam. "Not a day goes by that I do not envy my British colleague because of the prompt responses he receives from his Government," he complained, "while in my own case weeks go by with little or nothing to rely on except local possibilities for temporization." Certain that Communist terrorism and the recently enacted electoral law would produce a "hitlerian plebiscite" in the August 26 elections, Barnes nonetheless exhorted the department to impress upon Moscow its opposition to the political control exercised in Bulgaria by the Communists and their Agrarian, Socialist, and Zveno "stooges," including Prime Minister Kimon Georgiev, "a Simon pure totalitarian." The only difference between the present regime and its predecessor, he groused, was "merely that [the] masters of today look to Moscow for guidance and inspiration instead of to Berlin." Although now aware that Bulgarian elections would not result in a democratic government, Dunn advised Barnes "not to take a stand in opposition to the electoral law specifically." On August 11 Barbour drafted a cable to Barnes, initialled by Reber, Matthews, Bohlen, Dunn, and Durbrow, directing him to restate to Sofia the principles that determined America's recognition policy.[18]

Frustrated by this response, Barnes and British representative

Houstoun-Boswall instructed their respective military counterparts on the allied control commission to express their joint desire for a postponement of the proposed elections. The Soviets surprisingly complied. Delighted by this outcome, which he believed severely damaged Communist prestige, Barnes was puzzled by the reprimand he received from department officials, who, no less pleased by the "moral effect" of his *démarche,* cautioned him to consult with Washington before making further unauthorized proposals on the armistice commission. Barnes asserted that unless the United States continued to make her influence felt, "the term 'liberated countries' can in the end evoke only derision in eastern and southeastern Europe." In this agitated frame of mind he left for the London foreign ministers meeting "to assure those principles for which we have fought two wars on the continent of Europe and one in the Pacific" would be preserved in Bulgaria. In his absence Milton Rewinkel, equally bereft of hope for U.S.-Soviet ideological cooperation, informed Washington that any concessions offered by the Russians in London would be "mere dust deliberately thrown in [the] eyes of the western Democracies." Moscow's course—"complete control and communization of Bulgaria within the Soviet orbit"—was perfectly visible to him. As for the puppet Fatherland Front government, it was determined by all the force and chicanery employed by "the Fascist dictatorships" to impose "a regimentation of control and obedience which even Hitler's Nazi Party might have envied."[19]

Barnes was hardly consoled by the stalled foreign ministers meetings in London. In contrast to Barbour, Reber, Thompson, and others in the department, who felt it almost inconceivable that the Kremlin desired to perpetuate conditions in Bulgaria that repudiated the Yalta agreement, he became more sullen. The "election parody" of November 18, as he called it, solidified the position of the Fatherland Front, a "'new aristocracy,'" in his words, "drunk with power and carousing in a manner that those who went before them, bad as they were, did not dream of indulging themselves." So-called moderate elements, such as Kimon Georgiev, "will prove not only willing tools" of the government, he predicted, but will turn out to be star players on [the] Communist side." The December foreign ministers' gathering in Moscow was, therefore, the last chance to apply a "cold shower" to the activities of the Fatherland Front. "All eyes in Bulgaria today are turned to Moscow," Barnes wrote on December 13. The hopes of the Balkan peoples "for the realization of the larger objectives of [the] Second World war" rested with Byrnes and Bevin, "the spokesmen for world democratic leadership." Heedless of references to the Atlantic Charter and the Yalta declaration, Molotov consented only to give "friendly advice" to the Bulgarian parliament.[20]

Depressed by the perfunctory attention given Yugoslavia at Potsdam by

Truman and Byrnes, Shantz and Fraleigh languished in the same desolate environment as their colleagues in Rumania and Bulgaria. With the spectre of state confiscation of private property hanging over Yugoslavia, "all prospects [for the survival of individual enterprise] are filled with reasons for mental depression," Shantz noted. Unless a "strong moral example from the world of international commerce should intervene," the eradication of free trade seemed a virtual certainty. Given press censorship, the disfranchisement of half the electorate under the new electoral law, and the ubiquitous presence of OZNA agents and spies, who created a pervasive sense of fear throughout the country not unlike that which Shantz had perceived in Russia after the Kirov assassination in 1934, he considered it sheer folly to expect the forthcoming elections to improve political conditions. The National Front government and its "ruthless totalitarian police regime" was simply a "tool" of the Central Committee of the Communist party; and Tito was its local gauleiter. Moreover, traditional political passivity on the part of both Serbs and Croatians and the timorousness of Šubašić, who, as a Croatian, was an unacceptable political symbol to the Serbs, were unlikely to produce manifestations of public discontent. Consequently, he admonished the State Department to postpone the November 11 elections. "We here can see nothing we can do for the unfortunate people of Yugoslavia, except to use moral force to lighten [the] tyranny of the regime," he explained. The United States had an "obligation to make our position clear to [the] world and to attempt to redress [the] harm we have done by our part in establishing Tito in power." Thus, in late September, he asked the department to acknowledge publicly the urgency of a new provisional government and recommended the withdrawal of American recognition in case Tito objected. If this government also turned out to be a dictatorship, "it would at least be [an] indigenous one set up in line with [the] long-standing traditions under which the Yugoslav people lived before [the] war" in what Shantz thought was "relative happiness."[21]

Throughout this period of post-Potsdam depression, the department maintained minimal communications with the Belgrade embassy. Late in August, therefore, Ambassador Patterson went to Washington, where he received Truman's approval for an undefined "two-fisted policy" in Yugoslavia, including a preposterous plan to bring Tito to the United States "for a month of indoctrination," and Dunn's authorization to make local speeches, if necessary, in support of the Yalta declaration. Fearing that Patterson may have misunderstood the intent of these sanctions, careerists in Washington, skeptical as always of political appointees, thought it prudent to require him to consult with the department before taking any action. As one diplomat undiplomatically put it, "I wouldn't have given that idiot the discretion to do anything!" More important, however, was their concern that an injudicious remark might impede implementation of the Tito-Šubašić agreement. Despite appeals from the Belgrade embassy for a firmer policy, they still adhered to the belief that the policy of noninvolvement offered the best means to achieve the Atlantic Charter goals. Citing local opposition to Tito, the recently announced amnesty decree of the Yugoslav government, and its stated intention to end censorship as examples, Cannon, Huston, and Barbour concluded "that a sufficient field for maneuver still exists for the Yugoslavs to work out their transition to democratic government without United States or British intervention."[22]

By October, however, following the resignation of Šubašić from the provisional government and pressure from Serbian-Americans and former Yugoslav diplomats in the United States, career officers in the department had reevaluated their position. With the concurrence of Barbour, Matthews, Huston, Thompson, and Bohlen, parallel Anglo-American notes were transmitted to Belgrade urging postponement of the scheduled elections. Nevertheless, single-list elections were conducted. While embassy accounts indicated that the voting was outwardly free and unfettered, Reber told Byrnes that the preelection methods of intimidation were "repugnant to our conception of freedom." In the meantime, he and his fellow officers, pledged to uphold the Atlantic Charter and the Yalta declaration, found it difficult to accept the reality that Tito had obtained majority support. Even as they recognized the new Yugoslav republic in mid-December, they directed the embassy to inform Belgrade that American recognition "should not be interpreted as implying approval of policies of the regime, its methods of assuming control or its failure to implement the guarantees of personal freedom promised to its people." At the same time, they hoped that the "individualism" of the Serbian people would eventually produce conditions to bring about the political and economic relations "which we on our part most urgently desire to see." However, diplomats in Belgrade, who intimately experienced the impoverishment of American principles, could no longer take refuge in the diplomacy of silence.[23]

Meanwhile, in Moscow, Kennan also voiced concern about the threat of Soviet ideological exapnsionism. Shortly before Potsdam he had informed the department that the Comintern continued to function through a polycentric system in Paris, Cuba, Mexico, and Yenan, but he interpreted the spread of Soviet ideology as a tactic to achieve the old czarist strategic objective of geopolitical expansion. He believed that neither moral suasion, such as Washington advocated, nor the ideological remonstrations of diplomats in Eastern Europe would divert the course of Soviet aims. In his view, postwar coexistence with Moscow could only be achieved by recognizing the division of Europe. To preserve the status quo, however, the United States had to prevent further Soviet incursions, both ideological and military, into the Anglo-American sphere. Thus he counselled the American government to retain exclusive possession of the atomic bomb. "There is nothing—I repeat nothing—in the history of the Soviet regime," he wrote, "which could justify us in assuming that the men who are now in power in Russia, or even those who have chances of assuming power within the foreseeable future, would hesitate for a moment to apply this power against us if by doing so they thought they might materially improve their own power position in the world." He further urged Washington to strengthen the foundations of democracy in the West and to cease its humiliating attempts, as evidenced at the Potsdam and London conferences, to maintain "the facade of tripartite unity," by employing "some fig leaves of democratic procedure to hide the nakedness of Stalinist dictatorship." For such efforts Kennan "had nothing but contempt."[24]

Unhappily for Kennan, who had considered resigning from the Foreign Service after Potsdam until dissuaded by Bohlen and Durbrow, his colleagues in the department—including the Soviet specialists among them—uniformly rejected his realpolitik prescription for the postwar world. Henderson, who dismissed spheres of influence as little more than a "Maginot Line concept," agreed with Durbrow and Kohler that it was tantamount to abandoning the hapless peoples of Eastern Europe, whom Kennan, with his Great Russian bias, regarded with condescension. Whether these people were foolhardy or courageous, Barbour noted, the United States had "a moral obligation to them." While one had to be realistic about the Soviets, Yost added, the department was "faced as well with the reality of what kind of world it would be without any effort toward cooperation."[25]

Isolated from the dismal developments in Eastern Europe, diplomats in the department reflexively paid homage to the Atlantic Charter–Yalta ideals. The United States was "committed to the fulfillment of the principles and responsibilities" contained in the Atlantic Charter and the Crimea Declaration," Huston pointed out in October. "These policies and principles are right and good, and they are endorsed by the American people; they accordingly should not, and need not, be changed." While conceding that relations between the United States and the Soviet Union had taken "a potentially dangerous course," Bohlen cautioned against any action which would further estrange the two powers and abort the United Nations Organization. Indicative of the diplomats' enduring attachment to ideological cooperation, Bohlen and Stevens told representatives of the National Academy of Science on December 7 that the department continued to encourage interchange between Soviet and American scientists. Operating on the assumption that neither Russia nor Britain wished to demonstrate to the Iranian government that its trust in the United Nations Security Council had been misplaced, Henderson and Durbrow directed the Moscow embassy to relay to the Kremlin the department's hope that allied troops would be withdrawn from Iran by the beginning of 1946. And Dunn, Durbrow, and Reber still embraced the notion that the Soviets would relax their economic hold on Rumania and Hungary.[26]

Concurrent with the diplomats' lingering hope of postwar cooperation in accord with American ideals was the mounting apprehension that Moscow had opted for a policy of unilateralism. In their judgment, the results of the Potsdam and London conferences, added to the reports from Foreign Service officers in the field, gave little indication that the Kremlin sought to relinquish its hold on Eastern Europe. "The chief immediate and practical problem we face in our dealings with the Soviet Union in so far as Europe is concerned," Bohlen stated in mid-October, "is the question of Soviet expansion in Eastern Europe." Like Huston, he did not object to some measure of Soviet ascendancy in Eastern Europe along the lines of American politico-strategic influence in Latin America. After all, the states on Russia's western flank had provided the springboard for Germany's invasion. He felt, however, that Moscow's actions had "directed towards the establishment of complete Soviet domination and control over all phases of the external and internal life" of the countries in the area. "A continuance or an accentuation of present Soviet policies in the areas under consideration are unacceptable with the principle of cooperation in world affairs to which the Soviet Union had adhered during the war," Bohlen noted. It could only lead to a division of the world into spheres of influence and the formation of armed camps in preparation for the next war. In view of the unilateral actions taken by the Soviets in Eastern Europe and, to a lesser degree, in Iran, China, and Korea, Durbrow instructed Harriman to inform Moscow that it had not "given any important concrete evidence" to confirm its professed desire for cooperation since Yalta. If the Kremlin persisted in this behavior and in promoting the activities of the technically dissolved Comintern, "we of course must take cognizance of it and act accordingly."[27]

Clearly, diplomats in the department were in a quandary. On one hand, they continued to adhere to the concept of a postwar world based on the precepts of the Atlantic Charter in which Russia too would share. On the other hand, Soviet actions in violation of the Atlantic Charter ideals had progressively reduced the likelihood of postwar cooperation between the two states. To acknowledge Russia's predominance in Eastern Europe, which was virtually exclusive in Rumania, Bulgaria, and Poland, would secure postwar cooperation at the expense of the Atlantic Charter; to uphold to the letter the inviolability of the Atlantic Charter would assuredly worsen U.S.-Soviet relations and nullify Roosevelt's "grand design" of world peace and security. Caught in a void between equally unpalatable alternatives, and unable to suppress the foreboding that the United States, impossible and absurd as it seemed, faced the threat of another war, they decided to reexamine American postwar policy.

By the end of 1945 the feelings of uncertainty and anxiety that permeated the State Department had also cast a gloom upon Harry Truman. On the morning of December 17, he complained to his press secretary, Charlie Ross, that the Soviet Union confronted the United States with a fait accompli in Eastern Europe. Just as they had seized Poland and Bulgaria, he stated, they would some day capture the Black Sea Straits.
"There's only one thing they understand," the president said.
"Divisions?" asked Ross.
Truman nodded. But he realized at the same time that the American public was opposed to further involvement in Europe.
"I don't know what we're going to do."[28]

8. Estranged Allies: The Residue of the Past

Diplomats in the department shared little of Secretary of State Byrnes's revived hopefulness at the conclusion of the Moscow foreign ministers conference. To be sure, the Russians approved the American plan to internationalize control of atomic energy, which included the formation of a United Nations Atomic Energy Commission to exchange scientific information and to establish an inspection system that would ensure the peaceful rather than destructive use of atomic materials. They also accepted a minor role in the occupation of Japan. But persisting differences over Eastern Europe cast in stark relief the frangible Yalta accords. Dejected by the Kremlin's unrelenting control in Bulgaria and Rumania, Matthews brooded that the two powers appeared on a conflict course. As far as Durbrow was concerned, Russia's "real intentions" were now unmistakably clear.[1]

Telegrams from Eastern Europe repeated the same dirge of the previous year, alternately lamenting Russia's parasitic exploitation of the Balkan and east Central European peoples and entreating Washington to defend against further transgressions of American principles and prestige by a combination of diplomatic firmness and democratic propaganda. More unsettling was the Kremlin's sudden refusal to remove Soviet military forces from Iran by March 2, the withdrawal date Churchill and Stalin had set at the Teheran Conference. Unnerved by the flow of Russian arms to the separatist Tudeh (Communist) party in the northern Iranian province of Azerbaijan, the Teheran government lodged a formal complaint on January 19 before the Security Council of the United Nations. Although Byrnes and Near Eastern chief Henderson thought it wiser for Washington to offer support through the United Nations rather than to become directly involved in Iranian affairs, Moscow's action, combined with ominous reports from Barnes and Kennan of similar Soviet designs in the eastern Mediterranean, Korea, Manchuria, and China, gave rise to the spectre of Soviet penetration into other regions of the world. A further source of strain was the intensifying criticism of the government's foreign policy by Republican members of Congress, particularly Michigan Senator Arthur Vandenberg, erstwhile champion of congressional bipartisanship, who angrily described Byrnes's agreement at Moscow to subordinate international control of atomic weapons to the disclosure of scientific information as "one more typical American 'give away.'"[2]

The superimposition of the Iranian situation and congressional rumblings for a more resolute foreign policy on the backdrop of Russia's unilateral actions in Eastern Europe magnified the image of an aggressive, expansionist Soviet Union in the thinking of diplomats in the department. Barbour, Thompson, Reber, Durbrow, and Matthews opposed credits to Yugoslavia and the USSR so long as they continued to violate their Atlantic Charter–Yalta obligations. And although plans went ahead to establish diplomatic relations with the Rumanian government, which had broadened its representation in line with the agreement reached at the Moscow foreign ministers conference, careerists were averse to recognition of the Sofia government until it similarly implemented the Moscow decisions. Despite their hardening view of the Soviets, diplomats did not propose a shift in American foreign policy. This apparent incongruity can be explained in part by the fact that the concept of international cooperation they embraced remained intact. In addition, bureaucratic inertia acted as a brake on alternative foreign-policy options. Institutionally conditioned to conform to prevailing policies rather than to consider new courses of action, Foreign Service officers were not accustomed to making major policy recommendations. Finally, the Kremlin had not unequivocally demonstrated its future intentions.[3]

Perceptions of Moscow's objectives had also taken a turn for the worse in other quarters of the government. Concerned about the possible threat the Soviets posed to American security, James V. Forrestal and Robert P. Patterson, respective secretaries of the navy and war, and Admiral Leahy had recommended to President Truman in the fall of 1945 the creation of a commission to examine this question in light of new and future weapons technology. With the establishment of the central intelligence group the following January, Truman set into motion the planning, development, and coordination of all federal foreign intelligence activities. While this decision hardly reflected expectations of cooperation on the part of the Truman administration, so long as there was a shred of doubt about Russia's long-term intentions, American policy remained unchanged. As was noted at the end of 1945 in a report from the State Department's research and analysis division (formerly part of the disbanded OSS), however persuasive the evidence seemed, it could not be conclusively determined that the Soviet Union had charted a fixed course of military and ideological expansion. Similarly, the most recent policy statement approved by Truman harked back to the fundamental principles of the Atlantic Charter. Thus, notwithstanding its growing mistrust of Moscow, the American government clung to the position that it was to mutual U.S.-

Soviet advantage "to collaborate in all decisions in the international relations field."[4]

Meanwhile, in Moscow, Kremlin officials were experiencing similar anxieties about American intentions. Having acceded to Anglo-American control in Western Europe and to American predominance in the Pacific, they felt that they had kept their end of the Yalta bargain. Thus they suspected that the collective criticism of their actions in Eastern Europe, the termination of Lend-Lease, Washington's delay in approving postwar reconstruction credits, and Anglo-American attempts to gain oil concessions in Iran might evidence a plan to isolate and weaken the Soviet state. Remembering the attempt to isolate Russia after World War I, and sensing a renewed threat to national security, they introduced a new five-year plan to rebuild the Soviet economy and strengthen the Red Army. To mobilize the masses, they girded the country for another ideological offensive. Britain and the United States were attempting to lull the working class into a false sense of security with the United Nations and the rhetoric of peace, warned Eugene Varga, a leading party theoretician, while they secretly oppressed Communists by fascist methods and otherwise prepared for war.[5]

Such tirades intensified during the first part of February as the Kremlin prepared for elections to the Supreme Soviet. Like the propaganda drive of the late 1930s, campaign speeches were surfeited with allusions to national unity, industrial self-sufficiency, the restoration of Soviet cultural life, the lingering threat of fascism, and the infallibility of Stalin's policies. The days of frenzied oratory finally climaxed on February 9, the day before the elections, when Stalin himself appeared before the Russian people. In part an apologia for Moscow's failure to prepare for the war against Germany, Stalin's speech aimed mainly to prepare an exhausted, war-battered people for another grueling period of sacrifice to reconstruct the Soviet economy. To mobilize national support, however, he stressed the superiority of the Soviet system and the incompatibility of communism and capitalism. Echoing the post–World War I Marxist-Leninist line, he noted the continuing threat of capitalist encirclement and implied that future wars were inevitable until communism triumphed over the world economic system.[6]

Coming at precisely the historical moment when American anxieties about Soviet postwar intentions had reached a fever pitch, Stalin's remarks were interpreted by diplomats in the department as the ultimate renunciation of the wartime alliance and the clarion call to communist orthodoxy and revolutionary expansionism. In Bohlen's view, the speech resuscitated "all the harsh and antagonistic elements of Bolshevism." Matthews felt that it constituted "the most important and authoritative guide" to postwar Soviet policy. "It will henceforth be the communist and fellow-traveler Bible throughout the world" and "should be given great weight in any plans which may be under consideration for extending credits or other forms of economic assistance to the Soviet Union," he averred. "It is felt that in view of the clear indication of the new Soviet line," Durbrow chimed in, "we should be most diligent to counteract Soviet propaganda and political moves which in all probability will be directed primarily at dividing the British and ourselves in order to give the Soviets a freer hand to attain their own aims." Undersecretary Acheson, Leahy, Forrestal, and Harriman all agreed with these dire pronouncements. Byrnes too fell into a state of depression. Henry Wallace, now secretary of commerce, and a few others contended that the speech was intended primarily for public consumption. But their voices were muffled in the crescendo of fear which emanated from Washington and gradually swept the country.[7]

Stalin's speech prodded harried officials in the State Department to consider new policy alternatives to meet the perceived Soviet ideological challenge. Bohlen enumerated three: a modus vivendi based on Anglo-Soviet-American spheres of influence; nationalistic expansionism on the part of the United States, including the acquisition of strategic bases and the exertion of economic pressure on Moscow; and the legal-rational resolution of problems in the United Nations, the policy of world cooperation. A balance-of-forces alternative was ruled out because it violated American principles, lacked domestic support, and merely postponed an eventual clash under conditions of revived Soviet strength. For essentially the same reasons, narrower, nationalistic considerations were also discarded. In Bohlen's view, the universalistic approach offered the best solution because it assured that divisions between the Soviets and other nations "would be on a clear moral issue and not as a result of conflict of national interests between the great powers which would tend to divide world opinion." But since it was precisely the demise of world cooperation along Atlantic Charter lines which necessitated the policy reevaluation in the first place, Bohlen's analysis had simply come full circle to where matters currently stood.[8]

Others in the department who had nurtured the ideal of world cooperation were similarly unable to find a solution which at once met the Soviet threat and ensured national security without sacrificing American principles. "Recent developments throughout the world are sufficiently disquieting to induce the belief that American policy toward the Soviet Union should be carefully considered," Stevens, now assistant chief of the Eastern European division, pointed out to Matthews and Durbrow. "It is open to serious question whether the present method of dealing with crises in Soviet-American relations can ever be effective in dealing with

Soviet actions which are quite obviously geared to a long-term overall plan." If the State Department failed to coordinate with the War and Navy Departments to develop a new approach, he warned, the government "may again become subject to the type of criticism which has been made of its conduct of pre-Pearl Harbor relations with Japan." Cannon anxiously "hope[d] that our policy-makers have now some plan, for use when the best moment comes, to face up to the cold realities which have been staring us in the face this last year."[9]

Mired in a policy vacuum, diplomats in the department waited for some analysis from Kennan, chargé d'affaires in Moscow since Harriman's departure, of what they called "the new Soviet line." But the cables they received merely summarized the reemphasis of Marxist-Leninist doctrine in the Kremlin's rhetoric. Weary of his unsuccessful attempts over the past eighteen months to "pluck people's sleeves, trying to make them understand the nature of the phenomenon with which we in the Moscow embassy were daily confronted," suffering a congeries of cold, fever, sinus, and toothache, and the more dyspeptic for all of that, Kennan had decided to keep his thoughts to himself. This time, however, given the gravity of the situation, the department actually solicited his counsel. Even Dunn joined Matthews in asking Durbrow to draft "a polite" telegram requesting Kennan's analysis. Durbrow's overture, along with a similar appeal from the Treasury Department to explain Moscow's unwillingness to join the World Bank and the International Monetary Fund, finally coaxed Kennan to respond. "They had asked for it," he was to write later in his memoirs. "Now, by God, they would have it."[10]

Working furiously, Kennan emptied himself of his musings and memories, frustrations and rages. Eight thousand words later, he had produced a systematic, articulate analysis of the Kremlin's objectives and postwar outlook, which he sent to the department on February 22. As he had in the past, Kennan pointed out that the Soviets perceived the world with the same insecurity as their Russian ancestors, who faced constant threats to their existence from fierce nomadic peoples. Given their xenophobic history, it was not surprising that they responded enthusiastically to Marxism, he noted, which justified their neurotic fear of the outside world, clothed in moral and intellectual respectability their underlying dictatorship, and vindicated "the steady advance of Russian nationalism, a centuries-old movement in which conceptions of offense and defense are inextricably confused." But in his zeal to present a comprehensive picture of the Kremlin's outlook on world affairs, because he too was affected by "the bandwagon reaction," as he called it, to the communist threat, and possibly as well to ensure this time that he gained the department's ear, Kennan buried his realistic assessment of Russian objectives in a bog of Marxist-Leninist ideology. The USSR, he said, continued to live in "antagonistic 'capitalist encirclement'" and to await the fateful Armageddon of socialism and capitalism. Although they were unlikely to provoke a military conflict with the West, he observed, the Soviets would seek to enhance their strength in the world while exploiting conflicts between the capitalist states, particularly Britain and the United States. On the official level, this meant intensive military and industrial development, autarchy in economic matters, influence-peddling in backward, dependent nations, and secretiveness about internal Russian affairs. Kennan pointed out that, on the subterranean plane, Moscow would attempt to infiltrate racial, religious, and nationalistic movements, labor unions, women's organizations, the liberal press, and any other association through which it could promote world communism.[11]

The implications of Kennan's message were ominous. Since Soviet objectives derived wholly from internal conditions, and since the Kremlin was "committed fanatically" to the belief that no modus vivendi with the United States was possible, the American govenrment could do nothing to diminish Soviet hostility. In Kennan's view, Washington could only hope to contain Soviet expansionism by maintaining sufficient force (presumably military and moral) and demonstrating its willingness to use it, by enlightening the American public to the "malignant parasite" of world communism, and by presenting a democratic example for other nations to follow.

Telegram number 511 from Moscow rocked the State Department. "Magnificent!" Matthews gushed, the best Kennan had ever done. It "hits the nail on the head," Henderson added. For Kohler it dashed any lingering hope of U.S.-Soviet cooperation. Acheson called it "truly remarkable." Byrnes sent a message of commendation. William Benton, assistant secretary of state for public affairs, offered his congratulations and a job in the department. The telegram reverberated as well in other departments of the government. Secretary of the Navy Forrestal was so impressed that he had it reproduced and distributed to members of the Truman cabinet involved with foreign affairs and to upper-echelon officers in the military establishment.[12]

Until this time, Kennan's views had been dismissed as too abstract, impractical, and ethereal. Although everyone admired and respected his brilliance, Bohlen, Barbour, and others had agreed that "George's feet were 30 feet off the ground." But now that the department was floundering in its efforts to assess and respond to Soviet initiatives, his ideas assumed oracular significance. More importantly, they *encouraged* department officials to commit themselves to a new course of action. What shone through Kennan's exegesis to diplomats in the department, however, was not the image of realistic cooperation, which, considering his past endeavors to educate Washington officialdom, he ironically failed to stress; rather it was the image of ideological confrontation, which resonated their own perceptions, formed in the aftermath of the Bolshevik Revolution, developed in the socializing process of the Foreign Service, and reinforced, in varying degrees of durability, by the culture of their social experiences in the field during the interwar years and in the immediate postwar period. Ultimately, Kennan's analysis gave the lie to the department's efforts to fit the Russians into its Wilsonian concept of international relations, which had excluded them. By stressing Soviet containment, however, which on one level was a logical outgrowth of Wilsonianism, it went an important step further. Intrinsic to the notion of containment, of course, was the division of Europe into spheres of influence. Nevertheless, so long as diplomats perceived the Soviet Union more in the universalistic, moral terms of Wilsonianism than in the amoral and particularistic terms of power politics, they continued to anchor their opposition on the eternally viable principles of the Atlantic Charter.[13]

The American government's posture toward Russia noticeably hardened after the Stalin speech and Kennan's analysis. At his morning staff meeting on February 25, President Truman reportedly commented that "we were going to war with Russia or words to that effect." Three days later, partly because of a bristling Senate speech by Vandenberg, which demanded a vigorous defense of American principles and steadfast opposition to communist expansionism, Byrnes stated that the United States could no longer "stand aloof if force or the threat of force is used contrary to the purposes and principles of the [Atlantic] Charter." Dunn angrily wired from London, where the Council of Foreign Ministers continued efforts to conclude peace treaties with the former enemy states and to restore stability in Eastern Europe, "I don't suppose for a minute that the Soviet Union shares those objectives." On the contrary, they desired, in his view, "only puppet stooge governments in those countries."[14]

The emerging policy of confrontation received added confirmation on March 5 from Winston Churchill. While vacationing in the United States, the ex-prime minister delivered a speech at Fulton, Missouri, with the Truman administration's approval, which chillingly called attention to the "iron curtain" that had descended across Central and Eastern Europe and advocated what sounded like an Anglo-American alliance to inhibit Soviet expansion. Although a number of senators and sections of the American public viewed Churchill's speech as an attempt to lure the United States into pulling British chestnuts out of the fire in Europe, Acheson, Kohler, Durbrow, and others in the department glowed over the "get tough" approach with the Russians. At a dinner party the same evening, Bohlen scoffed at Henry Wallace's defense of Russia's capitalist-encirclement fears, noting that it was Russia rather than the

United States which was on the offensive. Kennan offered his plaudits for Churchill's speech from Moscow, scoring as he did the lukewarm response it received from the American public and, even more so, the criticism of British imperialism it provoked from Senators Claude Pepper, Harley Kilgore, and Glen Taylor. Congressional reaction was especially distressing to Kennan because it gave substance to Stalin's internal propaganda, which insidiously presented Moscow's refusal to remove its troops from Iran as a measure to preserve Soviet security. That the Fulton speech might well have exacerbated Stalin's suspicions of an Anglo-American combination directed against the Soviet Union was not mentioned.[15]

The presence of Soviet troops in Iran beyond the March 2 deadline for withdrawal, coupled with Churchill's timely address, proved similarly alarming to diplomats in the department. Likening Moscow's actions to German expansionism in Czechoslovakia during the late thirties, Henderson stated that he "was convinced that the Soviets were going into Iran with the intention of staying there and eventually working their way to the Persian Gulf." He further voiced the fear that this would place Moscow within easy reach of Middle Eastern oil. More important than power considerations, however, Soviet moves in Iran represented a violation of American, hence United Nations, principles. As a result of these views, the department issued a stern note to Moscow on March 6 demanding the removal of all Soviet troops. At the same time, precautions were taken to avoid the impression that the United States had overtly interfered in Iranian affairs. On March 8 Bohlen directed Ambassador Wallace Murray to remind the Shah that the American government's note was in response to a request from Prime Minister Ahmed es-Sultaneh Qavam, and that it would like to be informed whether Iran planned to bring the question before the Security Council.[16]

While the matter hung in the balance, the American embassy in Iran informed worried department officials of a Soviet troop build-up in the vicinity of Teheran directed toward Turkey and Iraq. Kennan's telegrams from Moscow, which presented a decidedly realpolitik orientation this time, aggravated the department's disquietude. "The USSR aims not only at acquiring [a] privileged position in northern Iran," he wrote in mid-March, "but at [the] virtual subjugation, penetration and domination of [the] entire country, and Bahrein and Kuwait as well, with the eventual denial of the resources of those territories to [the] western nations." Furthermore, he went on, the Kremlin was attempting to undermine the British Empire in India in "instinctive" pursuit of "ultimate political domination of [the] entire Asiatic mainland." As a consequence, he reviled the idealistic campaign undertaken by liberals such as journalist Walter Lippmann and Henry Wallace to convince Moscow of American good faith. This "reflects a serious misunderstanding about Soviet realities," he contended. Efforts of the United States to lessen Soviet suspicions required "nothing short of complete disarmament, delivery of our air and naval forces to Russia and [the] resigning of [the] powers of government to American communists." Even then, he cynically added, "Moscow would smell a trap and would continue to harbor most baleful misgivings."[17]

Finally, on March 25 Teheran decided to submit its dispute with Moscow to the United Nations. Although the Russians objected, the Iranian government, with the strong backing of the United States, refused to alter its decision. When the Security Council voted to include the issue on its agenda, Soviet representative Andrei Gromyko petulantly stalked out of the Council chamber. A week later, however, Moscow did agree to remove its troops and to recognize Iranian sovereignty in Azerbaijan.

The contretemps over Iran had simultaneously reinforced Washington's "get tough" policy and underscored the importance of Kennan's rationale for Soviet actions. Based on Kennan's "exhaustive and excellent analysis," Bohlen had stated on March 13, "there was no need to examine further the motives or the reasons for present Soviet policy." The United States was confronted with "an expanding totalitarian state" committed to the irreconcilability of the Soviet and non-Soviet camps. In those countries contiguous to Russia, this policy was implemented by force or the threat of force. Elsewhere, it was conducted through the medium of communist parties and front organizations. In the first instance, Bohlen proposed that the United States, fortified by the "unassailable platform" of the United Nations, "should use every method at its disposal" to check the Soviets if faced "with another wave of progressive aggression." "The Soviet Government should not be misled," he stated, as were Germany and Japan, "into believing that the U.S. is divided, weak, or unwilling to face its responsibilities." As for the surreptitious communist offensive, he recommended "a positive program designated to demonstrate to the peoples of these countries that the non-Soviet system offers more to them than the false promises of Communism." Later in the month, Bohlen, Admiral Forrest Sherman, deputy chief of naval operations, and General Deane summarized Kennan's analysis in a memorandum to Matthews. Fully in accord, Matthews in turn articulated these views at the April 1 meeting of the State-War-Navy Coordinating Committee, the body formed in December 1944 to facilitate military-civilian consultation on postwar policy. His memorandum confirmed the new direction of American foreign policy: to contain Soviet expansionism by a combination of ideological counteroffensive, diplomacy, and "military force if necessary."[18]

"I am sure you have felt the change in approach and atmosphere during the last month or so," Durbrow wrote to Kennan as the Iranian crisis was winding down. "It has been very gratifying for Chip [Bohlen] and me and others who have been associated with Russian matters for a long time to see the thing come into its proper perspective all along the line," he went on, "and it is our hope and feeling that the eyes that have been opened will remain open and thus," he added with unintended irony, "we can have a chance to place our relations on a much more realistic and healthy basis."[19]

Kennan was hardly impervious to the official stir caused by his "long telegram." Once a distant and lonely voice on the periphery of U.S.-Soviet relations, now he was the cynosure around which that policy revolved. With great satisfaction and relief, he recognized that his "voice now carried." Immersed in his personal success, however, and looking ahead to his new duties as deputy for foreign affairs at the National War College, it was unlikely that he appreciated the precise change in approach to which Durbrow referred. Physically removed from Washington, he continued during his remaining weeks in Moscow, even as he attributed Soviet aims to "power for its own sake" and "the most crudely chauvinistic tendencies in Russian character," to portray the USSR as a schizoid state instinctively antagonistic to rival ideologies.[20]

In the wake of the "long telegram," views such as these further crystallized the American government's image of ideological confrontation and strengthened its commitment to a hard-line Soviet policy. Undersecretary of State Acheson and other administration officials rallied congressional support in the spring for a $3.75 million loan to Britain to prevent the spread of communism. Byrnes, Dunn, and their associates adopted a tougher bargaining posture at the meetings of the Council of Foreign Ministers in Paris. And in May General Lucius D. Clay, American military governor in Germany, admittedly influenced by Kennan's contention that central German agencies could well serve "as a roadpaver for [the] Soviet Socialist state which is to follow" and by his recommendation to partition the country, halted reparations deliveries from the American zone to the east.[21]

The image of ideological confrontation and the emerging "get tough" policy accorded precisely with the views of Foreign Service officers in Eastern Europe. Yet, curiously, unlike their colleagues in the department, they were not heartened by the Truman administration's "new line." Since it was not intended to diminish Soviet Russia's domination of Eastern Europe, but rather to inhibit further expansionism, it rightly suggested to them Washington's implicit acceptance of a Soviet sphere of influence. Further contributing to their despondency was Moscow's increasing political and economic sovietization of the region, a reaction, at least in part, to the combined effect of the British loan, the suspension of reparations deliveries, and America's possession of the atomic bomb. As the Soviets tightened their grip, American diplomats once again joined forces with their British counterparts, who now had also deserted hope of conciliating Moscow, much less of establishing a postwar zone of influence in the Balkans, in a new struggle against a common foe. Notwithstanding their protestations, however, social and political conditions in Eastern Europe continued to deteriorate during 1946. Consumed by the meaninglessness of their diplomatic efforts to change the reality of their existence, some careerists, such as Schoenfeld, Bruins, and Melbourne, lifelessly conducted their diplomatic duties. By the end of the year, Jacobs, Shantz, and Berry repudiated their roles. And others, like Barnes and Lane, attempted to cope with their conditions by transforming their professional function into a personal crusade.

Upset by the breakdown of American policy in Bulgaria and offended because the State Department had not requested his assessment of the situation, Barnes was in a contentious state of mind. Perhaps the United States and British governments could not ameliorate the repressive and undemocratic state of Bulgarian affairs, he wired in February, but there was no reason to deliver the accolade of recognition so long as Moscow "shall be allowed to make of [the] Yalta Declaration exactly what Germany of [the] First and Second World War made of all international commitments to which Germany was a party." He further suggested that the department take steps to nullify the formula of "friendly advice" proposed by the Soviets at the Moscow foreign ministers conference. But department officials feared that this would impact adversely on the American government's legal-moral commitment to keep its agreements, which, after all, was the nub of the dispute with the Kremlin. Indeed, Vyshinski had pricked the department's sensitivity to this very issue three weeks earlier when he informed Byrnes and Bohlen—and probably not altogether inaccurately—that Barnes was attempting "to sabotage" American policies by advising Petkov and other noncommunist leaders in Bulgaria to reject the Moscow agreement. For a time, Byrnes did consider recalling Barnes for consultations. But in the end, Barbour and Matthews once again simply restrained him from making further statements on the subject, particularly since his view that Russia had conceived the compromise on Bulgaria was erroneous. However, at Barnes's request, Barbour did draft a note to the Kremlin repeating Washington's expectations of Bulgarian adherence to the Moscow agreement.[22]

Not surprisingly, the Kremlin ignored the note. Moreover, the Russian minister in Sofia, Stepan Pavlovich Kirsanov, after reading a translation of the message in Barnes's presence, personally attacked the disgruntled diplomat for "constantly interfering" in Bulgarian affairs "without any rhyme or reason and certainly without any right." Meanwhile, nationalization of local industry, political liquidation, and intensified anti-American propaganda continued unabated. In Barnes's mind, Moscow's sovietization program historically parallelled the exploits of "medieval knights in white armor slaying dragons that beset their way to winning beauteous and virtuous maidens who existed to prove [the] glory of chivalry." Only today "the combat is for the glory of communism and the people who have not yet learned to appreciate its blessings."[23]

Tensions in Sofia mounted as the first days of summer appeared. Repression was rife, Barnes observed, as the regime, in anticipation of national elections, "resorted to [the] police measures typical of Hitler and Mussolini." Although he recommended a statement of protest, Thompson and others in the department, intent on completing peace treaties with the former enemy states at the Paris peace talks, remained silent. Exasperated by the way the "Russians have been permitted to push us around," and by his own government's silence, Barnes entreated the department, in coordination with the British Foreign Office, to insist on a reorganization of the Bulgarian government before elections to the Grand National Assembly succeeded in "shaping, legalizing and consolidating [a] Bolshevik regime." "At least," he said, "we will have stood by our moral principles and proven seriousness of our faith to [the] democratic elements throughout [the] Balkan peninsula that do exist."[24]

Conditions were just as depressing in Rumania. If the Liberal and Peasant members of the Groza government were to become mere ciphers, Berry wrote his mother on February 4, "it is just as well that I not stay on, for it would be a contradiction to all that I have stood for since my arrival here 15 months ago." His suggestion that Washington issue a public note requesting Groza to confirm the assurances he gave in Moscow similarly met with silence from Barbour, Durbrow, and Matthews. Convinced that Moscow intended to alter the Transylvanian frontier in Rumania's favor, Berry urged the department to bring the matter before the United Nations. However, recognizing that the Russians were "fixed" in their course and that the case for rectification in Hungary's favor was debatable, the department, at Dunn's recommendation, asked Moscow only to consider the possibility of revision at some future date. When the Soviets rejected this compromise, the United States acceded to Rumania's claim.[25]

The American government's strong stand during the Iranian crisis momentarily raised sagging spirits in Bucharest. By spring, however, Berry and Melbourne ruefully concluded that the National Democratic Front, "a facade for the Communist Party," and the Soviets had no intention of honoring the Moscow guarantee for democratic freedoms, which Maniu, Brătianu, and King Michael now denounced as an Anglo-American "sell-out." Notes of protest from London and Washington produced diplomatic regrets from Groza and a personal reminder to Berry from Communist leader Emil Bodnaras that Rumania could not be bullied like the Philippines. Hopelessly distraught over the "gangster police force" that merrily continued its political and economic plundering, rumors of a Soviet troop build-up in the country, the "butchery" of former strong man Mihai Antonescu, and the unremitting obstruction of the American political mission's activities, Berry numbly told the king to accept the unconstitutional electoral laws promulgated by the Groza govenrment "in order to be able to fight again when his position is stronger." "It seems to me," he wired Washington on July 11, "we can do little more."[26]

Held prey by the same hopelessness as their colleagues in Bulgaria and Rumania, Fraleigh, Shantz, and Hohenthal chafed at the department's neglect to inform them promptly of changing developments, including major decisions such as recognition of the Yugoslav government, which they were informed about by the British ambassador in Belgrade. More demoralizing, however, was the state of diplomatic isolation in which they were confined by partisan officials and the expanding communization of the country. Accordingly, Shantz advised the department to consider "completely unacceptable" Tito's note of March 2 assuring democratic conditions in the country and to withhold diplomatic recognition. Nonetheless, Barbour and Matthews felt the note contained sufficient categoric assurances to warrant continued recognition of Yugoslavia. Weary of Washington's fruitless dialogue with Belgrade, "the most completely communist government outside Russia," Shantz reprovingly called for "some means more compelling" than international law to protest the Tito regime, whose program was "revolting in its unfairness to anyone brought up in the Western tradition." Since Yugoslav Communists had made no secret of their objective to destroy American and British capitalism, he strongly urged the denial of economic aid. Matthews and Barbour agreed that financial assistance should not be granted until Yugoslavia restored democratic conditions.[27]

Tito's visit to Moscow in the spring and the unrelenting admonitions of Šubašić and the prewar elite confirmed the embassy's view that Yugoslavia was simply the brightest star in the Soviet system. In spite of the "natural democratic tendencies" of the peasantry, the Communists would retain control of the country for the foreseeable future. So Shantz repeated his opposition to economic aid, advised educating the American public about conditions in Yugoslavia, and recommended that Washington offer assistance to other democratic governments. At the end of May, owing to Tito's refusal to allow American air communications with Yugoslavia, he exhorted the department to consider closing the American embassy in Belgrade. Fearing an escalation of hostilities with Moscow and a protracted impasse over the completion of peace treaties, Barbour, Matthews, and Thompson decided instead to issue a note of protest. To no avail Shantz and Hohenthal renewed their nonrecognition appeal in July following the execution of Mihailović. W. Perry George, who joined the mission in May, recommended at least the termination of UNRRA aid, "for it supports in power a regime which is our declared enemy." Rumored plans of a Serb uprising against Tito at the end of July met with human, if not political, sympathy from embassy officials. Immersed in their own sea of despair, Shantz and Fraleigh explained that "this typically Balkan plot" arose among people who had abandoned hope of change, "who feel they cannot go on suffering indefinitely, being themselves, and seeing their friends killed or imprisoned and their properties confiscated." [28]

The same feelings of defeatism encumbered the outlook of Jacobs after the arrival of Soviet military advisors in January. There was now "little doubt who was pulling [the] strings in Albania," he informed Washington; the former atmosphere "of goodwill and democratic spirit" had deteriorated into one of fear due to the actions of a small group of Communists "working hand in glove with Moscow." "This may be [the] last chance to befriend this honest industrious small people," he stated. Having suffered from centuries of Turkish oppression, then Italian opportunism, and finally Italo-German occupation, they "now face [the] prospect of exploitation under fear and terror by Soviet imperialistic swashbucklers," who would "cram their ideology down the throats of the [Tirana] government." As Soviet political, economic, and military influence grew during February and March, and as Tirana openly attacked United States policy and restricted the movement of American diplomatic representatives, Jacobs advised the department, in contrast to his earlier recommendations, to deny recognition to the Hoxha government unless it honored its treaty obligations and ceased its discourteous and insulting treatment of American diplomats; and if it appeared to Washington that another war were imminent, the American political mission should be withdrawn or reduced to custodial size. Furthermore, affected by the Iranian crisis and Churchill's Fulton speech, he believed that the United States and the United Kingdom, notwithstanding dubious British actions during the past year, were now driven "to [a] completely parallel policy." [29]

By spring Russian military and technical officials had settled into apartments and houses once the property of Albanian citizens; and the

Hoxha government, which had "gravitated entirely within the Soviet orbit," ceased to camouflage its dictatorship. Albanian servants and employees of the American political mission were intimidated, molested, and frequently conscripted nolens-volens into "volunteer" work on road construction or into "spontaneous" weekly demonstrations. Had the United States supported Albania's admission to the United Nations when the Hoxha regime was still responsive to Western influence, a disheartened Jacobs scolded the department, American principles and prestige might have survived recent Soviet actions. More disturbing still, Albanian forces, supplied by UNRRA aid, were massed along the Greek border with Yugoslav elements. Recalling how American supplies poured into Japan during the thirties, Jacobs "[failed] to see any common sense of patriotism" to aid a regime "which if war comes will add its bit to destroy us." Hoxha's visit to Belgrade the following summer, coming so soon after Tito's trip to Moscow, further alarmed Jacobs, who was impelled to believe that Stalin had given Yugoslavia a more important role in Albania. Because of his preeminent ideological focus and the confused state of affairs in the eastern Adriatic, Jacobs did not consider the possibility that Stalin and Tito had already sown the seeds of their own struggle for power in the Balkans. Neither, for that matter, did diplomats in Washington or Paris. Henderson, Reber, and Barbour continued to perceive Albanian and Yugoslavian designs on Greece as part of the Soviet-orchestrated policy of ideological expansion.[30]

The trend of events in the Balkans was not repeated in nearly the same grievous dimensions in Hungary or Czechoslovakia. To be sure, the Soviets had neither curtailed their efforts to gain control of the Hungarian economy nor moderated their support for the Czech government's program of nationalization. On the other hand, while the Kremlin remained acutely attuned to the slightest tremor of anti-Sovietism in those states, it permitted the Hungarians and Czechs, like the Finns, to control their own internal political affairs. Though none of this represented a change from previous policies, diplomats in these countries, affected by the general deterioration of political conditions in Eastern Europe, also tended to view local developments as part of a global plan of ideological confrontation with the United States and the Western democracies. Convinced that the USSR "bids fair to advance steadily in this area and elsewhere in Europe much as Nazi Germany advanced through the thirties," Schoenfeld urged American financial aid to Hungary to preclude the loss of Western investments. Having received no assurances from the Czech government that it intended to foster world trade and compensate American owners of nationalized property, Steinhardt conversely advised Washington to consider unfavorably Czech requests for reconstruction credits. The department took no action in either case.[31]

Schoenfeld's sagging spirits were dealt another blow in March when Hungarian Communist leaders, with Soviet encouragement, succeeded in pressuring Nagy and Tildy to expel from parliament twenty-one dissident members of the Smallholders party for disloyally denouncing the formation of a leftist Smallholder–Social Democrat bloc. While Barbour and Matthews sympathized with Nagy, who feared dissolution of the coalition would prolong the stay of the Red Army, Schoenfeld criticized his faint-hearted "appeasement," which, in Schoenfeld's judgment, sacrificed the will of the electors to the "expediency" of the coalition. Actually, Nagy's action did not significantly change the complexion of Hungarian political affairs. Even though Moscow clearly opposed any diminution of leftist influence in the country, it took no steps, which it well could have taken, to place the reins of government exclusively in the hands of the Communists, any more than its refusal to permit antigovernment criticism in Finland during the previous year had transmogrified the structure of the Finnish coalition.[32]

The Czech national elections in May provided a clearer illustration of Soviet intentions in the Danubian region. Although the Communist party received 38 percent of the vote and surprising majorities in Bohemia and Moravia, the elections were free of the terrorism, intimidation, and blackmail exercised in the Balkans. Indeed, the American embassy considered them democratic. Bruins, who had replaced Klieforth as counselor of embassy, informed Washington that "there have been no aspersions of unfairness and it cannot be said that the rather strong communist trend is attributable to intimidation by the Communists nor to its control of the election machinery. Leading persons are convinced that it was a secret and fair ballot."[33] And, significantly, the Soviets, while disappointed with the election results, did not attempt to reverse them. This hardly reflected complaisance on their part; rather it demonstrated the tentativeness of their approach in these westernmost salients of Eastern Europe, which still represented a political glacis between East and West.

No sooner had the American embassy acknowledged the fairness of the elections, however, than it began to worry about their untoward implications. Considering that the Communist party was now dominant in Bohemia and Moravia, Bruins was uncertain whether "democratic principles" would survive. His anxieties were not allayed when Prime Minister Klement Gottwald assured him that Czechoslovakia desired friendly ties with Russia and the West; for at the same time, "moderate" members of the political elite (unlike their counterparts in Finland) had impressed on him the tenuousness of their position, which, they feared, would be dangerously weakened without continued Western support. Steinhardt too grew more concerned about the harsher ideological orientation he detected in the leftist press. And by the end of July, he was again urging the

State Department to decline Czech requests for an Export-Import Bank loan until Americans were compensated for their confiscated property.[34]

Meanwhile, in Hungary, notwithstanding Stalin's personal assurance to Nagy that he would have a free hand to run his government, domestic conditions steadily worsened through the spring and summer. The economic malaise which afflicted the country appeared beyond cure. Agricultural and manufacturing production, adversely affected by land reform and the Soviet occupation, declined precipitously; the pengö was worthless as a medium of exchange. Continuing criticism of the Soviet occupation by Smallholder deputies and the outspoken opposition of the Hungarian clergy, led by Joseph Cardinal Mindszenty, decided Marshal Voroshilov, upon Moscow's instructions, to call for further expulsions from the national assembly. Powerless, Nagy again conceded Voroshilov's demands. Equally unable to alter the situation, and, as a result, all the more insensitive to Nagy's submissive response, Schoenfeld despondently resigned himself to further Soviet encroachment.[35]

In Poland, where Soviet political and ideological penetration was far more advanced than in Hungary or Czechoslovakia, Lane, like Barnes, continued to crusade against the foes of liberal-democratic principles. Neither he nor Keith were deterred by the animadversions of Polish officials, who accused them of internal interference and who challenged, in light of American discrimination against Negroes, their moralistic censure of Poland's domestic affairs. "I believe we have now reached the time when our policy towards Poland must remain completely firm," Lane counseled the department in February, to convince Warsaw and "their guiding authorities to the east" that "we do not intend to be backed against a wall." Neither was convinced. In March the Polish government postponed national elections, an action ostensibly provoked by Mikolajczyk's refusal to accept Stalin's offer of equal representation in parliament with the Communists and the Labor party. Rallying to Mikolajczyk's cause, Lane told Matthews that "unless we give publicity to what is going on in Poland and other nations in an analogous position, we will not be able to use our influence in these countries either politically or economically." In reply to possible charges that the United States threatened to provoke war by opposing Communist domination, he pointed out, in a marked departure from his attitude in the thirties, that unpreparedness nearly cost us the last war," that "appeasement will be just as dangerous today as it was at the time of Munich; and that we run much more danger of war if we ignore the dangers of aggression than of honestly facing facts."[36]

Outraged by the intensified political cleansing undertaken by Polish courts and police during the first two weeks of April, Lane and British ambassador Bentinck recommended that their governments issue parallel notes of protest and reaffirm their denial of credits until democratic practices were restored. Then, on April 18, Lane received word from Byrnes that the department had agreed to offer Poland credits of $40 million for the purchase of surplus coal cars and locomotives, a decision reached partly to alleviate Washington's guilt for having left Mikolajczyk to suffer his fate with the Soviets and partly to provide the economies of Western Europe with badly needed Polish coal. Almost apologetically, Durbrow assured Lane that no further credits would be granted without the promise of free elections. Lane was not mollified. Believing the department lacked understanding of the Polish situation, he literally begged it to retract its decision. Not only did it refuse to do so, but it further expressed its intention to conclude an additional Export-Import Bank credit agreement of $50 million. Crushed by the realization "that the Department has little confidence in my evaluation [of] Poland during my nine months here," Lane defiantly registered an "official protest" of Washington's action, which, in his opinion, would further encourage the minority government "to continue to flout the Yalta and Potsdam decisions." Still ignored, he flew to Paris on May 6 to present his case to Byrnes, whereupon the secretary of state suspended the deliveries of surplus equipment until Warsaw acceded to its political and economic agreements.[37]

Delighted by the news of Lane's triumph, Keith felt that withholding credits was "the best step we can take in the protection of our interests." After all, "time is running out in Poland," he observed. "A strong stand on our part will hearten and strengthen the 90% of the Poles who believe in the United States and I believe it is [the] one chance we now have of keeping Poland linked with the west." On June 14 Bierut reluctantly provided assurances that Warsaw would honor all its obligations. A week later the ban on the surplus war materials was lifted.

But Lane's feelings of satisfaction were soon erased by a new cloud of gloom. On June 30 the Polish government held a referendum to determine public preference for a unicameral or bicameral parliament, support for the Oder-Neisse boundary, and approval of the nationalization and land reform programs. Although reports from the Gdansk and Poznan consulates attested to the referendum's fairness, Lane was persuaded by Mikolajczyk that the government had employed intimidation and questionable methods of tabulation to produce the desired results. Then, on July 4, a pogrom was staged in Kielce, which left thirty-four Jews dead and forty-two injured. Notwithstanding the history of anti-Semitism among the Polish people, Lane, along wth Keith, contended that the government, if not directly responsible for the attack on Polish Jews, had encouraged it to legitimize its efforts to liquidate alleged reactionaries. Consequently, Lane combatively resumed his campaign to suspend credits. He further recommended the issuance of a note stressing the irregularities of the referendum and the rights of all parties to participate freely in the national elections, although he suggested that Washington first inform Molotov and Bevin of its intentions to see if joint action were possible. Thompson agreed. Departing from the rhetoric of political non-involvement of the war years, if not yet the traditional policy on which it was based, he wired Lane that the United States, as one of the powers who had helped to liberate Europe, was obliged to assume responsibility for the internal affairs of other states.[38]

Diplomats in the Moscow embassy believed that Soviet actions in Eastern Europe were motivated by considerations of power as much as by ideology. While it was uncertain to what extent Russia would dominate Hungary, Bulgaria, Rumania, Poland, even Finland, Davies and G. Frederick Reinhardt, a sovietologist who had previously served as political advisor to the military in the Mediterranean and Germany, pointed out that she possessed the will and the capacity to maintain control. Apart from Russia's geopolitical sway over Eastern Europe, however, embassy officials perceived her as an ideological expansionist elsewhere, a goal newly appointed Ambassador Walter Bedell Smith attributed to the Kremlin's belief in the incompatibility of capitalism and communism. Curiously, while Davies dismissed the department's concern about Soviet ideological ascendency in China, a country he knew well, as "a preoccupation with legalities rather than realities," he was certain that the recent establishment of diplomatic relations between Russia and Argentina, a country with which he was unfamiliar, signalled the establishment of "a major beachhead in South America" from which the Kremlin aimed to communize the Western Hemisphere. Considering Moscow's ideological objectives, Reinhardt advised Washington "to economically aid non-Russian countries struggling to establish real democracy." Similarly, Smith and Davies criticized the proposal of Andrei Gromyko to destroy existing atomic weapons and to regulate and control all other implements of war as a disingenuous ploy to arrogate moral leadership in the internationalization of the atomic bomb.[39]

For a variety of reasons—domestic opposition to America's postwar presence in Europe, the desire to conclude peace treaties with the former enemy states, the fear of provoking a clash between the USSR and the United States—diplomats in the department continued to couch their communications to Moscow in moderate language. Nevertheless, by the early summer of 1946 they felt much the same mistrust and antagonism toward the Soviets as did their colleagues in the field. Matthews recommended a stepped-up cultural and information program to combat Soviet propaganda in Russia and Eastern Europe. Barbour now belittled the idea of a joint U.S.-Soviet effort to reconstruct the European economy. The Russian specialists in the department, who considered themselves more qualified than their fellow officers to interpret and assess Soviet aims, were even more embittered by Moscow's behavior. Unlike Germany, which had operated on "a purely racial basis," the Soviet Union, contended Bohlen, Thompson, Stevens, and Henderson, strove to conquer the entire world by a combination of political, military, and diplomatic means mobilized by a "fanatic proselytizing religion." The June 7 lecture on fascism and capitalism by Fedor N. Oleshchuko, a member of the party's propaganda and agitation wing, left no doubt in Stevens's mind "that the United States is now regarded as the chief center of world reaction and as such will be regarded by the Soviet Government and held up to the Soviet people as the principal potential enemy of the Soviet Union." Reminiscent of the atmosphere of caution in 1940–41, Stevens urged SWNCC to prohibit visits of Russian nationals to any American overseas bases vital to national security.[40]

Through the summer months, the anti-Soviet attitudes of Foreign Service officers were repeatedly reinforced by Kennan, who had returned to Washington late in May to assume his duties at the War College. Actually, Kennan dissented from the emerging "get tough" policy of the Truman administration. It was pointless "to approach [the Russians] in a way that rules out cooperation," he told lecture audiences from the American Civil Liberties Union to the American Legion. The United States had to be frank, firm, and honest, but respectful of Russian power. However, intent on inculcating in Washington officials and the American public the mysterious ways of the Soviets, his attitude of realistic cooperation was overshadowed by the continued ideological orientation of his remarks. On occasion, Kennan even sounded as if he were willing to confront the Soviet Union militarily. Speaking before the department's division of Chinese affairs, he called Kremlin officials "fanatics" who were impervious to reason. But "while they are political gamblers, they are not gamblers when faced with the reality of military force." Consequently, he opposed relinquishing America's atomic monopoly. Unlike the United States, he warned Acheson, the Soviets would not hesitate to employ the bomb as a means of political extortion. Borrowing the Kremlin's "two irons in the fire" approach, he advised Washington to press for international control of the bomb, but to develop simultaneously the nation's ability to absorb an attack and offer retaliation.[41]

At the State Department's request, Kennan set out at the end of July on a six-city speaking tour of the Midwest and the West Coast. Although he endeavored to reduce the American public's growing fear of the USSR, his speeches incontinently rehashed the themes of Soviet aggressiveness and communist ideology. The road to better relations "lay only through a long, unpleasant process of setting will against will, force against force, idea against idea," he informed one audience, "through a process of conflict and dispute rather than through a happy collaboration for common ends." Impressed by his impassioned rhetoric, a Milwaukee clergyman remarked, "Boy, you missed your calling." Upon his return in August, he presented a summary of his tour to the department which reflected his distress over the many Soviet sympathizers he encountered on the West Coast, particularly among academics. Scornful of the scientific community's desire to enlighten the Russians about the dangers of atomic weapons, he found them politically "as innocent as six-year old maidens. In trying to explain things to them I felt like one who shatters the pure ideals of tender youth."[42]

The effect of Kennan's homiletics and the alarming reports from Eastern Europe, which increasingly likened Moscow's aims to those of Nazi Germany, served to rigidify the image of confrontation within the Truman administration and the military establishment. Their view was, in turn, reinforced by American journalists, members of Congress, and the public, who, as a result of the government's rhetoric of conflict, had become sensitized to the Russian threat. By August the White House construed Soviet moves outside Eastern Europe, however innocuous, as potentially expansionist. Thus, when the Kremlin renewed its proposal for a joint Soviet-Turkish defense of the Dardanelles, Truman, following the advice of his civilian and military advisors, including Near East and African chief Henderson, authorized a note of protest to the Russian embassy, warning against any interference with Turkey's exclusive right to defend the Straits. To assure Moscow that the United States was not bluffing, a powerful naval force was sent to the eastern Mediterranean.[43]

A second illustration of the administration's "get tough" attitude was the report on U.S.-Soviet relations prepared during the late summer of 1946 by Clark M. Clifford, special counsel to the president, in conjunction with the Departments of State, War, Navy, and other agencies including central intelligence. According to the report, which drew heavily on Kennan's "long telegram," considerations of realpolitik in Soviet foreign policy operated in the service of Marxist-Leninist ideology. Although Moscow did not anticipate immediate hostilities with the West, the report stated, Kremlin officials believed that conflict between the capitalist and socialist worlds was inevitable. Given this idée fixe, the United States should oppose—with atomic weapons, if necessary—any attempts to expand into regions vital to American security or to infringe on the rights of small nations. "It is our hope that they will change their minds and work out with us a fair and equitable settlement," the report concluded, "when they realize that we are too strong to be beaten and too determined to be frightened."[44]

On September 13, nearly two weeks before the report was submitted to Truman, Clifford sent a copy to Kennan along with a chit inviting his comments on its tone and substance. The main changes Kennan suggested—that successful containment of Soviet power would ultimately permeate and alter the Soviet system, that Kremlin leaders were not necessarily confident of their success in a struggle with the capitalist world, and that the actual use of biological or atomic weapons in the future by the United States required careful consideration under conditions prevailing at that time—were seemingly intended to deemphasize notions of ideological confrontation and realistic confrontation, while simultaneously placing more weight on a policy of realistic cooperation. Curiously, however, Kennan presented these points less as a major change in substance than as emendations. It is possible, of course, that he agreed with the underlying ideological thrust of the paper. But his long-suffering efforts to convert policy planners to a realpolitik perspective on international relations argue against this explanation. It is more plausible that he accepted this misreading of his views to retain his hard-won credibility, which would surely have been tarnished, if not destroyed altogether, had he revised at this juncture "his own policy," and to ensure his position of influence within the State Department. Even had he been so inclined, however, the crush of bureaucratic inertia in support of the realpolitik-in-the-service-of-ideology thesis had by then become too powerful to tolerate such a major change of emphasis. Quite likely, still basking in the success he had craved for so long, Kennan may have simply failed to appreciate the extent to which the administration's interpretation of his ideas as presented in the "long telegram" had set into motion plans for containment which deviated from his own policy preference and which threatened to escalate tensions between Washington and Moscow.[45]

A third significant development was Byrnes' September 6 speech at Stuttgart. Although the secretary of state enunciated the American government's continued interest in the unification of Germany, he clearly expressed Washington's willingness to live with a divided Germany to counteract future Soviet expansionism. Superficially, this was power politics par excellence; but, as was the case with the Turkish issue and the Clifford report, the underlying motive of this policy reformulation, following from the image of ideological confrontation, was to arrest the spread of communism. This was precisely the argument that Kennan presented, notwithstanding his intentions, in his March 6 telegram on Germany.[46]

By autumn Kennan had begun to feel troubled about the martial atmosphere that was developing in official circles and the American public's historical penchant for overreaction in international affairs. Peaceful coexistence between America and Russia, say in five or ten years, was still possible, he explained to his class at the National War College, if the United States remained politically and militarily strong, but diplomatically patient. Unfortunately his allusions to communist fanaticism and his furious attacks against Soviet sympathizers such as Henry Wallace, who was sacked by Truman on September 20 for his opposition to Washington's "get tough" policy, persisted. In any event, at this point Kennan was not likely to detach his fellow careerists or the administration from their hardening perceptions of ideological confrontation any more than he was able to tug them away from their wartime fancies of ideological cooperation. Cannon, Matthews, and others at the Paris peace conference grew daily more apprehensive of communist penetration into the eastern Mediterranean, Greece, and Western Europe. In October Henderson proposed financial and military aid to Iran, Turkey, and Greece and an expanded propaganda program to maintain the confidence of other nations that the American government was still committed to the United Nations principles. Should it ever come to a military test, he told Acheson, these principles and "the conviction that the United States is defending not only its cause but that of all free nations" would greatly strengthen American security.[47]

In fact, however, the Kremlin had not politically penetrated beyond those areas which it had militarily controlled during the war and which it had, therefore, de facto stipulated as part of its sphere of postwar influence at the Yalta Conference. In Eastern Europe, the focal point of U.S.-Soviet discord, the situation at the end of 1946 was not qualitatively different from that which obtained in the winter of 1944-45: save for Finland, which enjoyed a measure of independence, and the Baltic States, which lost their political identity, Russia continued to exercise formal control over those areas contiguous to her borders and informal influence in the Danubian region and in the eastern Adriatic. But Foreign Service officers and officials in the Truman administration perceived Soviet actions in the region as evidence of a calculated plan of rampant expansionism more far-reaching because of its Marxist-Leninist inspiration than that of Nazi Germany.

For diplomats in Eastern Europe, the waning months of 1946 presented a tragic denouement to the Atlantic Charter–Yalta scenario. Barnes and Rewinkel submitted that Bulgaria was a "Communist brain child" inextricably caught in the web of Soviet domination, just as she had been held captive by Germany in the thirties. Under the circumstances, Rewinkel "could only admire [the democratic Bulgarian leaders] for still having courage and hope in [the] belief that [the] principles of freedom and decency must somehow prevail in [the] end.'' The national elections of October 27 produced a predictable Communist victory. In an effort to justify to himself, if not the department, his activities of the past two years, Barnes noted that things could have been worse. At least the Agrarians had retained one-fourth of the seats in the national assembly. By 1947, with the execution of Petkov and the "fusion" of the Agrarians into the Communist party, even this consolation would be denied him.[48]

Pressured by the appeals of Maniu, Berry and Melbourne formally urged the department "to maintain [a] fighting front" with Great Britain by withholding recognition of the Groza regime and financial aid unless the Rumanian government complied with its assurances of free elections. But they realized that the Soviets and their Communist minions were intent on victory "regardless of what it costs in broken pledges and dead peasants." The election travesty that was perpetrated on November 19, which left the Peasants and Liberals scant representation in the new government, gave reality to this portent. Even as they advised the department to demand new elections, with which Thompson, Barbour, and others complied, Berry and Melbourne, having had their fill of Rumanian affairs, requested immediate transfers. The Rumanian elections "were the most fraudulent ever held in Rumania and we and the British had guaranteed free elections to the Rumanian people," Berry wrote his mother. "It makes us look pretty bad in their eyes." Berry and Melbourne departed in the spring of 1947. By the end of that year, the Peasant party was banned, the radical wing of the Liberals under Tâtârescu forced to resign, and King Michael compelled to abdicate.[49]

Periodic Yugoslav crossings of the Venezia-Guilia demarkation line during the summer of 1946 triggered anxieties within the Belgrade embassy of a possible attack on Trieste. Anxiety gave way to a fury of recrimination in August when Tito's aircraft gunned down two American transport planes, the second of which claimed the lives of five crew members. The augmentation of American troops in Venezia-Guilia and in northern Italy, along with Soviet reluctance to offer Belgrade its support, prompted Tito to satisfy the State Department's demands—although he impenitently maintained that the wind-blown planes had illegally entered Yugoslav territory—and to desist from any plans he might have secreted for the invasion of Trieste. These incidents, the expanding sovietization of the country, and the "deliberate impudence," as Shantz put it, toward the American diplomatic mission produced vehement outcries from Fraleigh, George, and Patterson to cut off UNNRA aid to Yugoslavia. As for Shantz, he had retreated from the war of words in Yugoslavia to the silence of private hates.[50]

Weary of the mounting anti-American tone of the Albanian press, the systematic campaign against political opposition and the Catholic Church, Hoxha's refusal to honor without revision the treaty agreements he inherited, and the discourtesies dispensed to the American political mission in Tirana, Jacobs too, in his case quite literally, fled from his Balkan purgatory. On October 10 he departed for the United States, three weeks before Acheson informed Tirana of the American government's decision to withdraw its mission. Completely reversing his view of the previous year, Jacobs advised Hickerson on November 14 to oppose admission to the United Nations of the "barbarous," "ruthless," and "unscrupulous" Hoxha regime.[51]

Meanwhile, Schoenfeld resigned himself to the seemingly irremediable economic situation in Hungary and to the intensified poaching on "reactionary" Smallholder deputies in parliament by Hungarian Communists and Soviet armistice officials. Critical of Nagy, Tildy, and Kovács for failing to provide moral leadership, and dismayed by Washington's apparent surrender of Hungary to the Soviet sphere, Schoenfeld, psychologically reposing himself in the "moral solidarity of [the] English speaking people" and in his government's traditional policy of political noninterference—"the best guarantee of spontaneous, virgorous and genuine democratic development"—told Cardinal Mindszenty on December 27 that further diplomatic representations were pointless. By this time, it would not have made any difference anyway. Communist charges of a fascist conspiracy within the political section of the army had already set into motion a sweeping purge of all Smallholder opposition, which climaxed early in 1947 with the arrest and "disappearance" of Béla Kovács. In due course, the Smallholder party was dissolved, paving the way for fraudulent elections in August and the establishment of a monolithic communist government the following year.[52]

Though conditions in Czechoslovakia remained relatively free of Soviet interference, Bruins and Steinhardt suspected that Soviet diplomats had established a clique within the Czech Foreign Office. Thus they evinced little surprise when the minister of foreign affairs accused the United States of granting France discriminatory rights to purchase American war surplus materials in Belgium, Germany, and Italy. Angered by Prague's display of cheek, especially since Washington had proposed a $50 million loan, the progressive anti-American–pro-Soviet orientation of the Czech press, and Vishinsky's imputation that the United States aimed to enslave the world economically, they helped persuade the State Department to suspended further sales of war materials. Depite the mounting strength of the Czech Communists and Beneš's willingness to propitiate them, Bruins urged the department not to abandon moderate elements in the government. By the summer of 1947, however, with the rigid polarization of the United States and Russia, American sustenance of Beneš and the Social

Democrats rapidly dissipated, and Bruins, like Schoenfeld, dejectedly and listlessly endured the functions of a caretaker diplomat.[53]

Unlike most of his colleagues, Lane was still inveighing against the Soviets and their Polish quislings as summer faded into autumn. Linked arm in arm with British ambassador Bentinck, he won the department's approval to protest the liquidation of Karol Popiel's Labor party, lauded Byrnes' Stuttgart speech, endorsed the assertive diplomatic position adopted by the American negotiating team in Paris, and strongly opposed any financial assistance to Warsaw until it guaranteed democratic elections. At the same time, Lane and Keith recognized that Mikolajczyk's Polish Peasant party could not possibly compete with the political forces marshalled against it. Nor, for that matter, could Lane effectively carry on his crusade against communist expansionism as an official representative of his government. "As I weighed in my mind the situation we were facing, I thought of my experience in Yugoslavia whence I had seen Hitler conquer country after country," he wrote. Although the ideologies, of course, were different, both Hitler and Stalin sought world domination, he noted. "The position I had supported about the elections having been definitely rejected by the Soviet and Polish governments, my usefulness as an Ambassador had ended." However, it was possible yet to do some good "by exposing Soviet objectives to the American people." On January 19, 1947, the Polish people cast their votes. The Peasant party secured 28 seats in the parliament. The Communists controlled 394. Four days later Lane submitted his resignation to General Marshall, who had become secretary of state in the same month, to bring his message, "without diplomatic evasion or reserve," to the American public.[54]

Telegrams from Moscow during the final months of the year conveyed the same combative tone. The intention of the Soviet propaganda offensive against the "lying," "spying," "war-mongering" American and British governments, commented Durbrow, who had cheerlessly replaced Kennan on July 1, was to extinguish in party circles "any lingering ideas or hopes that friendly relations are possible between [the] Anglo-Americans" and to condition the masses to perceive their former allies as new enemies no less menacing to Russian security than Nazi Germany. The public unrest created by the current "ideological house cleaning," the lack of housing, food, and consumer goods, reduced wages, and higher taxes was "hardly calculated to trouble [the] sleep of [the] Kremlin, with its long record of successful repression of non-conformism and its apparent disregard for human needs." While Stalin and Soviet party theoreticians such as Andrei Zhdanov appealed to "certain naive and unstable elements in the west" as an "injured innocent" people yearning for international collaboration, Durbrow wrote in November, it was only a tactical maneuver to divide the capitalist powers. As far as he was concerned, the vitreous postwar events and Soviet propaganda left no doubt "that [the] Kremlin has hit [the] sawdust trail in revival of [that] old-time Leninist religion." There was no reason to believe that Stalin had moderated Lenin's view that "memorial services will [inevitably] be sung over the Soviet Republic or over world capitalism." Moreover, Kremlin officials were now militarily equipped to realize their goal of world ideological supremacy. For this reason, Durbrow opposed American recognition of the Zionist state, which would only augment Soviet influence among the Muslim peoples from North Africa to the Levant, and possibly to India and Indonesia as well.[55]

Durbrow's belief that Moscow's expansionist aims were activated by a deep-seated eschatological imperative received affirmation from Davies and Reinhardt. Given the Kremlin's world outlook, Davies commented to Ambassador Smith in November, it was not surprising that Stalin had rejected the American proposal for the control and inspection of atomic energy production. "This outlook is inspired by and inextricably bound up with the Leninist-Stalinist interpretation of historical materialism," he explained. "The political philosophy of the men who rule Russia, despite its confusing tactical flexibility, is as intolerant and dogmatic as that which motivated the zealots of Islam or the Inquisition in Spain." Since Stalinist doctrine emphasized that the Soviet state must remain strong until capitalist encirclement was eliminated, it was "utterly naive to assume that the cessation of bomb production in the United States would induce the USSR either to abandon its own gigantic atomic research project or to participate sincerely in an effective program for atomic control and inspection." Lest it would be forgotten, he emphasized that the Kremlin's creed was "one of implacable hostility, not collaboration; unremitting preparation for war with the democratic west, not conciliation; the existence of two worlds now and the establishment of one world only when it will assuredly be a Soviet world."[56]

On December 17 Durbrow sent a letter to William Bullitt, who had carried in his *lettre d'agrément* to Moscow some thirteen years earlier the official and private hopes of the American government for a peaceful and cooperative relationship with the Soviet Union. Nothing had changed, he said. "It is the same old bologna, sold over the same counter, but cut a little bit thinner than before."[57]

The Bulgarian and Rumanian elections, the downing of American aircraft in Yugoslavia, the purge of democratic elements in Poland and Hungary, all these events further reified in the minds of diplomats in the department the polarization of the postwar world into irreconcilably opposed camps. For a fleeting moment in early December, however,

Moscow's agreement to conclude peace treaties with Italy, Bulgaria, Rumania, Hungary, and Finland and its endorsement of a General Assembly resolution to eliminate and control atomic weapons aroused speculation that the Soviets might embark on a more flexible foreign-policy course. A year earlier, the department would have seized with alacrity these concessions as indications of Moscow's peaceful intentions; but now, given the lens of suspicion and hostility through which the Russians were viewed, they were considered by Stevens and Bohlen possibly to be "tactical maneuvers" to exploit the non-Soviet world.[58]

9. Image and Reality: The Underlying Factors

Less than two years after the war in Europe had ended, relations between the United States and Russia had deteriorated into mutual suspicion and hostility of such intensity that each nation judged the other a threat to its very existence. Foreign Service officers in Eastern Europe and the USSR and in the corresponding geographic divisions of the State Department, who once considered the Soviets valiant comrades-in-arms and partners-to-be in the postwar world of peace and security, now viewed them as global expansionists even more menacing than the Nazis in their fanatic commitment to a revolutionary ideology. This tragic transformation, however precipitate, unidimensional, and inevitable it may appear from the perspective of the present, was actually a gradual, complex, and contingent one in which images of cooperation and confrontation, shaped by a complex of historical, cultural, social, and psychological antecedents, competed for dominance in the minds of professional diplomats.

The content of the "reality" that Foreign Service officers perceived derived from the liberal-internationalist culture of American foreign policy, specifically Wilsonianism, which sought to universalize American values of free trade, political democracy, and the rule of law. It was this world view which underlay the Atlantic Charter and its ideological offspring, the United Nations Declaration, the Moscow declaration of 1943, and the Yalta declaration on liberated Europe. Given the Russian military effort, Stalin's rhetoric of collaboration, and the apparent democratization of the Soviet Union, diplomats in the field and the department grew increasingly optimistic after 1943 that Moscow would support the Atlantic Charter principles. But once the Kremlin began to assert its control over Eastern Europe, their expectations of postwar cooperation progressively waned. The more the Soviets tightened their grip, the more passionately Foreign Service officers affirmed their allegiance to American postwar ideals and their hostility to the USSR. Just as diplomats had earlier altered the reality of Moscow's objectives to conform to their image of cooperation, they interpreted its actions in 1945–46 as an unmistakable sign of ideological confrontation.

A second influence from the past was the memory of the Bolshevik Revolution. The apocalyptic Marxist-Leninist vision of revolution and international conflict was completely antithetical to the Wilsonian world-view of peace, prosperity, and order. Of course, the global proletarian society did not emerge, as historically ordained, from the chaos of World War I. Nevertheless, the rhetoric of class conflict persisted, evoking in the United States, as in Europe, widespread fear of imminent revolutionary upheaval. Even though the pyrotechnics had subsided in the 1920s, Foreign Service officers who had lived through this turbulent period carried with them the memory of Bolshevik objectives and imparted it to junior diplomats. During the war, however, Foreign Service officers lost sight of Moscow's Bolshevik past. Not only had the Soviets proved loyal and courageous allies, but they had taken measures—the abolition of the Comintern, the reinstatement of the Orthodox Church, the veneration of Russian history—that suggested the abandonment of their radical faith. While the "Riga group" of sovietologists, having lived through the Soviet purges, remained somewhat more suspicious of the Kremlin than their colleagues, they too tended to view the Soviet Union more as a nation-state willing to cooperate with the West than as the seminary of communist revolution. Following the Soviet military advance into Eastern Europe in the latter part of 1944, their collective memory of Bolshevik revolutionary aims was revived. This became increasingly more distinct to career diplomats, reaching full clarity with Stalin's election address in February 1946.

The perceptions of Foreign Service officers were similarly affected by the more recent memory of military expansionism, fascism, and the policy of "appeasement" practiced by the democratic West in the thirties. They recalled Japanese and Italian aggression in Manchuria and Ethiopia and particularly the futile efforts to propitiate the Germans. During 1945–46 careerists grafted this residue from the past on to the memory of the Bolshevik Revolution to explain Soviet postwar actions. They accordingly advocated vigorous diplomatic resistance to prevent the Soviets from repeating their conquest of Eastern Europe elsewhere in the world, either by direct acts of aggression or intimidation.

Despite the parallel drawn between Nazi and Soviet aims, career diplomats judged the former to have been far less malevolent. For one thing, careerists felt that Germany had been harshly treated in the Treaty of Versailles. For another, Nazi objectives, and, in lesser magnitude, those of Italy and Japan, by virtue of their racist character, were believed to be limited. Germany had only consumed what was "digestible," Henderson pointed out, citing her decision to refrain from expanding into Scandinavia in illustration of the point. In addition, observed Kohler, the Nazis, apart from their liquidation of the Jews, had left intact local institutions, much like nineteenth-century colonialists. Finally, American diplomats viewed Germany as having been a stabilizing, modernizing force in Eastern Europe and a bulwark against the spread of communism. Even though the Nazis had applied their system with what Kennan called "ruthless monotony," Germany nonetheless had presented a model of efficiency and order (an aim of Wilsonianism) to the countries of Eastern Europe, and she had bidden fair to integrate them into the world economy (another Wilsonian objective). In the same way, Italy, as well as Japan, whose modernizing thrust of the 1930s had "occidentalized" her in the minds of American diplomats, had inspired hope of the same in Albania, Ethiopia, Manchuria, and northern China. Once world trade had revived, diplomats believed, these authoritarian aberrations would have disappeared and democracy would have been restored.[1]

Soviet aims, by contrast, driven by a universalistic, revolutionary ideology, were considered unlimited. Henderson further contended that Hitler's demands of France and Britain had been made during peace against declared enemies; Stalin's demands had been made during war against countries—Poland and the Baltic States—too small to present a threat to Soviet security. Moreover, the Soviets were methodically effacing the vestiges of Western civilization. Whereas the Germans, noted Kennan, had advanced the standard of living in the area, the Soviets were solely a "taking nation." Lane felt that it was his "apprehension of the Soviets [sic] disruptive designs, which I believe to be sincere," that partly accounted for Hitler's *Drang nach Osten*. Finally, unlike the polished, refined, and socially aware Germans, including the military, that the diplomats had encountered, the Soviets were uncivilized, barbaric orientals. The Soviets transformed social institutions and removed entire populations, Kohler stated. When the Germans had arrested a Pole, Lane pointed out, "you knew where he was, could send food and knew when to visit." But one never knew what happened to an individual after he was apprehended by the more "ruthless and cold-blooded" Soviets. Because of the publicity devoted to Hitler's extermination of European Jewry, Durbrow averred, little attention was focussed on Soviet atrocities: the Ukrainians who had starved in 1932–33 when they refused to join the collectives and the millions Stalin had killed during the purges. "Stalin made Hitler and Mussolini look like kindergarten kids!" The Germans, Barbour allowed, had been capable of "benevolence," as they had demonstrated in Bulgaria. The Nazis had controlled Eastern Europe with the "velvet glove," Roy Melbourne remarked, the Soviets with the "iron fist." "They lighted fires in the washbasins, stuck bayonets through paintings and cut our phone wires," Mrs. Arthur Schoenfeld stated. "They threw vases out, cut up oriental rugs to make softer seat covers for their jeeps and raped women, including our friends," Mrs. John H. Bruins remembered. Shortly after the end of the war, the Russian embassy had given a party, Mrs. Bruins recalled, but invited only a few ambassadors and a handful of attachés. "That wasn't much of a party," she noted with a lingering trace of incredulity.[2]

The process of socialization to which career diplomats were exposed and the experiences they shared as members of the Foreign Service also had an effect on their perceptions by providing a common framework through which they viewed the world. Periodic lectures by senior officers instilled in newcomers to the service the objectives of Wilsonianism and impressed upon them, in most cases—Bohlen's as an example—for the first time, Marxist-Leninist objectives of world revolution and ideological conquest. Although diplomats looked askance at the Utopian means of Wilsonianism, particularly the League of Nations, which ignored the competitive realities of international politics, they enthusiastically affirmed its idealistic goals of internationalizing American liberal values. Since most Foreign Service officers came from old-line American upper-class or upper-middle-class families, many of whom were prominent in their local communities, they readily identified with the elitest role of "peace-diplomat" into which they were indoctrinated. Those from humbler backgrounds, many of whom were "presocialized" in private secondary schools and Ivy League colleges, demonstrated a predisposition to their elitist roles.

For the most part, however, values and beliefs were communicated informally through the interaction of individuals from relatively homogeneous backgrounds in shared social experiences. Diplomats assigned to field missions closely associated with each other both professionally and socially, forming intimate personal bonds. These connections were particularly developed in socially and economically underdeveloped countries, where contacts outside the diplomatic community were more limited than, say, in England or France, or in the politically restrictive environments of the USSR and Eastern Europe. Deviations from shared perspectives entailed the loss of emotional contact with the group and jeopardized promotions. Thus beliefs tended to be anchored in what the group saw as real. Group ties, in short, engendered a clan mentality which psychologically detached the individual from the physical environment of the moment and inhibited independent judgments. Internal disturbances in the Western Hemisphere during the thirties, as an illustration, were uniformly perceived to have been fomented by foreign-based communist movements. And the authoritarian governments in Eastern Europe received unanimous approval from diplomats who regarded apprehensively the socially disruptive conditions of the region. Careerists who demonstrated intellectual independence—Kennan, most prominently, and Davies in China—did so at the expense of group support. In the department, on the other hand, where the network of social contacts was broader and more heterogeneous, *Gemeinschaft* ties were less pronounced. It was not uncommon when an individual was reassigned to the department, Elbridge Durbrow revealed, for someone to say, "Now when you cross the ocean, don't change your mind." Yet there, too, Foreign Service officers formed island communities, joined together by institutional and personal loyalties, by shared area and country specializations, and like their colleagues in the field, by the indifference and the hostility displayed toward the professional diplomat by the American public, Congress, and government officials.[3]

One manifestation of shared beliefs and values was the Foreign Service's Europocentric cultural bias. Career diplomats, many of whom had travelled and studied in Western Europe prior to entering the service, admired and identified with the glamour, elegance, and sophistication of London, Paris, Rome, Vienna, and Berlin, historic centers of Western tradition and civilization. Latin America, the Near East, the Far East, Eastern Europe, and the USSR were, by contrast, "primitive," "Asiatic," and devoid of the accustomed creature comforts in the civilized West, their peoples "unattractive," "pedestrian," "dull." Professional and personal attachments further facilitated the group's conformity to behavioral norms, the most important of which was its military-like obedience to higher authority. Career diplomats quickly learned that their "professional" role, like that of their nineteenth-century predecessors, was confined to reportorial and observational activities and to the implementation of prevailing policy. The analysis, formulation, and interpretation of policy flowed unidirectionally from the top of the foreign affairs bureacracy down. Component links in a hierarchical chain of authority, heads of missions and their staff, with few exceptions, dutifully followed the guidelines outlined by the department.[4]

The tendency to passivity and intellectual conformity on the part of Foreign Service officers was exacerbated during the 1930s by the American government's policy of political noninvolvement, cutbacks in State Department appropriations, and the public's view of diplomats as anachronistic survivors from some mythological world of "gold lace [and] bejewelled swords," all of which combined to foster a sense of professional purposelessness and to damage self-esteem. The diplomat's contribution to the military effort during World War II did help to restore his sense of purpose and to redeem his image in the public's mind. "Say what you like about the evils of State Department cooky pushers and scone shovers," read an article in the *Saturday Evening Post,* "the fact remains that the best of them are professionals in a trade that calls for patience, suavity, reliability, coolness and a faint dash of cynicism." Foreign Service officers, of course, underscored these sentiments. "I do not believe that there can be found anywhere," Henderson remarked, "persons who are more loyally, harmoniously, and effectively protecting and promoting the interests of the United States and serving the cause of world peace." Still, public criticism of the "aristocrat-diplomat" had not entirely abated. Letters of protest poured into the State Department upon the appointment of Dunn as ambassador to Italy in 1946, a man, so stated the *Nation*, "whose greatest diplomatic triumph remains the decision that a Vice-President's half sister is entitled to precede a Speaker's wife to the dinner table."[5]

While organizational morale, as a whole, improved during the war years, particularly among the group of officers who participated in post-war planning, career diplomats found disheartening the constriction of their professional role by the subordination of political objectives to military matters. Roosevelt's penchant for bypassing the secretary of state, a product of his personal style as well as his desire to conceal from public and official scrutiny his power-political "grand design," did not help matters. As late as February 1944, for example, Hull still had no knowledge of the decisions reached on postwar zones of occupation at the Teheran Conference, even though the Joint Chiefs of Staff had received Roosevelt's views in writing on November 18–19. As a consequence, Winant and Kennan functioned in a policy vacuum on the European Advisory Commission. Roosevelt's failure to keep the secretary of state informed resulted in similar communications gaps between the department and diplomats in Eastern Europe, who were often forced to depend on the British for information. To compound the problem, until Truman became president, information supplied by field missions was generally ignored. The Iranian crisis might have been averted, Henderson pointed out to Acheson in the summer of 1946, had Roosevelt taken "the recommendations of our people on the spot rather than those of foreign governments which have special interests at stake."[6]

The proliferation of competing bureaucratic entities such as the OSS, the Office of War Information, the Board of Economic Warfare, and the division of cultural relations also dispirited Foreign Service officers. The feeling that neither the public nor the government appreciated the career service ran through the pages of the *American Foreign Service Journal*, particularly after Truman's executive order late in 1945 to transfer technical specialists from OSS, OWI, and elsewhere into the once elite institution. The procession of diplomatic plenipotentiaries appointed by Roosevelt—Hopkins, Wallace, Hurley, and Harriman, "vagrant Pooh-Bahs" as John Paton Davies called them—further diminished the careerist's status by undermining his perceived authority as the representative of his government abroad. Cavendish Cannon took serious exception to Harriman's proposed fact-finding trip to Bucharest in the fall of 1944 lest it would appear to Rumanians that Washington had circumvented the diplomatic delegation under Burton Berry, which had not yet arrived, "to work through this high-powered but completely irregular channel." And everyone, of course, felt nothing but contempt for Hurley, who, frustrated by the continued civil war in China, intemperately charged that communist sympathizers within the Foreign Service had rendered ineffective Truman's policy to prevent the collapse of the Kuomintang. Since Hurley had already accused some Foreign Service officers—Davies for one—of being Communists, Durbrow capriciously wrote to Lane, "I am sure someone will come out and say there are a lot of fascists—so I'm glad to have known you."[7]

As a consequence of their shared values and beliefs, historical memories, social origins, and institutional experiences, Foreign Service officers tended to form common images of the Soviet Union. Yet they did not see the Soviets in the same way at the same time. This difference in perception resulted from variations in the social reality contingently experienced by diplomats in the field and the department.

Because of their direct contact with Russian-occupation forces or Soviet influenced political elements, careerists assigned to Eastern Europe in 1945 questioned almost immediately Moscow's willingness to support the Atlantic Charter-Yalta goals. Reluctant to abandon their hopes for the future, they sought information—Berry's and Melbourne's observation that Moscow had permitted free elections in Finland, as an example—to shore up their image of ideological cooperation. But as the Soviets and their puppets asserted political control of the region, particularly in countries on the perimeter of Russian borders, career officers implored Washington to assert diplomatically its commitment to the Atlantic Charter world and to preserve American prestige, which was identified with the internationalization of liberal-democratic ideals. Failure of the summit meeting at Potsdam to ameliorate Moscow's behavior eroded their image of Soviet cooperation and their expectations of postwar peace and harmony. To redress the anxiety produced by their inability to implement American foreign policy, they reinterpreted Soviet actions. The alternative of realistic cooperation was rejected because realpolitik was antithetical to the culture of foreign policy into which they had been socialized; realistic confrontation was unacceptable because it minimized the role of diplomacy. The historical memory of Moscow's post-World War I revolutionary aims and the more recent remembrance of Nazi expansionism provided a convenient model to satisfy cognitive and affective needs. Once Foreign Service officers adapted the framework of ideological confrontation and global expansionism, all Soviet behavior was overrationalized to fit their revised perception. Moreover, this image was self-perpetuating because the model on which it was based denied the existence of behavior—such as the Soviets demonstrated in Czechoslovakia and Hungary—that might disconfirm it.[8]

Diplomats in the field were also influenced by their contacts with the Eastern European political and social elite, with whom they identified, in the first instance, on the basis of shared class values, and with whom they spoke, they believed, a common political language. This is not to say that American diplomatic representatives, in spite of language deficiencies, had no contact with the peasantry, but rather that they filtered their impressions of these countries, in which most of them had had little, if any, prior experience, through the lens of the "thinking" people. The constant appeals of the prewar elite for American political intervention reinforced the image of ideological confrontation and exacerbated the diplomats' sense of guilt, as representatives of the United States, for having abandoned the defenders of democracy in Eastern Europe to their totalitarian fate. Eventually, Lane and Durbrow, among others, began to refer to the Crimea Conference as a "sell out" and a "capitulation." Bruins came to the view that the United States was "licked" from the day the military refused to liberate Prague. Shantz and Fraleigh traced the American government's postwar problems to its reluctance to launch an attack through the Balkans in 1944.[9]

In contrast to the way they viewed Groza, Bierut, and Tito, diplomats regarded Maniu, Mikolajczyk, and Šubašić as embattled democrats, "insiders-outside" their own governments, rendered impotent by forces beyond their control. In the same way, professional diplomats considered themselves "outsiders." Psychologically isolated because of Soviet imposed constraints on their activities, the State Department's failure to communicate regularly with them, and the lack of recognition for their efforts within the United States, they felt equally incapable of affecting the conditions of their existence, which likely strengthened their psychological identification with the prewar elite. Because of their personal and ideological identification with noncommunist political leaders and their mounting hostility toward the Soviet Union, Foreign Service officers tended to overlook the nondemocratic and, in some cases, Russophobic political histories of the Eastern European countries and the possibility that local leaders sought to use American support to advance their own political ambitions. Careerists were further inclined to stereotype the peoples of Eastern Europe, whose world view was determined by peasant traditions and historical fatalism, as struggling democrats awaiting political deliverance by their American saviors. Berry considered Rumania a "Latin island in a Slavic sea, [which] therefore furnishes a favorable soil in which the seeds of western democracy can take root and grow." Yet, virtually no mention was made of Moscow's extreme sensitivity to Rumania's antibolshevik–philofascist past and the intensity with which Rumanian armies had fought on the Russian front during the war. Despite the historic ties between the Bulgarians and Russians, Barnes was confident of the "natural friendship" the Bulgars felt for the United States. Bruins and Shantz expressed similar sentiments with regard to the Czechs and Yugoslavs, even though both peoples had demonstrated support for indigenous Communist parties.[10]

To a lesser degree Foreign Service officers received emotional and intellectual sustenance for their views from British diplomats in Eastern Europe. To be sure, careerists were suspicious of their British counterparts during much of 1945 because of their willingness to accede to a Soviet sphere of influence in the area. But they subsequently joined arms with them—Jacobs included—in a revival of the wartime alliance once Moscow tightened its hold on the region and the British began to express less reservedly their repugnance toward Soviet actions. Together they appealed to their respective governments to make joint representations to Moscow protesting its violation of the Yalta accords.

Diplomats in the department, on the other hand, were insulated from Soviet behavior. In Durbrow's words, "We didn't have to face the music."[11] Despite the flow of information from the field that deviated from the image of ideological cooperation, they were slow to alter their perceptions because they lacked their colleagues' firsthand experiences. Thus they reacted far more dispassionately than Berry or Barnes to the Rumanian coup and the Dimitrov episode.

Because of their participation in postwar planning, diplomats in the department tended to be more psychologically invested in the realization of the Atlantic Charter–Yalta goals. Since they believed that the policy of world cooperation was preferable to the alternatives of spheres of influence, nationalistic expansion, or military confrontation, they resisted dissonant evidence from the field that U.S.-Soviet cooperation was breaking down. As a case in point, Cannon was quick to recall Molotov's assurance that the Soviets would not intrude in Rumanian internal affairs, despite the flood of reports to the contrary from Bucharest. Of course, diplomats in the department—"outsiders-now-inside" the foreign-policy establishment—sympathized with the plight of their beleaguered colleagues in Eastern Europe, and after December 1945, once the costs of Washington's policy (the facilitation of communist expansionism) became clear to them, they reacted far more anxiously to incoming cables from the field.[12]

Since the United States had not yet formally reestablished diplomatic relations with the Balkan countries, diplomats in the department were not faced with the constant appeals from noncommunist leaders for American intercession, as were diplomats in the field. Nevertheless, they had to contend with bureaucratic pressures—analogous to the political force exerted on diplomats in the field by Eastern European officials—that constrained them from revising their estimate of Soviet postwar intentions. In the first place, they were sensitive to—and tried to compensate for—the criticism of Hopkins, Wallace, and others in the administration, who imputed to them, particularly the Russian specialists among them, reactionary, anti-Soviet biases. More importantly, the possible bureaucratic costs of recommending a policy change, namely, the loss of professional status, inhibited them from formulating alternative approaches. Given the negligible foreign-policy role they had played during the interwar years, they were understandably sensitive about their status within the foreign-policy establishment. Byrnes's penchant for confiding in a small circle of advisors and circumventing the department aggravated this natural bureaucratic caution and simultaneously depressed morale. Indicative of the South Carolinian's attitude, when a telegram reporting the proceedings of one day's meetings at the London foreign ministers conference was placed before him for his signature, he bellowed, "God Almighty, I might tell the President sometime what happened, but I'm never going to tell those little bastards in the State Department anything about it." Thus careerists frequently diluted the harsh and even belligerent cables from the field, which Matthews, for one, considered impractical and potentially dangerous, discredited the message source in some cases, such as that of Barnes, or simply did not pass them on to the secretary. "The men in the field viewed things from a narrow perspective," Charles Yost explained, "and didn't appreciate that the department was concerned with the entire world." Robert S. Folsom, second secretary in the Budapest legation, recalled, "For months I know we were regarded by those in the state department as Russo-phobes if not war mongers and that our reporting was discounted."[13]

Finally, Washington-based diplomats were affected by domestic opinion, or, better stated, their perceptions of the popular mood. Although the American public clearly influenced the decision to remove United States forces from Europe after the war, its attitude toward the Soviet Union—both in its manic and depressive phases—was basically shaped by government officials and the foreign-policy elite. Despite the amorphous nature of opinion polls during most of 1945, diplomats concluded that the American people would not tolerate deviation from the postwar policy of cooperation along Atlantic Charter lines. For the most part, however, public opinion provided a convenient rationalization for Foreign Service officers to maintain their attachment to prevailing policy, first cooperation, then, after the Moscow conference of December 1945, confrontation. In both instances, diplomats heard what they wanted to hear.[14]

A final distinction between diplomats in the department and the field was their state of psychological well-being. Sheltered from the conditions in Eastern Europe, careerists in Washington remained hopeful until the end of 1945 that divisions between the United States and the Soviet Union would be resolved. By early 1946, however, with the onset of the Iranian crisis and Stalin's election speech, they also concluded that the Soviets were incorrigibly opposed to the world of peace, prosperity, and harmony defined by the Atlantic Charter. But bogged down by the bureaucratic inertia of the department and ill-prepared by their training to suggest major policy alternatives, they were unable to transform their altered image of the Soviet Union into a new foreign-policy strategy. Branded as reactionaries when postwar cooperation seemed likely, now they were characterized by the likes of Admiral Leahy as "appeasers."[15] Kennan's "long telegram" and the containment policy it spawned rescued them from the policy vacuum in which they were mired and eased the demoralization they experienced following the erosion of their postwar expectations.

Witness to Soviet actions in the USSR and Eastern Europe, diplomats in the field increasingly despaired of postwar cooperation. The department's subsequent reassessment of Soviet aims and its gradual reformulation of American foreign policy did little to brighten their spirits. Psychologically incarcerated in the meaninglessness of their "Russian exile," their despair was only deepened by Washington's implicit renunciation of Eastern Europe to Moscow's sphere of influence. To cope with the anxiety of meaninglessness that they experienced, some careerists lifelessly accepted the conditions of their existence, ritualistically performing their diplomatic duties. This attitude was demonstrated by Schoenfeld and Bruins in Hungary and Czechoslovakia. Jacobs, Shantz, and by the winter of 1946–47, Berry and Melbourne as well, psychologically retreated from the conditions they encountered in Albania, Yugoslavia, and Rumania. Barnes and Lane tried to overcome their anxiety against the Soviets and their representatives in Bulgaria and Poland. Unlike their colleagues, they crusaded for American ideals, thereby provoking bitter resentment from the governments to which they were accredited.[16]

There was yet another response to the anxiety of self-estrangement aroused by developments in Eastern Europe, which manifested itself not in passive resignation, retreat, or febrile devotion to a cause, but in the active and creative participation in the conditions of one's existence. Kennan too experienced the futility of American efforts to win over the Soviets to the Atlantic Charter–Yalta principles, and he too found himself "obliged to fling his arms about," in Ortega's words, "to swim shipwrecked in that sea which is the world."[17] But, unlike his colleagues, who succumbed to the despair caused by their social and cultural disconnectedness from beliefs and values passionately affirmed, he constructed out of the meaninglessness which surrounded him a different explanation for the reality he encountered. There was still hope for cooperation with Moscow, he contended, provided American foreign policy were reoriented along balance-of-power lines. John Paton Davies, who was influenced by Kennan, also subscribed to this position. However, by the summer of 1946, coincidentally after Kennan had departed Moscow, his perceptions of the Soviets became more ideological in focus; and by the end of the year, he had grown increasingly disheartened by the Soviet challenge to American values.

Kennan, of course, was not unaffected by ideological considerations—as his telegrams of the 1930s and later attest—or by narrow, nationalistic concerns. His worldview was no more monolithic than that of his colleagues. Like them, he was disposed at any given time to see "reality" in one way as opposed to another. In this case, notwithstanding the ideological distortion of the "long telegram" and its famous sequel, the "Mr. X" article in *Foreign Affairs* that Kennan anonymously authored in 1947, the dominant perspective was realistic cooperation.[18]

Kennan did not despair of peaceful U.S.-Soviet postwar relations in part because he never emotionally committed himself, as his colleagues did, to the image of ideological cooperation. In addition, he had encountered psychological isolation and alienation all of his life. He was reared by a stern stepmother, who did not offer him much emotional intimacy; and he interacted little with his father, who was not a demonstratively affectionate person himself. As Kennan stated in his memoirs, he was obliged "to pick up my understanding of his [father's] mental world and reactions largely by bashful sidelong glances." Lonely, overly sensitive, and self-conscious of his own peripheral existence through his college years, he desperately sought—as his later behavior in Lisbon and in London with the European Advisory Commission revealed—personal recognition. In short, Kennan was accustomed to being an "outsider," and as a consequence, he was better prepared than his fellow careerists to reconcile himself to the difficult conditions experienced in the field. Reflecting on his Foreign Service years after the war, he wrote that the professional diplomat must develop sufficient emotional discipline to contend with the vicissitudes of life abroad, discipline which, he felt, began during one's formative years in the home. "Too often it is the man who in his college years basks in the sunlight of athletic success and student popularity who later wilts under the loneliness and frustrations of life abroad," he later wrote in what seems transparent self-revelation. "Sometimes it is the moody, unadjusted student, struggling to forge his own standards in a callous collegiate society, who develops within himself the thoughtfulness to comprehend a foreign environment and the self-discipline to adjust himself to it."[19]

What makes Kennan's realpolitik view—and more importantly, his consistent adherence to it—so significant is that it set him apart from other Foreign Service officers. Ironically, it was he whom Washington contacted for an analysis of Soviet aims when its postwar hopes were finally laid to rest in February 1946. It was tragic for America's future relations with the USSR that Kennan's "long telegram" did not present clearly the theme of realistic cooperation he had sounded during the previous several years. This is not to suggest that diplomats in the department, the Truman administration, or other members of the foreign-policy establishment would have suddenly divorced themselves from long-held cultural predispositions antagonistic to a power-political division of Europe into spheres of influences. To be sure, they were historically unprepared for a realpolitik paradigm of foreign affairs. But, admittedly in hindsight, they might well have tempered the rhetoric of ideological confrontation, which assured the continued estrangement of the two powers, and possibly have focused more on the realistic compromise reached at Yalta. Certainly Kennan was aware that the department's repeated requests for his views implied that his words would be read with intense interest. But in his eagerness to be heard, or perhaps in his resentment at not having been heard, he felt it incumbent on him to present the "whole truth." In so doing, he obscured the truth that he perceived. For him personally, however, the receipt of his epistle ended far more than his "official loneliness." With the eulogies of his superiors ringing in his ears, he was personally vindicated. Finally he counted. Finally he was recognized and approved.

Epilogue:
To the Truman Doctrine

By the winter of 1946–47 Foreign Service officers had become obsessed with the appearance of an ideologically expansionist Soviet Union. Convinced by past developments in Eastern Europe and Moscow's rhetoric of the universality of Soviet objectives, they braced themselves for the next challenge to the free world. It was this bipolar image of international politics, in which divergent ideologies were pitted against each other in a perpetual Cold War, if not armed struggle, that underlay the policy statement on U.S.-Soviet relations submitted by Matthews to the secretary of state on January 17, 1947. The USSR was not simply the only power that presented a threat to United States security, he wrote, it was also the only power that "today advocates a way of life based on a standard of values fundamentally at variance with our own" and that "openly proclaims" the inevitability of conflict between the two systems of government. "Lenin's slogan 'One step back, two steps forward' is still the gospel for the men of the Kremlin." Reiterating Kennan's analysis in the "long telegram," Matthews advocated a global policy to contain Soviet expansionism, which included the strengthening of American armed forces and the development of stable conditions within the United States. Possibly one day Kremlin leaders would recognize that "a policy of live and let live" was more advantageous "than a crusade for world communism which contains within itself the seeds of war, devastation and ruin."[1]

Fear of Soviet expansionism mounted in February. On the afternoon of the twenty-first, Henderson received word that the counselor of the British embassy wanted to meet with him immediately. Shortly thereafter, H. M. Sichel arrived at the department and handed Henderson two documents. They stated that Soviet-influenced communist elements in Greece and Turkey threatened to topple the governments of those countries unless massive economic assistance were extended. This came as no surprise to Henderson. Reports from Barnes, Jacobs, Durbrow, and others at the end of 1946 had informed the department that Greek Communists were being trained in Bulgaria under Russian supervision with the objective of subverting and overthrowing the Greek government and menacing nearby Turkey. What followed, however, did. Since His Majesty's government, which had shouldered most of the burden of assistance until then, was, in spite of the American loan of 1946, incapable of providing

211

the necessary aid, it had decided to pull out of both countries at the end of March. If Greece and Turkey and the entire eastern Mediterranean were to be saved from communist subversion, the United States would have to come to the rescue.[2]

As soon as Sichel had left, Henderson telephoned Hickerson. Recognizing the seriousness of the situation, they wasted no time in conveying the news to Acheson, who promptly directed them to prepare a preliminary position paper for presentation to Secretary of State Marshall on Monday morning. Henderson, Hickerson, and their staffs in the Near Eastern and European divisions worked feverishly through the weekend. At 11:00 A.M. on Sunday, they delivered their memorandum to Acheson at his Georgetown home. He approved it. At nine o'clock the following morning, it was on Marshall's desk.[3]

After Marshall had read the position paper and conferred with Lord Inverchapel (né Archibald Clark-Kerr), the British ambassador, he discussed the matter with the president. They agreed that the United States had no alternative. "The ideals and the traditions of our nation demanded that we come to the aid of Greece and Turkey," Truman observed. On the twenty-sixth the president, Marshall, and Acheson, joined by Admiral Leahy, met with legislative leaders before whom they announced their decision to request funds from Congress to aid Greece and Turkey. Marshall broached the issue in his characteristically laconic manner, which prompted the congressional gathering to question whether the United States had not been inveigled again to pull British chestnuts out of the fire. At this point, Acheson asked for the floor. It was not merely Soviet pressure on Greece and Turkey that concerned the administration, he dramatically explained, but the possibility that a breakthrough in those countries would lead to the penetration of China and Africa, the countries of the Middle East, and much worse, Western Europe, each of which, like the Eastern European states before them, would tumble over like so many little dominoes. What was at stake was the security and well-being of the entire world. The sense of dread he conveyed filled the vacuum of silence that followed his remarks, lingered on for a moment or two longer, and then prodded Senator Vandenberg to speak. "Mr. President," he solemnly intoned, "if you will say that to the Congress and the country, I will support you and I believe that most of its members will do the same."[4]

The following day intensive preparation began in the department on the special message the president would deliver to Congress fifteen days later "to put the world on notice that it would be our policy to support the cause of freedom wherever it was threatened." Career diplomats went about their work enthusiastically. Henderson, who was responsible for drafting the legislation for the Greek-Turkish aid bill, was delighted that

Truman had decided to extend American assistance worldwide. It was no longer possible to "cherish the hope that 'things will somehow get better.' " Durbrow remarked. "The Soviet Union is striving to attain a totalitarian secret police type of world subject to its control, and we want the world organized along the lines of western democracy in which the individual is accorded certain inalienable basic rights." To counteract Moscow's goal, he asserted, the United States must "resolve to continue on *our* One Democratic World course." Bohlen shared these sentiments. America's failure to assume responsibility abroad would affect millions around the world.[5]

Only Kennan opposed the new policy. Aid to Greece was one thing; but Turkey was not faced with the same communist threat. Moreover, in his opinion, the "doctrine" that the department and SWNCC had prepared was too sweeping, too moralizing, too inflexible. As he had stated to audiences within and without the government in January, Marxism-Leninism was not the driving force of Soviet actions; its function was "to distort and embellish" the reality that ultimately derived from the traditions and the deeper insecurity of the Russian past. "Ideology," in short, was "a product and not a determinant of social and political reality." But his remonstrations came too late. The postwar die, modelled on events in Eastern Europe and on Kennan's own assessment of Soviet objectives, was cast.[6]

After weeks of executive and public hearings, the Senate and House ratified aid to Greece and Turkey and, more importantly, launched the administration's program to support the cause of democracy around the world. Support for the Truman Doctrine gave congressional and public sanction to the imagery of ideological confrontation employed by career diplomats and administration officials after 1946 to define U.S.-Soviet relations. At the same time, it virtually ruled out the possibility of cooperation between the two powers in accordance with the realpolitik compromise reached at Yalta, which, notwithstanding the Cold-War rhetoric, remained intact. Having perceived Yalta more in terms of the Atlantic Charter and the declaration on liberated Europe, Foreign Service officers were jubilant over the public's reaction to the Truman Doctrine. In their judgment, the United States would now be able to protect other nations from falling victim to the same communized fate as had the Eastern European states. "Had we not acted promptly," Matthews averred, "there is little doubt that Greece would have become a Soviet satellite like Rumania, Hungary, Bulgaria and Czechoslovakia." In Kohler's words, the Truman Doctrine trumpeted to the world "that this permanent American revolution is the way to a better life for more and more of the earth's population."[7]

There is reason to suspect that Stalin was more than a little concerned about the direction American foreign policy was taking following the enunciation of the Truman Doctrine. In April, while the Moscow conference of foreign ministers was in session, the Soviet leader met with Minnesota Governor Harold Stassen.[8] Stalin was surprisingly amiable during their chat, much as he had been during the war years. He may well have been trying to intimate by his behavior that he wished to strike some mutually acceptable bargain with the United States on Germany and Eastern Europe. While this was certainly possible, American Foreign Service officers and administration officials alike paid no heed to his symbolic overture. At this late date, there was no turning back from the road to Armageddon.

Notes

Introduction

1. Joseph M. Jones, *The Fifteen Weeks*, pp. 17–19, 269–74; Dean Acheson, *Present at the Creation*, p. 297.

2. George M. Elsey, memorandum, March 9, 1947, George M. Elsey Papers, Box 17, Truman Library (hereafter Elsey Papers).

3. This existential definition of image, which fuses subject and object, differs from both the essentialist description of image as a mentalistic representation of reality and the empiricist notion of it as a veridical "copy" of the material world. For the philosophical foundation of existential psychology, see Edmund Husserl, *Ideas: General Introduction to Pure Phenomenology;* Martin Heidegger, *Being and Time;* Karl Jaspers, *Philosophy,* 3 vols.; and Jean-Paul Sartre, *The Transcendence of the Ego.* For psychological studies, see Ludwig Binswanger, *Being-in-the-World,* and Viktor Frankl, *The Doctor and the Soul;* and for more recent works, Rollo May, Ernest Angel, and Henri Ellenberger, eds., *Existence;* and Salvatore R. Maddi, "The Search for Meaning," in *Nebraska Symposium on Motivation.*

4. Although head of the division of Near Eastern and African affairs after 1944, Loy Henderson has been included in the sample because of his intimate association with Russian affairs from World War I to 1945.

Chapter 1

1. Recent histories of the origins and development of the diplomatic service include Robert D. Schulzinger, *The Making of the Diplomatic Mind,* and Warren R. Ilchman, *Professional Diplomacy in the United States.* For anecdotal histories written by former diplomats, see William Barnes and John Heath Morgan, *The Foreign Service of the United States,* and W. Wendell Blancké, *The Foreign Service of the United States.* See also Martin Weil's chatty account of the diplomatic elite, *A Pretty Good Club.* Smith Simpson, *Anatomy of the State Department,* pp. 1–7; J. Rives Childs, *American Foreign Service,* pp. 10–11.

2. Ilchman, p. 44.

3. Waldo Heinrichs, Jr., "Bureaucracy and Professionalism in American Career Diplomacy," in *Twentieth-Century Foreign Policy,* ed. John Braeman, Robert Bremner, and David Brody, pp. 142–53; Ilchman, pp. 51–64; Henry S. Villard, *Affairs at State,* p. 58.

4. The portrait presented here, based on data from the *Biographical Register of the Department of State,* parallels the detailed demographic analysis undertaken by James L. McCamy in *The Administration of American Foreign Affairs.*

5. Minutes of the Board of Review of Foreign Service Personnel, December 23, 1924, National Archives, Record Group 59 (hereafter NA, RG 59); Shaw to Berry, January 21, 1937, Box 7, Burton Berry Papers, Indiana University (hereafter Berry Papers).

6. Ilchman, pp. 225–37; Heinrichs, "Bureaucracy and Professionalism," pp. 179–203; Villard, pp. 145, 152; H. Freeman Matthews, "Memoirs of a Passing Era," p. 43; interviews with Rudolph Schoenfeld, January 16, 1976, Loy Henderson, January 24, 1976, and Jake Millar, Febraury 11, 1976, Washington, D.C.

7. Peter Blau and W. Richard Scott, *Formal Organizations,* pp. 60–63; Bernard Barber, "Some Problems in the Sociology of the Professions," *Daedalus* 92 (Fall 1963); 669–88;

William J. Goode, "Encroachment, Charlatanism, and the Emerging Profession: Psychology, Sociology, and Medicine," *American Sociological Review* 25 (December 1960): 902–14.

8. John Harr has identified an area specialist as an individual with five or more years of experience in a selected region. See *The Anatomy of the Foreign Service*, pp. 55–56. John Paton Davies, *Dragon by the Tail*, p. 211; interviews with Foy Kohler, September 13, 1976, Coral Gables, Fla., and Rudolph Schoenfeld; J. V. A. MacMurray to Arthur Bliss Lane, January 7, 1936, Box 11, Folder 218, Arthur Bliss Lane Papers, Yale University (hereafter Lane Papers).

9. Villard, pp. 34–35; James N. Gantebein, "Study by Foreign Service Officers in American Universities," *The American Foreign Service Journal* 16 (October 1939): 563 (hereafter *AFSJ*); G. Howland Shaw to Berry, February 22, 1930, and Berry to Shaw, April 5 and June 4, 1930, Box 3, Berry Papers.

10. Grew radio address, February 24, 1926, vol. 32, "Letters," Joseph C. Grew Papers, Harvard University (hereafter Grew Papers); Marriner speech, April 27, 1931, State Department Decimal File 111.24/48, NA, RG 59; Hughes, quoted in *AFSJ* 1 (November 1924): 38.

11. Hughes, quoted in *AFSJ, supra,* p. 37; George F. Kennan, *Memoirs, 1925–1950,* pp. 19–20; Loy Henderson, "Memoirs," 2:190.

12. See *AFSJ* for October, November, and December 1924 as examples. DeWitt Poole, "University Training for the Foreign Service of the United States," *AFSJ* 8 (September 1931): 344–45; J. Rives Childs, "Democraticized Diplomacy," *AFSJ* 11 (October 1934): 562; George V. Allen, "The Utility of a Trained and Permanent Foreign Service," *AFSJ* 13 (January 1936): 36.

13. Anthony Downs, *Inside Bureacracy,* pp. 228–36; Blau and Scott, p. 109; George C. Homans, *The Human Group,* pp. 112–20, 457–59; interviews with Mrs. H. F. Arthur Schoenfeld, October 25, 1975, and Edmund Dorsz, May 6, 1976, Washington, D.C.; Lord (William) Strang, *The Foreign Office,* pp. 161–62; Henderson, "Memoirs," 5:874.

14. Henderson, "Memoirs," 2:244–50.

15. Bruins speech, July 5, 1929, State Department Decimal File 123B835/78, NA, RG 59; interviews with Henderson (May 27, 1976), H. Freeman Matthews (May 20, 1976), and Rudolph Schoenfeld, Washington, D.C. The diplomat's sense of mission corresponds strikingly to the self-image of both the military and naval officers described by Peter Karsten in *The Naval Aristocracy* and Morris Janowitz in *The Professional Soldier.* Schulzinger, chap. 4, p. 93.

16. Tracy Hollingsworth Lay, *The Foreign Service of the United States,* pp. vii–x. Cliques tended to be formed by senior officers to promote the career interests of deserving younger men, whom Mrs. Schoenfeld referred to as "boot-blacks." Dorsz interview; Blau and Scott, pp. 121–23; Berry to Shaw, January 26, 1935, Box 5, Berry Papers. See Andrew M. Scott, "The Department of State: Formal Organization and Informal Culture," *International Studies Quarterly* 13 (March 1969): 1–19, and "Environmental Change and Organizational Adaptation: The Problem of the State Department," *International Studies Quarterly* 14 (March 1970): 85–95. Social distinctions based on rank within the service were not dissimilar from those in the military. See Janowitz, pp. 178–90.

17. See *AFSJ* for October 1924, August 1925, and June 1926; Charles E. Bohlen, *Witness to History, 1929–1969,* p. 7; Schoenfeld to William Castle, September 19, 1927, Schoenfeld Papers.

18. Interviews with Rudolph Schoenfeld, Henderson (May 15, 1976), and Elbridge Durbrow (January 29, 1976), Washington, D.C.; Shantz address, February 16, 1925, 123 Shantz, NA, RG 59.

19. Lay, p. x.

20. Graham Stuart, *American Diplomatic and Consular Practice,* p. 169; Cordell Hull, *The Memoirs of Cordell Hull,* 1:188–89; Bohlen, quoted in *Toward a Modern Diplomacy: A Report to the American Foreign Service Association,* p. 4; Durbrow interview, January 29,

1976; Villard, p. 67; Messersmith to Ben Cherrington, June 8 and November 24, 1939, State Department Decimal File 121.50/50 (hereafter designated by decimal number only), NA, RG 59.

21. Grew to Hughes, December 30, 1924, cited in Grew's memoirs, *Turbulent Era,* 1:644; Minutes of the Board of Review of Foreign Service Personnel, March 20, 1927, NA, RG 59; Henderson, "Memoirs," 2:258–59; Waldo Heinrichs, Jr., *American Ambassador,* chap. 8; Schoenfeld to Lane, March 9, 1928, and Lane to Schoenfeld, May 17, 1928, Schoenfeld Papers.

22. Henderson, "Memoirs," 4:530–31; Berry to Shaw, December 25, 1934, Box 5, Berry Papers; Schoenfeld to James W. Gantebein, October 23, 1934, Schoenfeld Papers.

23. Robert Bendiner, *The Riddle of the State Department,* pp. 109–19, 184–85.

24. Joseph H. Baird, "Professionalized Diplomacy," *AFSJ* 16 (October 1939): 542–43; William P. Cochran, Jr., "Ambassador Hugh Gibson on the Foreign Service," *AFSJ* 14 (June 1937): 375–76; Schoenfeld to Norman Armour, February 14, 1934, Schoenfeld Papers; see "H," "The Modern Diplomat," *Foreign Affairs* 15 (April 1937).

25. Villard, p. 163; Henderson, "Memoirs," 3:439; George to secretary, December 31, 1934, 120.7/390, NA, RG 59; Kennan, *Memoirs, 1925–1950,* p. 41; Berry to parents, July 18, 1932; to Shaw, October 28, 1934, and May 20, 1937; to Matthews, February 1947, Boxes 3, 4, 6, 15, Berry Papers; Schoenfeld to James R. Sheffield, November 30, 1935, Schoenfeld Papers; Bruins to son Bill, March 29, 1953, courtesy Mrs. John H. Bruins, Washington, D.C.

26. Wallace diary note, May 10, 1942, in John Morton Blum, ed., *The Price of Vision,* pp. 77–78; Roosevelt quoted in John F. Campbell, *The Foreign Affairs Fudge Factory,* p. 114; interviews with Charles Yost, May 6, 1976, and Henderson, January 24, 1976, Washington, D.C.; Bohlen, *Witness,* p. 129; Matthews, "Memoirs," pp. 257–58; diary entry of J. Pierrepont Moffat, January 14, 1941, vol. 45, J. Pierrepont Moffat Papers, Harvard University (hereafter Moffat Papers); Schoenfeld to Norman Armour, February 20, 1933, Schoenfeld Papers; Simpson, pp. 52–53.

27. Kennan quoted in Campbell, *Fudge Factory,* p. 49.

28. Hugh R. Wilson, *Diplomacy as a Career,* pp. 49–50; Kennan, *Memoirs, 1925–1950,* pp. 75–77; Charles W. Thayer, *Diplomat,* p. 270.

Chapter 2

1. Peter Filene, *Americans and the Soviet Experiment,* p. 67; Klieforth to Samuel Harper, November 26, 1923, Box 10, Folder 33, Samuel Harper Papers, University of Chicago (hereafter Harper Papers).

2. Press release of Secretary of State Charles Evans Hughes, March 21, 1923, Box 56, Folder 14, Harper Papers; Castle quoted in *AFSJ* 3 (February 1926): 43; memorandum prepared in office of Eastern European affairs, March 2, 1926, General Records of the Soviet Union, NA, RG 59.

3. Bohlen, *Witness,* pp. 8, 39; Kennan, *Memoirs, 1925–1950,* p. 84; see *AFSJ* 10 (February 1933); 54, 59. A number of Kelley's and Packer's speeches can be found in Box 4, Robert Kelley Papers, Georgetown University.

4. None of the diplomats interviewed remembered having opposed the decision; none recalled any strong positive reaction either. See William Phillips's diary entry of October 31, 1933, vol. 3, William Phillips Papers, Harvard University (hereafter Phillips Papers); Jacobs diary courtesy Mrs. Marjorie Riddle, Chapel Hill, North Carolina; Grew Diary entry, vol. 65, Grew Papers; *AFSJ,* December 1933, p. 430.

5. Bullitt speech, January 19, 1934, Records of the office of Eastern European affairs, staff studies, NA, RG 59.

6. Henderson letter to Hugh De Santis, September 13, 1976; interviews with Kennan and Kohler; Kennan, *Memoirs, 1925–1950,* pp. 31–32.

7. Interviews with Henderson (January 24, 1976) and Durbrow (January 29, 1976); Bullitt to MacMurray, December 12, 1933, Box 135, J. V. A. MacMurray Papers, Princeton University (hereafter MacMurray Papers); Henderson, "Memoirs," 3:612–14; Michael T. Ruddy, "Charles Bohlen and the Soviet Union, 1929–1969" (Ph.D. dissertation, Kent State University, 1973), p. 11; Ralph Block Oral History, Truman Library, pp. 20, 23; George V. Allen Oral History, Columbia University, p. 34; Bohlen personnel file 123Bohlen/36, May 29, 1931, NA, RG 59.

8. Henderson, "Memoirs," 2:366, 3:614–21; Louis Sussdorf, Jr., to secretary, 123H383/44, November 8, 1928, NA, RG 59; interviews with Henderson, January 24, 1976; Robert McBride, May 8, 1976, Charlottesville, Va.; and Kennan, September 7, 1976, Princeton, N.J.

9. Kennan to secretary, June 16, 1933, 861.00 Communist, All-Union Central Executive/43; Felix Cole to secretary (drafted by Kennan and A. S.), June 20, 1933, 661.00/175, NA, RG 59; Henderson, "Memoirs," 3:322–24, 480–81; Kennan interview.

10. Henderson, "Memoirs," 3:603, 5:909–10; interviews with Henderson (January 24, 1976) and Kennan; Bohlen, Witness, pp. 12, 21–23. Thomas Maddux has stated that the Moscow embassy viewed with suspicion Russia's entrance into the league. Actually, suspicions of Soviet intentions did not begin to mount until after the Kirov episode. See "Watching Stalin Maneuver between Hitler and the West: American Diplomats and Soviet Diplomacy, 1934–1939," Diplomatic History 1 (Spring 1977): 146–47.

11. John C. Wiley to secretary (Bohlen drafted), January 19, 1935, 861.00/11589, and February 9, 1935, 761.00/255, NA, RG 59; Bullitt to secretary, April 20, 1936, President's Secretary's File, Box 67, Franklin D. Roosevelt Papers, Roosevelt Library (hereafter FDR Papers); Beatrice Farnsworth, William C. Bullitt and the Soviet Union, pp. 152–53; Henderson, "Memoirs," 3:322–24, 5:883–86; Kennan memorandum, "The War Problem of the Soviet Union," March 1935, Box 1, George F. Kennan Papers, Princeton University (hereafter Kennan Papers); Henderson to secretary, January 17, 1936, 711.61/592, NA, RG 59; Shantz to secretary (Page drafted), September 21, 1935, 861.00-Congress, Communist International, VII/120, NA, RG 59.

12. Henderson to secretary, 861.011/33, 861.001/11629, 861.00/11636, 861.00/11637, and 861.011/40, respectively dated June 12, August 18, September 1, September 1, and September 28, 1936, NA, RG 59.

13. Henderson to secretary, November 16, 1936, 711.61/611; Bullitt to secretary (Kennan drafted), March 19, 1936, 761.00/269, NA, RG 59; Phillips diary entry, May 21, 1936, vol. 10, Phillips Papers.

14. Henderson to secretary, June 12, 1937, 861.20/389, and September 28, 1937, 761.90H/38, NA, RG 59; Henderson, "Memoirs," 5:955.

15. Kennan to secretary, March 18, 1937, 861.00 Party, All-Union Communist/186, NA, RG 59; Henderson to secretary, September 20, 1937, U.S. State Department, Foreign Relations of the United States: The Soviet Union, 1933–1939, pp. 391–94 (hereafter FRUS); December 23, 1937 (Norris B. Chipman drafted), 861.00 Party, All-Union Communist/193, NA, RG 59; Henderson, "Memoirs," 5:941–50; Henderson to Kelley, April 29, 1937, 861.00/11702; to secretary (Bohlen drafted), February 19, 1938, 861.00 Party, All-Union Communist/196; March 17, 1937, 861.01/2124, NA, RG 59.

16. Henderson to secretary, June 18, 1937, 861.20/385, and Henderson to Kelley, supra, NA, RG 59; Bohlen, Witness, p. 55; Kennan to secretary, February 18, 1937, 861.00/11675, NA, RG 59. Stalin's actions, as Kennan implied, were preceded by those of other well-known Russian despots, notably Ivan III and Ivan IV.

17. Henderson to secretary, December 22, 1937, 861.00/11745; Bohlen to secretary, 861.00 Supreme Soviet/2 and 5, respectively dated January 17 and February 2, 1938; Henderson to secretary (Page drafted), January 7, 1938, 861.00/11750, NA, RG 59; Henderson, "Memoirs," 5:888–908.

18. Henderson, "Memoirs," 3:597–98, 4:796–98; Kennan to Harper, June 7, 1938, Box 10, Folder 22, Harper Papers.

19. Henderson to secretary, January 26, 1938, 761.00/292, NA, RG 59; to Lane, May 19, 1937, Box 64, Folder 1148, Lane Papers; Henderson, "Memoirs," 5:969–73; Henderson to secretary (Bohlen drafted), February 18, 1938, 761.00/293; February 18, 1938, 861.00B/1680, NA, RG 59; Bohlen Oral History, Columbia University, p. 14; Kennan memorandum, December 23, 1937, 711.61/628, NA, RG 59.

20. Henderson to secretary, September 20, 1937, *FRUS*, 3:537–41; Page to secretary, December 7, 1937, 761.94/1005; Kennan memorandum, January 13, 1938, 761.93/1632, NA, RG 59; Kennan, *Memoirs, 1925–1950*, p. 72; Kennan memorandum, "The War Problem of the Soviet Union," *supra*.

21. Henderson to secretary, April 17, 1937, 861.01/2128; to Kelley, April 27, 1937, 761.00/284, NA, RG 59.

22. Henderson, "Memoirs," 7:1245; Bohlen, *Witness*, pp. 72–86.

23. Henderson, "Memoirs," 7:1283–84; Henderson to Harper, August 24, 1939, Box 21, Folder 17, Harper Papers; Bohlen, *Witness*, pp. 60, 63, 66, 82; Page memorandum, April 17, 1939, 661.6531/133, NA, RG 59.

24. Henderson memoranda, August 21, 1939, 661.6231/242, and August 25, 1939, 861.50/913, NA, RG 59; Kennan draft of paper, "German-Soviet Relations," ca. 1940, Box 4, Kennan Papers.

25. Bohlen to secretary, September 13, 14, 17 and October 4, 1939, Box 3, Charles E. Bohlen Papers, Library of Congress (hereafter Bohlen Papers); Steinhardt to secretary (Bohlen drafted), March 1, 1940, 661.6231/274, NA, RG 59.

26. Henderson, "Memoirs," 8:1369–77; Henderson to Hull, June 30, 1940, 711.61/6-3040, NA, RG 59.

27. Henderson and Page to Moffat, December 11, 1939, 711.61/691, NA, RG 59; Henderson to John Wiley, December 19, 1939, Box 7, John C. Wiley Papers, Roosevelt Library (hereafter Wiley Papers); Henderson memos of conversations with Welles and Oumansky, July 26, 1940, in records of office of Eastern European affairs, "Conversations and Related Memoranda," July 1940–April 1941; with Welles, Oumansky and Atherton, August 12, 1940, 711.61/746-1/2; to Welles, August 15, 1940, 861.20111/2; memo of conversation with naval and other defense officials, January 21, 1941, 611.6131/1-2141, NA, RG 59; memo to Welles, February 10, 1941, 861.74 Radio Corporation of America/36, NA, RG 59; Henderson memorandum, July 15, 1940, *FRUS*, 1:389–92; Henderson memo to Atherton, August 25, 1940, 840.01/8-2640; Page memorandum (Dunn and Henderson initialled), October 3, 1940, 711.61/782, NA, RG 59.

28. Bohlen, *Witness*, p. 102; Steinhardt to secretary (Bohlen drafted), November 10, 1940, 761.62/744, Box 3, Bohlen Papers.

29. Bohlen, *Witness*, p. 105; Henderson to Steinhardt, December 13, 1940, Box 29, Laurence A. Steinhardt Papers, Library of Congress (hereafter Steinhardt Papers).

30. Kennan, *Russia and the West*, p. 330; Henderson to Harper, June 27, 1941, Box 22, Folder 21, Harper Papers; to Steinhardt, August 18, 1941, Box 33, Steinhardt Papers.

31. Interviews with Henderson (January 24, 1976), Durbrow (January 29, 1976), Kennan, and Kohler; Bohlen undated notes on Soviet-American relations, Box 3, Bohlen Papers; Kennan draft of lecture, "Russia," May 20, 1938; "Some Fundamentals of Russian-American Relations," 1938?, Box 2, Kennan Papers; Kennan, *Memoirs, 1925–1950*, pp. 133–34.

Chapter 3

1. For a favorable interpretation of American objectives, see Bryce Wood, *The Making of the Good Neighbor Policy*. William Appleman Williams, *The Tragedy of American Diplomacy*, and Lloyd C. Gardner, *Economic Aspects of New Deal Diplomacy*, dispute

Washington's altruistic intentions. Dick Steward's analysis in *Trade and Hemisphere: The Good Neighbor Policy and Reciprocal Trade* falls somewhere in between. See also Robert Freeman Smith, *The United States and Cuba: Business and Diplomacy, 1917–1960*.

2. Lane to Grew, September 29, 1933, Box 57, Folder 1074, Lane Papers, Phillips diary entry, November 10, 1933, vol. 3, Phillips Papers; Vladimir Petrov, *A Study in Diplomacy*, pp. 8–9; Dorsz interview.

3. Lane to secretary, January 3, 1934, 817.00/7922, NA, RG 59; February 27, 1934, *FRUS*, 5:541–42; Petrov, pp. 30–31, 36–42.

4. Lane to secretary, May 22, 1934, *FRUS*, 5:559–60 and July 23, 1934, 5:511–15; March 26, 1934, 817.1051/834; May 14, 1935, 817.00/8225; October 9, 1935 (Guy W. Ray drafted), 611.1731/135, NA, RG 59; Petrov, p. 47, 54–58.

5. Lane to secretary, February 11, 1936, *FRUS*, 5:815–16; February 22, 1936 (Ray drafted), 817.00/8380, NA, RG 59; Lane to Welles, February 8, 1936, Box 62, Folder 1118, Lane Papers.

6. Petrov, p. 74.

7. Grew comments concerning Schoenfeld, December 29, 1924, vol. 26, "Letters," Grew Papers; Schoenfeld to James R. Sheffield, June 28, 1926, Schoenfeld Papers; Matthews, "Memoirs," pp. 97, 125; McBride interview; William L. Shirer, *The Collapse of the Third Republic*, p. 812.

8. Schoenfeld to J. Reuben Clark, October 12, 1931, Schoenfeld Papers; Matthews, "Memoirs," pp. 56–57, 76; Mrs. Schoenfeld interview.

9. Matthews, "Memoirs," pp. 116, 121–24; Matthews to secretary, May 2, 1934, 837.00/5042; July 30, 1935, 837.00/6467, NA, RG 59; Schoenfeld to William Castle, November 19, 1931, Schoenfeld Papers; and to secretary, February 16, 1932, 839.00/3547, NA, RG 59.

10. Schoenfeld to secretary, October 4, 1933, 839.00/3698, NA, RG 59; June 3, 1933, *FRUS*, 5:632–36, and July 3, 1936, 5:467–68; Schoenfeld to Welles, September 29, 1933, 839.00/3694, NA, RG 59.

11. Matthews to secretary, May 25, 1936, 837.00/7449; May 18, 1937, 837.00/8018, NA, RG 59.

12. Schoenfeld to secretary, September 8, 1933, 837.00/3833; October 6, 1933, 839.00/3700; October 9, 1933, 839.00/3701, NA, RG 59; Matthews to secretary (Fayette J. Flexer drafted), February 2, 1934, 837.00/4725; Caffery to secretary (Matthews drafted), March 16, 1934, 837.00/4932; Matthews to secretary, May 4, 1934, 837.00/5046, NA, RG 59; Schoenfeld to Sheffield, August 7, 1936, Schoenfeld Papers.

13. The most interesting account of American–East Asian relations during the Washington Conference period is Akira Iriye's *After Imperialism*. See also Dorthy Borg, *The United States and the Far Eastern Crisis of 1933–38*, and Dorthy Borg and Shumpei Okamoto, eds., *Pearl Harbor as History*. Alternative interpretations of the origins of the American-Japanese conflict are presented by Iriye, *Across the Pacific;* and by William Appleman Williams, *The Tragedy of American Diplomacy*, and Paul Schroeder, *The Axis Alliance and Japanese-American Relations*.

14. Hamilton conversation with Grew in Tokyo, September 29, 1933, 111.22/75; Hamilton diary entry, January 5, 1934, courtesy Mrs. Maxwell Hamilton, Roseburg, Oregon; Hamilton to Stanley K. Hornbeck, October 6, 1933, 761.94/646; Hamilton memorandum, March 3, 1933, 793.94 Advisory Committee/18, NA, RG 59.

15. Hamilton to secretary, March 20, 1934, 111.22/73, NA, RG 59; Hamilton diary entry, December 9, 1933; Hamilton to secretary, October 16–19, 1933, and January 21, 1934, 111.22/73 and 75, NA, RG 59.

16. Hamilton to secretary, March 20, 1934, *supra*. Hamilton memoranda, April 20, 1934, 793.94/6700, and November 11, 1935, 793.94/7378, NA, RG 59.

17. Joseph W. Ballantine Oral History, Columbia University, vol. 1, p. 38, Davies, *Dragon*, p. 210.

18. Hamilton memoranda, October 12 and 28, 1937, *FRUS*, 3:596–600, 646–48; October 10, 1938, 4:62–65.

19. Hamilton memorandum, November 13, 1938, *FRUS*, 3:569–72; Hamilton to Welles, June 28, 1939, *FRUS*, 2:529–30; to Grew, July 4, 1939, 2:217–18.

20. Davies to secretary, March 16, 1938, 693.001Manchuria/32; see Davies's reports from Mukden, May 1936 to April 1938, and from Hankow, November 1938 to September 1939, 893.00P.R. Mukden/102–25 and 893.00P.R. Hankow/135-46, NA, RG 59.

21. Davies, *Dragon,* p. 271; Hamilton lecture, pp. 13–14, 19, courtesy Mrs. Hamilton.

22. Interview with Mrs. Marjorie Riddle, September 9, 1976, Chapel Hill, N.C.; Jacobs to MacMurray, January 26, 1937, Box 157, MacMurray Papers.

23. Jacobs memoranda, April 8, 1937, 611.11B3/313, and April 21, 1937, 611.11B31/80; MacMurray and Jacobs to Feis, Dunn, Hornbeck, Pasvolsky, et al., December 17, 1937, 611.11B31/178; Jacobs memos of conversations with Paul V. McNutt, U.S. high commissioner to Philippines, MacMurray, Hamilton, et al., March 11, 1938, 711.B00/9; and Alger Hiss and Francis Sayre, January 20, 1939, 611.11B31/517, NA, RG 59.

24. Hamilton memorandum, June 23, 1941, 740.0011EW39/12389-1/2; Davies memorandum (Hamilton initialled), July 23, 1941, 740.0011PW/458, NA, RG 59.

25. Schoenfeld to Herbert Pell, April 20, 1936, Schoenfeld Papers.

26. Informative studies of Eastern Europe include Henry L. Roberts, *Eastern Europe: Politics, Revolution, and Diplomacy;* Hugh Seton-Watson, *Eastern Europe between the Wars, 1918–1941;* Joseph Rothschild, *East Central Europe between the Two World Wars;* René Ristelheuber, *Histoire des Peuples Balkaniques;* Hans-Erich Volkmann, ed., *Die Krise des Parlamentarismus in Ostmitteleuropa zwischen den Beiden Weltkriegen;* George D. Jackson, Jr., *Comintern and Peasant in East Europe, 1919–1930;* and Peter F. Sugar, ed., *Native Fascism in the Successor States.*

27. Lane to Herrera de Huerta, October 30, 1936, Box 63, Folder 1134, and to Dunn, June 18, 1937, Box 64, Folder 1148, Lane Papers.

28. Lane to Uncle Acosta Nichols, September 24, 1936, Box 63, Folders 1131, 1133; to Moore, June 17, 1936, Box 63, Folder 1125; and to Dunn, August 27, 1936, Box 63, Folder 1129, Lane Papers.

29. Lane to Moore, November 17, 1936, Box 63, Folder 1135, Lane Papers.

30. Lane to secretary, March 13, 1937, 860P.00B/104; April 17, 1937, 861.00/11686; May 10, 1937 (Page drafted), 861.00S.R.1/31, NA, RG 59; Lane to Roosevelt, October 8, 1936, Box 63, Folder 1125; Lane Papers; Lane to secretary, August 6, 1937, 123L24/504, NA, RG 59.

31. Schoenfeld to Norman L. Orme, September 13, 1937, Schoenfeld Papers; to secretary, December 15, 1936, 860D.00/836, NA, RG 59. With the dissolution of the Communist party in 1930 and the defeat of the fascist faction in the elections of 1933, the Finnish government, in contrast to the *étatisme* of its Baltic neighbors to the south, committed itself to the development of democratic institutions.

32. Schoenfeld to secretary, November 18, 860D.00/829, and September 29, 1939, 740.0011EW39/619, NA, RG 59.

33. Schoenfeld to secretary, 760D.61/556, 670, 665, and 957, respectively dated December 1, 6, and 7, 1939, and January 9, 1940, NA, RG 59.

34. Schoenfeld to secretary (Erkki Kapy drafted), August 1, 1940, 860D.00/893, NA, RG 59; March 19, 1941, *FRUS*, 1:14–16.

35. Schoenfeld to secretary, July 4, 1941, 740.0011EW39/12186, NA, RG 59; February 16, 1942, *FRUS*, 2:41–43, August 1, 1942, 860D.00/960, and September 18, 1942, 860D.00/965, NA, RG 59; Schoenfeld to Mrs. J. R. Sheffield, November 4, 1942, Schoenfeld Papers.

36. Richard Busch-Zantner, *Bulgarien;* Rothschild, chap. 7; interview with Walworth Barbour, June 2, 1976, Gloucester, Mass.; Barnes to secretary, March 30, 1933, 874.00/453; Henry Shoemaker to secretary (Barnes drafted), May 23, 1933, 874.00B/108, NA, RG 59.

37. Barnes to secretary, November 24, 1933, 874.00/468; February 2, 1934, 874.00/472; Barnes memorandum, April 23, 1935, 874.00/525, NA, RG 59.

38. McBride and Barbour interviews; Cannon to secretary, July 11, 1936, 874.00/559; June 30, 1937, 874.00/577, NA, RG 59.

39. Shantz to secretary, August 5, 1936, 868.00/983; August 8, 1936, 868.00/988; August 22, 1936, 868.00/989, NA, RG 59.

40. Shantz to secretary, September 5, 1936, 868.00/992; April 2, 1937, 868.00/1009, NA, RG 59.

41. McBride and Kohler interviews; Shantz to secretary (Kohler drafted), October 12, 1937, 868.42/12, NA, RG 59.

42. Barbour and McBride interviews; Huston to secretary, 875.00/399, 401 and 428, respectively dated November 16 and December 14, 1934, and August 31, 1935, NA, RG 59.

43. Huston to secretary, September 24, 1935, 875.20/85, and September 27, 1935, 875.00/430, NA, RG 59.

44. Shoemaker to secretary (Barnes drafted), March 31, 1933, 774.00/60; and Barnes memorandum, November 8, 1934, 768.74/328, NA, RG 59; Lane to Roosevelt, July 12, 1937, Box 64, Folder 1150, Lane Papers; Cannon to secretary, September 7, 1937, 874.00/580; and Shantz to secretary, October 14, 1937, 868.00/1015, NA, RG 59.

45. Shantz to secretary (Kohler drafted), December 7, 1938, 770.00/591, and December 9, 1938, 768.74/354; Leslie E. Reed to secretary (Kohler drafted), June 23, 1939, 868.00/1090, and August 4, 1939, 868.00/1096, NA, RG 59.

46. Franklin Mott Gunther and Huston to secretary, January 11, 1938, 871.00/591; Gunter to secretary (Huston drafted), June 10, 1939, 871.00/689, and December 12, 1939, 871.00/720; Frederick P. Hibbard to secretary (Huston drafted), July 8, 1939, 871.00/696, NA, RG 59.

47. Gunther to secretary (Huston drafted), March 9, 1940, 871.00/729; Huston and Gunther to secretary, November 20, 1940, 871.00/814, NA, RG 59.

48. Lane to Hugh Wilson, January 25, 1938, Box 65, Folder 1164; Lane "Confidential Analysis of Yugoslavia," Box 65, Folder 1167; Lane to Harold Tittman, January 24, 1938, Box 64, Folder 1174, Lane Papers.

49. Petrov, pp. 104–7; Lane to secretary, April 16, 1938, 760H.65/782; May 10, 1938, 770.00/525; May 11, 1938, 770.00/535; and May 20, 760H.65/785, NA, RG 59; Lane to Acosta Nichols, October 25, 1938, Box 65, Folders 1164–65, Lane Papers.

50. Lane to secretary, November 18, 1937, 860H.00B/42; December 2, 1937, 860H.00B/43; April 14, 1939, 860H.00/1015; October 31, 1939, 860H.00/1098; and June 4, 1940, 860H.00/1175, NA, RG 59.

51. Lane to secretary, December 28, 1939, 860H.24/139; January 4, 1940, 860H.6363Standard Oil Company/68; April 6, 1940, 611.60H31/209; Petrov, p. 200.

52. Lane to secretary, February 13, 1941, 740.0011EW39/8361, NA, RG 59; Ilija Jukić, *The Fall of Yugoslavia*, p. 57.

53. Lane speech, February 27, 1942, Box 67, Folder 1198, Lane Papers.

54. Interview with Mrs. John H. Bruins, December 12, 1975, Washington, D.C.; Bruins to secretary, October 6, 1938, 860F.50/102, and March 23, 1939, 860F.00/737, NA, RG 59; Bruins notes, summer 1938–1944, courtesy Mrs. Bruins.

55. Kennan to secretary, February 17, 1939, 860F.4016/68, and January 14, 1939, 860F.00/596, NA, RG 59; Kennan to Robert D. Coe, March 30, 1939, Box 1, Kennan Papers; Kennan interview.

56. Kennan interview.

57. Klieforth to secretary, 863.00/857, 860 and 877, respectively dated February 13, February 13, and February 22, 1934, NA, RG 59; Moffat diary entry, February 16, 1934, vol. 35; and Messersmith to Moffat, June 14, 1935, vol. 9, Personal Correspondence, Moffat Papers; Klieforth to Moffat, July 28, 1938, 862.00/3846, NA, RG 59.

58. Klieforth to secretary, June 25, 1941, 123K684/293, NA, RG 59; Klieforth, "Hitler Has You Card-Indexed," *Saturday Evening Post,* June 13, 1942, p. 18.

59. George to secretary, November 21, 1934, 765.84/80, NA, RG 59.

60. McBride interview, p. 28; James P. Warburg Oral History, Columbia University, vol. 6, p. 960; Dunn to Norman Armour, October 28, 1935, Box 4, John D. Hickerson Files, NA, RG 59; Dunn memos of conversations with Hugh Wilson, November 5, 1935, *FRUS,* 1:855–57, Ray Atherton, November 27, 1935, 1:859–62, and British ambassador, January 4, 1937, 741.65/332, NA, RG 59.

61. McBride and Barbour interviews; Roger Nash Baldwin Oral History, Columbia University, vol. 1, p. 601; Phillips to secretary (Reber drafted), July 8, 1937, 852.00/6039; Alexander Kirk to secretary (Reber drafted), July 22, 1937, 741.65/391; Edward L. Reed to secretary (Reber drafted), September 9, 1938, 865.00/1775; Phillips to secretary (Reber drafted), December 23, 1938, 865.00/1789; Reed to secretary (Reber drafted), May 19, 1939, 865.00/1821, NA, RG 59. More concerned with domestic economic conditions than with the acquisition of foreign territory, Neapolitans said, "We don't want Tunisia, we want cake."

62. Matthews, "Memoirs," pp. 135–36, 140–46, 152–57; letter from Matthews to Hugh De Santis, May 3, 1977; Robert Murphy to secretary (Barnes drafted), September 27, 1939, 851.00B/214, NA, RG 59.

63. Barnes to secretary, July 29, 1940, 740.0011EW39/5078; Matthews to secretary, September 30, 1940, 740.0011EW39/5816, NA, RG 59; Matthews, "Memoirs," pp. 178–204.

64. Barnes speech, March 1, 1940, 123B26/222, NA, RG 59; Matthews to secretary, December 30, 1940, 740.0011EW39/7335, NA, RG 59.

65. Policy statement on Russia, European division (Atherton drafted), June 21, 1941, 740.0011EW39/19382, NA, RG 59; interviews with Henderson (January 24, 1976) and Matthews (September 8, 1976).

66. Dunn to Welles (Henderson drafted), July 7, 1941, 861.51/2869, NA, RG 59; Harper to Walter Duranty, July 22, 1941, and Hazard to Harper, August 12, 1941, Box 22, Folders 23–24, Harper Papers.

67. Matthews Memorial Day address, June 1, 1937, 125M431/130, NA, RG 59; Bohlen to Phillips, December 3, 1935, vol. 8, Phillips Diary, Phillips Papers; Dunn-Moffat conversation, March 15, 1939, vol. 16, Personal Correspondence, Moffat Papers; Schoenfeld to Herbert Pell, April 20, 1936, and Sheffield, November 2, 1937, Schoenfeld Papers; Lane to Dunn, May 16, 1936, Box 2, vol. 3, John F. Montgomery Papers, Yale University; Henderson to Harper, May 6, 1937, Box 19, Folder 37, Harper Papers.

68. Schoenfeld to Sheffield, June 13, 1938, Schoenfeld Papers; Berry to parents, September 12, 1938, and August 22, 1939, Boxes 7–8, Berry Papers; Kennan, *Memoirs, 1925–1950,* p. 104; Henderson to Wiley, August 17, 1939, Box 7, Wiley Papers.

69. Henderson, "Memoirs," 8:1382, 1385–86; Lane to Roosevelt, May 17, 1940, 811.20/349, NA, RG 59; Schoenfeld to Mrs. Sheffield, March 20, 1941, Schoenfeld Papers.

70. Acheson, pp. 37–39, 66–67; Riddleberger Oral History, pp. 11–12.

71. G. Howland Shaw, "The Individualist and the Foreign Service," 9 (June 1932): 218; interviews with Matthews (September 8, 1976), Riddleberger and Durbrow (January 29, 1976); Mrs. Barnes to Berry, April 2, 1937, Box 6, Berry Papers; Klieforth to Moffat, December 27, 1939, vol. 18, Personal Correspondence, Moffat Papers; Kennan, *Memoirs, 1925–1950,* pp. 139–40; Henderson, "Memoirs," 5:876.

72. Henderson, "Memoirs," 4:803–10; 7:1107–9; Kennan memo of conversation with Colonel Coulter of military intelligence division, December 14, 1937, 121.5461/177; Kennan memorandum, February 2, 1938, 661.1115Amtorg Trading Corp./192, NA, RG 59; Henderson to Dunn and Hickerson, July 22, 1939, *FRUS: The Soviet Union, 1933–1939,* pp. 773–75.

73. Interviews with Mrs. Bruins, Rudolph Schoenfeld, Barbour, Matthews (May 20, 1976), and Durbrow (May 3, 1976); Schoenfeld speech, October 2, 1925, 123Schoenfeld62/135, NA, RG 59.

74. Durbrow interview, January 29, 1976; Berry to Miss Carp, November 24, 1934, and to minister in Iran (undated), Box 5, Berry Papers; George to secretary, November 9, 1934, 124.84/35, and November 28, 1934, 855.001Leopold/38, NA, RG 59; Klieforth to Wiley, July 29, 1938, Box 7, Wiley Papers; Hugh Fullerton to secretary, January 13, 1929, 123F951/122, NA, RG 59; Bohlen, *Witness*, pp. 69–79; Henderson, "Memoirs," 3:579–89; 6:1005–06, 1039, 1057; Henderson to secretary (Kennan drafted), December 9, 1935, 861.111/679; Durbrow memo, December 12, 1936, 123D101, NA, RG 59.

75. Moffat diary entries, December 12, 1933, and February 5, 1934, vols. 34 and 35, Moffat Papers; Matthews, "Memoirs," pp. 51–53; Lane to parents, April 12 and May 27, 1919, Box 56a, Folder 978, Lane Papers; Lane to secretary, March 22, 1939, 701.60F60H/8; Henderson to secretary (Bohlen drafted), December 31, 1936, 861.00Congress of Soviets, VII/6; Bohlen enclosure in Henderson letter to secretary, February 2, 1938, 861.00Supreme Soviet/5, NA, RG 59.

76. Interviews with Mrs. Bruins, Barbour and Durbrow (January 29, 1976); Hugh R. Wilson, *Diplomat between Wars*, pp. 302–3, 323.

77. Interviews with Kohler, Barbour, Henderson (January 24, 1976), and Durbrow (January 29, 1976).

Chapter 4

1. Samuel I. Rosenman, ed., *The Public Papers and Addresses of Franklin D. Roosevelt*, 10:418–19.

2. Rosenman, 11:268–69.

3. See the opinion polls taken by NORC, AIPO and OPOR from 1942 to the Yalta Conference in Hadley Cantril, ed., *Public Opinion, 1935–1946*, pp. 370–75. *Life*, March 29, 1943, pp. 20, 23 and 38; Bullitt to Roosevelt, January 29, 1943, President's Secretary's File, Box 111, FDR Papers. Across the Atlantic the British too joined in the euphoria. See Werth, *Moscow War Diary*, pp. 296–97; André Fontaine, *Histoire de la Guerre Froide*, 1:195–96.

4. See Forrest Davis, "Roosevelt's World Blueprint," *Saturday Evening Post*, April 10, 1943, pp. 20–21, 110–11. Still the best book on allied wartime relations is William H. McNeill's *America, Britain and Russia*. For an insider's view, see Herbert Feis, *Churchill-Roosevelt-Stalin*. Also illuminating are John Lewis Gaddis, *The United States and the Origins of the Cold War*; Gaddis Smith, *American Diplomacy during the Second World War*; Gabriel Kolko, *The Politics of War*; Acheson, *Present at the Creation*; and Robert A. Divine, *Second Chance*. I am grateful to Alexander George for suggesting the concept of a "benign" balance-of-power system.

5. David J. MacDonald Oral History, Truman Library, p. 57; Acheson, pp. 70–72.

6. Harley Notter, *Postwar Foreign Policy Preparation*, pp. 18–28, 41–65, 72–121; Bohlen, *Witness*, pp. 121–22; Wallace Oral History, 13:2311–12 and 11:2056–57; Henderson to Welles, April 9, 1942, *FRUS*, 3:435–37; Blum, *Wallace Diary*, entry of July 8, 1942, p. 95; Henderson interview, May 5, 1976.

7. Cannon memo of conversation with Hull and Brutus Coste, September 4, 1941, 740.0011EW39/14843, NA, RG 59; Bohlen to Hull, November 16, 1942, 711.61/11-1642, NA, RG 59; Bohlen to Harper, November 23, 1942, Box 1, Charles E. Bohlen Files, Department of State (hereafter Bohlen Files); Durbrow memo, October 28, 1942, *FRUS*, 3:764–65; and November 29, 1943, 810.0011EW39/31891, NA, RG 59.

8. Lane to secretary, September 7, 1943, 810.00/133; September 29, 1943, 821.00/1538; Keith to Livingston Satterthwaite, April 11, 1942, 821.00/1440; to division of American Republics, September 30, 1943, 821.00/1569, NA, RG 59.

9. Matthews to secretary, February 27, 1942, 740.0011EW39/19848; April 3, 1942 (Paul Reveley drafted); January 1, 1943, *FRUS*, 2:24–26; January 8, 1943, 2:33–35; Matthews to

Atherton, April 5, 1943, Box 13, H. Freeman Matthews Files, NA, RG 59 (hereafter cited as Matthews Files); and June 25, 1943, Lot File 53D246, division of European affairs, Department of State, Washington, D.C. (hereafter State Department Lot File).

10. Matthews to secretary, March 8, 1943, 861.00/11982; March 15, 1943, 851.01/1062; May 3, 1943 (Jacob D. Beam drafted), 841.00B/207; March 5, 1942, 740.0011EW39/20035; March 13, 1942, Matthews to Dunn (Bohlen initialled), August 24, 1943, 740.00119EW39/1657, NA, RG 59. For the British side, see Sir Ernest Llewellyn Woodward, ed., *British Foreign Policy in the Second World War,* 3:290–363.

11. Berry to parents, May 31, 1941; "Memo on German Atrocities in Crete," November 1, 1941; and "Hitler's New Order as Applied in Axis-Occupied Greece," October–December 1941, Box 9, Berry Papers; Berry to secretary (Melbourne drafted), 871.00/942 and 945, respectively dated January 30 and February 3, 1943; September 3, 1943 (Walter W. Birge drafted), 864.00/1102; October 24, 1943, 871.01/213; December 28, 1943 (Melbourne drafted), 871.00/1005; December 24, 1943 (Fraleigh drafted), 860H.01/651, NA, RG 59; Fraleigh to Berry, November 22, 1943, Berry to Cannon, February 16, 1943, Box 10, Berry Papers; Berry to secretary, March 1, 1943, 874.00/690; April 15, 1943 (Floyd H. Black drafted), 861.00/12006; September 17, 1943, 874.00/769; December 18, 1943 (Black drafted), 874.00/789, NA, RG 59.

12. Berry to secretary, March 3, 1943, 860H.00/1455, NA, RG 59; Berry to Cannon, May 19, 1943, Box 10, Berry Papers; Berry to secretary (Black drafted), September 16, 1943, 874.0111/397, NA, RG 59.

13. Henderson to secretary, October 15, 1942, *FRUS,* 3:464–66; October 31, 1942, 3:471–72; Henderson to secretary, November 8, 1942, 861.00/11963, and December 7, 1942, 861.9111/369, NA, RG 59; Henderson interviews, January 24 and May 21, 1969.

14. Henderson to secretary, November 9, 1942, 861.404/483; December 22, 1942, 861.00/11971, NA, RG 59.

15. Standley to secretary, March 11, 1943, *FRUS,* 3:636–38, Hull to Standley (Henderson drafted), March 17, 1943, 740.0011EW39/28434, NA, RG 59.

16. Hamilton to Mrs. Hamilton, August 7, August 22, September 29, October 13, 1943; Hamilton to secretary, August 8, 1943, 740.00119EW39/1565, NA, RG 59.

17. Interviews with McBride and Matthews (September 8, 1976); Lane to Leo J. Keena, June 4, 1937, Box 63, Folder 1147, Lane Papers; Standley to secretary (Stevens drafted), March 17, 1943, 740.0011EW39/29152, NA, RG 59; Thompson to secretary (Frederick C. Barghoorn drafted), January 27, 1943, 861.00/11991; Hamilton to secretary (Thompson drafted), February 8, 1944, 861.00/12055, NA, RG 59.

18. Kennan memorandum, "Russia and the Post-War Settlement," summer 1942, Box 2, Kennan Papers.

19. Bert Fish to secretary (Kennan drafted), February 4, 1943, 853.00/1064; April 21, 1943, 853.00/1075, NA, RG 59; Kennan to secretary, October 5, 1943, 841.34553B/4, NA, RG 59.

20. Edward Rice Oral History, Columbia University, p. 66; Brooks Atkinson, "America's Global Planner," the *New York Times Magazine,* July 13, 1947, pp. 9, 32–33; interview with Mrs. Jeanette Kennan Hotchkiss, Highland Park, Ill., May 21, 1977; Kennan, *Memoirs, 1925–1950,* p. 21; Kennan letter to Shaw, August 18, 1942, Box 3, Kennan Papers.

21. Kennan to secretary, October 18, 1943, 811.34553B/5; October 20, 1943, 811.34553B/6, NA, RG 59; Matthews, "Memoirs," pp. 155, 160–62, 259–60.

22. Henderson to Harper, March 23, 1942, Box 33, Folder 11, Harper Papers.

23. Thompson to secretary, December 29, 1941, 740.0011EW39/17728, NA, RG 59; memo prepared in the division of European affairs, approved by Dunn, February 4, 1942, *FRUS,* 3:505–12; Durbrow to Cannon and Atherton, December 14, 1942, 760F.61/12-1442, NA, RG 59; Cannon quoted in meeting of the subcommittee on security and technical problems, February 24, 1943, ST minutes 10, Box 79, Harley Notter Files, NA, RG 59 (hereafter Notter Files).

24. Durbrow memo of conversation with Messrs. Arlet and Lepkowski of Polish embassy, January 6, 1943, *FRUS,* 3:321–22; Henderson chit, June 2, 1943, 760C.61/7-1543, NA, RG 59. In a frank discussion with Averell Harriman, special envoy at the time to London, Prime Minister Sikorski conceded that it was injudicious for the Poles to request a Red Cross investigation. Sikorski's personal force might have resurrected Soviet-Polish relations, but he died in July in an airplane crash. See W. Averell Harriman and Elie Abel, *Special Envoy to Churchill and Stalin, 1941–1946,* pp. 199–201.

25. Durbrow to Atherton, Bohlen and Cannon, December 8, 1942, 860C.014/12-842, NA, RG 59; Bohlen memorandum, "Brief Summary of Indications of the Soviet Attitude toward Neighboring Countries," February 3, 1943, Box 1, Bohlen Files; see subcommittee meeting on security and technical affairs for Cannon, *supra.*

26. Durbrow memo of conversation with Davies, February 3, 1943, 711.61/2-243; Bohlen to Atherton and Dunn, May 19, 1943, 701.6112/85, NA, RG 59; Henderson, "Memoirs," 7:1112-25; Bohlen memorandum, "The Distinctive Character of the Soviet Government," August–September 1943, Box 2, Bohlen Files.

27. Cannon to Atherton, December 14, 1942, 851.01/12-1442, NA, RG 59; Cannon comments, subcommittee meeting on security and technical problems, April 27, 1943, ST minutes 15, Box 79, Notter Papers; Cannon memorandum, March 24, 1943, Box 31, Records of the European Advisory Commission, NA, RG 43.

28. Durbrow to Atherton, Henderson, and Dunn, April 9, 1943, 760.61/4-943, NA, RG 59; Bohlen and Henderson to Ambassador John G. Winant in London, May 1, 1943, Box 1, Bohlen Files; Durbrow memo of conversation with secretary British embassy, May 4, 1943, *FRUS,* 3:409–10; Hull to Standley in Moscow (Henderson and Durbrow drafted), June 28, 1943, 760.61/2047, NA, RG 59.

29. Dunn's views in minutes of subcommittee on political problems, February 12, 1943, P minutes 206; Cannon comments in meeting of subcommittee on security and technical problems, February 3, 1943, ST minutes 7, Boxes 57 and 79, Notter Files; Bohlen memo, "The Distinctive Character," Box 2, Bohlen Files.

30. Bohlen, "The Distinctive Character"; Kohler interview; Huston participation in departmental study on Albania, October 12, 1943, 800 Albania, Tirana Post Files, Records of Diplomatic and Consular Posts, Record Group 84, Washington National Record Center, Suitland, Maryland (hereafter WNRC, RG 84). Civil war erupted full force in October.

31. Durbrow memorandum, October 29, 1943, 860F.01/512-1/2, NA, RG 59. The first All-Slav Congress met in Moscow on August 14, 1941. Cannon quoted in Jukić, p. 133; Matthews to secretary (Waldemar G. Gallman drafted), January 5, 1943, *FRUS,* 2:969–70; Cannon memorandum, May 1, 1943, 860H.00/1477-1/2; Durbrow to Matthews, November 20, 1943, 870.00/39, NA, RG 59.

32. Cannon to Atherton and Dunn, August 6, 1942, 860H.00/1408; to Atherton, Dunn, and Welles, May 17, 1943, 860H.01/478, NA, RG 59; *Time,* October 18, 1943, p. 28; Dunn and Kohler to Roosevelt (Cannon initialled), September 24, 1943, 870.01A.M.G./1A; Cannon to Dunn and Atherton, June 25, 1942, 860H.00/1402-1/2, NA, RG 59.

33. Cannon and Bohlen remarks in meeting of subcommittee on security and technical problems, January 27 and February 3, 1943, ST minutes 6–7; meetings of the political subcommittee, February 12 and March 12, 1943, P minutes 206 and 214, Notter Files; Bohlen comment at meeting of subcommittee on territorial problems, January 29, 1943, T minutes 37, Box 59, Notter Files; Matthews unsigned memorandum, September 27, 1943, Box 17, Matthews Files, NA, RG 59. Bohlen's notion of moderate and extreme policy options appeared in an unsigned OSS report in May, which referred to a "military-imperialistic" versus "political" policy. Another study prepared in September by the research and analysis division of the OSS discussed the same concept in "minimum-maximum" terms. See OSS report 35339, RG 226, NA, RG 59; also report of Major General

Hildring, September 17, 1943, File CAD388, combined civil affairs committee, Records of the War Department General and Special Staffs, NA, RG 165.

34. Cannon quoted in ST minutes 7, *supra;* Cannon to Matthews, August 24, 1943, 760F.61/108; Matthews memo of conversation with R. E. Barclay, August 24, 1943, 760F.61/108, NA, RG 59; Bohlen to Dunn, August 26, 1943, Box 1, Bohlen Files.

35. Bohlen memo, "The Distinctive Character," *supra;* Bohlen memo, September 1943, Box 1, Bohlen Files, Dunn noting in the margin, "I agree with this memo;" Hull to Moscow embassy (Henderson drafted), July 29, 1943, 862.01/300; Durbrow memo of conversation with Monsignor Carroll, papal secretariat of state for foreign affairs, September 11, 1943, 865.00B/49, NA, RG 59.

36. Interviews with Durbrow (May 3, 1976), Yost, McBride, Kennan, Matthews (May 20, 1976), and Henderson (May 21, 1976); Bohlen to Hull, October 31, 1943, Box 52, Folder 162, Cordell Hull Papers, Library of Congress. Cordell Hull commented in his memoirs (2:1436–37) that the Moscow and Teheran conferences clearly signalled the Kremlin's desire for postwar cooperation with the United States.

37. Bohlen to Hull, October 18, 1943, 740.0011Moscow/10-1843, NA, RG 59.

38. Harriman quoted in Hamilton to Mrs. Hamilton, November 7, 1943; Harriman to Roosevelt and Stettinius, November 7, 1943, *FRUS,* 3:595–96; John R. Deane, *Strange Alliance,* p. 24; Hull, 2:1311; Hamilton to Mrs. Hamilton, November 15 and 18, 1943. Matthews "Memoirs," p. 303.

39. W. Averell Harriman, *America and Russia in a Changing World,* p. 21; Hamilton to Mrs. Hamilton, October 31, 1943.

40. Hamilton letter to Mrs. Hamilton, November 7, 1943; Harriman, *Special Envoy,* pp. 254–55; Werth, *Russia at War,* pp. 753–54.

41. Feis, *Churchill-Roosevelt-Stalin,* pp. 276–78; Winston Churchill, *Closing the Ring,* p. 706.

42. Bohlen memorandum, December 15, 1943, Box 1, Bohlen Files; *Witness,* pp. 150, 154; Durbrow to Matthews and Dunn, December 8, 1943, 861.24/1369, NA, RG 59; Hamilton to Mrs. Hamilton, December 2, 7, 12, and 19, 1943. Later, when the spirit of cooperation gave way to confrontation, the diplomats' recollections of Teheran would change. See, for instance, Robert Murphy, *Diplomat among Warriors.*

Chapter 5

1. Hull, 2:1448; Rosenman, 13:32; Frederick C. Barghoorn, *The Soviet Image of the United States,* pp. 46–47, 65–66, 87; Bohlen, *Transformation,* p. 26; Harriman, *Special Envoy,* pp. 295–96; Kohler interview.

2. Hamilton to Mrs. Hamilton, January 1 and February 2, 1944; to daughter Judy, May 4, 1944; Hamilton to secretary (Stevens drafted), January 24, 1944, 861.00/12051, NA, RG 59; Kohler interview for Thompson's reaction. Hamilton to Roosevelt and Hull, May 9, 1944, 760C.61/2296, NA, RG 59; to secretary (Stevens drafted), May 28, 1944, CCS350.05USSR, Records of the Joint Chiefs of Staff, National Archives, Record Group 218 (hereafter NA, RG 218).

3. Harriman, *Special Envoy,* pp. 296–97, 308; Hamilton to secretary, May 15, 1944, *FRUS,* 4:1171–73; to Mrs. Hamilton, May 25 and June 1, 1944.

4. Molotov's press release in Moscow embassy information bulletin, Elbridge Durbrow Papers (hereafter Durbrow Papers); Feis, *Churchill-Roosevelt-Stalin,* pp. 336–37; Berry to secretary (Lee Metcalf drafted), March 24, 1944, 871.9111/346, NA, RG 59; March 25, 1944, *FRUS,* 3:317–18, and April 21, 1944, 3:321–22; Berry to secretary (Homer W. Davis drafted), February 23, 1944, 868.00/1365, NA, RG 65; July 17, 1944, 860H.00/7-1744; July 22, 1944 (Davis drafted), 868.00/7-2244, NA, RG 59.

5. Berry to secretary, July 13, 1944, 871.00/7-1344; July 21, 1944 (Fraleigh drafted), 871.00/7-2144, NA, RG 59; Berry to mother, July 24, 1944, Box 11, Berry Papers.

6. Reber to G. Frederick Reinhardt, March 14, 1944, and Dunn, March 31, 1944, I711.9-ACC, Caserta Post Files, WNRC, RG 84; Reber comment in Reinhardt and Selden Chapin to secretary, March 11, 1944, *FRUS*, 3:1041–42. Reber's view was shared by Robert Murphy, United States political advisor in Italy, who equated Soviet communist infiltration with the rise of fascism two decades earlier. See Murphy to secretary, May 15, 1944, *FRUS*, 3:1112–14.

7. Kennan to Winant, February 7, 1944, and letter attached to E. Allan Lightner, Jr., to Hull, March 8, 1944, Box 16, Records of the European Advisory Commission, NA, RG 43.

8. Kennan to Winant, March, 1944, Box 3, Kennan Papers; diary note of conversation between Kennan and William Phillips, March 2, 1944, vol. 30, Phillips Papers; Matthews, "Memoirs," p. 229; Kennan, *Memoirs, 1925–1950*, pp. 164–66, 170–71. See Homans, pp. 287–88; also see Philip Selznick, "Foundations of the Theory of Organization," in Etzioni, p. 271.

Kennan's status as an "outsider" and his risk-oriented behavior fit the social-psychological pattern of the achievement-oriented military officer analyzed by Janowitz (*The Professional Soldier*). As Janowitz points out, unconventional careers "must be developed within the framework of existing institutions if officers expect to survive" (p. 12).

9. Durbrow memos, January 11, 1944, 760C.6115/29-1/2, and February 3, 1944, 761.00/2-344, NA, RG 59; Bohlen memos, March 24, 1944, "Current Problems in Relations with the Soviet Union," and March 25, 1944, Box 1, Bohlen Files.

10. Hull to Harriman (Bohlen drafted, Dunn and Matthews initialled), February 9, 1944, 711.61/977A, NA, RG 59.

11. This interpretation, unlike Davis's, stresses perceptual distortion, and it diverges from the position taken by Gaddis, who used selective poll data to substantiate the department's view. Matthews (September 8, 1976) and Barbour interviews. Milton Rosenberg has found that the public's foreign-policy attitudes tend to be shaped by social and political elites. However, once these attitudes are formed, the public constrains subsequent attempts to modify them. See Rosenberg, "Images in Relation to the Policy Process," in *International Behavior: A Social Psychological Analysis,* ed. Herbert Kelman, and "Attitude Change and Foreign Policy in the Cold-War Era," in *Domestic Sources of Foreign Policy,* ed. James N. Rosenau. Based on the January 18, 1944, AIPO poll, only 40 percent of Americans felt that Russia would cooperate with the United States after the war versus 51 percent the previous December. However, by April this figure had climbed back to 50 percent. Withal, an AIPO poll conducted on January 18—the day Moscow announced the Curzon Line boundary in eastern Poland—concluded that 41 percent of the public was sympathetic to Poland; but 29 percent supported Russia and 30 percent expressed no opinion. See Cantril, *Public Opinion,* pp. 370, 1169. For the department's reaction to public attitudes, see the office of public information reports, January 22, 1944, 760C.61/2197, and February 29, 1944, 711.61/988, NA, RG 59.

12. Unsigned memo to Stettinius, February 17, 1944, Box 17, Matthews Files; Durbrow memorandum, March 16, 1944, 760C.61/2248; Dunn memo of conversation with Ciechanowski, May 2, 1944, 760C.61/2305, NA, RG 59.

13. Memorandum, division of Southern Europe, March 1944, *FRUS*, 4:146–47; Cannon to Dunn, March 27, 1944, CCS387, Records of the Joint Chiefs of Staff, NA, RG 218; Huston memorandum, April 11, 1944, 740.0011EW(Peace)/3-2744, and Matthews to Hull, May 12, 1944, 871.001Carol II/368, NA, RG 59.

14. Bohlen to Hull, April 1, 1944, *FRUS*, 4:166; subcommittee meetings of February 18 and March 3, 1944, R minutes 13 and 14, Box 84, Notter Files.

15. Durbrow interview, January 29, 1976; Bohlen to Dunn, March 30, 1944,

740.0011EW39/33802, NA, RG 59; Bohlen memo, "Soviet War Aims," February 1944, and unsigned memorandum, spring 1944, Box 17, Matthews Files; Matthews interview, May 20, 1976; Dunn to Winant, February 15, 1944, Box 22, Records of the European Advisory Commission, NA, RG 43; Bohlen to Hull, April 3, 1944, 740.00119EW/2434, NA, RG 59.

16. State Department press releases of Hull radio comments, March 21 and April 8, 1944, and address by Assistant Secretary of State Breckinridge Long, Durbrow Papers. This sense of commitment—indeed, conversion in a number of cases—was conveyed in interviews with Durbrow, Henderson, Barbour, Yost, and McBride. Yergin is incorrect when he points out that the department did not accept Roosevelt's "grand design." However, given the president's reluctance to air his preferred policy openly, diplomats perceived it more in terms of ideological sharing than realistic accommodation.

17. See policy statements, PWC-139, 143, 151, 202, 204, and 216, Boxes 142–43, Notter Papers.

18. Roosevelt to Churchill, February 7 and 29, 1944, Box 1, Elsey Papers.

19. Matthews to secretary, May 29, 1944, 870.01/5, and Stettinius, June 6, 1944, 870.00/48, NA, RG 59; unsigned memo, "American Policy toward Spheres of Influence," May 1944, Box 17, Matthews Files; Kohler to Cannon, June 6, 1944, and Cannon to Stettinius, June 12, 1944, 870.00/48, NA, RG 59.

20. Cannon memo, May 19, 1944, 711.60H/33; Cannon to Kohler, June 14, 1944, 870.00/48, and Dunn, June 26, 1944, 870.00/6-2644, NA, RG 59; Walter F. Roberts, *Tito, Mihailović and the Allies, 1941–1945*, p. 208. State Department apprehensions about British policy in the Balkans were well-founded. As John O. Iatrides has described in *Revolt in Athens*, the British planned to support militarily the communist-dominated ELAS until the country was liberated, after which they intended to support the noncommunist nationalists and King George.

21. Winston Churchill, *Triumph and Tragedy*, p. 8.

22. Feis, *Churchill-Roosevelt-Stalin*, p. 311.

23. Shantz speech to American embassy in Cairo, July 20, 1944, 870.01A.M.G./8-144; Kennan to secretary (Stevens drafted), July 12, 1944, 861.9111/7-1244, NA, RG 59.

24. Hamilton's letters to his wife between December 30, 1943, and May 22, 1944, make clear that department politics, more than anything, influenced the decision.

25. Kennan, "Remarks to Lisbon Officer Staff," Box 2, Kennan Papers.

26. Kennan, *Memoirs, 1925–1950*, p. 224.

27. Feis, *Churchill-Roosevelt-Stalin*, pp. 373–75; Kennan, *supra*, p. 210.

28. Dunn to secretary, July 20, 1944, 760C.61/7-2044, NA, RG 59. Davis has interpreted Dunn's statement as a deviation from the policy of noninvolvement (pp. 107–8). Actually, American policy had not changed; it simply failed to respond to changing political realities.

29. Kennan, *Memoirs, 1925–1950*, p. 211; C. Ben Wright, "George F. Kennan; Scholar-Diplomat," pp. 255–56; Harriman to secretary, August 15, 1944, *FRUS*, 3:1376–77, and September 20, 1944, 4:992–98. Little of this vacillation appears in Harriman's memoirs. Kolko contends that military considerations alone dictated Soviet behavior, just as they determined Anglo-American reluctance to aid the related Slovakian revolt (pp. 115–20). However, it is naive to believe, as Kolko apparently does, that such a canny tactician as Stalin would have ignored the political implications of his actions.

30. Memorandum prepared by office of European affairs under Dunn's supervision, "Survey of Principal Problems in Europe," July 15, 1944, 840.00/7-1544, NA, RG 59; Bohlen memo, "Relations with the Soviet Union," September 1944, Box 1, Bohlen Files; Dunn quoted in Walter LaFeber, "Roosevelt, Churchill, and Indochina: 1942–45," *American Historical Review* 80 (December 1975): 1292; Arthur Bliss Lane, *I Saw Poland Betrayed*, pp. 66–67; Witness, p. 161.

31. Kennan, *Memoirs, 1925–1950*, pp. 218–20, 503–31.

32. Davies, *Dragon,* pp. 184, 274–77, 283.

33. Bohlen, *Witness,* pp. 41, 133, 156, 160; Wallace Oral History, diary note of May 9, 1944, vol. 19, p. 3328; Sherwood, pp. 774–75; Kennan, Barbour, and Matthews (September 8, 1976) interviews.

34. Hull, vol. 2, p. 1469; minutes of meetings of American group at Dumbarton Oaks, September 13 and October 4, 1944, Box 3, Leo Pasvolsky Papers, Library of Congress (hereafter Pasvolsky Papers); Dunn to Alger Hiss, October 28, 1944, Box 17, Matthews Files.

35. Harriman, *Special Envoy,* p. 354.

36. W. O. Baxter memo of conversation between Cannon, Kohler, Huston, Hohenthal, et al., August 8, 1944, 870.01A.M.G./8-844, NA, RG 59; Bohlen to Hopkins, October 3, 1944, Box 17, Matthews Files.

37. Churchill, *Truimph and Tragedy,* pp. 227–29.

38. Matthews to Hull, October 16, 1944, Box 17, Matthews Files; Bohlen, *Witness,* p. 163; Kohler memorandum, "United States Policy in Eastern Europe and the Near East," October 18, 1944, State Department Lot File 54D403.

39. American public opinion was also more critical of Britain than Russia at this time. See NORC poll results in Gabriel Almond, *The American People and Foreign Policy,* p. 99. Kohler memorandum, October 18, 1944, State Department Lot File 54D403, Near Eastern and African affairs; Cannon to Henry Labouisse, September 20, 1944, 840.50UNRRA/9-2044; and Hohenthal to Cannon, October 20, 1944, 860H.24/10-2044, NA, RG 59.

40. Matthews to Hull, October 16, 1944, *supra;* Harriman to secretary, September 19, 1944, *supra;* Hull, 2:1464.

41. Kennan memorandum, "Soviet Policy," September 18, 1944, Box 4, Kennan Papers; Kennan to secretary, November 11, 1944, 740.0011EW39/11-1144, NA, RG 59; and to Harriman, December 5 and 22, 1944, Box 3, Kennan Papers.

42. Stettinius to Moscow embassy (Thompson drafted, Matthews and Dunn initialled), January 3, 1945, 740.00119Control(Bulgaria)/1-345; Berry to secretary, November 23, 1944, 871.6363/11-2344 and December 4, 1944, 740.00119Control(Rumania)/12-444, NA, RG 59; Roy M. Melbourne, "Witness to the Start of the Cold War: The View from Rumania," paper presented at the Conference of the American Association for the Advancement of Slavic Studies, October 1975; Barnes to secretary, December 1, 1944, 871.01/12-144, NA, RG 59.

43. Berry to secretary, November 30, 1944, 871.01/11-3044, December 9, 1944, 871.01/12-944, and December 12, 1944, 871.01/12-1244; Stettinius to Berry, November 11, 1944, 123 Berry, NA, RG 59. See Melbourne, "Rumania: Nazi Satellite."

44. After King Boris's death in August 1943, a regency council exercised prerogatives on behalf of young King Simeon II. Besides the Communists, the front included Agrarian, Zveno, and Social Democratic representatives. Barnes to secretary, December 1, 1944, 871.01/12-144, and December 27, 1944, 740.00119Control(Bulgaria)/12-2744, NA, RG 59.

45. Kennan interpretative report, October 20, 1944, CCS350.05USSR, USJCS, NA, RG 218; January 10, 1945, 800USSR, Moscow Post Files, WNRC, RG 84; Kennan to secretary, November 7, 1944, 891.6363/11-744 and December 20, 1944 (Stevens drafted), 867N.01/12-2044, NA, RG 59; Henderson to secretary, November 1, 1944, 867N.01/11-144, and to Murray, November 4, 1944, 867N.01/11-444, NA, RG 59; Davies to secretary, November 15, 1944, 893.00/1-1049, NA, RG 59; and January 4, 1945, cited in *Dragon,* pp. 387–88.

46. Matthews to secretary, September 19, 1944, *FRUS,* 3:427; memo of conversation by chief of division of financial and monetary affairs Luthringer with Matthews, Cannon, Durbrow, et al., October 21, 1944, 3:917–18; Durbrow interview, May 3, 1976; Durbrow to Stettinius, November 20, 1944, 711.60N/11-2044, NA, RG 59. Opinion polls reveal that the American public basically perceived Russia as unaggressive and cooperative during and immediately after the war. During the Warsaw massacre, a NORC survey found only 20

percent of those sampled fearful of Soviet expansionism; 45 percent attributed Soviet behavior in Poland to security needs. By January 1945 approximately 70 percent of those surveyed expected U.S.-Soviet relations to be closer after the war than before. See Cantril, *Public Opinion,* p. 375; and Almond, pp. 92–99.

47. Bohlen memorandum, "United States–Soviet Relations, 1933–1944," December 11, 1944, Box 1, Bohlen Files; unsigned memorandum, "Russia's Postwar Foreign Policy," January 6, 1945, Box 17, Matthews Files. Most likely Bohlen drafted this statement.

48. Dunn quoted in *Newsweek,* December 25, 1944, p. 28.

Chapter 6

1. Bohlen, *Witness,* pp. 171–74; Kennan to Bohlen, January 26, 1945, Box 3, Bohlen Papers.

2. Bohlen to Kennan, February 3, 1945, Box 3, Bohlen Papers.

3. Frances Perkins, *The Roosevelt I Knew,* p. 142; Warwick Perkins letter to Hugh De Santis, May 6, 1976; Bohlen, *Witness,* pp. 180, 211; Hickerson to secretary, January 8, 1945, *FRUS: The Conferences at Malta and Yalta,* pp. 93–96; Bohlen to Hickerson, January 9, 1945, 501BC/1-945, NA, RG 59.

4. Feis, *Churchill-Roosevelt-Stalin,* pp. 556–58; Bohlen, *Witness,* p. 200; Matthews, "Memoirs," pp. 274, 283; interviews with Durbrow (January 29, 1976), Riddleberger, and Kohler.

5. Djilas, p. 114.

6. Berry to secretary (Melbourne drafted), February 3, 1945, 740.00119Control (Rumania)2-345; February 18 and 19, 1945, 740.00119Control(Rumania)/2-1845 and 12-1945; February 27, 1945, 740.00119Control(Rumania)/2-2745, NA, RG 59.

7. Grew to Berry, February 23, 1945 (Cannon drafted), 871.00/2-2345; February 24, 1945 (Cannon drafted; Thompson, Dunn, and Hickerson cleared in draft; Huston and Dunn initialled), 740.00119Control(Rumania)/2-2445; to Harriman, February 27, 1945 (Dunn signed; Huston drafted, Thompson, Matthews initialled), 740.00119Control(Rumania)/2-2545; February 27, 1945 (Cannon, Huston, Campbell drafted; Bohlen, Matthews, and Dunn initialled), 740.00119Control(Rumania)/2-2745; NA, RG 59.

8. Cannon had opposed the British embassy's recommendation for allied discussions on Rumania in Washington, preferring to wait instead for some assurance from Molotov. Unfortunately, Molotov's letters of March 4 and 7 gave no assurances. See Cannon to Matthews, Dunn, and Bohlen, March 3, 1945, Box 1, Bohlen Files. Berry to secretary, March 16 (Melbourne drafted) and 17, 1945, 740.00119Control(Rumania)/3-1645 and 3-1745; March 18, 1945, 871.00/3-1845, NA, RG 59. Melbourne was later to note that March 6 marked "the beginning of what would be called the cold war." See "Witness to Cold War," p. 5. Stettinius to Harriman (Huston drafted; Cannon, Dunn, Thompson, and Matthews initialled), March 8, 1945, 740.00119Control(Rumania)3-845, and Huston memorandum, March 19, 1945, 871.00/3-1945, NA, RG 59; Bohlen to Harriman (Cannon drafted), March 26, 1945, Box 1, Bohlen Files.

9. Barnes to secretary, February 2, 1945, 874.00/2-245; February 20, 1945, 740.0011EW/2-2045; February 27, 1945, 740.0011EW/2-2745, February 28, 1945, 874.50/2-2845, NA, RG 59.

10. Barnes to secretary, March 2, 1945, 874.00/3-245, NA, RG 59; March 21, 1945, *FRUS,* 4:176–77; March 23, 1945, 500CC/3-2345, NA, RG 59.

11. Acheson to Barnes (Cannon drafted), March 6, 1945, 740.00119Control(Bulgaria)3-645; Cannon to Matthews, March 19, 1945, 871.00/3-1945; Grew to Harriman (Cannon signed; Hohenthal, Huston, and Cannon drafted; Thompson, Dunn, and Matthews initialled), March 29, 1945, 874.00/3-2945, NA, RG 59.

12. Hohenthal memorandum, January 2, 1945, 860H.00/1-245; Stettinius to Richard C.

Patterson (Cannon drafted; Matthews and Dunn initialled), January 17, 1945, 860.H.01/1-1745; Cannon memorandum, January 29, 1945, 860H.01/1-2945; Grew to Winant (Dunn drafted), January 27, 1945, 860H.00/1-2745, NA, RG 59. Djilas recalled in his *Conversations with Stalin* how insensitive the Soviet leader was to the partisan struggle. As for Churchill, while he preferred a monarchy, he was willing to compromise the future role of Anglophiliac King Peter, who consented to the provisional government on January 29, to maintain some political influence in the country. "Do you intend to make Yugoslavia your home after the war?" Churchill barked at Brigadier Fitzroy Maclean in 1944. "No sir!" came the reply. "Neither do I. And that being that case, the less you and I worry about the form of Government they set up, the better." Quoted in Walter Roberts, p. 174.

13. Cannon memorandum (cleared in draft with Dunn and Hickerson), February 25, 1945, 860H.00/2-2545, NA, RG 59; Fraleigh to secretary, March 24, 1945, 800Yugoslavia, Belgrade Post Files, WNRC, RG 84.

14. Sherwood, p. 875. Opinion polls in February and March found that more than 50 percent of the American people still anticipated closer U.S.-Soviet ties after the war. This figure increasingly declined, save for an upswing during the Potsdam Conference, to less than 40 percent by the end of the war. See Cantril, *Public Opinion,* pp. 370–71, and the President's Secretary's File, Box 138, Truman Papers. Grew to Harriman (Thompson drafted; Bohlen, Matthews, and Dunn initialled), February 24, 1945, 860C.01/2-2445; March 3, 1945 (Thompson drafted), 860C.01/3-345; March 8, 1945 (Bohlen drafted; Thompson, Matthews, and Dunn initialled), 860C.01/3-845, NA, RG 59.

15. Churchill to Roosevelt, March 8, 1945, *FRUS,* 5:147–48; Churchill, *Triumph and Tragedy,* pp. 418–39. Bohlen and Leahy to Roosevelt, March 15, 1945, Map Room Files, Box 31, FDR Papers; Acheson to Harriman (Thompson drafted; Matthews initialled), March 18, 1945, 860C.01/3-1845, NA, RG 59.

16. Bohlen to Stettinius, March 13, 1945, Box 1, Bohlen Files; Churchill to Roosevelt, April 5, 1945, *FRUS,* 3:746–47; Roosevelt to Stalin, April 12, 1945, 3:756, and Harriman, April 12, 1945, 3:757. According to Durbrow and Matthews, Stalin's tirade so profoundly affected Roosevelt that he directed Bohlen, while in Hot Springs, to draft a new "game plan" for U.S.-Soviet relations. While this may be so, I have found no evidence to substantiate it either in personal or official records.

17. Sherwood, p. 881; Matthews, "Memoirs," p. 291; Records of Edward R. Stettinius, Jr., vol. 6, April 8–14, 1945, NA, RG 59 (hereafter Stettinius Record); Bohlen memo of conversation with Truman, Stettinius, Grew, and Harriman, April 20, 1945, *FRUS,* 5:231–34; Henderson Oral History, Truman Library, pp. 35, 237–38; interviews with Yost, Riddleberger and Barbour.

18. Harriman, *America and Russia,* p. 39; Henderson Oral History, p. 232. Harriman and Bohlen remembered Stalin as genuinely moved and quite obliging in his decision to send Molotov to San Francisco. Durbrow, by contrast, contended that Stalin was primarily motivated by his desire to assess the character of the new president. Both considerations probably influenced his decision.

19. Matthews, "Memoirs," p. 257; Bohlen, *Witness,* p. 166; minutes of the Secretary's Staff Committee meetings, February 9 and April 4, 1945, Boxes 88G-H, Records of Interdepartmental and Intradepartmental Committees, NA, RG 353, Lot 122; Stettinius Record, vol. 7, April 13–14, 1945; Dunn and Bohlen to president, April 23, 1945, 860C.01/4-2345, NA, RG 59. Bohlen, Thompson, and Kohler joined the American delegation.

20. Grew to Truman, April 10, 1945, *FRUS,* 4:1151–53; Stimson diary entries, April 2–3, 1945, vol. 51, Harry L. Stimson Papers, Yale University; Bohlen memo of conversation with Truman, Grew, and Harriman, May 15, 1945, Box 1, Bohlen Files; Bohlen, *Witness,* pp. 215–16.

21. Harriman, *Special Envoy,* pp. 474–75; Murphy, pp. 260–61; Theodore C. Achilles Oral

History, Truman Library, pp. 117–18; Grew to Dunn, June 14, 1945, vol. 21, Grew Diary, Grew Papers.

22. Ciechanowski, pp. 228, 361, 381, 383–84; Durbrow memos of conversations with Ciechanowski, 860C.01/6-1345 and 6-2945, respectively dated June 13 and 29, 1945, NA, RG 59; Durbrow interview, July 21, 1977.

23. Hamilton to secretary, March 15, 1945, *FRUS*, 4:607–8, and July 29, 1945, 4:618–19; July 13, 1945, 860D.00/7-1345, NA, RG 59; Feis, *Churchill-Roosevelt-Stalin*, p. 268. Since the United States was not at war with Finland, only Britain and Russia participated in the armistice commission. Finland was recognized by the United States on August 8, two days after Soviet recognition.

24. Jacobs diary entries, March 30 and May 9, 1945; Hamilton to Mrs. Hamilton, September 19, 1943; Jacobs to secretary, May 26, 1945, *FRUS*, 4:28–34; June 30, 1945, 875.01/6-3045, NA, RG 59.

25. Jacobs to secretary, July 1, 1945, 875.01/7-145, NA, RG 59.

26. Bohlen, *Witness*, p. 89; Bohlen to Steinhardt, December 28, 1944, Box 44, Steinhardt Papers.

27. Klieforth to Pasvolsky, July 21, 1943, Box 5, Leo Pasvolsky Files, NA, RG 59 (hereafter Pasvolsky Files) and March 23, 1944, 740.00119Control(Germany)/3-2344, NA, RG 59; Klieforth to Riddleberger, June 4, 1945, Box 47, Steinhardt Papers; Klieforth to secretary (Bruins drafted), June 4, 1945, 800Communist Control of Czech National Committees; June 12, 1945, 820 Military Affairs (General), Prague Post Files, WNRC, RG 84; June 15, 1945 (Bruins drafted), 860F.00/6-1545, NA, RG 59.

28. Klieforth to secretary, July 6, 1945, 860F.01/7-645, NA, RG 59.

29. Schoenfeld to secretary from Caserta, April 19, 1945, 800Hungary, Hungary Post Files, WNRC, RG 84; Schoenfeld to Matthews, May 30, 1945, 764.00/5-3045, NA, RG 59; Schoenfeld to secretary, June 16, 1945, 800Elections, Budapest Post Files, WNRC, RG 84; June 18, 1945, 864.00/6-1845, and June 19, 1945, 740.00119Control(Hungary)/6-1945, NA, RG 59.

30. Grew to Schoenfeld (Reber drafted), June 21, 1945, *FRUS: The Conference of Berlin*, 1:380; Schoenfeld to secretary, June 25, 1945, 740.00119Control(Hungary)/6-2545, NA, RG 59.

31. Harriman to secretary, June 30, 1945, 740.00119Control(Hungary)6 3045; Schoenfeld to secretary, July 6, 1945, 740.00119Control(Hungary)/7-645; Grew to Schoenfeld (Campbell drafted; Reber and Dunn initialled), July 13, 1945, 740.00119Control(Hungary)/7-1345; Schoenfeld to secretary, July 24, 1945, 864.00/7-2445, and July 26, 1945, 864.00/7-2645, NA, RG 59.

32. Berry to secretary, April 3, 1945, 871.00B/4-345; April 22, 1945, 871.00/4-2245, and April 24, 1945, 871.01/4-2445, NA, RG 59.

33. Berry to secretary, May 13, 1945, 871.00/5-1345, NA, RG 59; Bohlen to secretary, April 19, 1945, Box 2, Bohlen Files.

34. Melbourne to secretary, June 19, 1945, 761.71/6-1945, July 9, 1945, 871.00/7-945, July 10, 1945, 871.00/7-1045, NA, RG 59; and July 13, 1945, 800Rumania, Moscow Post Files, WNRC, RG 84.

35. Barnes to secretary, April 20, 1945, 740.00119Control(Bulgaria)/4-2045, NA, RG 59; May 9 and 13, 1945, 800Bulgaria, Sofia Post Files, WNRC, RG 84; 740.00119 Control(Bulgaria)/5-1045 and 5-1945, respectively dated May 10 and 19, 1945, NA, RG 59; Grew to president (Cannon drafted; cleared in draft with Matthews; Reber initialled), May 1, 1945, 740.00119Control(Bulgaria)/5-145, NA, RG 59.

36. Barnes to secretary, May 25, 1945, *FRUS*, 4:223; Grew to Barnes (Cannon drafted; Matthews and Reber initialled), May 25, 1945, 874.00/5-2545, NA, RG 59; Barnes to secretary, May 26, 1945, 874.00/5-2645, June 1, 1945, 874.00/6-145, and June 10, 1945, 874.00/6-

1045, NA, RG 59; Acheson to Barnes (Barbour drafted; Cannon and Reber initialled), June 10, 1945, 874.00/6-1045, NA, RG 59; Barnes to Caserta, June 12, 1945, 800Bulgaria, Caserta Post Files, WNRC, RG 84.

37. Barnes to secretary, June 16, 1945, 874.00/6-1645; June 23, 1945, 874.01/6-2345; June 28, 1945, 874.00/6-2845; July 6, 1945, 874.00/7-645, and July 9, 1945, 761.67/7-945, NA, RG 59.

38. Durbrow to Matthews, Phillips, and Dunn, May 30, 1945, 864.01/5-3045; Truman to Churchill (Durbrow drafted), June 2, 1945, 711.60/6-245; Cannon to Dunn, July 15, 1945, 870.00/7-1545, NA, RG 59; Thompson to Dunn, July 15, 1945, *FRUS*, 4:630; Grew to Barnes (Barbour drafted), July 17, 1945, 874.00/7-1745, NA, RG 59. According to Yergin (p. 92), Durbrow's statement exemplified the "Riga" approach. Davis contended (pp. 283–84) that he was more concerned with preserving the diplomacy of principle. Actually, he embraced both views.

39. Patterson to secretary (Fraleigh drafted), May 9, 1945, 860H.00/5-945, NA, RG 59.

40. Cannon to Matthews and Dunn, April 20, 1945, 860H.01/4-2045; Campbell to Huston, Hohenthal, and Cannon (Huston concurring), January 19, 1945, 760H.00/1-1945; Grew to Barnes (Hohenthal drafted), January 29, 1945, 760H.00/1-2945, NA, RG 59; Matthews memo of conversation with Truman, Grew, Leahy, and Phillips, April 30, 1945, *FRUS*, 4:1127–28; Matthews to Grew, May 2, 1945, 4:1132–33; Cannon to J. Wesley Jones, Southern European division chief, Reber and Matthews, May 6, 1945, 740.00119Control(Italy)/5-645, NA, RG 59; Reber to Matthews, May 10 and 21, 1945, Box 17, Matthews Files; Dunn to secretary (Thompson drafted), May 16, 1945, 860H.24/5-1445, NA, RG 59.

41. Grew to Truman (Cannon drafted), May 26, 1945, Official Files, Folder 364, Truman Papers; Thompson memo of conversation with Dunn and Šubašić, May 26, 1945, 500CC/5-2645, NA, RG 59.

42. Patterson to secretary (Shantz drafted), June 4, 1945, 860H.00/6-445; Shantz to secretary, June 18, 1945, 860H.00/6-1845, NA, RG 59; Shantz to secretary (Fraleigh drafted), June 23, 1945, 710-631/Yugoslavia-US, Belgrade Post Files, WNRC, RG 84; June 26, 1945 (Fraleigh drafted), 860H.00/6-2645; July 7, 1945, 860H.00/7-745; July 14, 1945, 860H.00/7-1445, July 29, 1945, 860H.00/7-2945, NA, RG 59.

43. Kennan to Harriman, February 24, 1945, Box 3, Kennan Papers; to secretary, January 30, 1945, 740.00119Control(Bulgaria)/1-3045, NA, RG 59; to Harriman, April 12, 1945, Box 3, Kennan Papers; Grew to Kennan (W. A. drafted; Matthews cleared in draft), April 30, 1945, 863.01/4-2645 and Kennan to secretary, May 2, 1945, 863.01/5-245, NA, RG 59.

44. Kennan to secretary, May 3, 1945, 740.00119EW/5-345, NA, RG 59; to Harriman, May 14, 1945, *FRUS*, 5:295–96; undated memorandum, ca. February 1945, Box 3, Kennan Papers; Kennan, *Memoirs, 1925–1950*, pp. 239–42, 253–58.

45. Stevens to Kennan, February 17, 1945, and ca. spring 1945, 710Russia, Moscow Post Files, WNRC, RG 84. Kennan altered this latter memo to read that the United States sought "workable arrangements" rather than "our objectives" in the postwar world. Their divergent views were confirmed in an interview with Kennan.

46. See Kennan-Davies to Harriman, April 23, 1945, 761.93/4-2345, NA, RG 59; Davies, *Dragon*, pp. 390, 405–7; see Bohlen Files, Box 2, for August 1945 memo from Davies; Davies to Harriman, July 26, 1945, 800Chinese Communists, Moscow Post Files, WNRC, RG 84.

47. Harriman, *Special Envoy*, pp. 413–14; Bohlen, *Witness*, p. 127; Davies, *Dragon*, p. 390; Deane, pp. 181, 285.

Chapter 7

1. Matthews, "Memoirs," p. 291; Churchill, *Triumph and Tragedy*, p. 603.

2. Herbert Feis, *From Trust to Terror*, p. 44; Churchill, *Triumph and Tragedy*, pp. 671–74; Harry S. Truman, *Years of Decision*, pp. 411–12.

3. Bohlen, *Witness*, pp. 238–39; Matthews Oral History, p. 8, Riddleberger Oral History, p. 23, Joseph C. Satterthwaite Oral History, p. 45, Truman Library; Durbrow interview, May 3, 1976.

4. Steinhardt despatches to secretary (Klieforth drafted), July 21, 1945, 860F.00/7-2145, 8-1045 and 8-2145, respectively dated July 21, August 10 and 21, 1945, NA, RG 59; Mrs. Bruins interview; Jacobs to secretary, August 15, 1945, 875.00/8-1545, NA, RG 59.

5. Klieforth to secretary, July 9, 1945, *FRUS*, 4:520–21; Steinhardt to secretary (Klieforth drafted), July 21, 1945, 860F.00/7-2145, NA, RG 59; Dunn to secretary from London, October 6, 1945, *FRUS*, 4:59–60; Byrnes to Jacobs (Acheson signed; McKisson drafted; Reber initialled), November 28, 1945, 875.01/11-2445; Jacobs to secretary, December 1 and 3, 1945, 875.01/12-145 and 12-345; December 11, 1945, 875.00/12-1145, December 18, 1945, 875.01/12-1845, NA, RG 59. All former Albanian treaties had been abrogated by the Anti-Fascist Congress at Permet in May 1944. Steinhardt to secretary (Bruins drafted), December 3, 1945, 860F.00/12-345, NA, RG 59.

6. Schoenfeld to secretary, 661.6431/10-545 and 10-645, respectively dated, October 5 and 6, 1945; Byrnes to Schoenfeld (Hickerson signed; Andrew E. Donovan drafted; Huston and Durbrow initialled), October 11, 1945, 661.6431/10-1145; Brynes to Schoenfeld (Willard L. Thorp signed; Campbell drafted; Reber initialled), November 7, 1945, 661.6431/10-3145, Schoenfeld to secretary, November 26, 1945, 740.00119EW/11-2645, NA, RG 59. Letter from Robert S. Folsom, Arlington, Virginia, to Hugh De Santis, April 19, 1975.

7. Schoenfeld to secretary, August 21, 1945, 864.00/8-2145, and Byrnes to Schoenfeld (Dunn signed; Donovan drafted; Matthews, Thompson, and Reber initialled), August 21, 1945, 864.00/8-1745, NA, RG 59; Schoenfeld to General William S. Key, August 27, 1945, 800 Hungarian Elections, Budapest Post Files, WNRC, RG 84; to secretary, September 11, 1945, 711.9 Allied Control Commission, Budapest Files, WNRC, RG 84.

8. Bohlen, *Witness*, p. 256; Matthews, *Memoirs*, p. 290. Formal recognition of Hungary came on October 11. Wallace, Archibald MacLeish, Lauchlin Currie, and others expressed regret at Dunn's influence in the department. See Wallace-Currie chat of December 28, 1944 in Blum, *Wallace Diary*, p. 418. MacLeish to Acheson, August 30, 1945, Box 1, Archibald MacLeish Papers, Library of Congress, Washington, D.C. According to Leslie Squires, a member of the Budapest mission temporarily in London, Dunn (supported by Cannon) successfully outlasted opposition to Hungarian recognition from Bohlen and John Foster Dulles. See Squires to Schoenfeld, October 11, 1945, *FRUS*, 4:886–87.

9. Schoenfeld to secretary, September 19, 1945, *FRUS*, 4:872–73; November 1, 1945, 864.00/11-145, NA, RG 59; Harriman, The Special Envoy, p. 510. The Smallholders received 57 percent of the vote in the national contest, versus 20 percent for the left, and 245 seats in the National Assembly, nearly twice the total of the Social Democrats and the Communists combined. See Schoenfeld to secretary (F. T. Merrill drafted), 864.00/10-1145, 11-945, and 11-1045, respectively dated October 11, November 9, and November 10, 1945, NA, RG 59.

10. Schoenfeld to secretary, November 15, 1945, 864.00/11-1545, NA, RG 59; November 23, 1945, 711.9ACC, Budapest Post Files, WNRC, RG 84; December 5, 1945, 864.50/12-545, NA, RG 59.

11. Lane to Grew, May 4, 1945, 860C.01/5-445, NA, RG 59; Lane, *I Saw Poland Betrayed*, pp. 26–27, 142; *Life*, July 16, 1945, pp. 14–15.

12. Lane to secretary, August 22, 1945, 860C.00/8-2245; August 18, 1945, 760C.00/8-1845; September 10, 1945, 860C.00/9-1045, NA, RG 59; Lane, *I Saw Poland Betrayed*, pp. 173–74; Lane to secretary; October 4, 1945, 860C.24/10-445, NA, RG 59; October 13, 1945, *FRUS*, 5:388–90, and October 14, 1945, 5:390; Lane to Durbrow, October 16, 1945, 860C.00/10-1645, and Lane to secretary, October 27, 1945, 860C.00/10-2745, NA, RG 59. Letters from Clifford Taylor, Pittsburgh, and John M. Cabot, Washington, to Hugh De Santis, April 24 and May 7, 1976.

13. Durbrow memos of conversation with Armand Berard, counsellor of French embassy,

October 11, 1945, *FRUS*, 5:386–88, and Mikolajczyk, November 9, 1945, 860C.00/11-945, NA, RG 59; Byrnes to Lane (THH drafted; Matthews and Bohlen initialled), November 9, 1945, *FRUS*, 5:411–12; Lane to Byrnes, November 13, 1945, 860C.51/11-1345, NA, RG 59. Interestingly, Durbrow told Lane that the department was impeded from taking a firmer position on the credits question due to the personal influence of Ludwig Rajchman, Polish minister of finance. Rajchman, a Jew and a bacteriologist by training, had lived in the United States and formed close ties with many New Deal reformers such as Samuel Rosenman, Hopkins, and MacLeish. See Durbrow to Lane, December 11, 1945, Box 23, Folder 1146, Lane Papers.

14. Lane to secretary, November 16, 1945, 860C.00/11-1645, Acheson to Lane (Durbrow drafted), November 16, 1945, 860C.00/11-1645; Byrnes to Lane (Durbrow and R. G. Hooker drafted), November 24, 1945, 123 Lane; Lane to secretary, 860C.51/11-3045, NA, RG 59; Lane to Norman Armour, December 5, 1945, Box 69, Folder 1247, and Durbrow to Lane, December 8 and 11, 1945, Box 23, Folders 437 and 446, Lane Papers.

15. Melbourne to secretary, August 7, 1945, *FRUS*, 5:562–64; August 17, 1945, 871.00/8-1745, NA, RG 59; August 22, 1945, 800 Rumania, Moscow Post Files, WNRC, RG 84; Byrnes to Melbourne (Dunn signed; Campbell drafted; Matthews initialled), August 25, 1945, 871.00/8-2545, NA, RG 59.

16. Melbourne to secretary, August 31, 1945, 800 Rumania, Moscow Post Files, WNRC, RG 84; Berry to secretary, 871.00/9-445 and 9-545, respectively dated September 4 and 5, 1945, NA, RG 59.

17. Berry to secretary, 871.00/11-2845, 12-1145, 12-1345, and 12-3145, respectively dated November 28, December 11, 13, and 31, 1945, NA, RG 59.

18. Barnes to secretary, 874.00/7-3145, 8-1145 and 8-1645, respectively dated July 31, August 11 and 16, 1945, NA, RG 59; Dunn to Byrnes, August 9, 1945, *FRUS*, 4:281; Byrnes to Barnes (Barbour drafted; Reber, Durbrow, Matthews, Bohlen, and Dunn initialled), August 11, 1945, 874.00/10-1145, NA, RG 59.

19. Barnes to secretary, 874.00/8-2245, 8-2345, 8-2445, and 8-2545, respectively dated August 22 through 25, 1945; Byrnes to Barnes (Barbour drafted; Matthews and Dunn initialled), August 23, 1945, 874.00/8-2345; Barnes to secretary, September 3, 1945, 874.00/9-345, and September 6, 1945, 874.00/9-645; Rewinkel to secretary, 874.00/9-1145, 9-1945 and 9-2145, respectively dated September 11, 19 and 21, 1945, NA, RG 59.

20. Barnes to secretary, October 25, 1945, 874.00/10-2545, November 13, 1945, 874.00/11-1445; Byrnes to Sofia (Barbour drafted; Reber, Durbrow, Thompson, Matthews, Bohlen, and Dunn initialled), November 14, 1945, 874.00/11-1445; Barnes to secretary, 874.00/11-2445, 12-545 and 12-1345, respectively dated November 24, December 5 and 13, 1945, NA, RG 59.

21. Shantz to secretary (Fraleigh drafted), August 13, 1945, 860H.00/8-1345, August 13, 1945 (Emil Kekich drafted), 860H.00/8-1345, and August 14, 1945, 860H.00/8-1445, NA, RG 59; August 22, 1945, *FRUS*, 5:1251–52; September 2, 1945, 860H.00/9-245, September 20, 1945, 860H.00/9-2045, and September 27, 1945, 860H.00/9-2745, NA, RG 59.

22. Patterson conversation with Truman, August 31, 1945, *FRUS*, 5:1252–53; Patterson meeting with Matthews, Reber, and Barbour, August 31, 1945, 710 Venezia Giulia, Belgrade Post Files, WNRC, RG 84; Huston to Matthews and Reber (Barbour drafted), October 8, 1945, 860H.01/9-2745, NA, RG 59; Barbour memorandum, division of Southern Europe, September 4, 1945, 710 Yugoslavia-US, Belgrade Post Files, WNRC, RG 84; Cannon to U.S. delegation, Paris peace conference, September 12, 1945, Box 6, Records of International Conferences, Commissions and Expositions, NA, RG 43; Huston to Matthews (Barbour drafted), October 15, 1945, 860H.01/10-1545, NA, RG 59; Barbour undated memorandum, "Situation in Yugoslavia," Box 17, Matthews Files.

23. Huston memos of conversation with Acheson, Mr. Duchich, president of Serbian Defense Council et al., October 16, 1945, 860H.00/10-1645, and Ivan Frangeš, October 30,

1945, 860H.00/10-3045; Byrnes to American embassies in Moscow, London, and Belgrade (Barbour drafted; Cannon, Thompson, Matthews, and Kennan initialled; Bohlen cleared in draft), October 17, 1945, 860H.01/10-1745, and October 26, 1945 (Barbour drafted; Cannon, Durbrow, Matthews, and Bohlen initialled), 860H.00/10-2245; Reber to secretary (Durbrow initialled), November 24, 1945, 860H.00/11-2445; Acheson to Belgrade, London, Paris, Sofia, and Bucharest (Reber and Barbour drafted), December 22, 1945, 860H.00/12-2245, NA, RG 59.

24. Kennan to secretary, July 15, 1945, 800C/820.02, Moscow Post Files, WNRC, RG 84; September 27, 1945, 761.67/9-2745, NA, RG 59; October 4, 1945, *FRUS*, 5:888–91, and September 30, 1945, 5:884–86; December 30, 1945, 840.4016/12-3045, NA, RG 59; Kennan, *Memoirs, 1925–1950*, p. 284.

25. Interviews with Kohler, Durbrow (January 29 and May 11, 1976), Barbour, Henderson (January 24, 1969), and Yost. The only realpolitiker in the administration, Secretary of War Stimson, had retired earlier in the year.

26. Huston to Hickerson, Matthews, Durbrow, and Bohlen, October 24, 1945, 711.61/10-2445, NA, RG 59; Bohlen memo, October 18, 1945, and Bohlen and Stevens memo of conversation with Dr. Frank Jewett, president of National Academy of Science et al., December 7, 1945, Box 1, Bohlen Files; Byrnes to Moscow (Henderson and George V. Allen drafted; Durbrow initialled), November 23, 1945, 891.00/11-2345; Acheson to Harriman, Dunn, Durbrow, and Reber initialled), November 18, 1945, 740.00119 Council/11-1845, NA, RG 59.

27. Bohlen memo, *supra;* Dubrow memo, November 27, 1945, 711.61/11-2245, NA, RG 59.

28. Eben Ayers diary entry, December 17, 1945, Box 25, Eben Ayers Papers, Truman Library.

Chapter 8

1. Byrnes, *Speaking Frankly*, p. 122; Acheson, p. 190; Harriman, *Special Envoy*, p. 525; Matthews, *Memoirs*, p. 298; Durbrow interview, January 29, 1976.

2. Henderson to secretary, Dunn, Cohen, and Acheson, January 3, 1946, 891.00/1-246, Henderson memo of conversation with Hussein Ala, Iranian ambassador, January 4, 1946, 891.00/1-446 and memo to secretary, January 5, 1946, 711.61/1-546; Byrnes to Murray (Henderson, Allen and H. B. Minor drafted), January 24, 1946, 891.00/1-2446, NA, RG 59; Barnes to secretary, January 15, 1946, 874.00/1-1546, NA, RG 59; Kennan to London, January 10, 1946, Box 6, NA, RG 43; Arthur H. Vandenberg, Jr., ed., *The Private Papers of Senator Vandenberg*, p. 233.

3. Acheson to Truman (Barbour drafted), January 12, 1946, 711.60H/1-446, NA, RG 59; Durbrow memo of conversation with Elbrick and Janusz Zoltkowski, January 12, 1946, *FRUS*, 6:376–79; Durbrow to Acheson, January 21, 1946; 861.24/1-1946; Brynes to Cohen in London (Barbour drafted; Thompson and Matthews initialled), January 30, 1946, 874.00/1-3146; Byrnes to Barnes (Barbour drafted), February 5, 1946, 871.01/2-546, NA, RG 59. The recognition of Rumania was announced on February 14.

4. Assistant Secretary of the Navy H. Struve Hensel to Forrestal, September 24, 1945; Leahy draft for review of Patterson and Forrestal to Truman, October 24, 1945; Forrestal to Truman, November 8, 1945, Folder 125, Leahy Files; Document 81a, "Functions of the Director of Central Intelligence," summer 1946, NA, RG 353, Lot 122; R & A report 3443.1, "The Capabilities and Intentions of the Soviet Union as Affected by American Policy," November 19, 1945, Records, Studies and Surveys of the Research Analysis Division of the Office of Strategic Services, NA, RG 59; unsigned State Department policy statement, "Foreign Policy of the United States," December 1, 1945, 711.00/12-145, NA, RG 59.

5. Kennan to secretary, January 15, 1946, 761.00/1-1546, and January 29, 1946, 611.4131/1-2946, NA, RG 59; Kennan to London, February 1, 1946, Box 6, NA, RG 43.

6. Kennan to secretary, February 2, 1946, *FRUS*, 6:688, and February 7, 1946, *FRUS*, 6:690–91; Charles Yost, *The Insecurity of Nations*, pp. 100–102.

7. Kohler, Matthews (May 20, 1976), Henderson (January 24, 1976), and Barbour interviews; Durbrow to Matthews, Acheson and G. Hayden Raynor, February 12, 1946, 861.00/2-1246, NA, RG 59; Bohlen, *Witness*, p. 272; Matthews memorandum, 761.00/2-1146, NA, RG 59; Acheson, p. 208. According to an AIPO poll of February 27, 1946, only 35 percent of the American people now expected U.S.-Soviet postwar cooperation. See Cantril, *Public Opinion*, p. 371.

8. Bohlen to Matthews, February 14, 1946, 711.61/2-1446, NA, RG 59. In "Paths not Taken: The United States Department of State and Alternatives to Containment, 1945–1946," *Diplomatic History* 1 (Fall 1977): 297–319, Robert Messer has argued that Bohlen's and Huston's views represented a potentially viable alternative policy to containment. But the clash of U.S.-Soviet political objectives in Eastern Europe had made this very universalistic policy of cooperation unattainable. Cooperation was still possible, but not on the globally idealistic basis American policymakers wished.

9. Stevens to Matthews and Durbrow (submitted by Matthews to SWNCC), February 18, 1946, Box 51, NA, RG 353, Lot 122; Cannon to Berry, February 25, 1946, Box 13, Berry Papers.

10. Kennan to secretary, February 12, 1946, 861.00/2-1246, NA, RG 59; February 19, 1946, Box 74, NA, RG 43; Kennan, *Memoirs, 1925–1950*, pp. 292–93; Durbrow interview, January 29, 1976.

11. Kennan to secretary, February 22, 1946, 861.00/2-2246, NA, RG 59. Given the emotional tenor of the postwar period, Kennan stated in an interview on September 7, 1976, it was difficult to detach oneself completely from the spectre of communist expansion. Indeed, this was the theme of his February 3 and 7 telegrams on Russian policy toward Spain and Argentina (Box 63, Folder 1, Elsey Papers). Even so, Kennan had not altered his view that Marxist ideology operated in the service of Russian military and political expansion, and that a policy based on the image of realistic cooperation offered the best chance for U.S.-Soviet coexistence. See Kennan to London, January 10, 1946, Box 72, NA, RG 43; and "The U.S. and Russia," winter or spring 1946, Box 3, Kennan Papers. Among the recent profusion of Kennanania, John Lewis Gaddis' "Containment: A Reassessment," *Foreign Affairs* 55 (July 1977): 873–88, stresses, perhaps too singlemindedly, Kennan's essential balance-of-power point of view. For a concise statement of Kennan's containment policy, see Jürgen Reiss, *George Kennans Politik der Eindämmung*.

12. Matthews, "Memoirs," pp. 260–61; Matthews chit to Kennan, February 22, 1946, 861.00/2-2246, NA, RG 59; Kohler interview; Benton to Kennan, March 7, 1946, and Henderson to Benton, March 20, 1946, 861.00/2-2246, NA, RG 59; Blum, *Wallace Diary*, p. 547; Harriman, *Special Envoy*, p. 548.

13. Barbour and Rudolph Schoenfeld interviews.

14. Truman quoted by Eben Ayers, February 25, 1946, Box 25, Ayers Papers; Vandenberg, pp. 246–49; U.S. State Department, the *Department of State Bulletin*, vol. 14, March 10, 1946, pp. 355–58; Dunn to Matthews, February 27, 1946, *FRUS*, 2:16–19.

15. Kohler and Durbrow (January 29, 1976) interviews; Blum, *Wallace Diary*, March 5, 1946, p. 557; Kennan to secretary, March 11, 1946, 741.61/3-1146 and March 22, 1946, 741.61/3-2246, NA, RG 59.

16. Henderson Oral History, Truman Library, pp. 52–54; Byrnes to Murray (Henderson drafted), March 24, 1946, 861.24591/3-2446, NA, RG 59; Byrnes to Kennan, March 5, 1946, *FRUS*, 7:340–42 (Kennan transmitted the note on March 6); Byrnes to Murray (Bohlen drafted), March 8, 1946, Box 1, Bohlen Files.

17. Kennan to secretary, March 21, 1946, 710India/710Iran/710Turkey, Moscow Post Files, WNRC, RG 84; March 20, 1946, Box 64, Folder 1, Elsey Papers.

18. Bohlen memos, March 13 and 14, 1946, and Bohlen (drafted with Admiral Sherman

and General Deane) to Matthews, March 22, 1946, Box 2, Bohlen Files; Matthews to SWNCC, April 1, 1946, 711/61/3-1446, NA, RG 59. Although the image of realistic confrontation was not reflected in Kennan's "long telegram," his fuzziness about containment left the door open for department officials, Secretary Forrestal, Leahy, and other military people to fill the void. On March 29 the Joint Chiefs of Staff impressed upon Byrnes that the United States must demonstrate to the Soviets by diplomacy and military might that notions of capitalist encirclement and irreconcilable hostility between the capitalist and communist worlds can only lead to "disaster" for Russia. See JCS to Byrnes, March 29, 1946, *FRUS*, 1:1165–66.

19. Durbrow to Kennan, March 22, 1946, Durbrow Papers.

20. Kennan, *Memoirs, 1925–1950*, p. 295; Kennan and Smith to secretary, April 22, 1946; 800Interpretive Political Reports, Moscow Post Files, WNRC, RG 84.

21. On the British loan, see Richard Freeland, *The Truman Doctrine and the Origins of McCarthyism;* Dunn to secretary from London, April 18, 1946, *FRUS*, 2:70–72; Clay's views in Gaddis, *The Origins of the Cold War*, pp. 318, 329–30. Acheson stated in his memoirs that 1946 was a year in which American officials recognized that the Kremlin worked exactly as Kennan had stated (p. 265).

22. Barnes to secretary, January 30, 1946, 874.00/1-3046, and February 11, 1946, 874.00/ 2-1146, NA, RG 59; Barnes to secretary, March 13, 1946, *FRUS*, 6:85–86. General Crane shared Barnes's malaise. See Crane to War Department, February 6, 1946, Folder 5, Leahy Files. Actually, both Petkov and Lulchev could have joined the government. However, they demanded control of the ministry of justice, which the Soviets refused. Bohlen (unsigned) memo of conversation with Byrnes and Vyshinski, January 23, 1946, 740.00.00119Council/ 1-2346; Byrnes to Kennan (Barbour drafted; Matthews and Durbrow initialled), February 14, 1946, 740.00119Control(Bulgaria)/2-446; Byrnes to Barnes, March 13, 1946, 874.00/3-1346; Matthews memo to Byrnes, March 22, 1946, 874.00/3-1346; Acheson to Barnes (Barbour drafted), March 26, 1946, 874.00/3-2646, NA, RG 59.

23. Barnes to secretary, March 29, 1946, 874.00/3-2946, and April 4, 1946, 874.00/4-446, NA, RG 59.

24. Barnes to secretary, June 8, 1946, 874.00/6-846; Byrnes to Barnes (G. L. West drafted; Thompson initialled), June 8, 1946, 874.00/6-846; Barnes to secretary, July 6, 1946, 874.00/ 7-646 and July 24, 1946, 740.00119EW/7-2446, NA, RG 59; July 26, 1946, 711ACC Bulgaria, Moscow Post Files, WNRC, RG 84.

25. Berry to mother, February 4, 1946, Box 13, Berry Papers; Berry to secretary, March 10, 1946, 871.00/3-1046, and March 29, 1946, 871.00/3-2946; Byrnes to Berry (Barbour drafted; Durbrow and Matthews initialled), February 11, 1946, 871.00/2-846; Byrnes to Berry (Barbour drafted; Durbrow, Bohlen, and Matthews initialled), March 6, 1946, 871.00/ 3-646; Berry to secretary (Melbourne drafted), April 6, 1946, 871.00/4-646; March 6, 1946, 740.00119Control(Rumania)/3-646; Brynes to Berry (H. J. Nickels drafted), March 19, 1946, 740.00119Council/3-1946, NA, RG 59. See also General Schuyler's reports of March 20, 1946 to the War Department, Folder 65, Leahy Files.

26. Byrnes to Berry (Barbour and Nickels drafted; Bohlen, Thompson, and Matthews initialled), May 20, 1946, 871.00/5-2146, Berry to secretary, June 4, 1946, 871.00/6-446, and July 11, 1946, 871.00/7-1146, NA, RG 59; June 5, 1946, *FRUS*, 6:599–601; June 8, 1946, 811.20200(D)/6-846, NA, RG 59; June 15, 1946, Box 120, NA, RG 43; July 4, 1946, *FRUS*, 6:611–12.

27. Fraleigh, Shantz, and Hohenthal to Patterson, February 17, 1946, Box 1, Richard C. Patterson Papers, Harry S Truman Library, Independence, Missouri (hereafter Patterson Papers); Shantz to secretary, March 2, 1946, 860H.00/3-246, and Matthews to secretary (Barbour drafted), March 6, 1946, 860H.01/3-246; Shantz to secretary, March 16, 1946, 860H.00/3-1646, and March 26, 1946, 860H.50/3-2646; Matthews to Acheson and Byrnes (Barbour drafted), February 11, 1946, 860H.24/2-1146, NA, RG 59. On January 30, 1946, the

former Constituent Assembly became the People's Assembly of the Federal People's Republic of Yugoslavia. A new constitution was proclaimed in the same month.

28. Hohenthal to Shantz, April 14, 1946, Moscow Post Files, WNRC, RG 84; Shantz to Paris, May 27, 1946, Box 80, NA, RG 43; Byrnes to Shantz (Barbour drafted; cleared in draft by Matthews), April 17, 1946, 860H.00/3-246, and Byrnes to Harriman (West and Barbour drafted; Thompson and Matthews initialled), May 29, 1946, 860H.7962/5-2946, NA, RG 59; Shantz to secretary (Fraleigh drafted), June 3, 1946, 710Yugoslavia, and June 6, 1946 (Hohenthal drafted), 801Recognition Yugoslavia, Belgrade Post Files, WNRC, RG 84; June 14, 1946 (Fraleigh drafted), 860H.00/6-1446, NA, RG 59; George to secretary, July 24, 1946, 848UNRRA, Belgrade Post Files, WNRC, RG 84; Shantz to secretary (Fraleigh drafted), July 31, 1946, 860H.00/7-3146, NA, RG 59.

29. Jacobs to secretary, January 29, 1946, *FRUS*, 6:1–3; February 8 and 5 and March 13, 1946, 701USMission-Albania/710, Tirana Post Files, WNRC, RG 84; Jacobs diary entries of March 6 and 26, 1946; Jacobs to secretary, February 28, 1946, *FRUS*, 6:12–15; March 6 and 22, 1946, 875.00/3-646 and 3-2246, March 6 and 22, 1946, February 21, 1946, 840.50UNRRA/2-2146; March 16, 1946, 124.753/3-1646, NA, RG 59.

30. Jacobs to secretary, 875.00/5-746, 5-2746 and 5-2846, respectively dated May 7, 27 and 28, 1946, NA, RG 59; April 20, 1946, 710Albania/701USMission-Albania, Tirana Post Files, WNRC, RG 84; May 9, 1946, 711.75/5-946, and May 8, 1946, 840.50UNRRA/5-846, NA, RG 59; June 24, 1946, Box 82, NA, RG 43; Barbour to Hickerson, July 18, 1946, 768.75/7-1346, NA, RG 59; Henderson memo of conversation (W. O. Baxter drafted) with Greek ambassador and Baxter, July 31, 1946, State Department Lot File 54D363; Barbour interview.

31. Schoenfeld to secretary, February 15, 1946, 710Hungary/USSR, Budapest Post Files, WNRC, RG 84; Steinhardt to secretary, February 26, 1946, *FRUS*, 6:185–88; Byrnes to Kennan (Durbrow and H. J. Hilton drafted; Barbour and Matthews initialled), March 5, 1946, 661.6431/3-546, NA, RG 59.

32. Schoenfeld to secretary, March 4 and April 3, 1946, 864.00/3-446 and 4-346; Byrnes to Schoenfeld (Barbour drafted; Matthews chit attached), March 6, 1946, 864.00/3-646, NA, RG 59; H. F. Arthur Schoenfeld, "Soviet Imperialism in Hungary," *Foreign Affairs* 26 (July 1948): 561. It also seems significant that Moscow entrusted the ministry of the interior in Hungary to Leslie Rajk, a pronounced anti-Semite and a leading member of the nationalist wing of the Hungarian Communist party, instead of to someone like Rákosi.

33. Steinhardt to secretary (Bruins drafted), May 29, 1946, 860F.00/5-2946, NA, RG 59.

34. Bruins to secretary, 860F.00/6-746 and 6-1046, respectively dated June 7 and 10, 1946, NA, RG 59; Bruins to secretary (Mirick drafted), July 11, 1946, 860F.00/7-1146, NA, RG 59; Steinhardt to secretary, July 30, 1946, *FRUS*, 6:209–10.

35. Schoenfeld to secretary, April 20 and May 2, 1946, 761.64/4-2046 and 5-246, NA, RG 59; Schoenfeld, "Soviet Imperialism," pp. 561–62; Schoenfeld to Paris, May 28, 1946, Box 80, May 10 and 16, Box 97, NA, RG 43; Schoenfeld to secretary, May 2, 1946, 864.51/5-246, NA, RG 59; Caffery to secretary (Matthews drafted), May 4, 1946, Box 99, NA, RG 43; see Bohlen, Matthews, and Kennan proposed note on Hungary at the USSR committee meeting, May 28, 1946, Box 15, NA, RG 353, Lot 122; Schoenfeld to secretary, 864.00/7-1146, 7-1246, and 7-1846, respectively dated July 11, 12, and 18, 1946, NA, RG 59.

36. Keith to secretary, February 2, 1946, 760C.00/2-246; Lane to secretary, February 22, 1946, 860C.00/2-2246, NA, RG 59; Lane to Matthews, March 1, 1946, in *I Saw Poland Betrayed*, pp. 193–96. Whether mainly to prevent further communization of the country or to enhance his own political ambitions, Mikolajczyk suicidally demanded 75 percent of the seats in parliament. He later lowered the figure to 40 percent.

37. Lane to secretary, April 3 and 16, 1946, 860C.00/4-346 and 4-1646; Byrnes to Warsaw embassy (Durbrow drafted), April 18, 1946, 860C.0014-1846; Lane to secretary, April 21, 1946, 860C.51/4-2146; Durbrow to Byrnes, April 22, 1946, 860C.51/4-2246, NA, RG 59; Lane

to secretary, April 25, 1946, 860C.51/4-2546, NA, RG 59; Lane, *I Saw Poland Betrayed,* p. 239; Lane to Elbrick, April 23 and May 14, 1946, Box 7, Folders 1252–53, Lane Papers.

38. Keith to secretary, May 14, 1946, 860C.00/5-1446; Thompson memo of conversation with Dr. Stefan Litauer, Minister Counselor Zoltkowski, and Elbrick, June 25, 1946, *FRUS,* 6:466–67; Lane to secretary, 860C.00/7-846, 7-946 and 7-1546, respectively dated July 8, 9 and 15, 1946; Lane to Elbrick (Dorsz drafted), July 5, 1946, 860C.00/7-546; Lane to secretary, July 20, 1946, 800Poland, Warsaw Post Files, WNRC, RG 84; Byrnes to Lane (Thompson drafted), July 26, 1946, 860C.00/7-2646, NA, RG 59; Thompson to Byrnes, July 26, 1946, Box 119, NA, RG 43. The American consular officers in question were Joseph Burt (Gdansk) and Howard Bowman (Poznan).

39. Davies unnumbered memorandum, June 6, 1946; Reinhardt unnumbered memos, June 17 and 27, 1946; Davies memos, April 20, 1946, 800Interpretive Reports, and unnumbered June 8, 1946; Reinhardt unnumbered memo, July 17, 1946; Smith to secretary (Davies drafted), June 26 and July 16, 1946, 713Atomic Energy, WNRC, RG 84.

40. Matthews to Benton, May 21, 1946, Box 9, Matthews Files; Barbour comments in meeting of USSR Committee, June 26, 1946, Box 16, NA, RG 353, Lot 122; Stevens memorandum, May 27, 1946, 861.00/5-2546, and Thompson to Hickerson, June 21, 1946, 711.61/6-2146, NA, RG 59; Hickerson to V. F. Field, executive secretary subcommittee for Europe (Stevens drafted), July 11, 1946, Box 136, NA, RG 353, Lot 122.

41. Kennan remarks, June 12, 1946, Box 2, Kennan Papers; H. Kullgren summary of talk by Kennan, "Soviet-American Relations," June 18, 1946, unnumbered document, NA, RG 59; Kennan to Acheson, July 18, 1946, *FRUS,* 1:860–65.

42. Kennan summary, August 23, 1946, in 123Kennan. Kennan acknowledged in his memoirs that his comments sounded like those later made by Senator Joseph McCarthy or the House Un-American Activities Committee (p. 301).

43. See Bernard Cohen, *The Public's Impact on Foreign Policy,* which substitutes for the myth about public opinion, rooted in normative democratic theory, a systematic examination of its relationship to foreign-policy formulation. The British loan is a good example of the administration's effect on congressional attitudes. In the Fortune poll of July 1946, 54 percent of the public believed that Russia sought to spread communism. See Cantril, *Public Opinion,* p. 133. See JCS to Patterson and Forrestal, August 23, 1946, *FRUS,* 7:857–58; also see R & A reports 3669A and 3540-3643A, NA, RG 59.

44. Elsey to Clifford, August 15, 1946, Box 63, Elsey Papers.

45. Clifford to Kennan, "American Relations with the Soviet Union," September 13, 1946, and Kennan to Clifford, September 16, 1946, Box 63, Elsey Papers. I am persuaded to this view by Kennan's memoirs and official correspondence, my personal impressions of him formed during our interview, and the responses of his sister, Mrs. Jeanette Kennan Hotchkiss, during our talk on August 20, 1977.

46. U.S. State Department, *Department of State Bulletin* (September 15, 1946): 496–501.

47. Kennan, *Memoirs, 1925–1950,* pp. 301–4; Kennan lectures, September 16 and October 1, 1946, Box 2, Kennan Papers; Henderson, Minor, and W. C. Dunn to Acheson, October 18, 1946, 891.00/10-1846, NA, RG 59. Henderson had encouraged aid to Iran and the Arab world since early summer, a position that provoked Jewish leaders and supporters of the Zionist cause to call for his dismissal. See Henderson, *Memoirs,* 2:366–69; and Blum, *Wallace Diary,* August 14, 1946.

48. Rewinkel to secretary, 874.00/9-746, 9-1946, and 9-2946, respectively dated September 7, 19, and 29, 1946; Barnes to secretary, November 30, 1946, 874.00/11-3046, NA, RG 59. Letter from John E. Horner, Girne, Turkey, to Hugh De Santis, October 5, 1976.

49. Berry to Paris, August 13 and 26, 1946, Box 123, NA, RG 43; Berry to secretary, September 23, 1946, 871.00/9-2346, and October 19, 1946, 871.00/10-1946; November 4, 1946, *FRUS,* 6:647–49; Berry diary entry, November 20, 1946, Box 13, Berry Papers;

Acheson to Berry (Hickerson signed; Nickels drafted; Barbour and Thompson initialled), November 22, 1946, 871.00/11-2246, NA, RG 59; Berry to mother, December 4, 1946, Box 13, Berry Papers; Melbourne, "Witness to Cold War," pp. 12–13.

50. Combined Chiefs of Staff to General Morgan (SACMED), July 5, 1946, *FRUS*, 6:907–8; Shantz to secretary, August 9, 1946, 811.2360H/8-946; Acheson to Patterson (Barbour drafted), August 20, 1946, 811.2360H/8-1946, and August 21, 1946 (Hickerson drafted), 811.2360H/8-2146; NA, RG 59; Patterson to Acheson, October 5, 1946, *FRUS*, 6:965, and Acheson to Patterson, October 17, 1946, 6:968–69; Fraleigh, George, and Patterson to secretary, September 4, 1946, 740.00119Council/9-446, NA, RG 59. Letter from John M. Cabot to Hugh De Santis.

51. Jacobs to Paris, September 8, 1946, Box 82, NA, RG 43; Jacobs to Hickerson, November 14, 1946, 501AA/11-1446, NA, RG 59.

52. Schoenfeld to secretary, November 23, 1946, 864.00/11-2346, NA, RG 59; "Soviet Imperialism," p. 558.

53. Steinhardt to secretary, August 14, 1946, *FRUS*, 6:213–14; Bruins to secretary (George F. Bogardus drafted), August 15, 1946, 860F.00/8-1546, NA, RG 59; Steinhardt to secretary (Bogardus drafted), September 3, 1946, 860F.00/9-346, and September 18, 1946, 860F.00/9-1846, NA, RG 59; Matthews to secretary (Clayton signed; Hickerson drafted), September 21, 1946, *FRUS*, 6:225; interviews with Yost and Mrs. Bruins; Steinhardt to secretary (Bruins drafted), December 31, 1946, 860F.00/12-3146, NA, RG 59; Bruins to Steinhardt, August 14 and 29, 1947, Box 54, Steinhardt Papers.

54. Lane to Secretary, 860C.00/8-2046, 10-246 and 10-846, respectively dated August 20, October 2 and 8, 1946, NA, RG 59; Lane to Paris, September 17, 1946, Box 119, NA, RG 43; Lane to Keith, October 14, 1946, Box 7, Folder 1258, Lane Papers; Keith to secretary, November 13, 1946, 860C.00/11-1346, NA, RG 59; Lane, *I Saw Poland Betrayed*, pp. 283, 288.

55. Durbrow to secretary, August 14, 1946, 711.41/8-1446, NA, RG 59; August 23, 1946, Box 63, Elsey Papers. Elsey noted on a chit to Clifford that Durbrow's reports confirmed their view of communist domination of every phase of Russian life. To counteract these anti–United States-United Kingdom articles, which filled the pages of *Pravda, Liternaturnaya Gazeta, Young Bolshevik, Culture and Life,* and other publications, Durbrow encouraged Washington to enlist the services of Kennan, Stevens, and other Soviet experts to produce an effective propaganda program of its own. See Smith to secretary (Durbrow drafted), October 10, 1946, 874 Information Broadcasts, Moscow Post Files, WNRC, RG 84. Durbrow to secretary, September 18, 1946, 711.61/9-1846, and November 2, 1946, 711.61/11-246; November 5 and 8, 1946, 861.00/11-546 and 11-846, NA, RG 59; Durbrow memorandum, "Mourning Thoughts on Soviet Economics," November 2, 1946, Durbrow Papers; Durbrow to secretary, August 2, 1946, Box 63, Folder 5, Elsey Papers.

56. Davies, Reinhardt, et al., to secretary, "Analysis of Soviet Strength and Weakness," September 1, 1946, 710Russia, Budapest Post Files; Davies to Smith (which Smith forwarded to department), November 18, 1946, 713Atomic Energy, Moscow Post Files, WNRC, RG 84.

57. Durbrow to Bullitt, December 17, 1946, Durbrow Papers.

58. Stevens and Richard H. Davis to Acheson and Matthews, December 23, 1946, and Bohlen to Matthews, December 27, 1946, Box 10, Matthews Files.

Chapter 9

1. Interviews with Henderson (January 24, 1976), Durbrow (January 29, 1976), Kohler, Kennan, and Mrs. Bruins; Schoenfeld to Reid, October 23, 1930, Schoenfeld Papers.

2. Henderson interview, January 24, 1976; Kennan memorandum, "The Techniques of

German Imperialism in Europe,'' April 1941, Box 3, Kennan Papers; Lane to Dunn, August 27, 1936, Box 63, Folder 1129, Lane Papers; Kohler interview; Lane, *I Saw Poland Betrayed,* p. 161; Durbrow (January 29, 1976) and Barbour interviews; letter from Melbourne, Newberry, South Carolina, to Hugh De Santis, April 21, 1976; interviews with Mesdames Bruins and Schoenfeld. See Katz and Cantril, ''An Analysis of Attitudes toward Fascism and Communism,'' *Journal of Abnormal and Social Psychology* 35 (1940): 356–66.

3. Durbrow interview, May 3, 1976. See Downs, p. 49, Homans, pp. 107–20, and Joseph de Rivera, *The Psychological Dimension of Foreign Policy,* p. 27.

4. Moffat diary entry, March 18, 1940, vol. 44, Moffat Papers. See Fraleigh comments on Arabs, Turks, and Jews in his diary of a trip to Cairo with Berry, December 30, 1943–January 26, 1944, Box 11, Berry Papers; on the appearance of Russian women, see Hamilton to Mrs. Hamilton January 30, 1944; Lane to Selden Chaplin on housing conditions in Poland, June 11, 1946, Box 70, Folder 1254, Lane Papers, Yost interview; Blau and Scott, p. 139; Homans, pp. 319–20; Chris Argyris, *Personality and Organization,* pp. 59–62; see Andrew Scott's interesting articles, ''The Department of State: Formal Organization and Informal Culture,'' *International Studies Quarterly* 13 (March 1969): 1–19, and ''Environmental Change and Organizational Adaptation,'' *International Studies Quarterly* 14 (March 1970): 85–95.

5. Marquis Childs, ''It Is Called Diplomacy,'' *Harper's* 176 (March 1938): 417–22. ''The Pros Make Better Diplomats,'' *Saturday Evening Post,* June 3, p. 104; F. H. Russell, chief of the office of public opinion, to Assistant Secretary Benton, January 16, 1946, State Department Lot File 54D202; Loy Henderson, *Foreign Policies: Their Formulation and Enforcement;* see M. E. McCallum to Truman, July 25, 1946, in 123Dunn, and ''The Shape of Things,'' *Nation,* August 3, 1946, p. 115.

6. Stettinius to Roosevelt, February 19, 1944, Box 1, Elsey Papers; Richard L. Connolly Oral History, Truman Library, vol. 2, p. 307; Henderson to Acheson, July 30, 1946, 891.00/7-3046, NA, RG 59.

7. Cannon to Matthews, September 28, 1944, in Cannon 123, NA, RG 59; Lane to Byrnes, and Claude Bowers to Byrnes, December 3, 1945, 120.1/12-345, NA, RG 59; Davies, *Dragon,* pp. 418–19; Durbrow to Lane, November 29, 1945, Box 23, Folder 484, Lane Papers.

8. de Rivera, pp. 28–29; Raymond A. Bauer, ''Problems of Perception and the Relations between the United States and the Soviet Union,'' *Journal of Conflict Resolution* 5 (1961): 223–29; Ole R. Holsi, ''Cognitive Dynamics and Images of the Enemy,'' in John C. Farrell and Asa P. Smith, eds., *Image and Reality in World Politics;* see also Leon Festinger, *A Theory of Cognitive Dissonance.*

9. This was confirmed by Charles Yost and, unintentionally, Mesdames Bruins and Schoenfeld during interviews. Lane, *I Saw Poland Betrayed,* pp. 172–73; Durbrow interview, May 3, 1976; Shantz to secretary (Fraleigh drafted), June 29, 1946, 710Yugoslavia/710 Bulgaria, WNRC, RG 84; Bruins to son Bill, January 9, 1954. Rudolph Schoenfeld admitted in an interview that diplomats in Eastern Europe (as elsewhere) suffered from an occupational malady known as ''localitis.''

10. Berry to secretary, May 23, 1946, 711.00/5-2346; Barnes to secretary, January 19, 1946, 874.01/1-1945, NA, RG 59; Mrs. Bruins interview; see Shantz views in chap. 10.

11. Durbrow interview, May 3, 1976.

12. Undersecretary Grew was especially sensitive to the feeling of diplomatic isolation experienced by diplomats in Eastern Europe. ''I myself,'' he later recalled, ''during my years in the field, suffered so much from the absence of such reactions that I felt my communications to the department were like throwing a pebble into a lake at night; we seldom even saw the ripples.'' Grew to James W. Webb, January 9, 1949, Box 25, James W. Webb Papers, Truman Library.

13. Blum, *Wallace Diary*, p. 470; Achilles Oral History, pp. 4–5; de Rivera, pp. 56–60, 232–42; Bohlen, *Witness,* pp. 248, 256–60; Matthews (September 8, 1976) and Yost interviews; letter from Robert Folsom to Hugh De Santis.

14. The findings of this study support Cohen's assertion that foreign-policy officials tend to be influenced more by the nexus of personal relations within the department than by the amorphous public (pp. 72, 80). Regarding relations within the bureaucracy, see Scott, "Environmental Change and Organizational Adaptation"; on the amorphous public, see Philip E. Converse, "The Nature of Belief Systems in Mass Publics," in David E. Apter, ed., *Ideology and Discontent;* concerning the indirect influence of public opinion on foreign policy, see de Rivera, pp. 343–60. As late as March 1945, a Princeton poll revealed that 40 percent of the public had never heard of the American government's proposals for the United Nations Organization and that barely 30 percent knew whether the United States had been a member of the League of Nations. See the special memorandum for United States delegation at San Francisco on public opinion, April 20, 1945, 500CC/5-745, NA, RG 59. Yet, a NORC poll during the same month showed that 64 percent, quite likely influenced by Washington's and Congress' "sales pitch," favored American entry into the United Nations. Similarly, a Princeton study in May concluded that only 58 percent of Americans thus far felt satisfied with Soviet cooperation, but 72 percent were in favor of postwar collaboration. When perceptions of the Soviet Union within the department altered during 1946, public attitudes similarly changed. In the Fortune poll of July 1946, for example, 54 percent surveyed believed Russia sought to spread communism throughout the world, double the figure in the sample tested the previous September. See the folder on public opinion trends in the President's Secretary's File, Box 138, Truman Papers.

15. Leahy diary entries, February 20 and 21, 1946, William D. Leahy Papers, Library of Congress, Washington, D.C.

16. This analysis draws from the psychological paradigm of Salvatore Maddi and the theoretical model of aberrant social behavior defined by Robert Merton. The lifeless undertaking of one's duties, abandonment of one's duties, and the elevation to a cause of one's duties roughly correspond to Maddi's states of nonmeaning, antimeaning, and extreme meaning and to Merton's ritualist, retreatist, and innovator social types. Actually, Merton's "innovator" becomes the "rebel" in this study, and vice-versa. It seemed semantically more appropriate to type Kennan as the former, although he would be defined as the latter in Merton's schema (rejection of goals and means and substitution of a new myth structure.) See Maddi, "The Search for Meaning," in *Nebraska Symposium on Motivation,* and Merton, *Social Theory and Social Structure,* chap. 7. Attitude is interpreted here—as is perception throughout the study—as an expression of behavior, that is, as the intentionality underlying behavior. See M. Brewster Smith, "Opinions, Personality and Political Behavior," *American Political Science Review* 52 (March 1958): 1–17, and Rollo May, *Love and Will,* chap. 9.

17. José Ortega y Gasset, *Man and Crisis,* p. 28; Paul Tillich, *The Courage to Be,* particularly chap. 2.

18. Kennan's views remain a source of controversy among historians. Yergin, for example, has labelled Kennan the "arch ideologue" of the Riga group (pp. 170–71). Had he traced Kennan's thinking beyond the Riga period, if only as a kind of null hypothesis, he would have seen that this analysis was shortsighted. Furthermore, he would not have had difficulty attempting to explain Kennan's later opposition to American militancy during the Berlin blockade, which he passes off as "surprising," given Kennan's ideological focus (p. 388). He would also have been forced, I suspect, to revise the enticingly simple Riga-Yalta typology: first, because Kennan and others, including Henderson and Durbrow in due course, did not always accord with the "Riga axioms," and second, because Kennan fit better as a representative of the "Yalta axioms," which, in any event, fail, as Yergin

presents them, to distinguish between images of ideological cooperation and realistic cooperation.

19. Hotchkiss interview, May 21, 1977; Kennan, *Memoirs, 1925–1950,* p. 17; Kennan, "The Needs of the Foreign Service," in Joseph E. McLean, ed., *The Public Service and University Education,* pp. 98–99.

Epilogue

1. Top secret memorandum, "Relations with the Soviet Union," prepared in division of European affairs and presented to secretary by Matthews, January 18, 1947, Box 17, Matthews Files.

2. Jacobs to secretary, September 21, 1946, *FRUS,* 7:222; Barnes to London, October 7, 1946, Box 82, NA, RG 43; Barnes to secretary, October 10, 1946, 710Yugoslavia/710 Great Britain/800Bulgaria, Sofia Post Files, WNRC, RG 84; Durbrow to secretary, October 10, 1946, *FRUS,* 7:233, and Barnes to secretary, November 26, 1946, 7:269–70.

3. Acheson, p. 290; Henderson Oral History, Truman Library, pp. 76–79.

4. Acheson, p. 293.

5. Harry S Truman, *Years of Trials and Hope,* p. 101; Henderson Oral History, Truman Library, pp. 87–88; Durbrow memorandum, "Comments on the International Policy of the Soviet Union in the Second Year of Peace," January 18, 1947, Durbrow Papers; Bohlen's comments in his draft of Truman's State of the Union message, Box 2, Bohlen Files.

6. Kennan remarks, Council on Foreign Relations, New York, January 7, 1947, and lecture at National War College, January 24, 1947, Box 2, Kennan Papers; Kennan, *Memoirs, 1925–1950,* pp. 314–21.

7. Matthews, "Memoirs," p. 313; Kohler, *Understanding the Russians,* p. 425; Kohler interview.

8. Episode excerpted from Adam Ulam, *The Rivals,* pp. 122–23.

Bibliography

Archival Records

National Archives

(Record Group 59)
H. Freeman Matthews–John D. Hickerson Files
Harley Notter Files
123 Files (Personnel Records)
Leo Pasvolsky Files
Edward R. Stettinius, Jr., Record
Records of the Board of Review of Foreign Service Personnel
Records of the Office of Eastern European Affairs, USSR Section, 1917–1941
Reports, Studies, and Surveys of the Research Analysis Division of the Office of Strategic Services
State Department Decimal Files

(Record Group 43)
Records of International Conferences, Commissions, and Expositions
Records of the European Advisory Commission

(Record Group 353, Lot 122)
Records of Interdepartmental and Intradepartmental Committees Maintained by the Secretariat, 1943–1951

(Record Group 218)
Records of the Combined Chiefs of Staff
Records of the United States Joint Chiefs of Staff
William D. Leahy Files

(Record Group 165)
Records of the War Department General and Special Staffs (Combined Civil Affairs Committee)

Washington National Records Center

(Record Group 84)
Records of Consular Posts
Records of Diplomatic Posts

246

Department of State

Charles E. Bohlen Files
Loy Henderson Files
Lot Files 54D202, Office of International Information and Cultural Affairs
Lot Files 54D363, Near Eastern and African Affairs
Lot Files 54D394, Division of European Affairs
Lot Files 54D403, Near Eastern and African Affairs
Lot Files 54D426, Eastern European Affairs
Lot Files 57D612, Eastern European Affairs
Lot Files 24, Near Eastern and African Affairs

Manuscripts

Library of Congress

Charles E. Bohlen Papers
Joseph E. Davies Papers
Leland Harrison Papers
Cordell Hull Papers
William D. Leahy Papers
Archibald MacLeish Papers
Leo Pasvolsky Papers
Laurence A. Steinhardt Papers

Harry S Truman Library

Dean Acheson Papers
Eben Ayers Papers
George V. Allen Papers
Clark M. Clifford Papers
George M. Elsey Papers
Richard C. Patterson Papers
Harry S. Truman Papers
James E. Webb Papers

Franklin D. Roosevelt Library

Adolf A. Berle Papers
Harry Hopkins Papers
R. Walton Moore Papers
Franklin D. Roosevelt Papers
John C. Wiley Papers
John G. Winant Papers

Harvard University

Joseph G. Grew Papers
J. Pierrepont Moffat Papers
William Phillips Papers

Yale University

Arthur Bliss Lane Papers
John F. Montgomery Papers
James R. Sheffield Papers
Henry L. Stimson Papers

Princeton University

John Foster Dulles Papers
James Forrestal Papers
George F. Kennan Papers
J. V. A. MacMurray Papers

Georgetown University

Robert Kelley Papers

University of Chicago

Samuel Harper Papers

Indiana University

Burton Y. Berry Papers

Private Collections

John F. Bruins letters, courtesy Mrs. John F. Bruins, Washington, D.C.
Elbridge Durbrow Papers, courtesy Elbridge Durbrow, Washington, D.C.
Maxwell M. Hamilton diary and letters, courtesy Mrs. Maxwell Hamilton, Roseburg, Ore.
Loy Henderson memoirs, courtesy Loy Henderson, Washington, D.C.
Joseph Jacobs diary, courtesy Mrs. Marjorie Riddle, Chapel Hill, N.C.
H. Freeman Matthews, "Memoirs of a Passing Era," courtesy H. Freeman Matthews, Washington, D.C.
H. F. Arthur Schoenfeld Papers, courtesy Mrs. H. F. Arthur Schoenfeld and Scott Schoenfeld, Washington, D.C.

Interviews

Walworth Barbour, Gloucester, Mass., June 2, 1976
Mrs. John H. Bruins, Washington, D.C., December 12, 1975

Edmund Dorsz, Washington, D.C., May 6, 1976
Elbridge Durbrow, Washington, D.C., January 29, May 3 and 11, 1976; July 21, 1977
Loy Henderson, Washington, D.C., January 24, May 5, 15, 21, and 27, 1976
Jeanette Kennan Hotchkiss, Highland Park, Ill., May 21, August 20, and September 9, 1977
George F. Kennan, Princeton, N.J., September 7, 1976
Foy D. Kohler, Coral Gables, Fla., September 13, 1976
Robert McBride, Charlottesville, Va., May 8, 1976
H. Freeman Matthews, Washington, D.C., May 20 and September 8, 1976
Jake Millar, Washington, D.C., February 11, 1976
Mrs. Marjorie Riddle, Chapel Hill, N.C., September 9, 1976
James W. Riddleberger, Washington, D.C., September 8, 1976
Mrs. H. F. Arthur Schoenfeld, Washington, D.C., October 25, 1975
Rudolph Schoenfeld, Washington, D.C., January 16, 1976
Scott Schoenfeld, Washington, D.C., October 25, 1975
Charles W. Yost, Washington, D.C., May 6, 1976

Oral Histories

Columbia University Oral History Collection

George V. Allen
Leslie Arends
Roger Nash Baldwin
Joseph Ballantine
Adolf A. Berle
Charles E. Bohlen
Lucius D. Clay
Will Clayton
Goldthwaite Dorr
Eleanor Lansing Dulles
Michel Gordey
Karl Harr
Loy Henderson
Nelson Trusler Johnson
Mary Pillsbury Lord
Robert Murphy
William Phillips
Edward E. Rice
Jacob Viner
Henry A. Wallace

James P. Warburg
James T. Williams

Truman Library Oral History History Collection

Theodore C. Achilles
Ralph Block
Richard L. Connolly
Mark Etheridge
Loy Henderson
Benjamin Hulley
David J. MacDonald
H. Freeman Matthews
James Riddleberger
Joseph Satterthwaite

Correspondence

Walworth Barbour, Gloucester, Mass.
Burton Berry, Rome, Italy
Donald F. Bigelow, Gstaad, Switzerland
Mrs. Charles E. Bohlen, Washington, D.C.
John M. Cabot, Washington, D.C.
Mrs. Antoinette Denny, Johnston, S.C.
Lady Julie Dodson, British Embassy, Brasilia, Brazil
James Clement Dunn, Rome, Italy
Elbridge Durbrow, Washington, D.C.
Mrs. Mabel Durkop, Genoa, Neb.
Robert S. Folsom, Arlington, Va.
Dr. J. Derchard Guess, Greenville, S.C.
Mrs. Maxwell M. Hamilton, Roseburg, Ore.
Loy Henderson, Washington, D.C.
John E. Horner, Girne, Turkey
Mrs. Paul H. Insinger, Columbus, Neb.
George F. Kennan, Princeton, N.J.
Alexander A. Klieforth, Bonn, West Germany
H. Freeman Matthews, Washington, D.C.
Roy M. Melbourne, Newberry, S.C.
Mrs. Harold Mouzon, Greenville, S.C.
Warwick Perkins, Owings Mills, Md.
James W. Riddleberger, Woodstock, Va.
Clifford Taylor, Pittsburgh, Pa.
Mrs. Llewellyn Thompson, Washington, D.C.
S. Roger Tyler, Jr., Washington, D.C.

Public Documents

Documents on American Foreign Relations Washington. Vols. 5–8. Boston and Princeton: World Peace Foundation and Princeton University Press, 1942–46.

Rosenman, Samuel I., ed. *The Public Papers and Addresses of Franklin D. Roosevelt.* Vols. 9–13. New York: Random House, 1941–50.

U.S., Department of State. *The Department of State Bulletin.* Vols. 5–15. 1941–46.

———. *Foreign Relations of the United States.* Annual vols., 1933–46. Washington, D.C.: U.S. Government Printing Office, 1950–69.

———. *Foreign Relations of the United States: The Soviet Union, 1933–1939.* Washington, D.C.: U.S. Government Printing Office, 1952.

———. *Foreign Relations of the United States: The Conferences at Cairo and Teheran, 1943.* Washington, D.C.: U.S. Government Printing Office, 1961.

———. *Foreign Relations of the United States: The Conference of Berlin (The Potsdam Conference), 1945.* 2 vols. Washington, D.C.: U.S. Government Printing Office, 1960.

———. *Foreign Relations of the United States: The Conferences at Malta and Yalta, 1945.* Washington, D.C.: U.S. Government Printing Office, 1955.

———. *The Foreign Service List.* Washington, D.C.: U.S. Government Printing Office, 1924–47.

———. *Register of the Department of State.* Washington, D.C.: U.S. Government Printing Office, 1933–47.

Woodward, Sir Ernest Llewellyn, ed. *British Foreign Policy in the Second World War.* Vols. 1–4. London: Her Majesty's Stationery Office, 1970–75.

Periodicals and Newspapers

The American Foreign Service Journal, 1924–47 (inclusive).
Life, 1933–50 (noninclusive).
Nation, 1933–50 (noninclusive).
Newsweek, 1933–50 (noninclusive).
New York Herald Tribune, 1933–50 (selected issues).
New York Times, 1933–50 (noninclusive).
New Republic, 1933–50 (noninclusive).
Time, 1933–50 (noninclusive).
U.S. News and World Report, 1933–50 (noninclusive).

Secondary Sources

Acheson, Dean. *Present at the Creation*. New York: New American Library, 1969.

Adler, Les K., and Thomas G. Patterson. "Red Fascism: The Merger of Nazi Germany and Soviet Russia in the American Image of Totalitarianism, 1930s–1950s." *American Historical Review* 75 (April 1970): 1046–64.

Allen, George V. "The Utility of a Trained and Permanent Foreign Service." *The American Foreign Service Journal* 13 (January 1936): 5–7, 32–36.

Almond, Gabriel. *The American People and Foreign Policy*. New York: Harcourt, Brace, 1950.

Argyris, Chris. *Personality and Organization*. New York: Harpers, 1957.

———. *Some Causes of Organizational Effectiveness within the Department of State*. Washington, D.C.: Center for International Systems Research, 1967.

Atkinson, Brooks. "America's Global Planner." *New York Times Magazine*, July 13, 1947, pp. 9, 32–33.

Auty, Phylis. *Tito*. London: Longman, 1970.

Baird, Joseph H. "Professionalized Diplomacy." *The American Foreign Service Journal* 16 (October 1939): 542–43.

Barber, Bernard. "Some Problems in the Sociology of the Professions." *Daedalus* 92 (Fall 1963): 669–88.

Barghoorn, Frederick C. *The Soviet Image of the United States*. New York: Harcourt, Brace and World, 1950.

Bauer, Raymond A. "Problems of Perception and the Relations between the United States and the Soviet Union." *Journal of Conflict Resolution* 5 (1961): 223–29.

Beloff, Max. *The Foreign Policy of Soviet Russia*. 2 vols. London: Oxford University Press, 1947, 1949.

Bendiner, Robert. *The Riddle of the State Department*. New York: Farrar and Rinehart, 1942.

Bendix, Reinhard. "The Age of Ideology: Persistent and Changing." In *Ideology and Discontent*. Edited by David E. Apter. New York: Free Press, 1964.

Bess, Demaree. "What Does Russia Want?" *Saturday Evening Post*, March 20, 1943, pp. 19, 91–94.

Binswanger, Ludwig. *Being-in-the-World*. New York: Basic Books, 1963.

Blancké, W. Wendell. *The Foreign Service of the United States*. New York: Frederick A. Praeger, 1969.

Blau, Peter, and W. Richard Scott. *Formal Organizations*. San Francisco: Chandler Publishing, 1962.

Blum, John Morton, ed. *The Price of Vision: The Diary of Henry A. Wallace, 1942–1946.* Boston: Houghton Mifflin, 1973.

Bohlen, Charles E. *The Transformation of American Foreign Policy.* New York: W. W. Norton, 1969.

———. *Witness to History, 1929–1969.* New York: W. W. Norton, 1973.

Borg, Dorothy. *The United States and the Far Eastern Crisis of 1933–38.* Cambridge: Harvard University Press, 1964.

Borg, Dorothy, and Shumpei Okamoto, eds. *Pearl Harbor as History: Japanese-American Relations, 1931–1941.* New York: Columbia University Press, 1973.

Briggs, Ellis. *Farewell to Foggy Bottom.* New York: David McKay, 1964.

Busch-Zantner, Richard. *Bulgarien.* Leipzig: W. Goldmann, 1941.

Byrnes, James F. *Speaking Frankly.* New York: Harper, 1947.

Campbell, A. E. "The United States and Great Britain: Uneasy Allies." In *Twentieth-Century American Foreign Policy.* Edited by John Braeman, Robert H. Brebner, and David Brody. Columbus: Ohio State University Press, 1971.

Campbell, John F. *The Foreign Affairs Fudge Factory.* New York: Basic Books, 1971.

Cantril, Hadley, ed. *Public Opinion, 1935–1946.* Princeton: Princeton University Press, 1951.

Carr, E. H. *The Twenty Years' Crisis, 1919–1939.* 2d ed. New York: Harper & Row, 1946.

Carsten, F. L. *The Rise of Fascism.* Berkeley: University of California Press, 1969.

Childs, J. Rives. *American Foreign Service.* New York: Henry Holt, 1948.

———. "Democratized Diplomacy." *The American Foreign Service Journal* 11 (October 1934): 562.

Childs, Marquis W. "It Is Called Diplomacy." *Harper's,* March 1938, pp. 417–22.

"Chinese Boy, The." *American Foreign Service Journal* 2 (October 1925): 44.

Churchill, Winston. *Closing the Ring.* Boston: Houghton Mifflin, 1951.

———. *The Grand Alliance.* Boston: Houghton Mifflin, 1950.

———. *The Hinge of Fate.* Boston: Houghton Mifflin, 1950.

———. *Triumph and Tragedy.* Boston: Houghton Mifflin, 1953.

Ciechanowski, Jan. *Defeat in Victory.* Garden City, N.Y.: Doubleday, 1947.

Clay, Lucius D. *Decision in Germany.* Garden City, N.Y.: Doubleday, 1950.

Clemens, Diane Shaver. *Yalta.* New York: Oxford University Press, 1970.

Clubb, O. Edmund. *China and Russia*. New York: Columbia University Press, 1971.

Cochran, William P., Jr. "Ambassador Hugh Gibson on the Foreign Service." *The American Foreign Service Journal* 14 (June 1937): 375–76.

Cohen, Bernard. *The Public's Impact on Foreign Policy*. Boston: Little, Brown, 1973.

Converse, Philip E. "The Nature of Belief Systems in Mass Publics." In *Ideology and Discontent*. Edited by David E. Apter. New York: Free Press, 1964.

Current Biography. New York: H. W. Wilson, 1940–65.

Davies, John Paton, Jr. *Dragon by the Tail*. New York: W. W. Norton, 1972.

———. *Foreign Affairs and Other Affairs*. New York: W. W. Norton, 1964.

Davis, Forrest. "Roosevelt's World Blueprint." *Saturday Evening Post*, April 10, 1943, pp. 20–22, 109–10.

Davis, Lynn Etheridge. *The Cold War Begins*. Princeton: Princeton University Press, 1974.

Deane, John R. *Strange Alliance*. New York: Viking Press, 1947.

Dedijer, Vladimir. *Tito Speaks: His Self-Portrait and Struggle with Stalin*. London: Weidenfeld and Nicolson, 1953.

de Rivera, Joseph. *The Psychological Dimension of Foreign Policy*. Columbus, Ohio: Charles E. Merill, 1968.

Destler, I. M. *Presidents, Bureaucrats, and Foreign Policy*. Princeton: Princeton University Press, 1972.

Deuel, Wallace R. "Why People Don't Like Diplomats." *The American Foreign Service Journal* 24 (February 1947): 11–13, 40–44.

Diggins, John P. *Mussolini and Fascism: The View from America*. Princeton: Princeton University Press, 1972.

Divine, Robert A. *Second Chance: The Triumph of Internationalism in America during World War II*. New York: Atheneum, 1967.

Djilas, Milovan. *Conversations with Stalin*. Translated by Michael B. Petrovich. New York: Harcourt, Brace & World, 1962.

Downs, Anthony. *Inside Bureaucracy*. Boston: Little, Brown, 1967.

Farnsworth, Beatrice. *William C. Bullitt and the Soviet Union*. Bloomington: Indiana University Press, 1967.

Feis, Herbert. *Churchill-Roosevelt-Stalin*. Princeton: Princeton University Press, 1967.

———. *From Trust to Terror: The Onset of the Cold War, 1945–1950*. New York: W. W. Norton, 1970.

Festinger, Leon. *A Theory of Cognitive Dissonance*. Evanston, Ill.: Row, Peterson, 1957.

Filene, Peter G. *Americans and the Soviet Experiment, 1917–1933*. Cambridge: Harvard University Press, 1967.

Fontaine, André. *Histoire de la Guerre Froide*. Vol. I. Paris: Fayard, 1965.

Frankl, Viktor. *The Doctor and the Soul*. Translated by R. Winston and C. Winston. New York: Alfred A. Knopf, 1965.

Gaddis, John Lewis. "Containment: A Reassessment." *Foreign Affairs* 55 (July 1977): 873–88.

————. *The United States and the Origins of the Cold War*. New York: Columbia University Press, 1972.

Gantebein, James W. "Study by Foreign Service Officers in American Universities." *The American Foreign Service Journal* 16 (October 1949): 541, 562–63.

Gardner, Lloyd C. *Economic Aspects of New Deal Diplomacy*. Madison: University of Wisconsin Press, 1964.

Gibson, Hugh. "Our Diplomatic Mess." *Colliers,* July 22, 1944, pp. 44–46.

Goode, William J. "Encroachment, Charlatanism, and the Emerging Profession: Psychology, Sociology, and Medicine." *American Sociological Review* 25 (December 1960): 902–14.

Grew, Joseph C. *Turbulent Era*. 2 vols. Boston: Houghton Mifflin, 1952.

"H." "The Modern Diplomat." *Foreign Affairs* 15 (April 1937): 509–15.

Halperin, Morton. *Bureaucratic Politics and Foreign Policy*. Washington, D.C.: Brookings Institution, 1974.

Hammond, Paul V. "NSC68: Prologue to Rearmament." In *Strategy, Politics and Defense Budgets*. Edited by Warner R. Schilling, Paul V. Hammond, and Glenn H. Snyder. New York: Columbia University Press, 1962.

Harr, John E. *The Anatomy of the Foreign Service*. Washington, D.C. Carnegie Endowment for International Peace, 1965.

Harriman, W. Averell. *America and Russia in a Changing World*. Garden City, N.Y.: Doubleday, 1971.

Harriman, W. Averell, and Elie Abel. *Special Envoy to Churchill and Stalin, 1941–1946*. New York: Random House, 1975.

Heidegger, Martin. *Being and Time*. Translated by J. Macquarrie and E. Robinson. New York: Harper, 1962.

Heinrichs, Waldo H., Jr. *American Ambassador: Joseph Grew and the Development of the United States Diplomatic Tradition*. Boston: Little, Brown, 1966.

————. "Bureaucracy and Professionalism in the Development of American Career Diplomacy." In *Twentieth-Century American Foreign Policy*. Edited by John Braeman, Robert H. Brebner, and David Brody. Columbus: Ohio State University Press, 1971.

Henderson, Loy. *Foreign Policies: Their Formulation and Enforcement*.

Washington, D.C.: U.S. Government Printing Office, 1946.

Holsti, Ole. "Cognitive Dynamics and Images of the Enemy." In *Image and Reality in World Politics*. Edited by John C. Farrell and Asa P. Smith. New York: Columbia University Press, 1968.

Homans, George C. *The Human Group*. New York: Harcourt, Brace, 1950.

Hopkins, Frank Snowden. "Psychological Tensions in the Foreign Service." *The American Foreign Service Journal* 24 (March 1947): 10–11, 40–46.

Hull, Cordell. *The Memoirs of Cordell Hull*. 2 vols. New York: Macmillan, 1948.

Husserl, Edmund. *Ideas: General Introduction to Pure Phenomenology*. Translated by W. R. Boyce Gibson. New York: Macmillan, 1931.

Iatrides, John O. *Revolt in Athens*. Princeton: Princeton University Press, 1972.

Ilchman, Warren F. *Professional Diplomacy in the United States, 1779–1939*. Chicago: University of Chicago Press, 1961.

Iriye, Akira. *Across the Pacific: An Inner History of American–East Asian Relations*. New York: Harcourt, Brace & World, 1967.

———. *After Imperialism: The Search for a New Order in the Far East, 1921–1931*. New York: Atheneum, 1965.

———. *The Cold War in Asia*. Englewood Cliffs, N.J.: Prentice-Hall, 1974.

Jackson, George D., Jr. *Comintern and Peasant in East Europe, 1919–1930*. New York: Columbia University Press, 1966.

Jackson, Senator Henry M., ed. *The Secretary of State and the Ambassador*. Jackson Subcommittee Papers on the Conduct of American Foreign Policy. New York: Frederick A. Praeger, 1964.

Janowitz. Morris. *The Professional Soldier*. 2d ed. New York: Free Press, 1971.

Jaspers, Karl. *Philosophy*. 3 vols. Translated by E. B. Ashton. Chicago: University of Chicago Press, 1969.

Jervis, Robert. *Perception and Misperception in International Politics*. Princeton: Princeton University Press, 1976.

Jones, Joseph M. *The Fifteen Weeks*. New York: Viking Press, 1955.

Jukić, Ilija. *The Fall of Yugoslavia*. Translated by Dorian Cooke. New York: Harcourt, Brace, and Jovanovich, 1974.

Karsten, Peter. *The Naval Aristocracy*. New York: Free Press, 1972.

Katz, Daniel, and Hadley Cantril. "An Analysis of Attitudes toward Fascism and Communism." *Journal of Abnormal and Social Psychology* 35 (1940): 356–66.

Kennan, George F. *From Prague after Munich: Diplomatic Papers, 1938–1940*. Princeton: Princeton University Press, 1968.

————. *Memoirs, 1925–1950*. Boston: Little, Brown, 1967.

————. "The Needs of the Foreign Service." In *The Public Service and University Education*. Edited by Joseph E. McLean. Princeton: Princeton University Press, 1949.

————. "Russia and the United States." *New Republic*, June 26, 1950, pp. 12–16.

————. *Russia and the West under Lenin and Stalin*. New York: New American Library, 1960.

Kertesz, Stefan, ed. *The Fate of East Central Europe*. South Bend: University of Notre Dame Press, 1956.

Klieforth, Alfred. "Hitler Has You Card-Indexed." *Saturday Evening Post*, June 13, 1942, p. 18.

Kohler, Foy D. *Understanding the Russians*. New York: Harper and Row, 1970.

Kohler, Foy D., and Mose L. Harvey, eds. *The Soviet Union: Yesterday, Today, Tomorrow*. Miami: Center for Advanced International Studies, University of Miami, 1975.

Kolko, Garbriel. *The Politics of War: The World and United States Foreign Policy, 1943–1945*. New York: Vintage Books, 1968.

LaFeber, Walter. *America, Russia and the Cold War, 1945–1975*. 3d ed. New York: John Wiley, 1976.

————. "Roosevelt, Churchill, and Indochina, 1942–1945." *American Historical Review* 80 (December 1975): 1277–95.

Lane, Arthur Bliss. "Conquest in Yugoslavia." *Life*, September 15, 1941, pp. 102–12.

————. *I Saw Poland Betrayed*. Indianapolis: Bobbs-Merrill, 1948.

Lay, Tracy Hollingsworth. *The Foreign Service of the United States*. New York: Prentice-Hall, 1928.

Lilienthal, David E. *The Journals of David E. Lilienthal: The Atomic Energy Years, 1945–1950*. New York: Harper and Row, 1964.

Livaneanu, Vasile. "Rolul Partidul Comunist Român in Pregatirea Insurecţiei Nationale Antifasciste Armate (in Lumina Izvoarelor Publicate in Anii 1944–1947)." *Revista de Istorie*, 27 (1974): 1145–65.

Lundestad, Geir. *The American Non-Policy towards Eastern Europe: Universality in an Area Not of Essential Interest to the United States*. Oslo: Universitetsforlaget, 1975.

McCamy, James L. *The Administration of American Foreign Affairs*. New York: Alfred A. Knopf, 1950.

McNeill, William H. *America, Britain and Russia*. London: Oxford University Press, 1953.

Maddi, Salvatore R. "The Existential Neurosis." *Journal of Abnormal Psychology* 72 (1967): 311–25.

————. "The Search for Meaning." In *Nebraska Symposium on Motiva-*

tion. Lincoln: University of Nebraska Press, 1970.

————, ed. *Perspectives on Personality: A Comparative Approach*. Boston: Little, Brown, 1971.

Maddux, Thomas R. "Watching Stalin Maneuver between Hitler and the West: American Diplomats and Soviet Diplomacy, 1934–1939." *Diplomatic History* 1 (Spring 1977): 140–54.

May, Ernest. *"Lessons" of the Past*. New York: Oxford University Press, 1973.

May, Rollo. *Love and Will*. New York: W. W. Norton, 1969.

May, Rollo, Ernest Angel, and Henri F. Ellenberger, eds. *Existence*. New York: Basic Books, 1958.

Melbourne, Roy C. "Rumania: Nazi Satellite." Ph.D. dissertation, University of Pennsylvania, 1951.

————. "Witness to the Start of the Cold War: The View from Rumania." Paper presented at the Conference of the American Association for the Advancement of Slavic Studies. Atlanta, Ga., October 1975.

Merton, Robert K. "Bureaucratic Structure and Personality." In *Complex Organizations*. Edited by Amitai Etzioni. New York: Holt, Rinehart & Winston, 1961.

————. *Social Theory and Social Structure*. New York: Free Press, 1968.

Messer, Robert. "Paths not Taken: The United States Department of State and Alternatives to Containment, 1945–1946." *Diplomatic History* 1 (Fall 1977): 297–319.

Murphy, Robert. *Diplomat among Warriors*. Garden City, N.Y.: Doubleday, 1964.

Nagy, Ferenc. *The Struggle behind the Iron Curtain*. Translated by Stephen K. Swift. New York: Macmillan, 1948.

Nietzsche, Friedrich. *The Use and Abuse of History*. 2d ed. Translated by Adrian Collins. Indianapolis: Bobbs-Merrill, 1957.

Notter, Harley. *Postwar Foreign Policy Preparation*. Washington, D.C.: Department of State, 1950.

Ortega y Gasset, José. *Man and Crisis*. Translated by Mildred Adams. New York: W. W. Norton, 1958.

Patraşcanu, Lucretiu. *Les Trois Dictatures*. Paris: Jean Vitiano, 1946.

Patterson, Thomas C. *Soviet-American Confrontation*. Baltimore: Johns Hopkins University Press, 1973.

"Peoples of the USSR, The." *Life,* March 29, 1943, pp. 23–26.

Perkins, Frances. *The Roosevelt I Knew*. New York: Harper and Row, 1946.

Petrov, Vladimir. *A Study in Diplomacy*. Chicago: Henry Regnery, 1971.

Phillips, William. *Ventures in Diplomacy*. Boston: Beacon Press, 1952.

Pinkerton, J. L. "The Land of the Wattle." *The American Foreign Service Journal* 1 (October 1924): 5, 28.

Ponomaryov, B., A. Gromyko, and V. Khostov, eds. *History of Soviet Foreign Policy, 1945–1970.* Translated by David Skvinsky. Moscow: Progress Publishers, 1974.

Poole, DeWitt, C. "University Training for the Foreign Service of the United States." *The American Foreign Service Journal* 8 (September 1931): 344–45, 374–77.

Prince, Gregory S., Jr. "The American Foreign Service in China, 1935–1941: A Case Study of Political Reporting." Ph.D. Dissertation, Yale University, 1973.

"Pros Make Better Diplomats, The." *Saturday Evening Post,* June 3, 1944, p. 104.

"Red Leaders." *Life,* March 20, 1943, pp. 38–42.

Reiss, Jürgen. *George Kennans Politik der Eindämmung.* Berlin: Coloquium Verlag, 1957.

Ristelheuber, René. *Histoire des Peoples Balkaniques.* Paris: Fayard, 1950.

Roberts, Henry L. *Eastern Europe: Politics, Revolution, and Diplomacy.* New York: Alfred A. Knopf, 1970.

———. *Rumania: Political Problems of an Agrarian State.* New Haven: Yale University Press, 1951.

Roberts, Walter F. *Tito, Mihailović and the Allies, 1941–1945.* New Brunswick, N.J.: Rutgers University Press, 1973.

Rosenberg, Milton. "Attitude Change and Foreign Policy in the Cold-War Era." In *Domestic Sources of Foreign Policy.* Edited by James N. Rosenau. New York: Free Press, 1967.

———. "Images in Relation to the Policy Process." In *International Behavior: A Social-Psychological Analysis.* Edited by Herbert Kelman. New York: Holt, Rinehart & Winston, 1965.

Rothschild, Joseph. *East Central Europe between the Two World Wars.* Seattle: University of Washington Press, 1974.

Ruddy, Michael T. "Charles Bohlen and the Soviet Union, 1929–1969." Ph.D. dissertation, Kent State University, 1973.

Sartre, Jean-Paul. *The Transcendence of the Ego.* Translated by Forrest Williams and Robert Kirkpatrick. New York: Noonday Press, 1957.

Schoenfeld, H. F. Arthur. "Soviet Imperialism in Hungary." *Foreign Affairs* 26 (July 1948): 554–67.

Schroeder, Paul. *The Axis Alliance and Japanese-American Relations.* Ithaca, N.Y.: Cornell University Press, 1958.

Schulzinger, Robert D. *The Making of the Diplomatic Mind.* Middletown, Conn.: Wesleyan University Press, 1975.

Scott, Andrew M. "The Department of State: Formal Organization and Informal Culture." *International Studies Quarterly* 13 (March 1969): 1–19.

————. "Environmental Change and Organizational Adaptation: The Problem of the State Department." *International Studies Quarterly* 14 (March 1970): 85–95.

Selznick, Philip. "Foundations of the Theory of Organization." In *Complex Organizations*. Edited by Amitai Etzioni. New York: Holt, Rinehart & Winston, 1961.

Seton-Watson, Hugh. *Eastern Europe between the Wars, 1918–1941.* 3d ed. New York: Harper and Row, 1962.

————. *The East European Revolution.* 3d ed. New York: Frederick A. Praeger, 1956.

"Shape of Things, The." *Nation*, August 1946, p. 115.

Shaw, G. Howland. "The Individualist and the Foreign Service." *The American Foreign Service Journal* 9 (June 1932): 218.

Sherwood, Robert. *Roosevelt and Hopkins.* New York: Harper, 1948.

Shirer, William L. *The Collapse of the Third Republic.* New York: Simon & Schuster, 1969.

Simpson, Smith. *Anatomy of the State Department.* Boston: Houghton Mifflin, 1967.

Smith, Gaddis. *American Diplomacy during the Second World War, 1941–1945.* New York: John Wiley, 1965.

Smith, M. Brewster. "Opinion, Personality, and Political Behavior." *American Political Science Review* 52 (March 1958): 1–17.

Smith, Robert Freeman. *The United States and Cuba: Business and Diplomacy, 1917–1960.* New York: Bookman Associates, 1960.

Smith, Walter Bedell. *My Three Years in Moscow.* Philadelphia: Lippincott, 1950.

"Stalin at 65." *Life*, January 1, 1945, pp. 62–68.

Stettinius, Edward R., Jr. *Roosevelt and the Russians: The Yalta Conference.* Garden City, N.Y.: Doubleday, 1949.

Steward, Dick. *Trade and Hemisphere: The Good Neighbor Policy and Reciprocal Trade.* Columbia: University of Missouri Press, 1975.

Strang, Lord (William). *The Foreign Office.* London: Allen & Unwin, 1955.

Stuart, Graham H. *American Diplomatic and Consular Practice.* New York: Appleton-Century-Crofts, 1952.

————. *The Department of State.* New York: Macmillan, 1949.

Sugar, Peter F., ed. *Native Fascism in the Successor States.* Santa Barbara, Cal.: ABC-Clio, 1971.

Taylor, A. J. P. *The Origins of the Second World War.* New York: Atheneum, 1961.

Thayer, Charles W. *Diplomat*. New York: Harper, 1959.

Tillich, Paul. *The Courage to Be*. New Haven: Yale University Press, 1952.

Toward a Modern Diplomacy: A Report to the American Foreign Service Association. Washington, D.C.: U.S. Government Printing Office, 1968.

Truman, Harry S. *Years of Decision*. Garden City, N.Y.: Doubleday, 1955.

———. *Years of Trial and Hope*. Garden City, N.Y.: Doubleday, 1956.

Ulam, Adam. *The Rivals: America and Russia since World War II*. New York: Viking Press, 1971.

"USSR, The." *Life,* March 29, 1943, pp. 20–22.

Vandenberg, Arthur H., Jr., ed. *The Private Papers of Senator Vandenberg*. Boston: Houghton Mifflin, 1952.

Villard, Henry S. *Affairs at State*. New York: Thomas Y. Crowell, 1965.

Volkmann, Hans-Erich, ed. *Die Krise des Parlamentarismus in Ostmitteleuropa zwischen den Beiden Weltkriegen*. Marburg/Lahn: Herder, 1967.

Weil, Martin. *A Pretty Good Club: The Founding Fathers of the United States Foreign Service*. New York: W. W. Norton, 1978.

Werth, Alexander. *Moscow War Diary*. New York: Alfred A. Knopf, 1942.

———. *Russia at War, 1941–1945*. New York: E. P. Dutton, 1964.

Williams, William A. *The Tragedy of American Diplomacy*. Rev. ed. New York: Dell, 1962.

Wilson, Hugh R. *Diplomacy as a Career*. Cambridge: Riverside Press, 1941.

———. *Diplomat between Wars*. New York: Longmans, Green, 1941.

Wolff, Robert Lee. *The Balkans in Our Time*. Cambridge: Harvard University Press, 1956.

Wood, Bryce. *The Making of the Good Neighbor Policy*. New York: Columbia University Press, 1961.

Wright, C. Ben. "George F. Kennan: Scholar-Diplomat." Ph.D. dissertation, University of Wisconsin, 1972.

Yergin, Daniel. *Shattered Peace*. Boston: Houghton Mifflin, 1977.

Yost, Charles W. *The Insecurity of Nations*. New York: Frederick A. Praeger, 1968.

Index

Acheson, Dean, 2, 76, 173, 176, 179, 189, 192, 194, 212
Albania, 5, 63–64, 72, 115, 124, 142–43, 157, 158, 183, 184, 193–94, 200, 208
Amau Doctrine, 51
American Consular Bulletin, 17
American Foreign Service Journal, 17–18, 20, 21, 23–25, 29, 204
Andrić, Ivo, 66
Antisemitism, 187
Antonescu, Ion, 65, 113, 127, 182
Argentina, 139, 140, 188
Atherton, Ray, 73, 94–95
Atlantic Charter, 2, 5, 81–82, 83, 85, 87, 91, 94, 95, 97–98, 101, 109, 111, 115, 122, 125, 127, 129, 130, 133, 136, 142, 147, 151, 157, 164, 166, 167, 168–69, 171, 173, 176, 192, 198, 204, 206, 207, 208, 213
Attlee, Clement, 156
Austria, 5, 150

Balkan Entente (1938), 65, 66
Balkans, 47, 47–49, 64, 65, 98, 99, 108, 111, 112, 113, 116, 117, 118, 124, 125, 128, 132, 135, 137, 145–46, 150, 151, 152, 158
Barbour, Walworth, 6, 112, 166, 180, 183, 185, 188–89, 200
Barnes, Maynard B., 77, 207, 208, 211; background of, 6; in Bulgaria, 61–64, 147–48, 149, 163–64, 180–81, 192, 193, 206; on Eastern European policies, 147; in France, 72, 73, 148; on Soviet expansionism, 126–27, 128, 135–36, 151, 152
Batista, Fulgencio, 48, 49
Beneš, Edvard, 69, 144, 157, 194–95
Bentinck, William, 186–87, 195
Berry, Burton Y., 14, 16, 22, 24, 180, 208; background, 6; on Eastern European policies, 108, 134–35; in Greece, 75; in Iran, 78; in Rumania, 146–47, 148, 162, 163, 181, 182, 193, 204, 205–6; on Soviet expansionism, 89, 126, 127, 135, 151, 152, 204

Bevin, Ernest, 188
Bierut, Boleslaw, 161, 205
Biryusov, Sergey Semenovich, 127
Bodnaras, Emil, 182
Bohlen, Charles E., 2, 21, 28, 29, 33, 36, 37, 39, 40, 42, 43, 75, 97, 141; background of, 6, 30; on Eastern European policies, 115, 116, 124, 163, 166; at peace conferences, 131, 133, 137, 155; personality of, 30; in Riga, 30–31; on Soviet expansionism, 78, 85, 87, 95–96, 97, 99, 100, 104, 110, 112, 113–14, 119, 120–21, 122, 128, 131–32, 139, 140, 154, 167–68, 172, 173, 176–77, 178, 179, 189, 197, 212
Bolshevik Revolution, 27–28, 198–99
Boris, King, 61, 62
Brătianu, Gheorghe, 65, 182
Bruins, John H., 19, 180; background of, 6; in Czechoslovakia, 68–69, 157, 185, 206, 208; on Eastern European policies, 194, 195, 205; on Soviet expansionism, 143–44
Bruins, Mrs., 200–201
Bulganin, Nikolai, 35
Bulgaria, 5, 42, 61–62, 64, 65, 109, 115, 124, 125, 126–28, 129, 135–36, 137, 142, 144, 145, 147–48, 149, 152, 155, 156, 163–64, 165, 168, 169, 170, 180–81, 182, 188, 192–93, 196, 197, 206, 208, 211
Bullitt, William, 29, 30, 31, 33, 72, 75, 82, 196
Byrnes, James F., 155, 159, 164–65, 170–71, 191, 207

Cannon, Cavendish W., 85–86, 89, 96, 97, 203–4; background of, 6; in Bulgaria, 62, 64; on Eastern European policies, 115, 116, 117, 124, 125, 147, 149, 150, 159, 160; education of, 61–62; at Potsdam, 155; in Rumania, 206; on Soviet expansionism, 95–96, 99, 112–13, 128, 134, 136, 173–74, 192; in Yugoslavia, 98
Carol, King, 105, 113, 127
Castle, William R., Jr., 28